Handbook of American Popular Culture

Handbook of

ANIMATION
THE AUTOMOBILE
CHILDREN'S LITERATURE
COMIC ART
DETECTIVE AND MYSTERY NOVELS
FILM
GOTHIC NOVELS
POPULAR MUSIC
THE PULPS
RADIO
SCIENCE FICTION
SPORTS
STAGE ENTERTAINMENT
TELEVISION
THE WESTERN

American Popular Culture

edited by
M. THOMAS INGE

VOLUME 1

GREENWOOD PRESS
WESTPORT, CONNECTICUT • LONDON, ENGLAND

Library of Congress Cataloging in Publication Data
Main entry under title:

Handbook of American popular culture.

    Includes index.
    1. United States—Popular Culture.
2. United States—Popular culture—Sources.
3. United States—Popular culture—Bibliography.
I. Inge, M. Thomas.
E169.1.H2643   301.2'1   77-95357
ISBN 0-313-20325-3 (v. 1)

Library of Congress Catalog Card Number: 77-95357
ISBN: 0-313-20325-3

First published in 1978

Greenwood Press
A division of Congressional Information Service, Inc.
88 Post Road West
Westport, Connecticut 06881

Printed in the United States of America

10 9 8 7 6 5 4

For Russel B. Nye

Contents

Preface

The serious, scholarly study of mass or popular culture is a fairly recent phenomenon, although some early investigations were first initiated within the established disciplines. For example, sociologists have long found the materials with which Americans amuse themselves fascinating for what they reflect about the people and their attitudes, morals, and mores. Popular culture, in other words, is a mirror wherein society can see itself and better understand its character and needs. One unresolved circular problem this approach presents is the question of whether the mass media merely reflect what society wants or influence it to want what the media provide. Is the violence commonly found on television there because we prefer to watch those shows that use it, or do we prefer to watch it because our baser instincts have been stimulated by its frequent use? Thus the sociological study of popular culture has often been initiated in the name of other causes: to deal with social problems, attempt to understand society and human nature, or engage in moral reform.

Some of the early film studies took place in English departments, where literary critics realized that some of the same techniques applied to the appreciation of fiction, poetry, and drama could be applied with great profit to the appreciation of motion pictures. In order to justify offering a course in film, however, all too often it was necessary to make a literary attachment explicit in the description, thus the now almost obligatory "Fiction and Film" course found in most English curricula. Such courses usually examine adaptations of novels and stories into film. If the instructor reaches the simple conclusion that the novel is always better than the film version (and I know a few who do), little has been accomplished. If, on the other hand, the instructor uses the separate art forms to elucidate each other through an examination of the necessarily different artistic techniques and creative strategies as applied to similar subject matter, the result can be increased respect for both forms of expression. Such an approach has encouraged the development of some perceptive film criticism.

It is no longer necessary to justify the study of the popular arts by an alliance with some other social or cultural purpose. We have come to recognize that each form or medium of expression has its own aesthetic principles, techniques, and ways of conveying ideas. Each has been subject to misuse and ineptitude, but each has also witnessed levels of artistic accomplishment remarkable by any standards, although finally each form must be evaluated within and by its own self-generated set of standards and objectives. There are hundreds of courses being taught in film, television, radio, science fiction, popular music, the detective novel, or comic art in American colleges and universities, sometimes with uneasy homes in departments of English, history, sociology, art history, mass communications, or American studies. The next decade will see the development of popular culture programs organized, as they should be, on an interdisciplinary basis. Already one degree-granting program has been established at Bowling Green State University in Ohio, also the seat of the Popular Culture Association and its publication, *Journal of Popular Culture*, established by Ray B. Browne in 1968. Scholars who have previously distinguished themselves in traditional fields are more frequently turning their attention to this new area of inquiry, as did Russel B. Nye in *The Unembarrassed Muse: The Popular Arts in America* (1970) and John Cawelti in *The Six-Gun Mystique* (1971).

This handbook is the first organized effort to assemble in one place the basic bibliographic data needed to begin the study of several of the major areas of popular culture. Each chapter, prepared by an authority on the subject, provides a brief chronological survey of the development of the medium; a critical guide in essay form to the standard or most useful bibliographies, reference works, histories, critical studies, and journals; a description of the existing research centers and collections of primary and secondary materials; and a checklist of works cited in the text. With this handbook, the student, scholar, librarian, or general reader can easily locate the kind of information needed to complete a research paper or project, answer a question, build a basic library, or read about a topic or personality as a matter of interest.

There are numerous areas of popular culture not covered here, although many of them will be discussed in volume two. Undoubtedly the essays contain oversights in terms of research collections and published materials. In future editions, however, we hope to remedy oversights and make the essays more comprehensive and accurate. To that end, corrections and suggestions should be directed to the editor in care of the Department of English, Virginia Commonwealth University, Richmond, Virginia 23284.

M. Thomas Inge

Handbook of
American Popular
Culture

CHAPTER 1 Animation
Thomas W. Hoffer

Animated motion pictures of the kind known to mass audiences in the United States from the early 1920s to the 1950s were literally created frame by frame. Of course, all moving pictures are photographed in this method, usually twenty-four frames taken in one second, processed and projected on a screen at the same rate, fused into the appearance of motion by our mind's "eye" in which the vision of a previous frame persists for a split second until the next frame is put in place on the screen. All of this happens so rapidly, we pay little heed to the technology involved or the psychology and physiology of our own mechanisms. However, the animated films considered here, while created frame by frame by a camera, are first drawn by an artist or groups of artists. With the creation of individual frames, their lines, form, perspective, mass, balance, color, and other dimensions of composition, including the orchestration of characters and objects, give the film animator the maximum control over the medium.

There are various kinds of animated drawings or objects that have evolved in film since the turn of the century. These include the stop-action tricks of Emile Cohl, silhouette cutouts of Lotte Reiniger, puppet films of George Pal, animated photographs by Bob Godfrey, and drawings of images and sound tracks on film by Norman McLaren. Our subject here is another type of animated material that reached mass audiences as the moving picture evolved in the United States and became a distinct product of our popular culture. These were the animated cartoons of Disney, Fleischer Brothers, Ub Iwerks, Tex Avery, Bob Clampett, Chuck Jones, Art Babbit, and hundreds of others who created their films frame by frame by drawing them individually for the camera through the use of celluloid overlays (cels). The works of those hundreds of artists resulted in more than movement of simple objects: they created characters, told stories, used and exploited stereotypes, and caricatured life and personalities.

HISTORIC OUTLINE

The following few highlights in the evolution of the animated cartoon in the United States after 1900 are certainly no substitute for a definitive history. Indeed, the field is in desperate need of more histories that attempt some assessment of the art form and organization in the context of the American moving picture and the broader social, economic, and political environments. More rigorous historical work is also needed simply to clarify the misstatements of fact and romanticism that sometimes creep into the literature, for which myths occasionally take on legendary form and are written as fact.

Depending upon whether you define animation as movement or photography, our story could start with successive drawings of animals on cave walls originating thousands of years ago or with early attempts around 1900 to fuse the moving picture camera and single drawings to create the illusion of movement. One likely contender for the first animated cartoon made in the United States was a project of the Edison studio entitled *The Enchanted Drawing*, registered for copyright on November 16, 1900. While running a bit over one minute at today's projection speeds of twenty-four frames-per-second, the story line consisted of a cartoonist interacting with a one-line caricature of a man drawn on a nearby easel. The cartoonist was J. Stuart Blackton, an employee of Edison, who would later become very prominent in the silent film industry.

Space does not permit tracing the evolution of the film cartoon through a series of characters, studios, principal directors, animators, or new techniques and technologies. One major characteristic of the period from 1900 to 1928 was a gradual diminishing of the sole animator as author into the formation of complex organizations relying upon divisions of labor to conceive, draw, photograph, and manufacture animated cartoons.

A number of important early animators influenced the medium with their individual styles, techniques, and inventions; they include Winsor McCay, John Bray, Earl Hurd, Raoul Barre, Max Fleischer, Paul Terry, Pat Sullivan, Sidney Smith, and Henry Mayer. At first, drawings were put on individual sheets of rice paper, but by 1914, John Bray and Earl Hurd were using celluloid overlays, or cels, with separately drawn backgrounds. Raoul Barre was instrumental in developing a technique for redrawing only the successive cels for those portions of the character that moved, using the same cel for the stationary portions of the character at any particular point in the animation sequence.

Soon, symbiosis set in; animated cartoons drew their content and characters from the comic strips. Animators also emulated each other as well as the characters created by such actors as Charlie Chaplin in the live action films of the day. In this period the animated cartoon was relegated to minor status on most playbills, sometimes used as a chaser at the end of a program and the start of another. Distributors and exhibitors placed little importance on them and in some instances with justification. Many cartoons had characters that were wooden and conveyed little personality through the silent medium. Others were strings of silent film visual gags with trite story lines. When the technologies of sound and then color were adopted, together with a more sophisticated method of manufacture, the animated cartoon began to attract an audience.

Much of the period from 1928 to 1950 has often been referred to as the "golden age" of film animation partly because it began with the exploitation of sound and, by 1932, color. The organizational genius of Walt Disney flowered during this time, streamlining the process of cartoon manufacture yet reinvesting and extending human and monetary profits toward higher quality through the ever complex divisions of labor embraced in his enterprise. Disney innovated the use of the story board in his organization, allowing his animators to plan entire films more efficiently. He reinvested money and effort in building a cadre of trained personnel who, according to some, were later exploited by him. Disney did not promote himself or his organization as a great contribution to American culture. He insisted on the best quality work and maximized every opportunity to strengthen the organization by maintaining every conceivable control over his product at a time when animating organizations were struggling against double features that tended to push cartoons out of theaters. Following the success of *Flowers and Trees* (1932), the first technicolor sound cartoon, and the popular *Three Little Pigs* (1933), which was promoted in other media with the hit tune "Who's Afraid of the Big Bad Wolf" (itself an appeal against the Depression), Disney resisted the general industry practice of following a winner with a duplicate offering, a practice still followed in today's phonograph, radio, television, and film industries. His shrewd deal with Technicolor, insuring exclusive use of the new process for two years, undoubtedly nourished new exhibitor and distributor interest in the animated film and seemed to be quite consistent with the high ideals of competitive bidding in the marketplace. Of course, his competitors did not think so.

The Disney organization also wrung every ounce of profit from merchandising activity and carried it to new heights, later emulated by Fleischer Brothers. Winsor McCay, however, was the master of such economic designs in the American cartoon. Such symbiotic activity was critically important for keeping Disney credit active for more investment, particularly for a feature length production in the form of *Snow White and the Seven Dwarfs* (1937). While it was not the first animated feature,

Snow White was the most economically and artistically successful for many years. In that picture and an earlier short subject, Disney innovated the multi-plane techniques that provided a greater sense of depth.

Today, in retrospect, most animators acknowledge Walt Disney's organizational and business skills, along with those of his brother Roy, as creating renewed interest in cartoon animation. Recognizing that individual animators could no longer start and complete whole cartoons on their own and yet maintain economically profitable enterprises, Disney acquired and managed his talent toward larger goals, although relationships among all were not always cordial. Checkpoints in the animation process were designed to help maintain quality and extend animation to new frontiers. These included the conference technique, key drawings, pencil tests, the Leica reel, and stereophonic sound. Initially, in the early 1940s, a film entitled *Fantasia* did badly at the box office but since has withstood the test of time, demonstrating that many of Disney's products now achieve new leases on life with new generations, enhanced by a weekly television program plugging Disney amusement parks and upcoming theatrical features. Few could lay claim to such longevity, but the secret was not attributed exclusively to art in animation.

World War II eclipsed commercial cartoon animation activity, but animated cartoons were released from other studios as well, including Warner Brothers, Metro Goldwyn Mayer, 20th Century Fox, Paramount, Universal, and Columbia. Like Mickey Mouse and other characters promoted in the silent era of cartoon making, the Fleischer studio animated Betty Boop (1930), Popeye (1933), and Superman (1941). In 1941 the Fleischer studios closed, but Paramount established Famous Studios and continued animating Superman, followed by Casper, the Friendly Ghost (1946), Herman and Katnip (1948), and Little Audrey (1949). Paul Terry's studio, eventually releasing through 20th Century Fox, animated Gandy Goose (1938), Dinky Duck (1939), Mighty Mouse (1943), and Heckle and Jeckle (1946). Following Andy Panda (1939), Walter Lantz, releasing through Universal, animated Woody Woodpecker (1940). Columbia's animation unit manufactured Krazy Kat (1930), Scrappy (1931), Barney Google in the mid-1930s, and The Fox and the Crow by 1941.

Following some labor troubles in the Disney organization in 1941, a number of artists left and set up United Production of America (UPA). Its cartoon style was in contrast to Disney's work. A looser organization at UPA resulted, for example, in far more abstraction as in the character and backgrounds of Mr. Magoo (1949) and Gerald McBoing Boing (1951); but the two-dimensionality of the UPA style, in considerable contrast to Disney's, did not bode well for the organization in their attempts at feature production. As more animators attempted to tackle feature production, a new word came into the vocabulary: "Disneyfication," which included the exploitation of strong story and personality, plus the realistic animation style Disney cultivated through constant training of his animation cadre and reinvestment in physical plant. Metro Goldwyn Mayer characters came later than those of other studios, but probably the most well-known were Tom and Jerry (1939). Warner Brothers began with Bosko (1930), Porky Pig (1935), and later introduced Bugs Bunny and Elmer Fudd (1940), Tweetie Pie (1944), Sylvester (1945), and the clever Roadrunner and the Coyote (1948).

With such a stable of characters and personalities competing for audiences, it was indeed a "golden era" for animation, not to be repeated again in the American marketplace.

The Disney characters were fewer in number compared to most studios but included Mickey Mouse (1928), Goofy (1932), Pluto (1930), Donald Duck (1934), and Chip and Dale (1943). Major efforts turned toward feature production, although the studio always had short subject cartoons in production until 1955. *Snow White* (1937) was an immediate box office success. Others followed, including *Pinocchio* (1940), *Fantasia* (1940), *The Reluctant Dragon* (1941), *Dumbo* (1941), *Bambi* (1942)—some live action, combinations of animation and live action, and all animation pictures. Despite the highly criticized but profitable animation style and "Disneyfication," Walt Disney's organization helped make the difference between survival and others who failed in feature animation. Of course, merchandising, television, and the new amusement parks also contributed toward reducing the large debt always held by the Disney organization until the 1960s.

Despite the end of the "golden era" after 1950, the curtain did not come down completely for the animated art. Television's capture of the nighttime radio and film audience was an important reason for the decline of film audiences. At the same time, film costs were increasing, and television provided animation substitutes and shortcuts in caricature and personality appeal similar to the way in which it absorbed the theatrical newsreel. While movie attendance is still very much a social event, it was much more a habit at this time compared to the present, with film audiences becoming specialized in being attracted to particular kinds of content. The mass medium is now electronic, not in acetate and color projected on screens in darkened theaters. While television has seemed to be the catalyst for providing children's programming fast, furiously, and frugally, its large appetite for material has also encouraged the resurrection, albeit occasionally in a heavily edited form, of many of the headliner cartoon characters of bygone years.

According to John Halas, the prolific animator and writer, today the opportunity for a new "golden age" is even riper. Admittedly, his view is contagious since more provocative graphic designs have displaced the

gags and story lines of the old animated products. Our new national poetry, the television commercial, has provided the topsoil for editorial ideas
to grow, exploiting new techniques and technologies. Joined by a much
larger flow of international contributors, nourished by television exposure
and the large capacity of the computer, the future of film animation continues to remain bright by generating and feeding audiences with visual
imagination and kinetic energy.

REFERENCE WORKS

Readers interested in animation will discover that a number of very
useful reference aids have been devised in the last decade to make library
research much easier. There are no such aids devoted exclusively to animation, but the general film literature has systematically encompassed
this topic.

Reference volumes designed to provide answers to brief questions include Leslie Halliwell's *The Filmgoer's Companion*, Roger Manvell and
Lewis Jacob's *International Encyclopedia of Film*, and Rim Cawkwell
and John M. Smith's *The World Encyclopedia of Film*. The Halliwell
work has the most entries, in excess of ten thousand. Manvell's effort has
fewer entries than Halliwell's, but lists an additional sixty-five hundred film
titles plus a bibliography, which Halliwell omits. The Cawkwell encyclopedia is available in paperback and, unlike the first two works, contains
long essays on film as well as biographical notations. *World* has a much
longer list of film titles, numbering over twenty-two thousand.

Translations of Georges Sadoul's works, *Dictionary of Filmmakers* and
Dictionary of Films, available in paperback, contain fewer listings of films
and filmmakers than volumes mentioned previously, but they are inexpensive resources. Containing sixteen hundred entries, with cross-refer-
ences, Raymond Spottiswoode's *Focal Encyclopedia of Film and Television Techniques* is an imposing contribution, especially with the additional one thousand diagrams and index of ten thousand references.

Peter Cowie's annual *International Film Guide* published by A. S.
Barnes is still the best way to keep updated on film generally, and a number of pages are devoted to animation on the world scene. Annual editions contain information on festivals, short films, animation, sponsored
films, services, schools, archives, magazines, books and a cinema directory.

While the initial release of the *American Film Institute Catalogue of
Motion Pictures: Feature Films, 1921-1930* (two volumes), edited by
Kenneth W. Munden, did not contain much data on animated features,
because there were very few at that time, future releases will provide

details on titles, credits, synopses, various indexes, and supplementary information. The second set released in the series was the *American Film Institute Catalogue of Motion Pictures: Feature Films 1961-1970* (two volumes), also edited by Munden. Additional volumes will also focus exclusively on short films, including animated subjects from 1911 to 1980.

Two important ongoing indexes are critically important to the scholar of animation desiring to keep up with new periodical material published in trade journals, critical magazines, and the popular press. Surveying the international scene is the *International Index to Film Periodicals* (annual since 1972 and published by the Federation Internationale des Archives du Film), which includes eighty of the most important film serials. The *Film Literature Index,* by Fred Silva, issued quarterly and in an annual accumulation, encompasses over three hundred film periodicals. With over one thousand subject headings, the alphabetical subject-author index is among the most comprehensive finding aids for contemporary data. Unfortunately, only three annual accumulations are currently available, precluding serious historical work.

Four additional bibliographic aids help overcome some of the shortcomings of the *Film Literature Index. The New Film Index,* by Richard Dyer MacCann and Edward S. Perry; *Retrospective Index to Film Periodicals* (1930-71), by Linda Batty; *The Critical Index* (1946-73), edited by John C. Gerlach and Linda Gerlach; and *The Film Index: A Bibliography,* Vol. 1: *The Film As Art* (silent era), edited by Harold Leonard will produce a substantial number of citations of animation materials published in a variety of film and general publications. All of the preceding titles, except the older *Film Index,* are compared by journal coverage, time coverage, and arrangement schemes in an article by Abigail Nelson, "Guide to Indexes of Periodical Literature on Film," *University Film Study Newsletter,* 6 (October 1975), 3.

With the exception of *Business Periodicals Index, Music Index,* and *Topicator,* none of the motion picture trade journals is currently indexed in any detail and certainly not back to their various years of inception. *Variety* is indexed in the first two sources from about 1948 to present, supplemented with *Topicator* in 1965, but all with different criteria for selection of material. *Moving Picture World,* a very important trade journal for the silent film era (1907-27), is loosely indexed on an annual basis but *Billboard, Variety,* and others require tedious issue-by-issue review.

Several additional indexes of the general film literature also include works on animation, including George Rehrauer's *Cinema Booklist* (with supplement), Frank Manchel's *Film Study: A Resource Guide,* Peter J. Bukalski's *Film Research: A Critical Bibliography With Annotations and Essay,* and Marietta Chicorel's *Chicorel Index to Film Literature.*

RESEARCH COLLECTIONS

Compared to general film collections, the number of archives containing even a fraction of animation material is very small. However, some libraries and museums across the United States do contain animated films, and a smaller number collect and have available papers, memorabilia, and ephemera in that subject area. This review begins with guides to these sources followed by a discussion of the most important collections and a closing section about commercial sources to animated films.

William C. Young's *American Theatrical Arts: Guide to Manuscripts and Special Collections in the United States and Canada* is a useful but slightly dated list of theater and film collections organized by name and subject area. One does need to read carefully when utilizing this directory and perhaps follow up hunches with a letter. For example, the references to the State Historical Society of Wisconsin Mass Communication History Center do not note animation subjects, but the center does indeed have a collection of several hundred animated films open to scholars. These are found under the Warner Brothers and United Artists Collections. The Margaret Young et al. *Subject Directory of Special Libraries and Information Centers* is a multi-volume collection of special libraries. Volume 2 (*Education and Information Science Libraries*) notes audiovisual collections and Volume 4 (*Social Sciences and Humanities Libraries*) lists art and theater collections.

Kemp Niver's exhaustive listing of early paper print films now in the Library of Congress describes a few surviving cartoon films and, moreover, a number of other films using stop action and other trick effects. Many titles held in the Library of Congress collection (described on p. 11) are listed in its *National Union Catalogue* series. A book catalog, *Library of Congress Catalogue: Films and Other Materials for Projection,* is another useful guide issued quarterly and in an annual accumulation. The Card Division of the Library of Congress issues a semiannual *Catalogue of Copyright Entries: Motion Pictures and Filmstrips* with additional volumes bringing together copyrighted films from 1894 to 1969. While there is no central listing of all films contained in the library's collection, the foregoing are of great help in isolating many animated titles.

Olga S. Weber's *North American Film and Video Directory* is a more comprehensive locator of film collections. Nineteen animation collections are separately listed in the index, and more can be located with careful reading. The directory is organized by states with references made to cities in alphabetical order. Each listing provides the full name and address of the repository and curator or librarian followed by broad descriptions of the film collections indicating by percentage the scope of animation holdings. While no specific titles are listed, this directory is a considerable accomplishment in providing leads to museums and libraries collecting animated films. Some collections are omitted (State Historical Society of Wisconsin Mass Communication History Center, for example), but the author had to rely on busy librarians to respond to her questionnaires, and some did not. Nevertheless, the guide is an extremely valuable tool for scholars and buffs seeking to view older animated films.

The fourth edition of *Subject Collections*, by Lee Ash, has numerous leads to film collections, some of which contain materials on animation. The listings are more detailed than the Weber work.

The Library of Congress, the National Archives, and the American Film Institute collections certainly constitute the largest film resources in the United States at the same location. Library of Congress holdings include the paper print collection of early United States and some foreign films (1894-1912) and over sixty thousand titles systematically gathered since 1942. Many major studios are represented in the copyright deposit holdings including animated cartoon makers, such as Warner Brothers, Metro Goldwyn Mayer, and Paramount. About five thousand short subjects and features are contained in special holdings seized from the Germans and Japanese during World War II. In the Motion Picture Section of the Prints and Photographs Division, projection facilities are available to individual scholars upon appointment. Reading room facilities containing extensive files on directors, production companies, yearbooks, press books, and other reference aids are also open to serious researchers.

The American Film Institute deposits its holdings, numbering about thirteen thousand in 1977, in the Library of Congress. The institute was established in June 1967 to preserve the heritage and advance the art of film and television in the United States. Major programs include the location and preservation of films, financial aid to filmmakers, the publication of film books, periodicals, and reference works, and the support of basic research in film. At the institute's West Coast Center for Advanced Studies, the Charles K. Feldman Library archives contain some animation materials for research. There, researchers may review the Max Fleischer collection of original patents for motion picture apparatuses used for animation and the Dave Fleischer oral history with Joe Adamson. The library also has over fifty Metro Goldwyn Mayer animation scripts.

The National Archives hold United States government produced films in a collection exceeding forty million feet of film. All photographic and paper holdings in the National Archives are organized under more than four hundred Record Groups representing several hundred past and present United States government agencies. Interested parties should write to the General Services Administration, National Archives and Records Service, Washington, D.C. 20408, for a list of Record Groups in addition to raising specific research questions. For animation, the Motion Picture and Sound Recording Branch of the Audiovisual Archives Division has direct control over film subjects. An inquiry for this chapter produced useful leads to three Record Groups (Record Groups 111, 56, and 306) on Private Snafu cartoons produced by United States agencies during World War II and several Walt Disney films, such as *New Spirit* and *Der Fuehrer's Face* (Record Groups 56 and 306). Reservations are required for use of viewing machines, and prints of animated subjects are available at moderate costs. Occasionally, preliminary inventories are available for public distribution, but often researchers will have to await arrival at the National Archives in order to use "in-house" inventories.

The Film Department of the Museum of Modern Art, New York City, has about 250 animated films, of which less than one-half are from the silent period. Special materials include scripts, sketches, production information, and notebooks in the Paul Terry Collection and similar matter in the Isadore Klein Collection. Additionally, the library has voluminous files under the animation subject heading, containing newspaper clips, articles, program notes, and miscellaneous materials. Access is available to scholars who make advance appointments. Many films in the museum's collection circulate; write the Circulation Department, Museum of Modern Art, 11 West 53rd Street, New York, New York 10019.

Also available in New York City are the Anthology Film Archives, 80 Wooster Street, New York, New York 10012, and the New York Public Library. The latter houses a large collection of materials in American theater of which a small part is comprised of animation materials of the book and nonbook sort. Holdings include a collection of press books, posters, the George Kleine Collection of scrapbooks, and the Robinson Locke Collection. The catalog to the nonbook material, entitled *Catalogue of the Theater and Drama Collection: Research Library of the New York Public Library, Part III*, provides an alphabetical listing by person and subject. Researchers should write: Library Museum of the Performing Arts, New York Public Library at Lincoln Center, 111 Amsterdam Avenue, New York, New York 10023.

An overlooked resource for animation material is housed in the New York State Library, Manuscripts and Special Collections Division (Albany, New York 12234). While there are no films in this collection, there are some forty thousand scripts of all films reviewed by the defunct New York State Board of Censors. When the board was in operation, they used scripts to help evaluate films proposed for exhibition in the state. When abolished, board files went to the New York State Library, including all scripts separately filed by title.

The George Eastman House was among the earliest formed collections of films in cinema and is among the very few privately endowed archives functioning in the United States where public screenings are a regular part of their research and acquisition activities. Animation films are a small part of the Eastman collection. Scholars should write: Curator, George Eastman House, Inc., Library, Rochester, New York 14607.

Established in 1974, the Museum of Cartoon Art in Greenwich, Connecticut, is a collector of original art work but also provides film programs in a small theater upon request or reservation. This project is financed by the cooperative effort of cartoonists, foundations, and private enterprise to preserve the best of cartoon art in the United States. Memberships and book lists are available to interested persons. Their film holdings include the productions of John Bray, Winsor McCay, Pat Sullivan, Paul Terry, Walt Disney, Ub Iwerks, Max and Dave Fleischer, Tex Avery, Chuck Jones, Fritz Freleng, Bob Clampett, and others. Researchers should make advance appointments by writing the museum at Comly Avenue, Town of Rye, Port Chester, New York 10573.

The major research collection of films and miscellaneous materials in animation between both coasts is housed in the State Historical Society of Wisconsin, Mass Communication History Center, 816 State Street, Madison, Wisconsin 53706. While no films circulate, researchers can have a visual feast on hundreds of animated subjects from the Warner Brothers and United Artists collections, which include films featuring Daffy Duck, Bugs Bunny, Porky Pig, Elmer Fudd, and Popeye, among others. Special inventories listing release dates, call numbers, titles, and special classifications, such as war, minorities in cartoons, and gangster cartoons, are available at the center. As a part of the several thousand feature, television print, and short subject collections, the center houses much of the early work of Tex Avery, Bob Clampett, Robert McKimson, Chuck Jones, Fritz Freleng, Paul Smith, Ben Hardaway, Cal Dalton, Frank Tashlin, Jack King, Ben Clopton, Sandy Walker, Ub Iwerks, and many others. There is a very large sample of the Looney Tunes and Merrie Melodies series in addition to other cartoon characters already noted. The Warner Brothers cartoon collection is extensive. Paramount holdings include a comprehensive list of Popeye titles from 1933 to 1957. Additional materials from the press, broadcasting, film, theater, and television collections are among the holdings of the center. For a detailed list of holdings, write the center, Susan Dalton, film archivist.

The major archives and libraries for animation research on the West Coast include the Animated Film Study Collection at the Film and Television Study Center, the University of California at Los Angeles (Theater Arts), the American Film Institute (Charles K. Feldman Library, mentioned earlier), and the Walt Disney Archives.

The Film and Television Study Center is intended to be facilitative rather than acquisitional in helping researchers tap large resources of the sixteen-member institutions under its banner. With regard to animation, two collections coordinated by the center should be mentioned here. Chuck Jones donated numerous materials covering his association with Metro Goldwyn Mayer during the 1960s, with 150 cartons of cels, backgrounds, and other materials. Films, such as his feature *The Phantom Tollbooth*, and his noted short *Dot and the Line*, are included in the collection. Partially funded by the National Endowment for the Arts, the center (6233 Hollywood Boulevard, Hollywood, California, Mr. Ed Goff, Director) completed a union catalog of film and television manuscript collections in eleven Western states, including California, Oregon, Washington, Utah, Colorado, Nevada, Montana, Wyoming, New Mexico, Idaho, and Arizona.

The Animated Film Study Collection, also coordinated by the Film and Television Study Center, comprises more than one hundred examples of animation from around the world. The principal organizer and sponsor of the collection is the Education and Training Trust Fund of the Professional, Technical and Clerical Employees Union, Local 986. Studios and other organizations and persons have added to the collection, which includes the traditional Winsor McCay and Paul Terry examples, but a major thrust of the collection is on post-World War II work. Works by Peter Burness, Paul Jullian, and Robert Cannon are represented as well as Avery, Jones, and Hanna-Barbera. International artists are also represented, such as Norman McLaren, Ryan Larkin, Jiri Brdecka, Bob Godfrey, John Halas, Richard Williams, Paul Grimault, Giulio Gianini, and John Hubley. A recent acquisition includes the George Pal Collection, available for viewing at UCLA. For a list of films in the collection, write: Steven Paul Leiva, International Animated Film Society, 6233 Hollywood Boulevard, Suite 203, Hollywood, California 90028. Access to these materials may be obtained by contacting the Film and Television Study Center, at the same address as the International Animated Film Society.

The Theater Arts Library and Film Archives, UCLA (Los Angeles, California 90024), have long been known by film scholars as among the most significant collections of papers and films through their published catalog *Motion Pictures: A Catalogue of Books, Periodicals, Screenplays and Production Stills*, which represents material collected through March 1976. For animation interests, there is a small collection of twenty-three Walt Disney cartoon continuities and shooting scripts from the period 1937-39. The Film Archive, in Melnitz Hall on the UCLA campus, has a catalog of holdings obtained by writing archivist Robert Epstein.

The University of Southern California's Library and Special Collections houses thousands of cinema books and over one hundred manuscript collections. Although less than one-third of the collections have been cataloged and organized, a generalized list of all collections and detailed guide to the cataloged materials is contained in *Primary Cinema Resources: An Index to Screenplays, Interviews and Special Collections at the University of Southern California* (1975), by Christopher D. Wheaton and Richard B. Jewell.

The Walt Disney Archives are a completely separate department from the Disney Library, which contains virtually all of the major books on animation. Under the direction of David R. Smith, the archive collection was established in 1970 to collect and preserve the historical materials relating to the Disney enterprises. Primary files deal with Disney, and supplementary material includes live action and animated theme, amusement parks, merchandising, publicity and promotion matter, publications of Disney enterprises, and disc recordings. Researchers will find most Disney correspondence from 1930 until his death in 1966, with some earlier files from the 1920s. Most of the eight hundred Disney books published in the United States are cataloged and housed in the archives, along with all phonograph music put out by the Disney organization, comprising some thirteen hundred recordings. In addition to thousands of clips and articles in vertical files, five hundred thousand still negatives, and production files for all Disney films, taped oral histories of key Disney employees including Walt and Roy Disney are available. Advance notice is required for access from Disney Archives, 500 South Buena Vista Street, Burbank, California 91521.

Public libraries in Anaheim, California, and Orlando, Florida, also collect Disney material, such as books, press releases, maps, operating manuals, newsletters, posters, press books, handbills, and other ephemera.

The University of California Art Museum, Pacific Film Archive (2625 Durant Avenue, Berkeley, California 94720) ranks among the three major archives in the United States which have regular exhibitions. The other two are the Museum of Modern Art Film Library and the American Film Institute. The Pacific Film Archive has been called the most spirited and inventive of the three, holding about 15 percent of its three thousand titles in animated film.

Probably the most widely available reference guide for 8mm and 16mm films currently in print and distribution is James L. Limbacher's *Feature Films on 8mm and 16mm*, which has information on more than fifteen thousand films. However, this guide has limitations for those with interests in animation. Others, with modest budgets and Super 8mm equipment, will find a 1976 compilation by Leonard Hollman in *Film Collector's World* (Nos. 2, 3, and 4, unpaged) to be a very useful aid in locating more than seven hundred animated cartoons in the inexpensive gauge. Fifteen of the major distributors are coded to long lists of cartoons grouped by character, series title, and studio. A number of very early Disney materials, several compilations, and feature highlights are available. Others listed include Famous Studios, Fleischer Studio, Hanna-Barbera, Ub Iwerks, Walter Lantz, Metro Goldwyn Mayer, Winsor McCay, Screen Gems, Terrytoons, UPA, Van Buren, Warner Brothers, and a number of miscellaneous entries. Hollman's listing is a valuable service to scholars of animation and deserves to be reprinted in a medium of more lasting quality.

Additional listings of films about animation are found in the Library of Congress National Union Catalogue series described earlier. The Bukalski work, cited in the literature section, contains detailed listings of rental and sales agencies.

A number of private collectors, some of whom are retired animators, still retain a great deal of animation art, scripts, and other memorabilia. In the last decade, a cult of animation collectors has grown in the United States, furnishing a ready-made market for consuming animation art or artifacts of animators. Often, such material is offered for sale in comic or cartoon fanzines (specialized, limited-run magazines for film enthusiasts) or film periodicals. Thomas W. Hoffer's previous contact with commercial collectors revealed the location of several hundred of Winsor McCay's original paper cels from *Gertie the Dinosaur*, many of which were reported to be locked in a vault in New York City, presumably accruing value with each year. This review of sources will not contribute to the inflation and greed such private archiving nourishes, but will merely remind the reader that animation art in the commercial marketplace can often be very expensive.

Some of those sources are contained in two periodicals, *Film Collector's World* and the *Classic Film Collector*. *World* is published biweekly and is full of commercial and trading information on 16mm and 8mm films, many animated. There are occasional columns about trading, the film industry (past and present), featured stars, animation, and, of course, considerable advertising. *Classic* is more of a tabloid newspaper, published quarterly and featuring news of the film collecting industry, obituaries, biographies, distributor news, film reviews, historical materials, film society news, clips from other publications, and advertisements, many for animated films.

HISTORY AND CRITICISM

Useful books and periodicals focusing exclusively on animation in the American film industry can still be counted on two hands. While there are signs that this literature is growing, there have been very few first-rate works about the evolution of animation. Studies drawing upon something more than anecdotes, but emphasizing individual animators and their organizations as well as their art, are coming into the publishing marketplace, but slowly. Animation buffs and scholars will find more revealing information within the general film literature, discussed on pp. 121-49 in the sections dealing with reference works and major research centers.

Not surprisingly, Walt Disney is the subject of several books on animation. One of the earliest, which attempted a serious review of his art and organization, was *The Art of Walt Disney*, by Robert D. Feild, with an emphasis on the process of animation through a studio system. However, the definitive book about Disney, his animators, and the organization is Bob Thomas' more recent *Walt Disney: An American Original*. Thomas drew from interviews with Disney and others, interoffice memoranda, verbatim minutes of studio meetings and Disney correspondence, revealing for the first time a more realistic picture of the Disney evolution. While quoting from these documents, sometimes at great length, Thomas has provided a much more accurate recollection of events than interviews permit, although personal interviews, as a research tool, certainly fulfill other functions in historical research. But, the Thomas book, through its documentation and other material, provides the reader with a more accurate and fuller perspective on the Disney enterprises than previously available. Thomas' earlier book, *The Art of Animation*, was aimed at a young adult audience with easy-reading narration, glossary, and excellent illustrations. A more official, family-oriented biography was provided by Disney's daughter, Diane, and Pete Martin, in a book published in 1956, a decade before Mr. Disney's death, *The Story of Walt Disney*. In considerable contrast, *The Disney Version*, by Richard Schickel, attempts to cut through the so-called Disney myths and present an objective overview of cartoon content and organization in American culture. Schickel surveyed much of the enormous periodical material on the Disney organization, and numerous references are included in the concluding bibliography. Readers who want to dip into this other view might also want some perspective provided by Al Kilgore in "The Disney Assault," and Leonard Maltin in "More on the Disney Version," published in *Film Fan Monthly*.

There have been a number of other works emphasizing the techniques of animation while sandwiching in a historical overview. One of the most useful was the 1941 work of Nat Falk, *How to Make Animated Cartoons: The History and Technique*, which begins first with history, then a description of the 1940 studios, followed by a detailed "how-to-draw cartoons" chapter. The most recent of this kind of hybrid book dealing with animation history and the "how-to" focus is Donald Heraldson's *Creators of Life: A History of Animation*. The technique sections are certainly more informative and competently done than the historical chapters, which contain some inaccurate statements and lack documentation. The author claimed he interviewed several animators for the book, but there was no direct attribution to any of them in the text. A review of Heraldson's work is given in *Film Collector's World*, No. 2 (October 1976), and his reply is printed in the following issue, No. 3 (November 1976), indicating, among other things, that the publisher and author had different ideas about the thrust of the work.

Among the technique books, the fourth edition of *The Technique of Film Animation* by the prolific John Halas and Roger Manvell is probably the most up-to-date and thorough, including a short history as preface material. The authors explicate factors influencing animation, such as style, timing, aesthetic principles, the kinds of sound tracks, and color and the more practical matters, such as advertising agents and public relations requirements. The last half of the book is devoted to pure technique, taking animation from story board stages, characterization, and sound, through the production process, and concluding with a review of various forms of animation, such as puppet, silhouette, and drawing-on-film animation. Film measurement tables and an animation glossary are also included. Other texts focusing upon techniques include Roger Manvell's *The Animated Film*, Roy Madsen's *Animated Film: Concepts, Methods, Uses*, Eli L. Levitan's *Animation Art in the Commercial Film*, Zoran Perisic's *The Animation Stand*, and John Halas' *Visual Scripting*.

Other recent and important books reviewing the Disney experience include *The Art of Walt Disney*, by Christopher Finch, and *The Disney Films*, by Leonard Maltin. Finch's work was originally published in a 458-page deluxe edition in 1973, but in 1975 a briefer version numbering 160 pages was reedited and published. The shorter version is still lavishly illustrated with pictures conveying the charm of Disney characters, but a rather superficial text highlights the background of the Disney enterprises, such as Disney World in Florida. However, Maltin's book is considerably different and provides a detailed listing of the credits for Disney features and short subjects through 1967. The features are described in considerable detail in 258 of the total 312 pages, with the remaining pages listing all short subjects in theatrical release and episode titles of Disney's ABC and NBC television programs from October 1954 through the 1966-67 television season. The encyclopedic scope of the Maltin work enhances its value as a reference tool as well.

Until very recently, other studios and animators were long neglected in the literature of American animation. Leslie Cabarga's *The Fleischer Story* attempts to fill a void concerning Dave and Max Fleischer, animators of Betty Boop and Popeye. While his scrapbook approach is appealing to the eye with hundreds of model drawings, cartoons, magazine reprints, and film frames, it lacks documentation and direct attribution to the large number of animators and studio personnel interviewed. Then there is the mystery of the parting of the Fleischer brothers, which apparently was so legally incendiary that the publisher, Woody Gelman, refused to print it, leaving a relatively large hole in Cabarga's story. The work ends abruptly without much reflection on how the Fleischer experience fits in the animation scheme of things or the industry. Still, the anecdotes and ephemera add some unity to the previously fragmented story spread over various periodical articles.

Emphasizing personality, style, frame enlargements, and detailed background interviews, Joe Adamson has reviewed the life and work of a major animator in *Tex Avery: King of Cartoons*. Adamson has a refreshing sense of accuracy in his work, coupled with definite views on the state of animation research and writing, including his favorite fault in animation writing, the "sociological sidestep." He takes several authors to task, such as Lewis Jacobs, Richard Schickel, Ralph Stephenson, and Roger Manvell. Model drawings are adequately reproduced in the text, but the film frame enlargements are of poor quality. The enthusiasm of the author in describing Avery's work, supplemented with numerous drawings and cels, drives one to reach for a theoretical supplement Super 8mm reel in the pocket part, placed there by a thoughtful publisher who finally recognized that writing about animation requires viewing as well. But, alas no publishers have yet taken the risk or invested money in Super 8mm supplements to texts of this sort, despite the importance the Adamson text places on the films. Significant pluses in Adamson's book include the filmography at the end, the detailed interview with Tex Avery, and another interview with Avery's long-time associate, Heck Allen.

The most recent lavishly illustrated case study of an animated film is John Canemaker's *The Animated Raggedy Ann and Andy*, a step-by-step documentary about the making of the film released in April 1977. This work also has the traditional historical review of animation in a shorthand version, but the bulk of the book concentrates on the fascinating production process. Canemaker provides the best informed and intimate view of animated feature production on a film that was intended to "rank with Disney" while striving not to imitate a Disney product. For other types of animation, Lotte Reiniger in *Shadow Puppets, Shadow Theatres and Shadow Films* reviewed the history of silhouette animations and described her techniques. Puppet animation was described in Bruce Holman's *Puppet Animation in the Cinema*.

Bruno Edera's work *Full Length Animated Feature Films* is a broad but detailed worldwide survey of animated features which reviews celluloid, collage, film painting, silhouette, puppet, and computer-generated animation. For the first time, this long form is placed into global perspective from the United States, Asia, Middle East, Australia, Eastern and Western Europe, together with hundreds of illustrations. The 187-page catalog in the last half of the work, listing credits and a synopsis for each animated feature, establishes this work as an important reference source. Surveying the same worldwide environment but with a decided thrust to the future is John Halas and Roger Manvell's volume *Art in Movement: New Directions in Animation*. Finely chosen and reproduced monochrome and color stills dominate the book, and the authors' survey of contemporary animation, embellished with a review of new techniques and visual effects beyond the approach that established Disney, is thorough. From a pictorial standpoint, this is an eye-dazzling work, expensively priced.

Computer Animation, edited by John Halas, helps to fill a gap in the animation literature concerning these new techniques. Twenty contributors help reduce the mystery in computer animation while providing detailed recommendations for harnessing the machine. Whether the future of animation production involves memory banks, interactive systems, and automated drawing, anyone contemplating an interest in the field should review this work for a better grasp of the future of the form, which promises to free the artist for creativity.

Ralph Stephenson's *The Animated Film*, a somewhat pretentious survey of world animation history, is nevertheless the only paperback overview of the field within reach of most budgets. While undocumented, Stephenson scans the horizon from animation in the 1920s, Disney and his contemporaries, to the animation cartoon in the post-World War II era. French, Canadian, Polish, British, Yugoslavian, Russian, German, Japanese, and Scandinavian animation traditions are also explored in the remaining chapters. A filmography listing numerous films by animators is especially useful for the beginner.

There are, of course, several general histories of film that devote a few pages to animation, but the subject is treated lightly. In all instances, Disney is mentioned most often. References to these works can be found in the bibliographies already noted.

In the last decade or two, in selected periodicals, there has been a new emphasis on animation subjects, focusing on animators, their techniques, and often descriptions of their works. Important periodical articles include *The American Film Institute Report* (Summer 1974), which devoted its entire issue to the subject of animation, including new material on Winsor McCay, Richard Huemer, Chuck Jones, and the Hollywood cartoon. *Film Comment* (January-February 1975) consisted of another twelve pieces on Warner Brothers' cartoons, contemporary and early animators, and television animation. Controlled circulation magazines, such as *Millimeter* and *Filmmakers' Newsletter*, have also featured well researched animation articles. Other articles have regularly appeared in *Films and Filming, Ecran, Print,* and a journal no longer published, *Film Fan Monthly.*

Films and Filming has featured an animation column by David Rider. *The American Film,* published by the American Film Institute, has placed renewed emphasis on animation. *American Cinematographer* has occasionally published animation materials, especially combined animation and live-action work. Other relevant periodicals regularly available include *Films In Review, Journal of Popular Film, Velvet Light Trap, Journal of the University Film Association, Film Comment,* and *Cartoonist Profiles.*

Lately a great deal of material, consisting of anecdotes and frequently undocumented case studies, has been irregularly published in a form called "fanzines"—magazines printed in limited runs for buffs and potential scholars. Some of this unrefereed material is of marginal quality, both in substance and in writing. But, the growth of these magazines indicates a renewed interest and audience in films of specialized types, including animation. Unless one subscribes to a favored fanzine at the outset, obtaining copies of back issues is very difficult since most libraries do not obtain these materials. A recent fanzine devoted exclusively to the animated Hollywood film has the dubious title of *Mindrot.* Others, such as *Photon, Monster Times,* and a more professionally printed *Cinefantastique,* have also contained articles on animation.

In late 1977, Mike Barrier and Mark Lilien revived the authoritative *Funnyworld* (P.O. Box 1633, New York, N.Y. 10001), an infrequently published animation periodical. Now, with a sharply focused editorial policy promising to remain in animation, and publishing on a quarterly schedule, Editor Barrier expects to remove *Funnyworld* ". . . from the fanzine ghetto . . ." (as he put it in an editorial of the first revived issue No. 17). Back issues of this lively and serious animation periodical are promised from University Microfilms.

While not put squarely into the fanzine category, some advertising media, such as *Film Collector's World* and *Classic Film Collector,* do provide very useful material, such as animation news, book reviews, announcements of upcoming animated television specials, new fanzines, and one-time-only publications. However, their chief value remains in advertising, Super 8mm and 16mm sound, silent, monochrome, and color films of animated and other subjects.

The history of animation has been given short shrift in most film histories. Even a casual perusal of the animation literature reveals a distinct lack of historical studies. The current publication emphasis is on individual animators, studios, and case studies. While animation history is certainly reviewed in many texts, there is seldom any effort to document fully factual information on given organizations and artists or to put those activities in the larger context of the film industry. Occasionally a few writers ignore the larger contexts entirely, choosing to emphasize personalities and artistic concerns, sometimes tending to romanticize their subject matter. Animation hymns, hero worship, adulation of personalities and style, and other questionable approaches to animation art and organization cloud important assessments still to be made concerning this abstract medium, which has proceeded to stages far beyond the traditional "golden age." Whether audiences for new computer-generated animation are conditioned for new styles and forms remains to be seen. We know little about changing styles in the so-called golden age or why "Disneyfication" was a formula that worked, for example. Certainly much more ought to be written about those problems since audience acceptance of any given form is an important precondition toward the maintenance of the medium for communication, whether it is for political propaganda, the marketing of consumer products, or ambiguous "entertainment." The artistic factors are important to be sure, but resurrection of animation art can be especially meaningful in these larger contexts if we understand the economic and organizational conditions under which it was produced and the political, psychological, and social environments within which it is consumed by mass audiences.

BIBLIOGRAPHY

BOOKS AND ARTICLES

Adamson, Joe. *Tex Avery: King of Cartoons.* New York: Popular Library, 1975.
The American Film Institute Report. Vol. 5. (Summer 1974). Special issue devoted to animation.
Ash, Lee. *Subject Collections: A Guide to Special Book Collections and Subject Emphases as Reported by University, College, Public, and Special Libraries and Museums in the United States and Canada.* 4th ed. New York: R. R. Bowker, 1974.
Batty, Linda. *Retrospective Index to Film Periodicals.* New York: R. R. Bowker, 1975.
Bukalski, Peter J. *Film Research: A Critical Bibliography With Annotations and Essay.* Boston: G. K. Hall, 1972.
Cabarga, Leslie. *The Fleischer Story.* Franklin Square, N.Y.: Nostalgia Press, 1976.
Canemaker, John. *The Animated Raggedy Ann and Andy.* Indianapolis: Bobbs-Merrill, 1977.

Catalogue of the Theater and Drama Collection: Research Library of the New York Public Library. Part III. Boston: G. K. Hall, 1967.

Cawkwell, Rim, and John M. Smith. *The World Encyclopedia of Film*. New York: A-W Visual Library, 1972.

Chicorel, Marietta. *Chicorel Index to Film Literature*. New York: Chicorel Library Publishing Corp., 1975.

Cowie, Peter. *International Film Guide*. Cranbury, N.J.: A. S. Barnes, 1964-

Disney, Diane, and Pete Martin. *The Story of Walt Disney*. New York: Henry Holt, 1956.

Edera, Bruno. *Full Length Animated Feature Films*. New York: Hastings House, 1977.

Falk, Nat. *How to Make Animated Cartoons: The History and Technique*. New York: Foundation Books, 1941.

Federation Internationale des Archives du Film. *International Index to Film Periodicals*. New York: R. R. Bowker, 1972- .

Feild, Robert D. *The Art of Walt Disney*. New York: Macmillan, 1942.

Film Comment. Vol. 11. (January-February 1975). Special issue devoted to animation.

Finch, Christopher. *The Art of Walt Disney*. New York: Harry N. Abrams, 1973, 1976.

Gerlach, John C., and Linda Gerlach. *The Critical Index*. New York: Teachers College Press, 1974.

Halas, John. *Computer Animation*. New York: Hastings House, 1974.

————. *The Great Movie Cartoon Parade*. New York: Bounty, 1976.

————. *Visual Scripting*. New York: Hastings House, 1976.

————. *The Technique of Film Animation*. 4th ed. New York: Hastings House, 1976.

————, and Roger Manvell. *Art In Movement: New Directions In Animation*. New York Hastings House, 1970.

Halliwell, Leslie. *The Filmgoer's Companion*. 4th ed. New York: Hill and Wang, 1974.

Heraldson, Donald. *Creators of Life: A History of Animation*. New York: Drake, 1975.

Hollman, Leonard. "Film List." *Film Collectors World*. No. 2-4 (1976), unpaged.

Holman, Bruce. *Puppet Animation in the Cinema*. Cranbury, N.J.: A. S. Barnes, 1975.

Kilgore, Al. "The Disney Assault." *Film Fan Monthly*, No. 87 (September 1968), 3-4.

Leonard, Harold, ed. *The Film Index: A Bibliography*, Vol. 1: *The Film As Art*. New York: Arno Press, 1970. Reprint.

Levitan, Eli L. *Animation Art in the Commercial Film*. New York: Reinhold, 1960.

Library of Congress. *Library of Congress Catalogue: Films and Other Materials for Projection*. Washington, D.C.: Library of Congress, 1973-1975. (With supplements)

———. *Motion Pictures, 1894-1959.* 4 vols. Washington, D.C.: Library of Congress, 1951-1960.

———. *National Union Catalogue 1953-1957,* Vol. 28: *Motion Pictures and Film Strips.* Ann Arbor, Mich.: J. W. Edwards, 1958.

———. *National Union Catalogue 1958-1962,* Vols. 53, 54: *Motion Pictures and Film Strips.* Ann Arbor, Mich.: J. W. Edwards, 1963.

———. *National Union Catalogue 1963-1967, Motion Pictures and Film Strips.* 2 vols. Ann Arbor, Mich.: J. W. Edwards, 1969.

Limbacher, James L. *Feature Films on 8mm and 16mm.* 5th ed. New York: R. R. Bowker Co., 1977.

MacCann, Richard Dyer, and Edward S. Perry. *The New Film Index.* New York: E. P. Dutton, 1975.

Madsen, Roy. *Animated Film: Concepts, Methods, Uses.* New York: Interland Publishing Co., 1969.

Maltin, Leonard. "More on the Disney Version." *Film Fan Monthly,* No. 87 (September 1968), 5-6.

———. *The Disney Films.* New York: Harry N. Abrams, 1973.

———, and Frank Manchel. *Film Study: A Resource Guide.* New Jersey: Associated University Press, 1973.

Manvell, Roger. *The Animated Film.* New York: Hastings House, 1955.

———, and Jacob Lewis. *International Encyclopedia of Film.* New York: Crown, 1972.

Mehr, Linda Harris. *Motion Pictures, Television and Radio: A Union Catalogue of Manuscript and Special Collections in the Western United States.* Boston: G. K. Hall, 1977.

Munden, Kenneth W., ed. *American Film Institute Catalogue of Motion Pictures: Feature Films, 1921-1930.* New York: R. R. Bowker, 1971.

———. *American Film Institute Catalogue of Motion Pictures: Feature Films, 1961-1970.* New York: R. R. Bowker, 1976.

Niver, Kemp. *Motion Pictures from the Library of Congress Paper Print Collection: 1894-1912.* Berkeley: University of California Press, 1967.

Perisic, Zoran. *The Animation Stand.* New York: Hastings House, 1976.

Rehrauer, George. *Cinema Booklist.* Metuchen, N.J.: Scarecrow Press, 1972. (With supplement, 1974).

Reiniger, Lotte. *Shadow Puppets, Shadow Theatres and Shadow Films.* London: B. T. Batsford, 1970. Reprint. Boston: Plays, 1975.

Sadoul, Georges. *Dictionary of Films.* Translated by Peter Morris. Berkeley: University of California Press, 1972.

———. *Dictionary of Filmmakers.* Translated by Peter Morris. Berkeley: University of California Press, 1972.

Schickel, Richard. *The Disney Version.* New York: Simon and Schuster, 1968.

Silva, Fred, et al. *Film Literature Index.* Albany, N.Y.: Filmdex, 1974-.

Spottiswoode, Raymond. *Focal Encyclopedia of Film and Television Techniques.* New York: Hastings House, 1970.

Stephenson, Ralph. *The Animated Film.* Cranbury, N.J.: A. S. Barnes, 1973.

Theater Arts Library, University of California (Los Angeles). *Motion Pictures:*

A *Catalogue of Books, Periodicals, Screenplays and Production Stills.* Boston: G. K. Hall, 1976.
Thomas, Bob. *The Art of Animation.* New York: Simon and Schuster, 1958.
————. *Walt Disney: An American Original.* New York: Simon and Schuster, 1976.
Weber, Olga S. *North American Film and Video Directory.* New York: R. R. Bowker, 1975.
Wheaton, Christopher D., and Richard B. Jewell. *Primary Cinema Resources: An Index to Screenplays, Interviews and Special Collections at the University of Southern California.* Boston: G. K. Hall, 1975.
Young, Margaret Labash, et al. *Subject Directory of Special Libraries and Information Centers.* Vols. 2 and 4. Detroit: Gale, 1975.
Young, William C. *American Theatrical Arts: Guide to Manuscripts and Special Collections in the United States and Canada.* Chicago: American Library Association, 1971.

PERIODICALS

American Cinematographer. Los Angeles, 1919-.
American Film: Journal of the Film and Television Arts. Washington, D.C., 1975-.
American Film Institute Report. Washington, D.C., 1970-.
Billboard. Cincinnati, Ohio, 1894-.
Cartoonist Profiles. Fairfield, Conn., 1969-.
Cinefantastique. Oak Park, Ill., 1970-.
Classic Film Collector. Indiana, Pa., 1962-.
Ecran. Montreal, Canada, 1961-.
Film Collector's World. Rapids City, Ill., 1976-.
Film Comment. New York, 1962-.
Film Fan Monthly. Teaneck, N.J., 1959-73.
Filmmakers' Newsletter. New York, 1967-.
Films and Filming. London, 1954-.
Films in Review. New York, 1950.
Funnyworld. Little Rock, Ark., 1973-.
Journal of Popular Film. Bowling Green, Ohio, 1972-.
Journal of the University Film Association. Philadelphia, 1949-.
Millimeter, New York, 1973-.
Mindrot, Minneapolis. 1975-.
Monster Times. New York, 1972-.
Moving Picture World. New York, 1907-27.
Photon. Brooklyn, N.Y., 1963-.
Print. Aspley Guise, England, 1964-.
University Film Study Newsletter. Cambridge, Mass., 1972-.
Variety. New York, 1905-.
Velvet Light Trap. Cottage Grove, Wis., 1971-.

CHAPTER 2 The Automobile
Maurice Duke

HISTORIC OUTLINE

Although man had dreamt of a self-propelled vehicle for centuries, it was not until the end of the nineteenth century that a practical road machine capable of sustained distances emerged for general use. Historians disagree on the actual inventor of the first American automobile, but it is widely known that men such as George B. Selden, Charles E. Duryea and J. Frank Duryea, John William Lambert, Gottfried Schloemer, Charles Black, Charles Brady King, and Ransom Eli Olds, among others, were constructing and testing gasoline engine vehicles in the last two decades of the century.

It was not until the first decade of the twentieth century, however, that the automobile emerged as a commercially practical business and industrial venture. Still sought after by collectors, the early Oldsmobile, followed shortly by a host of other American automobiles, was the first successfully produced and marketed motorcar in the United States. From an inauspicious beginning in 1901, the year in which 425 Oldsmobiles were manufactured and sold, the automobile industry grew to become a giant that has influenced our physical, intellectual, and moral lives in a way that is unequalled in modern times. By mid-century, nearly fifty million automobiles were registered in the United States. There are indeed few Americans who can truthfully claim that the motorcar has had no place in their lives.

When the automobile first appeared, it was treated as a curiosity, a plaything for the rich and a tinkering project for the inventors or the hapless blacksmith who might be called upon to aid a motorist who by some mechanical malfunction had suddenly become a pedestrian. The automobile quickly took hold, however, capturing people's minds as well as their imaginations. Born into an America that had virtually no road system, it soon began to shrink the size of the continent of whose vastness and inexhaustibility St. Jean deCrèvecoeur had boasted just over a century before. Although still not completely trustworthy for long distance touring, automobiles became popular for cross-country expeditions— giving rise, incidentally, to a number of early automobile travel narratives and novels—and for exploring places that mere decades before were out of range of the traveller or adventurer who had to rely on the horse, the ship, or the train.

When the automobile emerged from its novelty stage, its influence on American life became markedly greater. The mass production of Henry Ford's Model T, which began in 1908, ushered in a new era of attitudes and convictions about the motorcar. Ford proved that his vehicle—and presumably others as well—could be produced cheaply and could be made to operate efficiently. Both the joys and woes of owning self-propelled wheels had now come to mid-America. Although sudden death might lurk around the next curve and the neighborhood horses might be terrified, not to mention the emerging noise and pollution problems, there was a new sense of freedom across the land. Urban dwellers could escape to the country for a day; isolated rural residents could visit each other and the nearby towns and cities more easily; lovers had a ready-made mobile bedroom; and businessmen could move more quickly in their daily routines.

As the automobile became a way of life in America, so American life had to adjust to accommodate it. While the motorcar was shrinking the size of the continent, it was also altering both its physical and moral landscape as well. Service stations, garages, and parts warehouses popped up around the country at the same time that legislators and judges were pondering complex problems about how the use of the automobile should be governed. Also, both culturally and socially other changes were taking place. Society took a negative attitude to women driving automobiles, for example, steering wheels sometimes carrying a warning sign that read "Men and Boys Only." Clothes styles were altered to be more in keeping with what the motorist would need. Hotels began giving way to the more modern motel, a combination of the words *motor* and *hotel*, and city dwellers found they could live outside urban areas and motor to work, thus creating America's vast and sprawling suburbs.

When America emerged, chauvinistic and sassy, from World War I, the automobile, already firmly planted in American life, was there to help it celebrate its victory. In the decade of the 1920s, important social distinctions began to be made between owners and drivers of the myriad cars available in the country. Ford's Model T had been superseded by the more manageable and sleeker Model A; the rumble seat came into its own; and the owner of expensive cars, such as Cadillacs, Buicks, Chryslers, and Packards, set them aside from those who drove the more plebian Fords and Chevrolets. The female driver also came into her own, with such automobile manufacturers as, for example, Jordan, actually making a sales pitch to women. The liberated woman, so the ads implied, should choose a Jordan; and advertising pictures of this sleek car would often show a woman driving, with a man sitting beside her on their way to the club, tennis, or golf. And the Dusenberg, one of the great prestige cars of the era, is still preserved in an outdated phrase in our language: "It's a Doosy!"

Throughout the 1920s and 1930s, the automobile continued to be the great emancipator of middle America. It was not until the belt-tightening occasioned by World War II that serious thoughts about the longevity of the automobile began to be considered. Entering their first period of gasoline rationing, Americans now had to queue up to receive rationing stickers. "Is this trip necessary?" became the question of radio newscasters and politicians alike. The wheels of the country began to turn more slowly, but the speed was destined to be regained and even vastly accelerated in the next decade.

Emerging victorious from World War II, the American, as Lewis Mumford would later write in *The Highway and the City*, "sacrificed his life as a whole to the motorcar." Freeways and interstates took the place of the prewar highways, which now became relegated to secondary road status. Drive-in movies, dubbed passion pits by their critics, drive-in restaurants, drive-in churches, and even drive-in funeral parlors made their appearance across America. And the cars of yesteryear began reappearing on the nation's roads after having been reworked into custom vehicles, whose youthful creators steadfastly maintained reflected their innermost personalities. Although he applied the term to different cars at a later date, as cultural critic Tom Wolfe said, the 1950s and early 1960s marked the era of "the kandy°kolored, tangerine°flake, streamline baby." America was the car and the car was America.

Then something happened. In the early 1970s Americans began to face the reality that fossilized fuels might indeed be depleted in the foreseeable future. Moreover, the motorcar, long suspected as a serious atmospheric pollutant, came under the study of scientists who proved such to be the case. Adding to the already major problems the one of safety, the automobile thus became a political issue, and Detroit car manufacturers found themselves dictated to more by Washington than by their own boards of directors. Suddenly, the automobile became in many people's minds the great enemy, and ominous rumblings from the federal government were a portent of intentions to break up the American's love affair with his wheels. One can only guess as to where such sentiments will eventually lead. As *Car and Driver* magazine speculated some months ago, America might be waking up with a hangover from the greatest party in human history.

From the beginning of recorded history, man has been a competitive creature. One aspect of this competition has manifested itself in sports, the leisure-time play world of the adult. Sports are surveyed elsewhere in this book; but because the automobile has occupied a unique role in American sports, its place in competition has been reserved for this section.

The automobile had hardly emerged as a functioning mechanical entity from the small factories of America than one of its special uses came to be competition. That competition has grown, and the groups that sponsor it have become so organized, that automobile sports in America is now a multi-million dollar entertainment industry. Whether it is a local businessman racing in amateur weekend events, or A. J. Foyt making his bid for an unprecedented fourth career win at Indianapolis, the automobile has changed the sports pages of America's newspapers and the Monday morning quarterbacking in America's offices in a permanent way.

Historians agree that the first officially recognized American automobile race occurred in November 1895 when the Chicago *Times-Herald* Race, from Chicago to nearby Evanston, Illinois, was run over a distance of just fifty-five miles. Quite naturally, other sanctioned races soon followed in great numbers. During these early days of racing, competitors took to the open public roads to stage their events, but legislators quickly identified and acted against this kind of racing because of the dangers that it imposed upon life and property. Accordingly, sanctioned racing, using specially made cars that were usually modifications of those available to the public, took to horse racing tracks, where they could run in an orderly circle before grandstand-seated spectators.

With the passage of time, however, the automobile manufacturers recognized the need for specialized courses that would accommodate the peculiar needs of automobile racing as distinct from horse racing. This included hard-surface tracks, provisions for spectator safety, and an area where the cars could be worked upon before, or often during, a race. Accordingly, large wooden oval tracks were constructed. Similar in design to the present-day Indianapolis track, they were widely used throughout the 1920s. Later, when better surfacing materials became available, these kinds of tracks gave way to the conventionally paved courses, such as those now widely in use in all parts of the country. The best known of these courses is undoubtedly the Indianapolis Motor Speedway, although the annual race there is only one on the yearly circuit sponsored by the United States Auto Club (USAC). One of the major sponsors in American racing, the USAC also sponsors sprint car, dirt car, midget, stock, and road-racing events.

Until the close of World War II American automobile racing was conducted almost exclusively on the oval tracks of the Indianapolis type. Following the war, however, other forms of racing began to emerge. They now include stock-car racing, road racing, drag racing, and off-road racing. Each form has contributed markedly to the overall sport of motor racing.

Stock-car racing had its beginnings in the South and is an outgrowth of the illegal whiskey industry, which has permeated Southern culture for years. Moonshiners, who of necessity had to produce their wares out of the view of the law enforcement officers, early discovered methods of engine and chassis preparation that would allow them maximum speed and minimum risk. For this operation, they chose inconspicuous American sedans and then set about preparing them for their unique duty. Often the drivers of these cars would run whiskey during the week and then show up at a local track on the weekend to race against each other.

In the early 1950s, stock-car racing, as it came to be called, underwent marked changes. In the first place it was organized on a national level by the National Association of Stock Car Racing (NASCAR). Further, it took on a new respectability and spread nationwide with headquarters in Daytona Beach, Florida. With the proliferation of this popular form of racing came an interest on the part of the Detroit manufacturers. Precisely how much sponsorship is involved between the top NASCAR teams and the companies that make the cars they race is not known. Indeed, the manufacturers constantly and categorically deny involvement in racing, but the influence is surely there. National advertising alone is enough to suggest that such is the case.

At the same time that stock-car racing was moving from the backwoods brush country of the South and into national prominence, another form of racing was introduced to America. This was road racing, which brought to the American racing scene not only a new kind of motorized competition, but also the influence of and interest in international racing, long popular in Europe. It was not long before the names of such great European drivers as Tazio Nuvolari, Rudolf Caracciola, Graham Hill, Mike Hawthorne and the South American Juan Manuel Fangio became, if not household words, common enough to racing across America.

The revival of road racing in America, where it had been virtually unknown since before the days of the wooden race courses of the pre-1920s, came about as the result of the introduction of the now legendary MG-TC sports car following World War II. Upon their return from duty in Europe, many GI's brought with them these small English sports cars, a kind of vehicle that was unknown to Americans of the time. Nimble and swift if operated by a seasoned driver, these machines quickly came to be used in competitive events. Soon the town of Watkins Glen, New York, today internationally known for its support of road racing, became the site of races that were run through the streets of the village. About this time the Sports Car Club of America (SCCA) was formed to promote both amateur and professional competition. In order to be a member of this organization, the applicant had to own a sports car; he was dropped from membership when he divested himself of it.

Over the years the SCCA has grown to the point that it sponsors major professional road races throughout the country on closed courses designed to simulate actual road conditions and, in addition, all the amateur road racing events that are conducted each year from coast to coast. International in flavor, road racing is now one of the major spectator events on the American racing scene.

Drag racing, another popular form of American automobile sport, had its origins at the same time that road racing was being reintroduced to America, although the two groups are quite different.

Automotive writer Brock Yates, the iconoclastic senior editor of *Car and Driver* magazine, has speculated that drag racing had its beginning in California, where city fathers attempted to slow down traffic by installing traffic lights at intersections that normally would not need them. The outcome was, Yates speculated, that youthful hot-rodders would stop beside each other at a red light and then race to the next one, and so on down the street.

No matter what the precise origin of this form of racing, which involves driving a specially prepared car in a straight line to its maximum speed, its early forms doubtless took place on public streets and highways. With the passing of time, however, the drag racers moved to special straight tracks prepared for this kind of sport and became organized under the National Hot Rod Association (NHRA). This form of racing, in which the cars regularly run at speeds in excess of two hundred miles per hour, is often said to be a mechanic's sport rather than a driver's sport, since the preparation of the car rather than driving skill, some maintain, is more crucial.

Off-road racing is a relatively new and highly controversial kind of motorized competition. It involves competing in vehicles specially prepared to negotiate rough terrain, but not on a prepared course, and withstand the mechanical strain for hundreds, often thousands, of miles.

One other kind of racing deserves mention here, before we turn to the myriad material available for the study of the automobile. That is the Grand Prix circuit, one or two of whose races are conducted yearly on American soil.

The Grand Prix, consisting of a series of races run throughout the year in various countries, is considered by many to be the pinnacle of motorcar racing. The world champion driver is decided each year from the ranks of this group, and its drivers regularly receive more international publicity than those on any other circuit. Each year, in October, one of the Grand Prix races is run at Watkins Glen, and recently there has been added a Grand Prix West, which is run through the streets of Long Beach, California. Because the drivers on the Grand Prix circuit have played so crucial a part in the American racing scene, any study of the American automobile that omitted them would be less than complete.

Whether the future of American automobile racing is inextricably intertwined with the future of the American passenger car is impossible to say. There is the likelihood that even if the American family car as we know it disappeared from the landscape, automobile racing would still continue. After all, the spectators at the chariot races of antiquity were not themselves drivers of chariots. At this point it is safe to say that American automobile racing is not suffering the same illnesses as the automobile at large in our society. The hangover from the party of racing is one confined largely to escalating costs, not to a general malaise and disenchantment with the automobile that now permeate a large segment of society.

RESEARCH COLLECTIONS

This section centers on the major American collections of published and/or manuscript materials about the automobile, not on collections of specimens of actual automobiles, of which hundreds exist. For a list of where such vehicles can be located and viewed one should consult "Automobile Museums of the World," in *Automobiles of the World*, by Albert L. Lewis and Walter A. Musciano.

By far the most nearly complete collection of materials available for the study of the automobile in America is housed in the Automotive History Collection of the Detroit Public Library. This enormous collection, over thirteen thousand books and eight thousand bound periodicals, which spans the history of the automobile, is the starting place for anyone interested not only in the cultural and social significance of the motorcar, but also in its entire history and development. The collection is concerned with all aspects of the automobile. Fortunately for researchers, it has been cataloged and a description, by subject and author, of its contents is readily available in *The Automotive History of the Detroit Public Library: A Simplified Guide to Its Holdings*, 2 volumes.

Another major collection is housed in the Free Library of Philadelphia. Although there is no published guide to its holdings, this collection contains a total of some thirteen thousand volumes and is concerned with all aspects of automotive industry and its history. Included also are shop manuals and periodicals centering on the automobile. Of particular importance are the seventeen thousand photographs of automobiles, ranging from the late nineteenth century to the present.

The DeGolyer Foundation Library of Southern Methodist University holds some ninety thousand volumes concerning the automobile, along with first editions by prominent authors, as well as manuscripts, photographs, and maps. The Cleveland Public Library and the New York Public Library also have extensive holdings on the automobile, as does the San Diego Public Library, which houses five thousand volumes. In the Stuart A. Work Collection on automobile history at the University of California at Los Angeles, one can locate materials not only historical in nature, but also centering on racing, automobile shows, and promotional events concerning the automobile. Other materials can be located in the Flint Public Library in Flint, Michigan, and in the Highway Safety Research Institute Library of the University of Michigan, which houses some twenty-six thousand items centering on the automobile.

The Library of Vehicles in Garden Grove, California, deserves special mention. W. Everett Miller, automotive engineer and curator, reports that there are millions of individual items in the collection, which covers vehicles of transport on land, worldwide through all ages, their makers, users, and repairers. Miller reports, for example, some thirteen thousand vehicle catalogs, fourteen thousand magazines, and six thousand books. This is only a part of that vast collection.

HISTORY AND CRITICISM

The researcher attempting to uncover the history of the American automobile will find that his task is a relatively easy one, inasmuch as a number of good historical studies are readily available. Such, however, is not the case when one attempts to find those writings about the social and cultural significance of the automobile, the reason being that much of that material lies buried in random chapters of longer histories. Thus, in identifying materials of the latter kind, the present essay often directs the reader to individual chapters in books.

Among the general histories of the American automobile, one most often cited is John Henry Mueller's "The Automobile," a thesis completed at the University of Chicago in 1928. In *The Gasoline Age: The Story of the Men Who Made It*, C. B. Glasscock presents a general history with a bibliography and a list of more than fifteen hundred automobiles of various names and makes that have been produced in the United States, while J. Frank Duryea writes of his own invention in *America's First Automobile*.

Lawrence J. White writes factually in his *The Automobile Industry Since 1945*, while Rudolph E. Anderson presents many little-known stories about the history of the American automobile from its beginnings to about 1920 in *The Story of the American Automobile*. The early history of the automobile in terms of its developers is the subject of *The Road Is Yours*, by Reginald McIntosh Cleveland and S. T. Williamson, which also contains a useful chronology of important dates in the development of the American automobile.

A book that centers more closely on English cars than American ones, but is invaluable for the information it gives about the pre-gasoline era, is Anthony Bird's *The Motor Car, 1765-1914*. Another, which contains a worthwhile "Suggested Reading'" list, is John B. Rae's *The American Automobile: A Brief History*. Other general studies include *Great American Automobiles*, by John Bentley, and *The Automobile: How It Came and Grew, and Has Changed Our Lives*, by Frank Ernest Hill. A general book that contains information and descriptions of over four thousand various makes of automobiles, many of them American, is *The Complete Encyclopaedia of Motor Cars*, edited by G. N. Georgano.

Rich Taylor, former managing editor of *Car and Driver* and former editor of *Special-Interest Author*, is currently bringing to completion his book, *The Complete Automobile Almanac*, to be published by Scribner's Sons. The book is scheduled for a fall 1978 publication and is advertised as offering "*everything* you would ever want to know about cars." Useful addresses and manufacturing and racing data are planned for this book.

Anyone interested in the overall moral implications of the automobile would do well to consult the pioneer work by Leo Marx, *The Machine in the Garden: Technology and the Pastoral Ideal*, which chronicles the dilemma when the fruits of the industrial revolution have to be weighed against the damage the machine can cause. In order to understand the chronological development of the internal combustion engine in its larger relationship to human evolution, one can find valuable information in chapter 8, "The Drive for Power," of Jacob Bronowski's *The Ascent of Man*. No one who attempts to understand the automobile as a positive moral and aesthetic force in human life should neglect Robert M. Pirsig's *Zen and the Art of Motorcycle Maintenance*. Although Pirsig ostensibly writes about motorcycles, he actually builds a historical, moral, and philosophical context from which to view and comprehend the vast network of machinery with which our daily lives are filled. A study of the social significance of the automobile in American culture can be found in chapter 8, "The Automobile Revolution," of Frederick Lewis Allen's *The Big Change: America Transforms Itself, 1900-1905*.

Almost as soon as the automobile became prominent in American life, references to specific social and moral questions that it posed began to appear in print.

In 1905 R. T. Sloss included such chapters as "The Automobile in Commerce," "The Automobile in Sport," and "Touring," in his *The Book of the Automobile*, a study that includes information about early automobile legislation as well. In 1916, James R. Doolittle and others included a germinal chapter in their book *The Romance of the Automobile Industry.* In chapter 11, "The Romance of Progress," for example, they consider the automobile as a force in eugenics, hygenics, the improvement of the quality of food, and the emancipation of women. Again, Herbert Lee Barber, in his 1917 book *The Story of the Automobile: Its History and Development from 1760 to 1917*, includes in chapter 5, "Benefits Conferred by the Automobile," a study of the social and cultural significance of the automobile in American society during the early years of the century. (Historians will also find valuable information in Barber's price list for automobiles and trucks, included at the end of the book.)

Passing references to various social and cultural aspects of the automobile in books published during the 1920s and 1930s may also be found in Ralph C. Epstein's *The Automobile Industry* and in Robert S. Lynd and Helen M. Lynd's *Middletown: A Study in Contemporary American Culture*, and *Middletown in Transition: A Study in Cultural Conflicts*, by the same authors.

Following World War II John Kouwenhoven was concerned with the aesthetics of the automobile and America's attitude toward it, as is evidenced in passing references in his *Made in America: The Arts in Modern Civilization*. Although published in England and therefore concerned primarily with the English automobiles, *The Internal Combustion Engine and Its Effects Upon Society*, by John Theodore Brabazon and Cuthbert Moore, presents observations that are as valid in America as in Great Britain; and Frank Donovan's *Wheels for a Nation* explores the ways in which the automobile has changed and is changing our lives, socially, culturally, physically, and economically.

Several books published in this decade also center on the automobile as a social, cultural, and moral force. James J. Flink in *America Adopts the Automobile, 1895-1910* explores the sociocultural milieu within which the automobile came of age, while *The Car Culture*, by the same author, studies the influence of the automobile as a synthesizing force in American history. A more particularized study is Reynold M. Wik's *Henry Ford and Grass-Roots America*, an appraisal of the impact that the Model T Ford made on rural American life. A similar study, but one of considerably broader scope, is John B. Rae's *The Road and the Car In American Life*, which deals with the impact of these two subjects on Americans from the beginning of the mass-produced automobiles of the first decade of the century to 1970. Finally, P. M. Townroe's *The Social and Political Consequences of the Motor Car* treats in admirable fashion just what the title promises. Unseen at this writing is *Driven: The American Four-Wheeled Love Affair*, by Leon Mandel. Advertised as "a psychological, sociological, and economic appraisal of the car's impact on society," this book is scheduled for forthcoming publication.

Despite the generally positive attitudes toward the automobile as expressed by society and its writers alike, there are a number of published negative appraisals of which the researcher should be aware. These books, which are proliferating with the passing of time, began in the 1950s. More will doubtless appear in the future.

One of the first among the studies that views America's motorcars as less than desirable is John Keats' *The Insolent Chariots*, which surveys the history, advertising, and problems of automobile maintenance of the great Detroit industry. It also discusses that industry's failure to hear and heed the voice of the public where the automobile is concerned. Two other books by one of America's most respected scholarly writers, which continue in the same vein, are *The City in History: Its Origins, Its Transformations, and Its Prospects* and *The Highway and the City*. Written by Lewis Mumford, these books—especially the latter one—judge the automobile to be a devastatingly negative force on America's cities.

One of the most controversial, if specialized, books that attacks the motorcar in America came from consumer advocate Ralph Nader in 1965. *Unsafe at Any Speed* is in particular an indictment of the General Motors Corvair, the small rear-engined automobile designed to counter the enormous success of the imported Volkswagen. Nader, who parleyed the circumstances surrounding the publication of this book into a national *cause célèbre* that launched his self-appointed mission, presents statistical information and testimony to buttress his belief that the designers and manufacturers were callously negligent in designing the Corvair. Because of Nader's general indictment of the automobile industry as a whole, the student of the automobile's history will find this book central to his study.

Several important studies in the 1970s deserve the attention of the researcher because they point out the new way in which the automobile is being perceived in America. In *Beyond the Automobile: Reshaping the Transportation Environment*, Tabor R. Stone offers tentative methods of transportation that would supersede the motorcar. Kenneth R. Schneider, in *Autokind Vs. Mankind*, boldly asserts his thesis that "challenges the automobile for what it does to life in the cities and the stranglehold it has on society." He continues "against the fradulent claims of technology," as he calls them, concluding that the automobile must be removed from society. Automobile journalist John Jerome clearly announces that "the premise of this book is that the automobile must go," in *The Death of the Automobile*, while Emma Rothschild foresees the time that the automobile will be gone in *Paradise Lost: The Decline of the Auto-Industrial Age*. In *From Main Street to State Street: Town, City, and Community in*

America, Park Dixon Goist treats the negative impact of the automobile on middle America. In this regard, chapter 3, "Automobility and Community," is particularly useful. For an antidote to this strain of negativism in current writings about the automobile one should consult *The War Against the Automobile,* by B. Bruce-Biggs. In this book the author attacks the anti-automobile forces, including Ralph Nader.

A number of books treat in whole or in part specialized topics within the development of the automobile in American life. In chapter 18, "Milady at the Wheel," of *Get a Horse! The Story of the Automobile in America,* M. M. Musselman charts the emergence of the female driver in the United States, while Tom Wolfe's *The Kandy*Kolored Tangerine*Flake Streamline Baby* centers on the fad of automobile customizing and hot rod building on the West Coast. Although basically a cultural study, Cynthia Golomb Dettelbach's *In the Driver's Seat: The Automobile in American Literature and Popular Culture* should not be overlooked by anyone interested in the literary use to which many authors have put automobiles. In *Man and Motor: The 20th Century Love Affair,* editor Derek Jewell collects and reprints myriad writings about the automobile from authors as distant in time as Rudyard Kipling and as contemporary as Henry Miller. Covered also in this book is the motorcar in movies and in art. Raymond Lee's *Fit For the Chase: Cars and the Movies* deals with the use to which automobiles have been put in popular films.

Although primarily a history of styling changes in the automotive industry to about 1970, Paul C. Wilson's *Chrome Dreams: Automobile Styling Since 1893* includes sections about popular tastes regarding automobiles. In *American Funeral Cars and Ambulances Since 1900,* Thomas A. McPherson traces in minute detail, replete with photographs of each specimen, the history of the hearse and ambulance for the entire twentieth century. The appendix to this book contains a helpful list of names and addresses of all the manufacturers discussed and illustrated in the text.

Relying on court and corporation records, family histories, and autobiographies, as well as trade journals and newspapers, George S. May attempts to uncover the reasons for the American automobile industry's having begun in Michigan in *A Most Unique Machine: The Michigan Origins of the American Automobile Industry.* And George Barris, in *Cars of the Stars,* prints a number of captioned photographs of the specialized vehicles that have been owned or used by Hollywood celebrities. Finally in prose that tells us much about the motoring public of yesteryear, a number of original advertisements are reproduced in *The Poster Book of Antique Auto Ads—1898-1920,* compiled by Howard Garrett, as well as in *Automobiles: 1900-1905, Automobiles: 1906-1912,* and *The Roaring 20's,* all of which reproduce posters.

Anyone interested in charting the historical, cultural, and social significance of the automobile, be it domestic or imported, should not overlook the importance of the biographies and autobiographies of central figures in the industry. Listed here is a selection of the major books on that subject. They are presented chronologically by publication date, because in that order they represent not only the stories of the men who have produced our cars but also the history of the industry at large: Lyman Horace Weeks, *Automobile Biographies: An Account of the Lives . . . of Those . . . Identified With the . . . Vehicles* (1904); Henry Ford, with Samuel Crowther, *My Life and Work* (1922); Walter P. Chrysler and Boyden Sparkes, *Life of An American Workman* (1937); J. C. Long, *Roy D. Chapin*, the founder of the Hudson Company (1945); Edwin Corle, *John Studebaker: An American Dream* (1948); Allan Nevins, *Ford*, 3 volumes, (1954, 1957, and 1963); W. O. Bentley, *W. O.* (1958); Alfred P. Sloan, Jr., *My Years With General Motors* (1963); W. Robert Nitske and Charles Morrow Wilson, *Rudolf Diesel* (1965); Edward John Montagu, *Rolls of Rolls-Royce* (1966); Z. E. Lambert and R. J. Wyatt, *Lord Austin—The Man* (1968); Richard Crabb, *Birth of a Giant* (1969), which contains brief biographies of early American car makers and the stories of their cars; Anthony Rhodes, *Louis Renault* (1969); Lawrence R. Gustin, *Billy Durant: Creator of General Motors* (1973); Richard M. Langworth, *Kaiser-Frazer: The Last Onslaught of Detroit* (1975); Sol Sanders, *Honda: The Man and His Machines* (1975); Ferry Porsche, with John Bentley, *We at Porsche: The Autobiography of Dr. Ing. h.c. Ferry Porsche* (1976); and George S. May, *R. E. Olds: Auto Industry Pioneer* (1977). The researcher should not overlook the fact that many of the listed books contain valuable bibliographies.

So much has been written on racing, some of it excellent and unfortunately some of it of dubious quality, that it is difficult to know where to begin research on the topic. The intent of this section is to send those interested to the books that will yield the most information on the subject.

Anthony Pritchard and Keith Davey's *The Encyclopaedia of Motor Racing* states that it contains "the results of every important international motor race from the first event in 1894 to 1973," while Robert Cutter and Bob Fendell's *Encyclopedia of Auto Racing Greats* offers a compendium of information about drivers in the sport, along with statements on racing from many of them. In *Great American Automobiles: A Dramatic Account of Their Achievements in Competition*, John Bentley concentrates more on the machines than the men who drive them.

A comprehensive story centering on the American scene, from its beginning to the early 1970s, can be found in veteran automobile racing writer Albert R. Bochroch's *American Automobile Racing*, while coverage of the scene to about 1930 is presented in *The Golden Age of the American Racing Car*, by Griffith Borgeson, a volume that contains useful appendices on the early tracks, drivers, races, and cars. Another book that centers on the early years of American competition is *Great Auto Races*, a handsome volume written and lavishly illustrated by Peter Helck. A useful introduction to the whole topic of racing can be found in *The New York Times Complete Guide to Auto Racing*, by John Radosta. Much additional information is contained in Charles Fox's *The Great Racing Cars and Drivers* and in Brock W. Yates' *Racers and Drivers. A History of the World's Racing Cars*, by Richard Alexander Hough, offers additional information about the machines used in competition over the years.

The annual Indianapolis race, often dubbed the greatest spectacle in racing, has been the subject of uncounted articles, as well as a number of books. Among the more useful are *The Indy 500: An American Institution Under Fire*, by Ron Dorson, and a remarkably complete and well-illustrated study is *The Indianapolis 500: A Complete Pictorial History*, by John and Barbara Devaney. *The Indianapolis Records*, by Alan C. Hess, presents information about its subject up to 1949, while Lyle Kenyon Engle's *132 of the Most Unusual Cars That Ever Ran at Indianapolis* discusses "the greatest and most unusual cars that ever ran at the Indy track." The famous New York to Paris race is the subject of J. F. Clymer's *The Story of the New York to Paris Race*. And *Motor Racing*, edited by Peter Berthon, contains essays by various experts writing on different aspects of the sport.

Two of America's best known automobile manufacturers who have competed against each other in sales of cars as well as on the track form the subject of *The Racing Fords*, by Hans Tanner, and *Chevrolet=Racing . . . ?: Fourteen Years of Raucous Silence!!*, by Paul Van Valkenburg. *The Model T Ford in Speed and Sport*, by Daniel Roger Post, offers a nostalgic look into racing's past.

Two studies of contemporary American racing from unique points of view are worth the attention of those interested in looking behind the scenes of the sport. They are *Sunday Driver*, by Brock Yates, and *The Stainless Steel Carrot*, by Sylvia Wilkinson. Automotive journalist Yates decided that in order to write well about racing he needed the actual experience on the track, and *Sunday Driver* chronicles his year in racing in the Trans Am series. Wilkinson's book follows the ups and downs of a professional driver during an entire season.

Although European Grand Prix racing was long known on the continent before it made its mark on American fans, drivers, builders, and mechanics, its history is influential in the background of American racing. Numerous Americans have been and still are involved in the sport, and the American racing fan remains keenly interested in the careers of the drivers on this circuit.

Several books that take the reader into the world of Grand Prix competition include William Court's *A History of Grand Prix Motor Racing, 1906-1951*; L. J. K. Setright's *The Grand Prix*; Richard Garrett's *Fast and Furious: The Story of the World Championship of Drivers*; Robert Daley's *Cars at Speed: The Grand Prix Circuit*; Giovanni Lurani's *History of the Racing Car*, which concentrates mostly on the Grand Prix; and Barré Lyndon's *Grand Prix*, a study of that form of racing in the mid-1930s. A book that deserves special mention here is Sir Malcolm Campbell's *The Romance of Motor Racing*. Sir Malcolm, himself one of racing's greats, presents in this book one of the first behind-the-scenes looks at the early years of the sport, including the competition at Indianapolis.

In the category of American road racing, one finds three books that are especially useful in understanding this particular form of competition. They are Raymond Yates and Brock W. Yates' early study titled *Sport and Racing Cars*, Anthony Pritchard's *The Racing Sports Car*, and Lyle Kenyon Engle's *Road Racing in America*, which describes the state of the sport in the early 1970s.

Other books on various aspects of American racing include Eugene Jaderquist and Griffith Borgeson's *Best Hot Rods*, one of the earliest books on this form of racing. Done in the early 1950s, it is useful today because it gives reference data about the beginning of hotrodding. *The Complete Book of Fuel and Gas Dragsters*, by Lyle Kenyon Engle and the editorial staff of *Auto Racing* magazine, is self-explanatory, as is *The Complete Book of Stock-Bodied Drag Racing*, by the same authors. Two other books in the same category are Wally Parks' *Drag Racing Yesterday and Today* and *The Sox & Martin Book of Drag Racing*, by Bill Neely and the editors of *Hot Rod* magazine. *The Roar of the Mighty Midgets* provides data on this popular kind of racing just following World War II. Joe Scalzo's *Stand on the Gas: Sprint Car Racing in America* admirably covers this popular sport.

Two books on stock-car racing, one of America's most popular spectator sports, are Jerry Bledsoe's *The World's Number One, Flat-Out, All-Time Great, Stock Car Racing Book*, which provides an overview of the sport, and Lyle Kenyon Engle's *The Complete Book of NASCAR Stock Racing*, done with the assistance of the editorial staff of *Auto Racing* magazine. Another book on this subject is Bloys Britt's *The Racing Flag: NASCAR*. Off-road racing is the subject of still another book by Lyle Kenyon Engle, *Off-Road Racing*, the story of men and machines in this form of the sport.

From the beginning of racing, fans and others have wanted to know

about the men, sometimes women, who raced the cars. Included here is a
list of biographies and autobiographies, drawn from the enormous amount
of published material on the subject. The intent in compiling this list has
been twofold. In the first place, the lives of many of the greatest drivers
are told in these books; second, the history of the sport is also drama-
tized. The list has been arranged chronologically, in an attempt to follow
the history of racing as well as of the lives of those who made it:

J. Wentworth Day, *Speed: The Authentic Life of Sir Malcolm Camp-
bell* (1932); Russ Catlin, *The Life of Ted Horn* (1949); Wilbur Shaw,
Gentlemen, Start Your Engines (1955); Alf Francis, *Alf Francis: Racing
Mechanic* (1958); Giovanni Lurani, translated by John Eason Gibson,
Nuvolari (1959); Rudolf Caracciola, translated by Sigrid Rock, *A Racing
Car Driver's World* (1961); William F. Nolan, *Barney Oldfield* (1961);
William F. Nolan, *Phil Hill: Yankee Champion* (1962); Stirling Moss, *All
But My Life* (1963); Jim Clark, *Jim Clark at the Wheel* (1965); Don
Garlits and Brock Yates, *King of the Dragsters: The Story of Big Daddy
(Don) Garlits* (1967); Pat Moss, *The Story So Far* (1967); Graham Gauld,
Jim Clark (1968); Anthony Granatelli, *They Call Me Mister 500* (1969);
Graham Hill, *Life at the Limit* (1969); Bill Libby, *Parnelli: A Story of
Auto Racing* (1969); Mario Andretti, with Bob Collins, *What's It Like
Out There?* (1970); Craig Breedlove, as told to Bill Neely, *Spirit of Amer-
ica* (1971); Heinz Prüller, with Jocen Rindt, *Jocen Rindt* (1971); Jack
Brabham, *When the Flag Drops* (1971); Richard Petty, as told to Bill
Neely, *Grand National: The Autobiography of Richard Petty* (1971);
Eoin S. Young, *Bruce McLaren: The Man and His Racing Team* (1971);
Jeanne Beeching, *The Last Season: The Life of Bruce McLaren* (1972);
Jacques Deschenaux, *Jo Siffert* (1972); Jackie Stewart and Peter Manso,
Faster!: A Racer's Diary (1972); Emerson Fittipaldi and Elizabeth Hay-
ward, *Flying on the Ground* (1973); Denis F. Jenkinson, editor, *Fangio*
(1973); Jim Hunter, *Racing to Win* (1974); Bill Libby, *Foyt* (1974); Peter
Revson and Leon Mandel, *Speed with Style* (1974); Mark Donohue, with
Paul Van Valkenburg, *The Unfair Advantage* (1975); Sam Posey, *The
Mudge Pond Express* (1976); Bill Libby, with Richard Petty, *"King
Richard": The Richard Petty Story* (1977).

BIBLIOGRAPHY

Allen, Frederick Lewis. *The Big Change: America Transforms Itself, 1900-1950.*
    New York: Harper and Row, 1952.
Anderson, Rudolph E. *The Story of the American Automobile.* Washington,
    D.C.: Public Affairs Press, 1950.
Andretti, Mario, with Bob Collins. *What's It Like Out There?* Chicago: Henry
    Regnery, 1970.

Automobiles, 1900-1905. Dallas, Tex.: Highlands Historical Press, n.d.

Automobiles, 1906-1912. Dallas, Tex.: Highlands Historical Press, n.d.

The Automotive History Collection of the Detroit Public Library: A Simplified Guide to Its Holdings. 2 vols. Boston, Mass.: G. K. Hall, 1966.

Barber, Herbert Lee. *The Story of the Automobile: Its History and Development from 1760 to 1917*. Chicago: A. J. Munson, 1917.

Barris, George. *Cars of the Stars*. Middle Village, N.Y.: Jonathan David, 1974.

Beeching, Jeanne. *The Last Season: The Life of Bruce McLaren*. Newfoundland, N.J.: Walter R. Haessner, 1972.

Bentley, John. *Great American Automobiles: A Dramatic Account of Their Achievements in Competition*. Englewood Cliffs, N.J.: Prentice-Hall, 1957.

Bentley, W. O. *W. O.* London: Hutchinson, 1958.

Berthon, Peter, ed. *Motor Racing*. London: Seeley Service, 1939.

Bird, Anthony. *The Motor Car, 1765-1914*. London: B. T. Batsford, 1960.

Bledsoe, Jerry. *The World's Number One, Flat-Out, All-Time Great, Stock Car Racing Book*. Garden City, N.Y.: Doubleday, 1975.

Bochroch, Albert R. *American Automobile Racing*. New York: Viking, 1974.

Borgeson, Griffith. *The Golden Age of the American Racing Car*. New York: W. W. Norton, 1966.

Brabazon, John Theodore, and Cuthbert Moore. *The Internal Combustion Engine and Its Effect Upon Society*. London: Oxford University Press, 1971.

Brabham, Jack. *When the Flag Drops*. London: William Kimber, 1971.

Breedlove, Craig, as told to Bill Neely. *Spirit of America*. Chicago: Henry Regnery, 1971.

Britt, Bloys. *The Racing Flag: NASCAR*. New York: Pocket Books, 1965.

Bronowski, Jacob. *The Ascent of Man*. Boston: Little, Brown, 1973.

Bruce-Biggs, B. *The War Against the Automobile*. New York: E. P. Dutton, 1977.

Campbell, Malcolm. *The Romance of Motor Racing*. London: Hutchinson, n.d.

Caracciola, Rudolf. *A Racing Car Driver's World*. Translated by Sigrid Rock. New York: Farrar, Straus and Cudahy, 1961.

Catlin, Russ. *The Life of Ted Horn*. Los Angeles: Floyd Clymer, 1949.

Chrysler, Walter P., and Boyden Sparkes. *Life of an American Workman*. New York: Dodd, Mead, 1937.

Clark, Jim. *Jim Clark at the Wheel*. New York: Coward-McCann, 1965.

Cleveland, Reginald McIntosh, and S. T. Williamson. *The Road Is Yours*. New York: Greystone Press, 1951.

Clymer, J. F. *The Story of the New York to Paris Race*. Los Angeles: Floyd Clymer, 1951.

Corle, Edwin. *John Studebaker: An American Dream*. New York: E. P. Dutton, 1948.

Court, William. *A History of Grand Prix Motor Racing, 1906-1951*. London: Macdonald, 1966.

Crabb, Richard. *Birth of a Giant*. Philadelphia: Chilton, 1969.

Cutter, Robert, and Bob Fendell. *Encyclopedia of Auto Racing Greats*. Englewood Cliffs, N.J.: Prentice-Hall, 1973.

Daley, Robert. *Cars at Speed: the Grand Prix Circuit*. Philadelphia: Lippincott, 1961.

Day, J. Wentworth. *Speed: The Authentic Life of Sir Malcolm Campbell*. London: Hutchinson, 1932.

Deschenaux, Jacques. *Jo Siffert*. London: William Kimber, 1972.

Dettelbach, Cynthia Golomb. *In the Driver's Seat: The Automobile in American Literature and Popular Culture*. Westport, Conn.: Greenwood Press, 1976.

Devaney, John, and Barbara Devaney. *The Indianapolis 500: A Complete Pictorial History*. Chicago: Rand McNally, 1976.

Donohue, Mark, with Paul Van Valkenburg. *The Unfair Advantage*. New York: Dodd, Mead, 1975.

Donovan, Frank. *Wheels for a Nation*. New York: Thomas Y. Crowell, 1965.

Doolittle, James R., et al. *The Romance of the Automobile Industry*. New York: Klebold Press, 1916.

Dorson, Ron. *The Indy 500: An American Institution Under Fire*. Newport Beach, Calif.: Bond/Parkhurst Books, 1974.

Duryea, J. Frank. *America's First Automobile*. Springfield, Mass.: Donald M. Macaulay, 1942.

Engle, Lyle Kenyon. *Off-Road Racing*. New York: Dodd, Mead, 1974.

———. *132 of the Most Unusual Cars That Ever Ran at Indianapolis*. New York: Arco, 1970.

———. *Road Racing in America*. New York: Dodd, Mead, 1971.

——— and the editorial staff of *Auto Racing* magazine. *The Complete Book of Fuel and Gas Dragsters*. New York: Four Winds Press, 1968.

——— and the editorial staff of *Auto Racing* magazine. *The Complete Book of NASCAR Stock Car Racing*. New York: Four Winds Press, 1968.

——— and the editorial staff of *Auto Racing* magazine. *The Complete Book of Stock-Bodied Drag Racing*. New York: Four Winds Press, 1970.

Epstein, Ralph C. *The Automobile Industry*. Chicago and New York: A. W. Shaw, 1928.

Fittipaldi, Emerson, and Elizabeth Hayward. *Flying on the Ground*. London: William Kimber, 1973.

Flink, James J. *America Adopts the Automobile, 1895-1910*. Cambridge, Mass.: M.I.T. Press, 1970.

———. *The Car Culture*. Cambridge, Mass.: M.I.T. Press, 1975.

Ford, Henry, and Samuel Crowther, *My Life and Work*. 1922. Reprint, New York: New York Times/Arno, 1973.

Fox, Charles. *The Great Racing Cars and Drivers*. New York: Grosset and Dunlap, 1972.

Francis, Alf. *Alf Francis: Racing Mechanic*. London: G. T. Foulis, 1958.

Garlits, Don, and Brock Yates. *King of the Dragsters: The Story of Big Daddy (Don) Garlits*. Philadelphia: Chilton, 1967.

Garrett, Howard, comp. *The Poster Book of Antique Auto Ads—1898-1920*. Secaucus, N.J.: Citadel Press, 1974.

Garrett, Richard. *Fast and Furious: The Story of the World Championship of Drivers*. New York: Arco, 1969.

Gauld, Graham. *Jim Clark*. New York: Arco, 1968.

Georgano, G. N., ed. *The Complete Encyclopaedia of Motor Cars.* London: Ebury Press, 1968.

Glasscock, C. B. *The Gasoline Age: The Story of the Men Who Made It.* Indianapolis: Bobbs-Merrill, 1937.

Goist, Park Dixon. *From Main Street to State Street: Town, City, and Community in America.* Port Washington, N.Y.: Kennikat Press, 1977.

Granatelli, Anthony. *They Call Me Mister 500.* Chicago: Henry Regnery, 1969.

Gustin, Lawrence R. *Billy Durant: Creator of General Motors.* Grand Rapids, Mich.: Wm. B. Eerdmans, 1973.

Helck, Peter. *Great Auto Races.* New York: Harry N. Abrams, 1975.

Hess, Alan C. *The Indianapolis Records.* London: Stuart and Richards, 1949.

Hill, Frank Ernest. *The Automobile: How It Came, Grew, and Has Changed Our Lives.* New York: Dodd, Mead, 1967.

Hill, Graham. *Life at the Limit.* New York: Coward-McCann, 1969.

Hough, Richard Alexander. *A History of the World's Racing Cars.* New York: Harper and Row, 1965.

Hunter, Jim. *Racing to Win.* New York: Arco, 1974.

Jaderquist, Eugene, and Griffith Borgeson. *Best Hot Rods.* New York: Arco, 1953.

Jenkinson, Denis F. *A Story of Formula 1, 1954-1960.* London: Grenville, 1960.

————, ed. *Fangio.* New York: W. W. Norton, 1973.

Jerome, John. *The Death of the Automobile.* New York: W. W. Norton, 1972.

Jewell, Derek, ed. *Man and Motor: The 20th Century Love Affair.* New York: Walker and Co., 1967(?).

Keats, John. *The Insolent Chariots.* Philadelphia: Lippincott, 1958.

Kouwenhoven, John. *Made in America: The Arts in Modern Civilization.* New York: W. W. Norton, 1948.

Lambert, Z. E., and R. J. Wyatt. *Lord Austin—The Man.* London: Sidgwick and Jackson, 1968.

Langworth, Richard M. *Kaiser-Frazer: The Last Onslaught of Detroit.* Kutztown, Pa.: Automobile Quarterly Publications, 1975.

Lee, Raymond. *Fit For the Chase: Cars and the Movies.* Cranbury, N.J.: A. S. Barnes, 1969.

Lewis, Albert L., and Walter A. Musciano. *Automobiles of the World.* New York: Simon and Schuster, 1977.

Libby, Bill. *Foyt.* New York: Hawthorn Books, 1974.

————, with Richard Petty. *"King Richard": The Richard Petty Story.* Garden City, N.Y.: Doubleday, 1977.

————. *Parnelli: A Story of Auto Racing.* New York: E. P. Dutton, 1969.

Long, J. C. *Roy D. Chapin.* N. p.: n. p., 1945.

Lurani, Giovanni. *History of the Racing Car.* New York: Thomas Y. Crowell, 1974.

————. *Nuvolari.* Translated by John Eason Gibson. London: Cassell, 1959.

Lynd, Robert S., and Helen M. Lynd. *Middletown: A Study in Contemporary American Culture.* New York: Harcourt, Brace, 1929.

————. *Middletown in Transition: A Study in Cultural Conflicts*. New York: Harcourt, Brace, 1937.

Lyndon, Barré. *Grand Prix*. London: John Miles, 1935.

McPherson, Thomas A. *American Funeral Cars and Ambulances Since 1900*. Glen Ellen, Ill.: Crestline Publishing, 1973.

Mandel, Leon. *Driven: The American Four-Wheeled Love Affair*. New York: Stein and Day (forthcoming).

Marx, Leo. *The Machine in the Garden: Technology and the Pastoral Ideal in America*. Oxford, Eng.: Oxford University Press, 1964.

May, George S. *A Most Unique Machine: The Michigan Origins of the American Automobile Industry*. Grand Rapids, Mich.: Wm. B. Eerdmans, 1975.

————. *R. E. Olds: Auto Industry Pioneer*. Grand Rapids, Mich.: Wm. B. Eerdmans, 1970.

Montagu, Edward John. *Rolls of Rolls-Royce*. Cranbury, N.J.: A. S. Barnes, 1966.

Moss, Pat. *The Story So Far*. London: William Kimber, 1967.

Moss, Stirling. *All But My Life*. New York: E. P. Dutton, 1963.

Mueller, John Henry. "The Automobile." Ph.D. dissertation, University of Chicago, 1928.

Mumford, Lewis. *The City in History: Its Origins, Its Transformations, and Its Prospects*. New York: Harcourt, Brace and World, 1961.

————. *The Highway and the City*. New York: Harcourt, Brace and World, 1963.

Musselman, M. M. *Get a Horse! The Story of the Automobile in America*. Philadelphia: Lippincott, 1950.

Nader, Ralph. *Unsafe at Any Speed*. New York: Grossman, 1965.

Neeley, Bill, and the editors of *Hot Rod* magazine. *The Sox & Martin Book of Drag Racing*. Chicago: Henry Regnery, 1975.

Nevins, Allan. *Ford: The Times, the Man and the Company, 1865-1915*. New York: Charles Scribner's Sons, 1954.

————. *Ford: Expansion and Challenge, 1915-1933*. New York: Charles Scribner's Sons, 1957.

————. *Ford: Decline and Rebirth, 1933-1962*. New York: Charles Scribner's Sons, 1963.

Nitske, W. Robert, and Charles Morrow Wilson. *Rudolf Diesel*. Norman: University of Oklahoma Press, 1965.

Nolan, William F. *Barney Oldfield*. New York: G. P. Putnam's Sons, 1961.

————. *Phil Hill: Yankee Champion*. New York: G. P. Putnam's Sons, 1962.

Parks, Wally. *Drag Racing Yesterday and Today*. Los Angeles: Trident Press, 1966.

Petty, Richard, and Bill Neely. *Grand National: The Autobiography of Richard Petty*. Chicago: Henry Regnery, 1971.

Pirsig, Robert M. *Zen and the Art of Motorcycle Maintenance*. New York: William Morrow, 1974.

Porsche, Ferry, with John Bentley. *We at Porsche: The Autobiography of Dr. Ing. n. d. Ferry Porsche*. Garden City, N.Y.: Doubleday, 1976.

Posey, Sam. *The Mudge Pond Express.* New York: G. P. Putnam's Sons, 1976.

Post, Daniel Roger. *The Model T Ford in Speed and Sport.* Arcadia, Calif.: D. R. Post Publications, 1956.

Pritchard, Anthony. *The Racing Sports Car.* London: Pelham Books, 1970.

————, and Keith Davey. *The Encyclopaedia of Motor Racing.* London: Robert Hale, 1969, 1973.

Prüller, Heinz, with Jocen Rindt. *Jocen Rindt.* London: William Kimber, 1971.

Radosta, John S. *The New York Times Complete Guide to Auto Racing.* New York: Quadrangle Books, 1971.

Rae, John B. *The American Automobile: A Brief History.* Chicago: University of Chicago Press, 1965.

————. *The Road and the Car in American Life.* Cambridge, Mass.: M.I.T. Press, 1971.

Revson, Peter, and Leon Mandel. *Speed with Style.* New York: Doubleday, 1974.

Rhodes, Anthony. *Louis Renault.* New York: Harcourt, Brace and World, 1969.

The Roar of the Mighty Midgets. Paterson, N. J.: Rocco Press, 1948.

The Roaring 20's. Dallas, Tex.: Highlands Historical Press, n. d.

Rothschild, Emma. *Paradise Lost: The Decline of the Auto-Industrial Age.* New York: Random House, 1973.

Sanders, Sol. *Honda: The Man and His Machine.* Boston: Little, Brown, 1975.

Scalzo, Joe. *Stand on the Gas: Sprint Car Racing in America.* Englewood Cliffs, N.J.: Prentice-Hall, 1975.

Schneider, Kenneth R. *Autokind Vs. Mankind.* New York: W. W. Norton, 1971.

Setright, L. J. K. *The Grand Prix.* London: Thomas Nelson and Sons, 1973.

Shaw, Wilbur. *Gentlemen, Start Your Engines.* New York: Coward-McCann, 1955.

Sloan, Alfred P., Jr. *My Years With General Motors.* Garden City, N.Y.: Doubleday, 1963.

Sloss, R. T. *The Book of the Automobile.* New York: D. Appleton, 1905.

Stewart, Jackie, and Peter Manso. *Faster!: A Racer's Diary.* New York: Farrar, Straus and Giroux, 1972.

Stone, Tabor R. *Beyond the Automobile: Reshaping the Transportation Environment.* Englewood Cliffs, N.J.: Prentice-Hall-Spectrum, 1971.

Tanner, Hans. *The Racing Fords.* New York: Meredith Press, 1968.

Townroe, P. M. *Social and Political Consequences of the Motor Car.* North Pomfret, Vt.: David and Charles, 1974.

Van Valkenburg, Paul. *Chevrolet = Racing . . .?: Fourteen Years of Raucous Silence!!* Newfoundland, N.J.: Walter R. Haessner, 1972.

Weeks, Lyman Horace. *Automobile Biographies: An Account of Lives and the Work of Those Who Have Been Identified with the Invention and Development of Self-Propelled Vehicles.* New York: The Monograph Press, 1904.

White, Lawrence J. *The Automobile Industry Since 1945.* Cambridge, Mass.: Harvard University Press, 1971.

Wik, Reynold M. *Henry Ford and Grass-Roots America.* Ann Arbor: University of Michigan Press, 1972.

Wilkinson, Sylvia. *The Stainless Steel Carrot*. Boston: Houghton Mifflin, 1973.

Wilson, Paul C. *Chrome Dreams: Automobile Styling Since 1893*. Philadelphia: Chilton, n. d.

Wolfe, Tom. *The Kandy*Kolored Tangerine*Flake Streamline Baby*. New York: Farrar, Straus, and Giroux, 1965.

Yates, Brock W. *Racers and Drivers*. Indianapolis: Bobbs-Merrill, 1968.

———. *Sunday Driver*. New York: Farrar, Straus, and Giroux, 1972.

Yates, Raymond, and Brock W. Yates. *Sport and Racing Cars*. New York: Harper and Brothers, 1954.

Young, Eoin S. *Bruce McLaren: The Man and His Racing Team*. London: Eyre and Spottiswoode, 1971.

CHAPTER 3   Children's Literature*
R. Gordon Kelly

The relationship between children's literature and the mainstream of the nation's literary and intellectual life was particularly close in the late nineteenth century, when, for example, three successive editors of the *Atlantic Monthly*, Thomas Bailey Aldrich, Horace Scudder, and William Dean Howells, all, at one time or another, wrote expressly for children. In this century, however, there has been significantly less overlap. Few major twentieth-century American authors have written for children, and in the development of higher education, the study of children's books was relegated to the intellectual periphery of schools of education and library science. Until recently, writing about children's books, as well as the books themselves, issued with a few notable exceptions from a cozy enclave cut off in large measure from modern literary and intellectual trends. As a consequence, "children's literature" all too often designates a narrowly belletristic tradition that excludes much that is of interest in the history of books for children, including works of great popularity. From the ubiquitous primers of the seventeenth and eighteenth century to the phenomenally popular stories of Horatio Alger in the nineteenth and the adventures of Nancy Drew and the Hardy boys in the twentieth, some children's books, however undistinguished in literary quality, have reached very large numbers of readers. Moreover, much of the literature directed to children is "popular" literature in the sense that it is highly conventional and intended to appeal to the largest possible audience. This is as true of the moral tale, the principal form of antebellum fiction for children, as it is of the works of Alger and the numerous series books produced early in this century under the direction of Edward Stratemeyer, to cite only three of the most conspicuous examples of popular children's literature. Thus there is ample justification for including a chapter on children's literature in a handbook on popular culture.

*Portions of this chapter appeared as "American Children's Literature: An Historiographical Review," *American Literary Realism*, 6 (Spring 1973), pp. 89-108. Reprinted by permission.

Although there has been an increasing interest in the history and criticism of children's literature in the last ten years, much of the work that
has appeared reflects a conventional and unimaginative belletristic orientation, lacking scope and theoretical sophistication. Fortunately, the
most interesting and promising work in the field deals with the cultural
significance of popular books for children: the antebellum moral tale, the
novels of Alger, and the Oz fantasies of L. Frank Baum. Children's books
are especially deserving of a contextualist approach because they give
form and specificity in ways considered appropriate for impressionable
minds to matters of crucial importance: cultural definitions of what *is*;
what is good, true, and beautiful; what things go together. Children's
books are an accessible, readily available feature in an elusive enterprise—
the creation, maintenance, and modification of meaning in society. We
have hardly begun to examine children's books in America from this perspective and to locate them in the cultural contexts in which they were
written, read, and selectively preserved and made available to successive
generations of American children.

HISTORIC OUTLINE

The following summary of the history of books for children in the
United States departs in two important ways from the capsule histories
to be found, for example, in most textbooks on children's literature. First,
it emphasizes changes in the social and intellectual factors shaping the
creation of children's books. One does not have to be a philosophical
idealist to admit that concepts of the child and his or her needs constitute
crucial aspects of an author's intention, nor need one be a Marxist to
accept that changes in technology can significantly affect the production
of books, including books for children. Second, I have not assumed that
the development of literature for children can easily or unambiguously
be interpreted as an increasingly faithful delineation of social reality appropriate to the child's needs and interests, for the very concept of these
needs and interests has undergone significant change in the last two centuries and is changing even now.

Histories of children's literature have often been written as if fidelity
to life and a due regard for the true nature of the child are asymptotic
with the present—that as we approach the present, books for children,
with numerous exceptions duly noted, are, on balance, both truer to life
and truer to what we take to be the essence of childhood than books
published decades or centuries ago. The view is understandable though
scarcely pardonable. The children's books of colonial America especially
lie on the far side of a cultural divide that few would-be historians of
children's literature have endeavored to cross, being content to dismiss

books written before the first quarter of the nineteenth century as narrowly sectarian, gloomy, and morbid, to name a few of the charges leveled at them by modern commentators. What is being condemned, however, is not the literature so much as the view of human nature, including child nature, that pervades the primers and catechisms, those most popular of children's books produced in the seventeenth and eighteenth centuries. However, literature for children was more diverse than that, for in addition to the religious manuals and conduct books, there was biography, fiction, animal stories, riddles, fables, nursery rhymes, fairy tales, and picture books. A leading historian of early books for children only slightly overstates the situation when he observes: "Speaking broadly, I know of no kinds of children's books published today which were not also published in the seventeenth century."[1] Moreover, it is clear that writers for children sought in a variety of ways to appeal to and to influence the mind of the child reader—as they understood it—since a major aim was to arouse in the child the desire for saving knowledge.

The emergence of modern children's literature is conventionally dated from the middle of the eighteenth century and credited, rather too narrowly, to the entrepreneurial genius of John Newbery, whose first venture in colorfully printed books written to amuse as well as edify children was *Pretty Little Pocket Book* (1742), by which time books for children had been highly vendible for several decades. From the 1750s, Newbery's little books were imported or pirated by American printers and booksellers, most notably Isaiah Thomas in Worcester, Massachusetts.

Americans remained heavily dependent on British books for children until well into the nineteenth century, but in the 1820s, the spirit of literary nationalism began to stir interest in the creation of a truly American literature for children. Much of the literature was religious, though not narrowly sectarian. Interdenominational tract societies, such as the American Sunday School Union, established in 1818, and the American Tract Society, founded the following year, produced vast quantities of books and pamphlets for the religious and moral edification of American youth, most of it presented in the attractive format that derived from Newbery and his American imitators.

The future of American children's literature, however, did not lie in the efforts of the tract societies but in the work of such popular and prolific antebellum moralists as Jacob Abbott and Samuel Griswold Goodrich, better remembered as the genial, avuncular "Peter Parely." Goodrich eventually wrote over one hundred books designed to introduce his young readers to the facts of geography, history, and natural science in an informal and entertaining way—often by employing a travelogue format. Abbott, trained as a Unitarian minister, was even more prolific than Goodrich. In a series of books devoted to the educational and moral development of a good boy, Rollo, Abbott managed to hint at how an individualized child character might be created, and in a later series, the *Franconia* stories, he drew on his childhood memories of Maine in describing a group of children growing up in a rural village.

Until the 1850s, the moral tale, designed primarily to instruct the young in the civic virtues of obedience, piety, self-reliance, and self-discipline, was the principal form of secular fiction addressed to American children, but in the decade before the Civil War, there was a perceptible broadening of children's literature. William Taylor Adams, writing as "Oliver Optic," introduced more adventure into boys' books while still adhering, in an early book like *The Boat Club* (1855), to the moral values of the day. Like the adventure tale, stories of family life, later a staple of girls' fiction, also have their origins in the 1850s in such popular works as *The Wide, Wide World* (1850) of "Elizabeth Wetherell" (Susan Bogart Warner) and Maria Cummins' *The Lamplighter* (1854), both of which illustrate the rewards accruing to faith, fortitude, and patience. Even fantasy, a form generally uncongenial to the New England temperament, can be traced to the 1850s in the work of the minor transcendentalist Christopher Pearse Cranch, *The Last of the Huggermuggers* (1855).

After the Civil War, American children's literature flowered in a manner that surprised even the most hopeful critics of children's books a decade before. Most of the differences that set off early nineteenth-century books for children from their counterparts in the 1870s and 1880s can be traced in large measure to the altered views about the nature and needs of children typically held by children's authors, publishers, and later librarians. By 1850, the concept of infant depravity ceased to be a major factor in shaping books for children and was replaced by a conception of the child as innocent and good.

Childhood came to be acknowledged as a separate stage of life valuable in itself, a time during which the child's capacity for wonder and imagination could be freely and safely indulged. This view of childhood affected virtually every aspect of child nurture from discipline to clothing and diet and had a profound effect on books for children. The extraordinary achievements in children's literature from 1865 to the turn of the century are owed directly and decisively to widespread acceptance of this altered view of the child.

Other factors of a more mundane sort also contributed to the expansion, diversification, and specialization of publishing for children that occurred after the Civil War. Population increases and comparatively high levels both of income and of literacy in the United States contributed to a rapid expansion of audiences for books of all kinds. Developments in printing technology speeded up the process of publication, making possible more attractive books at lower prices. Improvements in transportation, especially the creation of a continental rail system, meant that the market for children's books could be organized on a national basis. The growth of public education and the founding of public libraries also stimulated the demand for children's books.

To these demographic and technological factors, which in isolation merely describe a capacity for growth, must be added factors of belief and value. The development of literature for children after the Civil War was owed not only to the new views of childhood described earlier but also to the profound faith in the social and individual benefits of education—a faith deeply rooted in democratic thought—and to a conception of art, which, in its more exalted formulations, promised a kind of secular salvation through works of imaginative genius.

As a consequence of these views, writers for children, as well as editors and publishers, rejected the overt didacticism that had characterized the antebellum moral tale and sought to shift the emphasis in children's books from instruction to entertainment and pleasure. Nevertheless, this shift in emphasis can be overstated. The rejection of a particular form of moralizing after 1860 did not entail rejecting the moral values espoused by earlier writers, such as Goodrich and Abbott. Self-reliance, courage, and independence, if not religious faith, composed a core of values that underwent little change in the course of the century, although the literary forms in which they were expressed changed markedly. An astute student of the change correctly observes: "The assertion of freedom from moral didacticism, far from being a move toward aesthetic autonomy, was made within a definite and circumscribed moral framework."[2]

Much of the history of children's literature in the last third of the nineteenth century is foreshadowed in books and periodicals that appeared in the five years following the Civil War. The most notable single work is Louisa May Alcott's *Little Women* (1867), which provided a model for much subsequent fiction centered on family life. Earlier practitioners of the boys' adventure story, such as "Oliver Optic," were joined by "Harry Castlemon" (Charles Austin Fosdick) and Horatio Alger, Jr., whose *Ragged Dick* (1868) was the first of more than one hundred novels depicting the rise (or, often, the restoration) to respectability of impoverished, often homeless, boys. A popular sentimental girls' series began in 1867 with the publication of *Elsie Dinsmore* by Martha Farquharson Finley.

The works of "Castlemon," Alger, and Finley defined a gray area of literary and moral respectability—not as objectionable as the dime novels and story papers, a rank undergrowth of cheap, sensational fiction that flourished despite the contempt heaped upon it by custodians of the nation's cultural life—but certainly not as praiseworthy as the work of Harriet Beecher Stowe, John Townsend Trowbridge, Louisa May Alcott, and a host of other, mainly New England, writers who dominated the quality juvenile periodicals of the period: *Our Young Folks, The Riverside Magazine, Wide Awake, Youth's Companion,* and preeminently *St. Nicholas.* In the thirty years following its establishment in 1873, *St. Nicholas,* under the able editorship of Mary Mapes Dodge, made available to American children the work of the best regarded juvenile authors in Britain and the United States.

With the turn of the century, new types of children's books appeared, but there was little change in the social and intellectual factors underlying the creation of children's literature. Interest in folk and fairy tales, formerly limited almost exclusively to British materials and the work of the Grimm brothers and Hans Christian Andersen, broadened to include the traditional tales of other countries. Animal stories became popular after the turn of the century, with the publication of Jack London's *The Call of the Wild* (1903), Alfred Ollivant's *Bob, Son of Battle* (1898), and the work of Ernest Thompson Seton. An even more popular new form was the school sports story, which reflected the increasing prominence of athletics in the national life in the 1880s and 1890s. The Frank Merriwell stories of "Burt L. Standish" (Gilbert Patten), derived in large measure from the dime-novel tradition, but the work of more ambitious juvenile novelists, such as Ralph Henry Barbour, owed much to Thomas Hughes' widely read story of life at Rugby, *Tom Brown's School Days* (1857).

Such books as Kate Douglas Wiggins' *Rebecca of Sunnybrook Farm* (1903) and Dorothea Canfield Fisher's *Understood Betsy* (1917) were notable contributions in the early twentieth century to the well-established domestic story tradition inaugurated by *Little Women,* while L. Frank Baum enriched the rather thin tradition of American fantasy with *The Wonderful Wizard of Oz* (1900) and more than a dozen sequels. Another staple of juvenile publishing, the series adventure for boys, underwent development at the turn of the century at the hands of Edward Stratemeyer, who followed up his success with the Rover Boys by creating the Motor Boys, the Bobbsey Twins, and Tom Swift, among others. Retaining control of each series' concept, Stratemeyer hired writers willing to work to his formula and published their work under a series pseudonym. Following his death in 1930, Stratemeyer's production-line methods of quality control were successfully continued by his daughter, Harriet Stratemeyer Adams, who created Nancy Drew.

Stratemeyer's rationalization of series book production has an analogue in the world of quality publishing for children. The growth of children's libraries and the professionalization of children's librarianship in the late nineteenth and early twentieth century, together with the establishment of National Book Week in 1919, the appointment in the same year of Louise Seaman Bechtel as children's book editor at Macmillan, and the concentration of children's book reviewing in the hands of librarians and educationists—all influenced the creation of children's literature, especially after 1920, in ways that are not yet well understood. Part of the effect, however, has been to maintain critical standards that appear to have changed little since the 1880s.

The decade of the 1930s saw the publication of some notable examples of the family story and the juvenile historical novel as well as some excellent retellings of traditional folk tales. The picture book, however, is the principal form of children's book in which there has been dramatic improvement, owing largely to new color printing processes. The achievements of writers in the 1930s notwithstanding, the history of American children's literature in the century following the Civil War is marked by a proliferation of types but a singular continuity of underlying cultural values and assumptions.

It is not really until the 1960s that significant changes occur in American children's books, changes that have their origins in a heightened sensitivity to racial, ethnic, and gender discrimination as well as in the emergence of alternative concepts of the child that permitted, indeed demanded, franker and more explicit treatment of social problems: divorce, drug abuse, and mental illness, for example. Although it is possible to point to the kind of apparent qualitative changes that characterize any period—the emergence recently of more sophisticated science fiction and fantasy for young people is an example—major changes in children's books involve a shift in the concept of childhood as occurred in the middle of the nineteenth century and appears to be occurring now in efforts to define the rights of children, including the right of access to children's books of unprecedented frankness.

REFERENCE WORKS

The best general guide to the field of children's literature is Virginia Haviland's *Children's Literature: A Guide to Reference Sources*, a selective annotated bibliography of books, articles, and pamphlets concerning the history, selection and evaluation, illustration, authorship, and types of books for children. The scope of the volume is limited largely to the professional literature of librarianship and education; there are few references to the substantial body of writing about children's literature by historians, literary scholars, and the occasional psychologist or sociologist who has ventured into the field. Regular supplements to *Children's Literature* are planned, the first of which appeared in 1972 with citations to books and articles published from 1966 to 1969.

An equally basic reference work is Anne Pellowski's *The World of Children's Literature*, a world bibliography of monographs, series, and multi-volume works, organized by country, relating to various aspects of writing for children, including the history and criticism of children's books, library work with children, criteria and techniques of writing for children, lists of recommended books, and children's reading interests. An elaborate index permits the reader to locate items about a given author, type of children's book, or theme. The brief historical introduction to children's literature in the United States is unusual for its account of social factors shaping the production of books for children. In press at the time of this writing, a very promising handbook, *The Penguin Companion to Children's Literature*, edited by Brian Alderson, is principally comprised of biographical and critical essays on notable British and American children's authors and illustrators, supplemented by topical entries and aimed at providing accurate introductory information on the development of children's leisure reading.

W. Bernard Lukenbill's *A Working Bibliography of American Doctoral Dissertations in Children's and Adolescents' Literature, 1930-1971* is a welcome reference tool, despite the author's selective, cursory annotations. *Research in Children's Literature*, compiled by Dianne Monson and Bette Peltola, annotates 332 studies, undertaken between 1960 and 1974, of the content of children's books as well as of the influence of literature, the reading interests of children, and their response to selected books. Lukenbill's "Research in Children's Literature" in the textbook *Children and Books* unfortunately lacks comprehensiveness and is uncritical and out of date, especially regarding historical research. The best source of information on current research in children's literature is *Phaedrus: An International Journal of Children's Literature Research*, edited by James Fraser. Published biannually, *Phaedrus* aims at calling attention to research, conducted throughout the world and in various academic disciplines, into children's literature, defined broadly as "the media environment of the child and adolescent." Recent issues have been devoted to German language, Scandinavian, and Soviet research in children's and young people's periodicals and television.

In addition to *Phaedrus*, several periodicals are devoted to the study of children's literature. A more narrowly literary and critical focus characterizes *Children's Literature*, a collection of articles and reviews issued annually under the auspices of the Modern Language Association Seminar on Children's Literature and the Children's Literature Association. Although some excellent articles have appeared in *Children's Literature* since its inception in 1972, too many are of indifferent quality. A similar but consistently better journal is *Children's Literature in Education*, an Anglo-American quarterly that occasionally publishes articles on American children's books. *The Horn Book Magazine*, long the only periodical devoted exclusively to children's literature, publishes critical articles and reviews of children's books as well as occasional 'historical studies. These, unfortunately, are rarely the work of professional historians and all too frequently fail to add measurably to our understanding of the history of children's books in the United States. Articles on children's lierature also appear regularly in *Top of the News*, the quarterly journal of the Children's Services Division and Young Adult Services Division of the American Library Association.

A valuable biographical reference work is Dennis La Beau's recently published index to biographical dictionaries, *Children's Authors and Illustrators*, which covers thirty-two sources of biographical information and indexes 17,686 articles on some ten thousand authors and illustrators. Standard sources of biographical information include Stanley Kunitz and Howard Haycraft's *The Junior Book of Authors*, supplemented by Muriel Fuller's *More Junior Authors*, and Doris deMontreville and Donna Hill's *Third Book of Junior Authors*; Anne Commire's continuing series *Something About the Authors*; and Miriam Hoffman and Eva Samuels' *Authors and Illustrators of Children's Books: Writings on Their Lives and Works*, containing articles on or by fifty notable contemporaries. In press at this writing is *Twentieth Century Children's Writers*, edited by Daniel Kirkpatrick, a collection of six hundred entries consisting of a brief biography, complete bibliography, and a brief critical essay on English language authors of fiction, poetry, and drama for children. Brian Doyle's *The Who's Who of Children's Literature* provides brief accounts of over four hundred British and American authors, from 1800 to the present, some of whom, like L. Frank Baum, creator of the Wizard of Oz books, are rarely mentioned in histories of children's literature. Two articles in an ongoing series by David L. Greene provide bibliographical information on a variety of limited circulation, special interest periodicals devoted to children's authors, such as *Newsboy*, the journal of the Horatio Alger Society, and *The Baum Bugle*, published by the International Wizard of Oz Club: "Author Society Journals and Fanzines" and "Children's Literature Periodicals on Individual Authors, Dime Novels, Fantasy." Using biographical data from *Something About the Author*, W. Bernard Lukenbill presents a simple profile of contemporary children's authors in "Who Writes Children's Books."

The standard biographical source, *Illustrators of Children's Books, 1744-1945*, by Bertha E. Mahoney, Louise P. Latimer, and Beulah Folmsbee, provides information on five hundred illustrators whose work has appeared in picture books in this country. Supplements appeared in 1958 and 1968. Martha E. Ward and Dorothy Marquardt's *Illustrators of Books for Young People*, with 750 entries, supplements but does not supplant the more comprehensive *Illustrators of Children's Books* series.

The most complete listing of contemporary books for children is *Chil-*

dren's Books in Print, a trade bibliography published annually since 1970. The companion volume, *Subject Guide to Children's Books in Print*, lists books under seven thousand subject categories. Other indexes include: *Subject and Title Index to Short Stories for Children; Subject Index to Poetry for Children and Young People*; and Norma O. Ireland's *Index to Fairy Tales, 1949-1972, Including Folklore, Legends, and Myths in Collections. Children's Catalogue* is a highly selective, classified listing of books found useful in school and children's libraries. First published in 1909, the 13th edition, listing over fifty-four hundred titles, appeared in 1976. For years this annotated catalog was used by librarians as the basic tool for selecting books for children's libraries, but it is now generally used in conjunction with other selection aids. Annual supplements to *Children's Catalogue* are planned for the period 1977-80.

The most comprehensive historical bibliography of books for children is D'Alté Welch, "A Bibliography of American Children's Books Printed Prior to 1821," originally published serially in the *Proceedings of the American Antiquarian Society* and then reprinted as a single volume in which, unfortunately, the valuable notes on the British originals of American books were eliminated. Primarily interested in books intended for leisure reading, Welch excluded from his bibliography school books, catechisms, conduct manuals, and other popular materials that were intended solely or primarily for instruction. The usefulness of the bibliography is enhanced by Welch's survey of private and institutional collections of early American juveniles as well as by notes indicating libraries that own copies of the books listed and titles that appear also in the National Union Catalogue.

A number of specialized bibliographies are also available. Charles Bragin, *Dime Novels, 1860-1964*, is a valuable guide to an enormous body of popular literature. Jacob Blanck's *Peter Parley to Penrod* provides bibliographical information on a noted bibliophile's choice of the best-loved American juvenile books. *Young People's Literature in Series* by Judith and Kenyon Rosenberg is a two-volume work that extends the coverage provided by Frank M. Gardner's earlier *Sequels*. Volume 1 lists over fourteen hundred works of fiction, arranged by author and published, with few exceptions, since 1955. Omitted, however, are series intended for children under the age of seven and series that the compilers, in their wisdom, deemed lacking in literary quality, such as the Hardy Boys and Nancy Drew mysteries and even the venerable Oz books. Volume 2 is devoted to publishers and nonfiction series books.

A useful, though now somewhat dated, guide to historical fiction for children is Seymour Metzner, *American History in Juvenile Books*, which covers trade books (but not texts) available in 1964-65 and permits researchers to assemble works of fiction set in particular historical periods. Augusta Baker, *The Black Experience in Children's Books*, lists books that in the judgment of the compiler, provide an accurate picture of Negro life throughout the world. Jean S. Kujoth's *Best-Selling Children's Books* cites nearly one thousand titles with sales of one hundred thousand and lists them by author, title, illustrator, year of original publication, total sales, and type and age level.

A useful but now somewhat out-of-date guide to contemporary children's periodicals is Lavinia Dobler, *The Dobler World Directory of Youth Periodicals*, a highly selective international listing. No very comprehensive bibliography of historical children's periodicals is readily accessible. (The most comprehensive is in Betty L. Lyon's dissertation, "A History of Children's Secular Magazines Published in the United States from 1789 to 1899.") Still useful for magazines published before 1900 is Harriet L. Matthews, "Children's Magazines." Despite limitations of coverage, the best account of American children's periodicals is to be found in Frank Luther Mott's *A History of American Magazines*. Access to the contents of *St. Nicholas*, the preeminent American children's periodical of the nineteenth century, has been simplified by two indexes: Anna L. Guthrie, *Index to St. Nicholas, Volumes 1-45* and John McKay Shaw, *The Poems, Poets and Illustrators of St. Nicholas Magazine, 1873-1943*.

Some students of children's literature have argued that the serious reviewing of children's books does not really begin until just after World War I with the work of Anne Carroll Moore in the New York *Herald Tribune*. This view is rendered indefensible by Richard Darling's excellent monograph, *The Rise of Children's Book Reviewing in America, 1865-1881*. Darling demonstrates beyond cavil that children's books were widely reviewed in periodicals of all kinds and frequently judged by critical standards not significantly different from those in use during the last sixty years.

In recent years the reviewing of children's books has been increasingly restricted to a handful of specialized professional periodicals, of which the most important in terms of affecting a book's commercial success are *School Library Journal, Booklist*, and *Subscription Books Bulletin*, the latter published by the American Library Association as a guide to materials worthy of consideration for purchase by small and medium-sized public libraries, as well as schools and junior colleges. The *New York Times Book Review, The Horn Book Magazine, Language Arts, English Journal*, and the *Bulletin of the Center for Children's Books*, published at the University of Chicago, also do extensive reviewing of children's books. Much of this reviewing activity is superficial, however, with few reviews in excess of three hundred words. Access to recent reviews is enhanced by *Children's Book Review Index* and by *Children's Literature Review*, edited by Ann Bloch and Carolyn Riley, the latter a digest of commentary organized by author and cross-referenced to *Contemporary Authors* and *Something About the Authors*. Forthcoming children's books are announced, though not reviewed, semi-annually (February and July) in *Publishers Weekly*.

Lists of selected children's books are legion. The following citations merely hint at the number and diversity of available selection aids. *Bibliographic Index*, under the heading "Children's Literature," provides the best general guide to children's book lists, since pamphlets and periodical articles are cited here in addition to books. *Aids to Media Selection for Students and Teachers* is available from the United States Office of Education. A comparable guide, Ingeborg Boudreau's *Aids to Choosing Books for Children*, is published by the Children's Book Council. Ellin Greene and Madalynne Schoenfeld's *A Multi-Media Approach to Children's Literature* lists films, records, and other nonprint materials generally neglected by list makers who restrict their definition of children's literature to books. *Notable Children's Books, 1940-1970* is an influential compilation of annual lists prepared by a committee of the Children's Services Division of the American Library Association. Similar compilations from the Center for Children's Books at the University of Chicago are Mary K. Eakin, *Good Books for Children* and Zena Sutherland, *The Best in Children's Books*. *Best Books for Children*, compiled by Eleanor Widdoes, lists some four thousand titles that are reevaluated yearly against such standard guides to book selection as ALA *Booklist*, *School Library Journal*, and *Children's Catalogue*. *Issues in Children's Book Selection* is an illuminating collection of twenty-nine essays reprinted from *School Library Journal* and chosen by Lillian Gerhardt, the journal's editor. The articles, principally by librarians and teachers of librarianship, discuss the assumptions, the professional and social context, and the dilemmas of evaluating books for children in a period characterized by increasingly realistic delineations of social problems in books for children. The historical development of approved lists of books has not received the systematic attention the subject deserves, but Esther Carrier's *Fiction in Public Libraries, 1876-1900*, especially the chapter "Fiction for Young People," reveals the terms of the debate over appropriate principles of selection that concerned late nineteenth-century librarians and documents the various positions taken regarding the values and dangers of fiction for children.

Material on the Newbery and Caldecott awards, given annually to the best work of fiction for children and best illustrated book respectively, is available in Bertha Mahony Miller and Elinor W. Field, *Newbery Medal Books, 1922-1955 and Caldecott Medal Books, 1938-1957*; and Lee Kingman, *Newbery and Caldecott Medal Books, 1956-1965*. These volumes are especially valuable for the author's acceptance papers reproduced in them.

Irene Smith, *A History of the Newbery and Caldecott Medals*, describes the initiation of the awards and the criteria used and gives brief biographical accounts of the winners.

Books and the Teen-age Reader, by Robert G. Carlsen, is the standard guide to literature written especially for adolescents. Nancy Larrick's popular *A Parent's Guide to Children's Reading*, now in its fourth edition, is a comprehensive manual for parents seeking to foster and sustain a love of reading and good books in their children.

The presence of sexism and racism in children's literature has been an issue for almost two decades. Representative studies dealing with the nature and incidence of stereotypes are discussed on pp. 68-69, but several guides to literature purportedly free of stereotypes deserve to be noted here. Recently published by the Council on Interracial Books for Children, *Human—and Anti-human—Values in Children's Books* presents both an evaluation of selected children's books and a values checklist procedure for determining the presence of sexism, racism, and elitism. The procedure deserves careful scrutiny since it involves matching aspects of a book's content, mainly elements of characterization, to predetermined stereotypes and indicating the presence or absence of a match—a relatively inflexible and crude form of values analysis. Compilations of materials deemed non-sexist are *A Guide to Non-Sexist Children's Books*, edited by Judith Adell and Hilary D. Klein, and *Positive Images: A Guide to Non-Sexist Films for Young People*, edited by Linda Artel and Susan Wengrof.

Two textbooks have dominated the field of children's literature until very recently. May Hill Arbuthnot's *Children and Books* was first published in 1947. A fifth edition, edited by Zena Sutherland following Hill's death, appeared in 1977. *Children's Literature in the Elementary School* by Charlotte Huck and Doris A. Young, published in 1961, was most recently revised in 1976 and is aimed at introducing prospective elementary teachers to the various types of literature for children and presenting an outline for a classroom literary program. Other textbooks include William Anderson and Patrick Groff's *A New Look at Children's Literature*, an interesting but seriously flawed effort to found a literary approach to books for children on the principles of archetypal criticism; and James Steel Smith's *A Critical Approach to Children's Literature*, a similarly motivated attempt to show how books for children could be judged primarily on literary rather than nonliterary criteria. Neither book is convincing; in both cases, the authors find it necessary to consider factors of social context at some point in the process of evaluating books for children. Rebecca J. Lukens, *A Critical Handbook of Children's Literature*, approaches the evaluation of children's books by defining and illustrating fundamental literary concepts, such as plot, character, and setting, and then attempting to establish prescriptive norms for what constitutes a good plot, effective characters, etc., in an abstract and absolute sense. It is an effort that tells us more about Lukens than about literary values or good books for children.

Several recent textbooks are oriented more toward contemporary social issues and the depiction of social reality in children's books than toward considerations of literary merit. *Now Upon a Time,* by Myra P. Sadker and David M. Sadker, and *Children's Literature: An Issues Approach,* by Masha K. Rudman, are both organized by topic and concerned with the representation of such matters as the life cycle, minority groups, and sexuality in books for children.

The broadest and most extensive collection of essays on children's literature is Virginia Haviland's *Children and Literature: Views and Reviews,* which contains over seventy essays concerning the history, major genres, and the development in several foreign countries of children's literature. *Only Connect,* edited by Sheila Egoff, reprints, with few exceptions, articles published in the 1960s that deal with children's literature as "an essential part of the whole realm of literary activity." Matters of principal concern are the relationship between children and books, fantasy in children's literature, the relationship of children's authors to their work, and the contemporary literary situation. Sara I. Fenwick, *A Critical Approach to Children's Literature,* reprints papers of the Thirty-first Annual Conference of the Graduate Library School at the University of Chicago. The conference, taking its theme from Lillian H. Smith's influential *The Unreluctant Years,* emphasized approaches to the study and evaluation of literature "that can provide for children satisfying and worthwhile experiences of joy, inspiration, self-imagination and increased wisdom." *The Hewins Lectures, 1947-1962,* edited by Siri Andrews, is a collection of addresses given annually in commemoration of the efforts of the pioneer children's librarian Caroline M. Hewins. Most are devoted to historical topics, especially the work of female New England children's authors of the last century such as A. D. T. Whitney, Eliza White, Laura Richards, and Lucretia Hale. Nicholas Tucker's *Suitable for Children? Controversies in Children's Literature* draws heavily on British writing but brings together a fine set of essays on fairy stories, comics, children's classics, and the fears engendered in children by reading. Several pieces on the value of children's literature round out the collection. Somewhat dated now, and drawn largely from journals in education and library science, Evelyn R. Robinson's *Readings About Children's Literature* reprints articles and excerpts on such topics as book selection and evaluation, the history of children's books, illustration, fairy tales, and fiction. Some fifty articles on all phases of children's literature that appeared originally in

The Horn Book Magazine between 1949 and 1966 are collected in *Horn Book Reflections*, edited by Elinor W. Field.

A particularly lively collection of personal essays is Selma Lanes' *Down the Rabbit Hole: Adventures and Misadventures in the Realm of Children's Literature*. Concerned with the quality of children's books but not given to repeating pious inanities or suffering fools gladly, Lanes is a sensitive, informed, and incisive commentator on topics ranging from the demise of *St. Nicholas Magazine* in the 1930s to the recent proliferation of picture books and the value of Dr. Seuss. Lanes also has some acute and useful things to say about the constraints imposed by the economics of the children's book trade. Louise Seaman Bechtel, *Books in Search of Children*, consists of speeches and essays by Macmillan's pioneer children's editor. Jean Karl, *From Childhood to Childhood*, reflects upon the making of children's books from the vantage point of twenty years as an editor. Two books by influential children's librarians are Frances Clarke Sayers' *Summoned by Books* and Lillian H. Smith's *The Unreluctant Years*, arguably the most influential statement of the standards and goals for the criticism of children's books that has appeared since World War II.

RESEARCH COLLECTIONS

Brief overviews of the history and diversity of collections of children's literature are provided in two recent articles: James Fraser, "Children's Literature Collections and Research Libraries" and Frances Henne, "Toward a National Plan to Nourish Research in Children's Literature." The best single source of information about collections, Carolyn Field's *Subject Collections in Children's Literature*, is currently undergoing a much needed revision and expansion. In the meantime, articles on collections are appearing regularly in *Phaedrus*, e.g.: "Research Collections in New England," by Ruth Hayes, Priscilla Moulton, and Sarah Reuter, an excellent description of nearly fifty collections of children's books held by New England colleges, universities, historical societies, public libraries, and religious associations.

The rich holdings of the Library of Congress are described by Virginia Haviland in "Serving Those Who Serve Children: A National Reference Library of Children's Books." A two-volume catalog, *Children's Books in the Rare Book Division of the Library of Congress*, has recently been published. The origins and development of the outstanding collection of colonial and antebellum books for children at the American Antiquarian Society is described by Frederick E. Bauer, Jr., "Children's Literature and the American Antiquarian Society." A similar survey of the Pierpont Morgan Library collection is Gerald Gottlieb's "Keeping Company with the

Gutenbergs." *Early Children's Books and Their Illustration*, with text by Gerald Gottlieb and a fine introductory essay by the noted British social historian J. H. Plumb, describes few American books, but this sumptuously produced catalog of an exhibit at the Morgan Library is essential to any serious student of American children's literature. Another of the outstanding collections of children's books in the country is at the Free Library of Philadelphia. *Early American Children's Books*, by A. S. W. Rosenbach, catalogs some 680 items printed before 1836 that form the nucleus for a new greatly augmented collection. A *Checklist of Children's Books, 1837-1876* of the Free Library's collection of children's books was recently completed by Barbara Maxwell.

Unlike Rosenbach and other notable collectors of children's books, Irvin Kerlan, who gave his collection to the University of Minnesota, concentrated his efforts primarily on twentieth-century materials (initially, award-winning books), but in addition to books, he also collected correspondence, original illustrations, manuscripts, book dummies, and press proofs, thus permitting the study of a work from its inception to its final form.

HISTORY AND CRITICISM

In an earlier article, "American Children's Literature: An Historiographical Review," R. Gordon Kelly described and evaluated the development of historical writing on children's literature in America. Owing to limitations of space, that discussion cannot be reproduced here, and interested readers are referred to it. The most comprehensive work in the field is still *A Critical History of Children's Literature*, by Cornelia Meigs, Anne T. Eaton, Ruth Hill Viguers, and Elizabeth Nesbitt. Although outdated, often in error, and primitive in conceptualization, the work remains an indispensable starting point for anyone interested in the history of children's literature. The most authoritative brief account of the development of literature for children in this country is Fred Erisman's essay "Children's Literature in the United States, 1800-1940," but several older discussions of children's books in America are still useful: Algernon Tassin, "Books for Children"; Charles Welsh, "The Early History of Children's Books in New England"; and especially Elva S. Smith, *A History of Children's Literature: A Syllabus with Selected Bibliographies*, and Rosalie V. Halsey, *Forgotten Books of the American Nursery*.

Fortunately, there are several monographs and recent articles that partially offset the inadequacies of Meigs' *A Critical History*. William Sloane's *Children's Books in England and America in the Seventeenth consensus among most librarians cum historians of children's literature, Century* demonstrates for all but the most obtuse that, contrary to the seventeenth-century books for children were varied both in subject matter and the means chosen to appeal to youthful minds. Still the best historical analysis of the popular primers of the eighteenth century, Paul Leicester Ford's *The New England Primer* includes a reprint of a 1727 edition, the oldest copy extant. Monica Kiefer's *America Children Through Their Books, 1700-1835*, based on research undertaken in the Rosenbach collection, relies uncritically on early, unreliable historians of children's books and is more concerned with changing conceptions of childhood, revealed in an array of historical documents and artifacts, than with books for children.

Anne Scott MacLeod's *A Moral Tale: Children's Fiction and American Culture 1820-1860* is a sensitive, intelligent, and gracefully written description of the didactic fiction of the antebellum period. Particularly valuable are MacLeod's efforts to relate the moral tales to the social dislocation of the period. *A Moral Tale* largely overshadows John C. Crandall's "Patriotism and Humanitarian Reform in Children's Literature, 1825-1860," but "Values Expressed in American Children's Readers: 1800-1850," by Richard DeCharms and Gerald H. Moeller, is still useful, in part for the method of content analysis employed in the study.

The thirty-five years between the end of the Civil War and the turn of the century saw an expansion and diversification of children's literature as well as a shift in emphasis from instruction to entertainment. Many of the changes are mirrored in the children's periodicals of the period. John Morton Blum's *Yesterday's Children* is both an excellent anthology compiled from *Our Young Folks*, the prototypical New England literary magazine for children, and a cogent analysis of the social values expressed in its pages. "*None But the Best*," by Louise Harris, is an inept attempt to deal with a major periodical of the period, *Youth's Companion*, its editor, Daniel Sharp Ford, and a prolific contributor, C. A. Stephens. Lovell Thompson's *Youth's Companion* is a useful anthology of articles and stories from the pages of the most popular and longest-lived of American juvenile periodicals. R. Gordon Kelly's *Mother Was a Lady* analyzes the structure of values exemplified in the major children's periodicals of the post-Civil War period, including *St. Nicholas, Youth's Companion*, and *Our Young Folks*. Although thin and impressionistic, the essays in Alice M. Jordan, *From Rollo to Tom Sawyer*, contain some useful information on authors and children's periodicals, and a number of addresses collected in *The Hewins Lectures, 1947-1962*, cited earlier, contain valuable material. Alice B. Cushman's "A Nineteenth Century Plan for Reading," for example, examines religious literature for children, an aspect of the field that has been severely neglected.

Much factual information about publishing for children can be uncovered in Raymond Kilgour's three studies of nineteenth-century publishers notable for children's booklists: *Lee and Shepard: Publishers for the People; Messrs. Roberts Brothers, Publishers;* and *Estes and Lauriat*. A year-by-year account of books published and prices paid to authors, the Lee and Shepard study includes biographical information, material on the public reception of particular children's books, and brief descriptions of the more notable titles brought out by the firm.

A good overview of changes in children's literature at the end of the nineteenth century is Russel B. Nye's "The Juvenile Approach to American Culture, 1870-1930." Arthur Prager, in *Rascals at Large; or, the Clue in the Old Nostalgia*, writes affectionately but incisively about the popular heroes of his childhood reading: the Hardy boys, Tom Swift, Don Sturdy, Bomba the Jungle Boy, and a host of other series characters whose exploits go unsung in the standard histories. In *Golden Multitudes*, a history of bestsellers, Frank Luther Mott gives incidental coverage to the popular reading taste of American youth from colonial times through the 1930s.

Good interpretive and critical studies of children's authors are not numerous, despite the recent increase of scholarly interest in the field. *A Sense of Story*, by the British critic and children's author John Rowe Townsend, is something of a pioneer effort at describing and evaluating the literary achievement of children's writers, in this case nineteen contemporary British, American, and Australian writers. Even so venerated an author as Louisa May Alcott has attracted little first-rate commentary. Much of the best work on individual children's authors has been done not by literary scholars but by historians interested in popular authors who, like Horatio Alger and L. Frank Baum, have considerable cultural significance but, in the view of the custodians of children's literature, little if any literary significance. Especially neglected are the popular and prolific antebellum writers like Jacob Abbott. Carl J. Weber, *A Bibliography of Jacob Abbott*, contains a biographical sketch, but the best account of Abbott's work is in MacLeod's *A Moral Tale*.

The most notable student of Louisa May Alcott's writing is Madeleine Stern, whose most recent contribution, *Louisa's Wonder Book*, prints the text of a heretofore unknown Alcott juvenile as well as a revised bibliography of Alcott's writings. Earlier work by Stern and other commentary on Alcott's writings are described and evaluated in Alma Payne's bibliographical essay "Louisa May Alcott."

The immense popularity of the juvenile novels of Horatio Alger has resulted in a relatively extensive interpretive literature. Though dated, John Seelye, "Who Was Horatio?" and Robert Falk, "Notes on the Higher Criticism of Horatio Alger," are still useful overviews, and both have the added virtue of discrediting the "biography" of Alger published by Herbert Mayes in 1928 but only recently admitted by him to have been intended as a hoax. The prosaic facts of Alger's life are accurately and succinctly presented in Frank Gruber, *Horatio Alger, Jr.: A Biography and a Bibliography*. Still the best single essay on Alger, R. Richard Wohl's "The Rags to Riches Story: An Episode in Secular Idealism" can be supplemented by John Cawelti's discussion of Alger in *Apostles of the Self-Made Man*, which places Alger in the context of earlier fiction about street children, and Michael Zuckerman, "The Nursery Tales of Horatio Alger, Jr." Dee Garrison, "Custodians of Culture in the Gilded Age: The Public Librarian and Horatio Alger," describes efforts to counter Alger's popularity in the late nineteenth century by proscribing his works.

The popular Oz books of L. Frank Baum have also attracted the interest of cultural historians. Baum's life and work are ably described in *The Wizard of Oz and Who He Was*, by Martin Gardner and Russel B. Nye. Fred Erisman, "L. Frank Baum and the Progressive Dilemma," analyzes the difference between the Oz books and Baum's more realistic series, Aunt Jane's Nieces. Henry Littlefield, "The Wizard of Oz: Parable on Populism," attempts to demonstrate a coherent pattern of political reference in *The Wonderful Wizard of Oz*, Baum's first Oz book. S. J. Sackett, "The Utopia of Oz," reconstructs the Utopian vision allegedly underlying the Oz series.

Commentary on other popular children's authors varies considerably in quality. Fred Erisman writes incisively on the school sports stories of Ralph Henry Barbour, "The Strenuous Life in Practice," and the books of Kate Douglas Wiggin, "Transcendentalism for American Youth"; but Jacob Blanck's *Harry Castlemon, Boys' Own Author* is disappointingly brief in its discussion of Castlemon's widely read adventure stories; and R. W. Cummins' book on Palmer Cox and the Brownies, a favorite feature of *St. Nicholas* for many years, is an uncritical appreciation. The vastly popular Elsie Dinsmore books are given an indifferent and unsympathetic analysis by Janet Brown, *The Saga of Elsie Dinsmore*. Hawthorne's contributions to children's literature are ably, if briefly, discussed by Alexander Kern, "A Note on Hawthorne's Juveniles," and more recently and at greater length by M. Mattfield, "Hawthorne's Juvenile Classics."

Daniel Roselle's *Samuel Griswold Goodrich* is the best account of the life and work of the prolific and influential antebellum children's author who created the appealing persona of "Peter Parley." John L. Cutler's *Gilbert Patten and His Frank Merriwell Saga* is a sympathetic biographical and literary analysis of a popular author generally ignored in the standard histories of children's literature. The work of Frank R. Stockton, a frequent contributor to *St. Nicholas* and one of the few American fantasy writers for children in the nineteenth century, is competently examined by Martin I. J. Griffin in *Frank R. Stockton, A Critical Biography*.

Several studies have dealt with genres of types of children's literature. A particularly fine example is *The Uses of Enchantment*, a Freudian inquiry into the significance of fairy tales for the psychological development of young children, by the gifted psychotherapist Bruno Bettelheim. An earlier, little-known study on the same topic is Julius E. Heuscher, *A Psychiatric Study of Fairy Tales*. The efflorescence of the picture book in the last decade or so has stimulated an interest in the historical development of this form of children's book. Barbara Bader, *American Picture Books from Noah's Ark to the Beast Within*, is a comprehensive survey, while Irene Whalley's *Cobwebs to Catch Flies* is limited to illustrated books of the eighteenth and nineteenth century. Also valuable is Donnarae Mac-Cann and Olga Richard, *The Child's First Books: A Critical Study of Pictures and Texts*. Bobbie Ann Mason gives a feminist reading of the Nancy Drew mystery books in *The Girl Sleuth*.

Carolyn T. Kingston's *The Tragic Mode in Children's Literature* is an interesting and ambitious effort to delineate a form of tragedy, based on an Aristotelean framework, that is appropriate to children's literature, one occupying a middle ground between ignoring suffering and offering the too complete exposure to "life's rawness" that characterizes great tragedy, according to Kingston.

The last fifteen years have seen a number of studies undertaken to determine the presence and nature of stereotypes in books for children. In "The All-White World of Children's Books," Nancy Larrick reports that fewer than 10 percent of the five thousand trade books for children published in 1962-64 included Negro characters. The most comprehensive analysis of black characters in books for children is Dorothy Broderick's *Image of the Black in Children's Fiction*, which draws on Sterling Brown's *The Negro in American Fiction* for its typology of black stereotypes and describes their appearance in books for children from 1827 to 1967. Black stereotypes in series fiction are described by Paul Deane, "The Persistence of Uncle Tom." *The Black American in Books for Children*, edited by Donnarae MacCann and Gloria Woodward, is a collection of readings on the topic, while Jane Bingham's "The Pictorial Treatment of Afro-Americans in Books for Young Children, 1930-1968" summarizes the author's doctoral research.

Analyzing an ill-defined sample of books popular in the last one hundred years, J. P. Shepard, "The Treatment of Characters in Popular Children's Fiction," finds that villains in the selected books are typically ugly, non-Caucasian, and either very rich or very poor. A more elaborate research effort, using books published between 1945 and 1962, is reported by D. K. Gast in "Minority Americans in Children's Literature." His content analysis procedures yielded evidence of widespread stereotyping of ethnic minorities in children's literature, although Gast suggests that much of it is positive and complimentary. His conclusions were subsequently challenged by G. T. Blatt, however, in an essay, "The Mexican-American in

Children's Literature." Taken together, these representative articles suggest that the problem of typification in children's literature has hardly begun to be resolved at a conceptual level. Neither Gast nor Blatt, for example, provide a basis for discriminating necessary typification from unwarranted stereotyping.

On the delineation of sex roles in children's literature, the following are helpful: Lenore J. Weitzman and others, "Sex Role Socialization in Children's Picture Books"; Alleen P. Nilson, "Women in Children's Literature," a survey of two decades of Caldecott Award books; and Susan K. Rachlin and Glenda Z. Vogt, "Sex Roles as Presented to Children by Coloring Books."

NOTES

1. William Sloan, *Children's Books in England and America in the Seventeenth Century* (New York: King's Crown Press, 1955), pp. 4-5.
2. E. Geller, "Somewhat Free: Post-Civil War Writing for Children," *Wilson Library Bulletin,* 51 (1976), p. 175.

BIBLIOGRAPHY

BOOKS AND ARTICLES

Adell, Judith, and Hilary D. Klein, eds. *A Guide to Non-Sexist Children's Books.* Chicago: Academy Press Ltd., 1976.

Aids to Media Selection for Students and Teachers. Washington, D.C.: United States Office of Education, 1976.

Alderson, Brian, ed. *The Penguin Companion to Children's Literature.* New York: Penguin Books, in press.

Anderson, William, and Patrick Groff. *A New Look at Children's Literature.* Belmont, Calif.: Wadsworth Publishing Co., 1972.

Andrews, Siri, ed. *The Hewins Lectures, 1947-1962.* Boston: Horn Book, 1963.

Arbuthnot, May Hill, and Zena Sutherland. *Children and Books.* 5th ed. Glenview, Ill.: Scott, Foresman, 1977.

Artel, Linda, and Susan Wengrof, eds. *Positive Images: A Guide to Non-Sexist Films for Young People.* San Francisco: Booklegger Press, 1976.

Bader, Barbara. *American Picture Books from Noah's Ark to the Beast Within.* New York: Macmillan, 1975.

Baker, Augusta. *The Black Expeirence in Children's Books.* New York: New York Public Library, 1971.

Bauer, Frederick E., Jr. "Children's Literature and the American Antiquarian Society." *Phaedrus,* 3 (Spring 1976), 5-8.

Bechtel, Louise Seaman. *Books in Search of Children.* New York: Macmillan, 1969.

Bettelheim, Bruno. *The Uses of Enchantment: The Meaning and Impotrance of Fairy Tales.* New York: Alfred A. Knopf, 1976.

Bingham, Jane. "The Pictorial Treatment of Afro-Americans in Books for Young Children, 1930-1968." *Elementary English,* 48 (November 1971), 880-85.

Blanck, Jacob. *Harry Castlemon, Boys' Own Author.* New York: R. R. Bowker, 1941.

——. *Peter Parley to Penrod: A Bibliographical Description of the Best-Loved American Juvenile Books.* New York: R. R. Bowker, 1938.

Blatt, G. T. "The Mexican-American in Children's Literature." *Elementary English,* 45 (April 1968), 446-51.

Bloch, Ann, and Carolyn Riley, eds. *Children's Literature Review.* Detroit: Gale, 1976.

Blum, John Morton, ed. *Yesterday's Children: An Anthology Compiled from the Pages of Our Young Folks, 1865-1873.* Boston: Houghton Mifflin, 1959.

Boudreau, Ingeborg. *Aids to Choosing Books for Children.* New York: Children's Book Council, 1967.

Bragin, Charles. *Dime Novels, 1860-1964.* Rev. ed., Brooklyn, N.Y.: Dime Novel Club, 1964.

Broderick, Dorothy. *Image of the Black in Children's Fiction.* New York: R. R. Bowker, 1973.

Brown, Janet Elder. *The Saga of Elsie Dinsmore: A Study in Nineteenth Century Sensibility.* Buffalo, N.Y.: University of Buffalo, 1945.

Brown, Sterling. *The Negro in American Fiction.* Washington, D.C.: Associates in Negro Folk Education, 1937.

Carlsen, Robert G. *Books and the Teen-age Reader: A Guide for Teachers, Librarians, and Parents.* 2nd ed. New York: Harper and Row, 1971.

Carrier, Esther Jane. *Fiction in Public Libraries, 1876-1900.* Metuchen, N.J.: Scarecrow Press, 1965.

Cawelti, John G. *Apostles of the Self-Made Man.* Chicago: University of Chicago Press, 1965.

Children's Book Review Index. Detroit: Gale, 1975-.

Children's Books in Print. New York: Bowker, 1970-.

Children's Books in the Rare Book Division of the Library of Congress. 2 vols. New York, N.Y.: Rowman & Littlefield, 1976.

Children's Catalogue, 13th ed. New York: H. W. Wilson, 1976.

Commire, Anne, ed. *Something About the Authors.* Detroit: Gale, 1971-.

Crandall, John C. "Patriotism and Humanitarian Reform in Children's Literature, 1825-1860." *American Quarterly,* 21 (Spring 1969), 3-22.

Cummins, R. W. *Humorous but Wholesome: A History of Palmer Cox and the Brownies.* Watkins Glen, N.Y.: Century House, 1973.

Cutler, John L. *Gilbert Patten and His Frank Merriwell Saga: A Study in Sub-Literary Fiction, 1896-1913.* Orono: University of Maine, 1934.

Darling, Richard L. *The Rise of Children's Book Reviewing in America, 1865-1881.* New York: R. R. Bowker, 1968.

Deane, Paul C. "The Persistence of Uncle Tom: An Examination of the Image of the Negro in Children's Fiction Series." *Journal of Negro Education*, 37 (Spring 1968), 140-45.

De Charms, Richard, and Gerald H. Moeller. "Values Expressed in American Children's Readers: 1800-1850." *Journal of Abnormal and Social Psychology*, 64 (February 1962), 136-42.

DeMontreville, Doris, and Donna Hill, eds. *The Third Book of Junior Authors.* New York: Wilson, 1972.

Dobler, Lavinia G. *The Dobler World Directory of Youth Periodicals.* 3rd ed. New York: Citation Press, 1970.

Doyle, Brian. *The Who's Who of Children's Literature.* New York: Schocken, 1968.

Eakin, Mary K., comp. *Good Books for Children: A Selection of Outstanding Children's Books Published 1950-1965.* Chicago: University of Chicago Press, 1966.

Egoff, Sheila, ed. *Only Connect.* Toronto: Oxford University Press, 1970.

Erisman, Fred. "Children's Literature in the United States, 1800-1940." In *Lexicon Zur Kinder- und Jugendliteratur,* edited by Klaus Doderer. Vol. 2. Weinheim and Basel/Pullachbei. Munich, Ger.: Beltz Verlag and Verlag Dokumentation. In press.

————. "L. Frank Baum and the Progressive Dilemma." *American Quarterly,* 20 (Fall 1968), 616-23.

————. "The Strenuous Life in Practice: The School and Sports Stories of Ralph Henry Barbour." *Rocky Mountain Social Science Journal,* 7 (April 1970), 29-37.

————. "Transcendentalism for American Youth: The Children's Books of Kate Douglas Wiggin." *New England Quarterly,* 41 (June 1968), 238-47.

Falk, Robert. "Notes on the Higher Criticism of Horatio Alger." *Arizona Quarterly,* 19 (Summer 1963), 151-64.

Fenwick, Sara I., ed. *A Critical Approach to Children's Literature.* Chicago: University of Chicago Press, 1966.

Field, Carolyn W., ed. *Subject Collections in Children's Literature.* New York: R. R. Bowker, 1969.

Field, Elinor Whitney, ed. *Horn Book Reflections.* Boston: Horn Book, 1969.

Ford, Paul Leicester, ed. *The New England Primer.* Reprint. New York: Teachers College Press, 1962.

"Forecast of Children's Books." Spring, Fall Children's Book Numbers, *Publishers Weekly.*

Fraser, James. "Children's Literature Collections and Research Libraries." *Wilson Library Bulletin,* 50 (October 1975), 128-30.

Fuller, Muriel, ed. *More Junior Authors.* New York: H. W. Wilson, 1963.

Gardner, Frank M., comp. *Sequels.* 4th ed. London: Association of Assistant Librarians, 1955.

Gardner, Martin, and Russel B. Nye. *The Wizard of Oz and Who He Was.* East Lansing: Michigan State University Press, 1957.

Garrison, Dee. "Custodians of Culture in the Gilded Age: The Public Librarian and Horatio Alger." *Journal of Library History,* 6 (October 1971), 327-36.

Gast, D. K. "Minority Americans in Children's Literature." *Elementary English,* 44 (January 1967), 12-23.

Gerhardt, Lillian, ed. *Issues in Children's Book Selection.* New York: R. R. Bowker, 1973.

Gottlieb, Gerald. *Early Children's Books and Their Illustration.* Brookline, Mass.: David R. Godine, 1975.

————. "Keeping Company with the Gutenbergs." *Wilson Library Bulletin,* 50 (October 1975), 154-56.

Greene, David L. "Author Society Journals and Fanzines." *Phaedrus,* 2 (Spring 1975), 16-20.

————. "Children's Literature Periodicals on Individual Authors, Dime Novels, Fantasy." *Phaedrus,* 3 (Spring 1976), 22-24.

Greene, Ellin, and Madalynne Schoenfeld. *A Multi-Media Approach to Children's Literature: A Selective List of Films, Filmstrips, and Recordings Based on Children's Books.* Chicago: American Library Association, 1972.

Griffin, Martin I. J. *Frank R. Stockton: A Critical Biography.* Philadelphia: University of Pennsylvania Press, 1939.

Gruber, Frank. *Horatio Alger, Jr.: A Biography and a Bibliography.* West Los Angeles, Calif.: Grover Jones, 1961.

Guthrie, Anna Lorraine. *Index to St. Nicholas, Volumes 1-45.* New York: H. W. Wilson, 1920.

Halsey, Rosalie V. *Forgotten Books of the American Nursery.* Boston: Goodspeed, 1911.

Harris, Louise. *"None But the Best."* Providence, R.I.: Brown University Press, 1966.

Haviland, Virginia, ed. *Children and Literature: Views and Reviews.* Glenview, Ill.: Scott, Foresman, 1973.

————. *Children's Literature: A Guide to Reference Sources.* Washington, D.C.: Library of Congress, 1966.

————. "Serving Those Who Serve Children: A National Reference Library of Children's Books." *Quarterly Journal of the Library of Congress,* 22 (1965), 300-16.

Hayes, Ruth; Priscilla Moulton; and Sarah Reuter. "Research Collections in New England." *Phaedrus,* 3 (Spring 1976), 13-21.

Henne, Frances. "Toward a National Plan to Nourish Research in Children's Literature." *Wilson Library Bulletin,* 50 (October 1975), 131-37.

Heuscher, Julius E. *A Psychiatric Study of Fairy Tales: Their Origin, Meaning, and Usefulness.* 2nd rev. ed. Springfield, Ill: Charles C. Thomas, 1974.

Hoffman, Miriam, and Eva Samuels. *Authors and Illustrators of Children's Books: Writings on Their Lives and Works.* New York: R. R. Bowker, 1972.

Huck, Charlotte, and Doris A. Young. *Children's Literature in the Elementary School.* 3rd ed. New York: Holt, Rinehart & Winston, 1976.

Human—and Anti-Human—Values in Children's Books: A Content Rating Instrument for Educators and Concerned Parents. New York: Council on Interracial Books for Children, 1976.

Ireland, Norma O., ed. *Index to Fairly Tales, 1949-1972, Including Folklore,*

Legends, and Myths in Collections. Westwood, Mass.: Faxon, 1973.

Jordan, Alice M. *From Rollo to Tom Sawyer.* Boston: Horn Book, 1948.

Karl, Jean. *From Childhood to Childhood.* New York: John Day, 1970.

Kelly, R. Gordon. "American Children's Literature: An Historiographical Review." *American Literary Realism,* 6 (Spring 1973), 89-108.

———. *Mother Was a Lady: Self and Society in Selected American Children's Periodicals, 1865-1890.* Westport, Conn.: Greenwood Press, 1974.

Kern, Alexander C. "A Note on Hawthorne's Juveniles." *Philological Quarterly,* 39 (April 1960), 242-46.

Kiefer, Monica M. *American Children Through Their Books, 1700-1835.* Philadelphia: University of Pennsylvania Press, 1948.

Kilgour, Raymond. *Estes and Lauriat.* Ann Arbor: University of Michigan Press, 1957.

———. *Lee and Shepard: Publishers for the People.* Hamden, Conn.: Shoe String Press, 1965.

———. *Messrs. Roberts Brothers: Publishers.* Ann Arbor: University of Michigan Press, 1952.

Kingman, Lee, ed. *Newbery and Caldecott Medal Books, 1956-1965.* Boston: Horn Book, 1965.

Kingston, Carolyn T. *The Tragic Mode in Children's Literature.* New York: Teachers College Press, 1974.

Kirkpatrick, Daniel, ed. *Twentieth Century Children's Writers.* London: St. James; New York: St. Martin's, in press.

Kujoth, Jean S. *Best-Selling Children's Books.* Metuchen, N.J.: Scarecrow Press, 1973.

Kunitz, Stanley J., and Howard Haycraft, eds. *The Junior Book of Authors.* 2nd ed. New York: H. W. Wilson, 1951.

La Beau, Dennis, ed. *Children's Authors and Illustrators: An Index to Biographical Dictionaries.* Detroit: Gale, 1976.

Lanes, Selma G. *Down the Rabbit Hole: Adventures and Misadventures in the Realm of Children's Literature.* New York: Atheneum, 1971.

Larrick, Nancy. *A Parent's Guide to Children's Reading.* 4th ed. Garden City, N.Y.: Doubleday, 1975.

———. "The All-White World of Children's Books." *The Saturday Review of Literature,* 68 (September 11, 1965), 63-64.

Littlefield, Henry. "The Wizard of Oz: Parable on Populism." *American Quarterly,* 16 (Spring 1964), 47-58.

Lukenbill, W. Bernard. *A Working Bibliography of American Doctoral Dissertations in Children's and Adolescents' Literature, 1930-1971.* Champaign: University of Illinois Graduate School of Library Science, 1972.

———. "Research in Children's Literature." In *Children and Books,* edited by Zena Sutherland. 5th ed. Glenview, Ill.: Scott, Foresman, 1977.

———. "Who Writes Children's Books?" *Journal of Communication,* 26 (1976), 97-100.

Luken, Rebecca J. *A Critical Handbook of Children's Literature.* Glenview, Ill.: Scott, Foresman, 1976.

Lyon, Betty Longeneker. "A History of Children's Secular Magazines Pub-

lished in the United States from 1789-1899." Ed.D. dissertation, Johns
Hopkins, 1942.

MacCann, Donnarae, and Gloria Woodward. *The Black American in Books for
Children: Readings in Racism.* Metuchen, N.J.: Scarecrow Press, 1972.

———, and Olga Richard. *The Child's First Books: A Critical Study of Pictures
and Texts.* New York: H. W. Wilson, 1973.

MacLeod, Anne Scott. *A Moral Tale: Children's Fiction and American Culture,
1820-1860.* Hamden, Conn.: Archon, 1975.

Mahoney, Bertha E.; Louise P. Latimer; and Beulah Folmsbee. *Illustrators of
Children's Books, 1744-1945.* Boston: Horn Book, 1947.

Mason, Bobbie Ann. *The Girl Sleuth: A Feminist Guide.* Old Westbury, N.Y.:
Feminist Press, 1975.

Mattfield, M. "Hawthorne's Juvenile Classics." *Discourse,* 12 (1969), 346-64.

Matthews, Harriet L. "Children's Magazines." *Bulletin of Bibliography,* 1 (April
1899), 133-36.

Maxwell, Barbara, comp. *Checklist of Children's Books, 1837-1876.* Philadelphia: Free Library of Philadelphia, 1975 (mimeo).

Meigs, Cornelia, et al. *A Critical History of Children's Literature.* Rev. ed. New
York: Macmillan, 1969.

Metzner, Seymour. *American History in Juvenile Books: A Chronological Guide.*
New York: H. W. Wilson, 1966.

Miller, Bertha Mahoney; Ruth Hill Viguers; and Marcia Dolphin. *Illustrators
of Children's Books, 1946-1956.* Boston: Horn Books, 1958.

———, and Elinor W. Field, eds. *Newbery Medal Books, 1922-1955.* Boston:
Horn Book, 1955.

———. *Caldecott Medal Books 1938-1957.* Boston: Horn Book, 1957.

Monson, Dianne, and Bette Peltola. *Research in Children's Literature.* Newark,
Del.: International Reading Association, 1976.

Mott, Frank Luther. *Golden Multitudes: The Story of Best Sellers in the United
States.* New York: Macmillan, 1947.

———. *A History of American Magazines.* 6 vols. Cambridge, Mass.: Harvard
University Press, 1938-68.

Nilson, Aileen P. "Women in Children's Literature." *College English,* 32 (May
1971), 918-26.

Notable Children's Books, 1940-1970. Chicago: American Library Association,
1977.

Nye, Russel B. "The Juvenile Approach to American Culture, 1870-1930." In
New Voices in American Studies, edited by Ray B. Browne. West Lafayette,
Ind.: Purdue University Press, 1966.

Payne, Alma. "Louisa May Alcott." *American Literary Realism,* 6 (Winter
1973), 27-43.

Pellowski, Anne. *The World of Children's Literature.* New York: R. R. Bowker,
1968.

Prager, Arthur. *Rascals at Large; Or, the Clue in the Old Nostalgia.* Garden
City, N.Y.: Doubleday, 1971.

Rachlin, Susan K., and Glenda L. Vogt. "Sex Roles as Presented to Children by Coloring Books." *Journal of Popular Culture*, 8 (1974), 549-56.

Robinson, Evelyn R. *Readings About Children's Literature*. New York: David McKay, 1966.

Roselle, Daniel. *Samuel Griswold Goodrich, Creator of Peter Parley: A Study of His Life and Work*. Albany: State University of New York Press, 1968.

Rosenbach, A. S. W. *Early American Children's Books*. Portland, Maine: Southworth, 1933.

Rosenberg, Judith K., and Kenyon C. Rosenberg. *Young People's Literature in Series*. 2 vols. Littleton, Colo.: Libraries Unlimited, 1972-73.

Rudman, Masha K. *Children's Literature: An Issues Approach*. Lexington, Mass.: D. C. Heath, 1976.

Sackett, S. J. "The Utopia of Oz." *Georgia Review*, 14 (Fall 1960), 275-91.

Sadker, Myra P., and David M. Sadker. *Now Upon a Time: A Contemporary View of Children's Literature*. New York: Harper and Row, 1977.

Sayers, Frances Clarke. *Summoned by Books*. New York: Viking, 1968.

Seelye, John. "Who Was Horatio?" *American Quarterly*, 17 (Winter 1965), 749-56.

Shaw, John McK., comp. *The Poems, Poets and Illustrators of St. Nicholas Magazines, 1873-1943: An Index*. Tallahassee: Florida State University Press, 1965.

Shepard, J. P. "The Treatment of Characters in Popular Children's Fiction." *Elementary English*, 39 (November 1962), 672-76.

Sloane, William. *Children's Books in England and America in the Seventeenth Century*. New York: King's Crown Press, 1955.

Smith, Elva S. *A History of Children's Literature: A Syllabus with Selected Bibliographies*. Chicago: American Library Association, 1937.

Smith, Irene. *A History of the Newbery and Caldecott Medals*. New York: Viking, 1957.

Smith, James Steel. *A Critical Approach to Children's Literature*. New York: McGraw-Hill, 1967.

Smith, Lillian H. *The Unreluctant Years: A Critical Approach to Children's Literature*. Chicago: American Library Association, 1953.

Stern, Madeleine B. *Louisa's Wonder Book: An Unknown Alcott Juvenile*. Mt. Pleasant, Mich.: Clarke Historical Library, Central Michigan University, 1975.

Subject Guide to Children's Books in Print. New York: R. R. Bowker, 1970-

Subject Index to Poetry for Children and Young People. Chicago: American Library Association, 1957.

Subject and Title Index to Short Stories for Children. Chicago: American Library Association, 1955.

Sutherland, Zena, ed. *The Best in Children's Books: The University of Chicago Guide to Children's Literature, 1966-72*. Chicago: University of Chicago Press, 1973.

Tassin, Algernon. "Books for Children." *Cambridge History of American Litera-*

ture. 4 vols. Cambridge, Eng.: Cambridge University Press, 1917-21.

Thompson, Lovell, ed. *Youth's Companion.* Boston: Houghton Mifflin, 1954.

Townsend, John Rowe. *A Sense of Story.* Philadelphia: Lippincott, 1971.

Tucker, Nicholas. *Suitable for Children? Controversies in Children's Literature.* Berkeley: University of California Press, 1976.

Viguers, Ruth Hill. *Margin for Surprise: About Books, Children and Librarians.* Boston: Little, Brown, 1964.

Ward, Martha E., and Dorothy Marquardt. *Illustrators of Books for Young People.* 2nd ed. Metuchen, N.J.: Scarecrow Press, 1975.

Weber, Carl J. *A Bibliography of Jacob Abbott.* Waterville, Maine: Colby College, 1948.

Weitzman, Lenore J. et al. "Sex Role Socialization in Children's Picture Books." *American Journal of Sociology,* 77 (May 1972), 1125-50.

Welch, D'Alté. "A Bibliography of American Children's Books Printed Prior to 1821." *Proceedings of the American Antiquarian Society,* 73 (1963), pt. 1:121-324, pt. 2:465-596; 74 (1964), pt. 2:260-382; 75 (1965), pt. 2:271-476; 77 (1967), pt. 1:44-120, pt. 2:281-535.

Welsh, Charles. "The Early History of Children's Books in New England." *New England Magazine,* n.s. 20 (April 1899), 147-60.

Whalley, Irene. *Cobwebs to Catch Flies: Illustrated Books for the Nursery and Schoolroom, 1700-1900.* Berkeley: University of California Press, 1975.

Widdoes, Eleanor B., comp. *Best Books for Children: A Catalogue of 4000 Titles.* 13th ed. New York: R. R. Bowker, 1971.

Wohl, R. Richard. "The Rags to Riches Story: An Episode in Secular Idealism." In *Class, Status and Power,* edited by Reinhard Bendix and Seymour M. Lipset. Glencoe, Ill.: Free Press, 1953.

Zuckerman, Michael. "The Nursery Tales of Horatio Alger, Jr." *American Quarterly,* 24 (May 1972), 191-209.

PERIODICALS

Bibliographic Index. New York, 1937-.

Booklist and Subscription Books Bulletin. Chicago, 1905-.

Bulletin of the Center for Children's Books. Chicago, 1948-.

Children's Literature. Philadelphia, 1972-.

Children's Literature in Education. London, England, 1970-.

Elementary English. Champaign, Ill., 1924-.

English Journal. Urbana, Ill., 1912-.

The Horn Book Magazine. Boston, 1924-.

Language Arts (formerly *Elementary English*). Urbana, Ill., 1924-.

New York Times Book Review. New York, 1896-.

Phaedrus: An International Journal of Children's Literature Research. Boston, 1973-.

School Library Journal. New York 1954-.

Top of the News. Chicago, 1946-.

CHAPTER 4 Comic Art *
M. Thomas Inge

Except for the attention of a few psychologists, sociologists, educationists, and media specialists, American comic art has been the most generally neglected area of popular culture until very recently. What has been written in the past has usually been of a disparaging and condescending nature by critics who at least recognized the broad popular appeal of the comics but who also often viewed them as subversive threats to highbrow culture and social stability. Very few were the writers who found more than ephemeral value in the funnies and comic books, and even fewer who recognized the unique aesthetics of this hybrid form of narrative art.

The daily and Sunday comic strips, and comic books, are part of the reading habits of more than one hundred million people at all educational and social levels in the United States. Any mass medium that plays so heavily on the sensibilities of the populace deserves study purely for sociological reasons, but comic art is important for other reasons as well. While the roots of comic art may be partly European, the comics as we know them today are a distinctively American art form that has contributed heavily to the culture of the world, from Picasso to the pop art movement. They derive from popular patterns, themes, and concepts of world culture— just as Dick Tracy was inspired by Sherlock Holmes (notice the similarity in noses), Flash Gordon and Superman draw on the heroic tradition to which Samson, Beowulf, Davy Crockett, and Paul Bunyan belong. The comics also serve as revealing reflectors of popular attitudes, tastes, and mores, and they speak directly to human desires, needs, and emotions.

Historical studies, biographies, anthologies, and periodicals have begun to proliferate rapidly in this subject area in the past few years, partly because some publishers have wished to tap the lucrative nostalgia market, but in many cases because others have begun to recognize the importance of documenting this part of our national heritage. Much of the best work has originated in amateur and limited press run publications authored by

*Portions of this chapter appeared as "American Comic Art: A Bibliographic Guide," *Choice*, 11 (January 1975), 1581-93. Reprinted by permission.

collectors and devotees of the art form. The study of comics has become a part of high school, college, and university curricula throughout this country and abroad, and annual conventions are held on a national and regional scale for collectors, dealers, artists, writers, and fans. This essay will provide a brief historic summary of the development of comic art in America and a guide to the most useful reference works and resources for those who wish to study the subject.

HISTORIC OUTLINE

While some historians would trace the comic strip to prehistoric cave drawings, the medieval Bayeux tapestry, the eighteenth-century print series of such artists as William Hogarth, the illustrated European broadsheet, the nineteenth-century illustrated novels and children's books, or European and American humorous periodicals, the American comic strip as we know it may have been influenced by all of these antecedents, yet it remains a distinct form of expression unto itself and primarily is an American creation. It may be defined as an open-ended dramatic narrative about a recurring set of characters, told with a balance between narrative text and visual action, often including dialogue in balloons, and published serially in newspapers. The comic strip shares with drama the use of such conventions as dialogue, scene, stage devices, gesture, and compressed time, and it anticipated such film techniques as montage (before Eisenstein), angle shots, panning, close-ups, cutting, and framing. Unlike the play or the film, however, the comic strip is usually the product of one artist (or an artist and a writer) who must be a combined producer-scriptwriter-director-scene designer at once and bring his characters to life on the flat space of a printed page, with respect for the requirements of a daily episode that takes less than a minute's reading time. It is these challenges that make fine comic art difficult to achieve and contribute to its distinct qualities.

Identifying the first comic strip is not easy. Some would suggest James Swinnerston's 1895 feature for the San Francisco *Examiner, Little Bears and Tykes,* in which bear cubs, who had been used in spot illustrations for the newspaper since 1893, adopted the human postures of small children. Others more commonly suggest Richard Outcault's *The Yellow Kid,* who first appeared in the May 5, 1895, issue of the New York *World,* a street urchin in the middle of riotous activities set in the low-class immigrant sections of the city and identified by the title "Hogan's Alley." Unlike Swinnerston, Outcault developed a central character in his use of the Kid, always clad in a yellow shift on which his dialogue was printed, and by 1896 had moved from a single panel cartoon to the format of a progressive series of panels with balloon dialogue, which would become the definitive form of the comic strip.

Outcault's use of contemporary urban reality in his backgrounds, which had counterparts in the naturalistic novels of Stephen Crane, Frank Norris, and Theodore Dreiser, would not reappear in the comics for over two decades (and even then in the safe Midwestern environment of Sidney Smith's *The Gumps* of 1917, which emphasized the pathos of lower middle-class life, and Frank King's *Gasoline Alley*, a year later, where the use of chronological time first entered the comics in following the growth of a typical American family). Most of the popular strips that came on the heels of the Kid in the following three decades used humor and fantasy as their major modes, such as Rudolph Dirks' *The Katzenjammer Kids*, now in its eightieth year and the longest running comic strip in existence; Frederick Burr Opper's several wacky creations *Happy Hooligan*, *Maude the Mule*, and *Alphonse and Gaston*; Richard Outcault's penance for his illiterate outlandish Kid, *Buster Brown*; Winsor McCay's *Little Nemo in Slumberland*, the most technically accomplished and aesthetically beautiful Sunday page ever drawn; Bud Fisher's *Mutt and Jeff*, the first daily comic strip and the first successful comic team in the funnies; George Herriman's classic absurdist fantasy and lyrical love poem *Krazy Kat*; Cliff Sterret's abstractly written and drawn family situation comedy, *Polly and Her Pals*; George McManus's *Bringing Up Father*, whose central characters, Maggie and Jiggs, became a part of American marital folklore; Billy DeBeck's tribute to the sporting life, *Barney Google*; Elzie Segar's *Thimble Theater*, which in 1929, after a ten-year run, introduced Popeye to the world; and Frank Willard's boarding house farce, *Moon Mullins*. These were the years when the terms *comics* and *funnies* became inseparably identified with this new form of creative expression, even though comedy and humor were not to remain its primary content.

Although some adventurous continuity and suspense had been used in C. W. Kahles' burlesque of melodrama, *Hairbreadth Harry* in 1906, Roy Crane's *Wash Tubbs* of 1924 and George Storm's *Phil Hardy* and *Bobby Thatcher* of 1925-27 established the adventure comic strip, and Harold Gray's *Little Orphan Annie* also of 1924 drew on the picaresque tradition in a successful combination of exotic adventure and homespun right-wing philosophy. The adventure strip would not become a fully developed genre, however, until 1929 and the appearance of the first science fiction strip, *Buck Rogers*, by Richard W. Calkins and Phil Nowlan, and the successful translation of the classic primitive hero from the novels of Edgar Rice Burroughs, *Tarzan* (most beautifully drawn in those years first by Harold Foster and later by Burne Hogarth). The 1930s and 1940s were to be dominated by adventure titles, such as Chester Gould's *Dick*

Tracy, Vincent Hamlin's *Alley Oop*, Milton Caniff's *Terry and the Pirates* and his postwar *Steve Canyon*, Alex Raymond's *Flash Gordon*, Lee Falk's *Mandrake the Magician* (drawn by Phil Davis) and *The Phantom* (drawn by Ray Moore), Harold Foster's *Prince Valiant*, Fred Harman's *Red Ryder*, Fran Striker's *The Lone Ranger* (drawn primarily by Charles Flanders), Alfred Andriola's *Charlie Chan* and *Kerry Drake*, Will Eisner's *The Spirit*, and Roy Crane's second contribution to the tradition, *Buzz Sawyer*. Related by the use of the same devices of mystery and suspense and also developed during these years were the soap opera strips, among the best known of which were *Mary Worth*, by Allen Saunders and Dale Connor (a reincarnation of Martha Orr's 1932 antidote for the Depression, *Apple Mary*); writer Nicholas Dallis' *Rex Morgan, M. D.* (drawn by Marvin Bradley and Frank Edgington), followed in 1952 by *Judge Parker* (drawn by Dan Heilman and later by Harold LeDoux), and in 1961 by *Apartment 3-G* (drawn by Alex Kotzky); and Stanley Drake's 1953 collaboration with writer Eliot Caplin on *The Heart of Juliet Jones*.

The 1950s proved to be the era in which satire flourished in the comics. As early as 1930, Chic Young's *Blondie* had gently satirized at first the flappers and playboys of the jazz age and later the institution of marriage, but Al Capp's *Li'l Abner* of 1934 would eventually become a significant forum for illustrating the hypocrisies and absurdities of the larger social and political trends of the nation. Just as Capp used the hillbilly life in Dogpatch as his main vehicle for satire, his successors would use other and often more imaginative vehicles, such as the fantasy world of children in *Barnaby* by David Johnson Leisk and *Peanuts* by Charles Schulz, the ancient form of the animal fable by Walt Kelly in *Pogo*, military life in *Beetle Bailey* by Mort Walker, the world of prehistoric man by Johnny Hart in *B. C.*, and the fanciful world of a medieval kingdom in *The Wizard of Id* by Hart and Brant Parker. The most recent entries in this tradition, however, demonstrate two radical trends for the 1970s, with Russel Myers' *Broomhilda* moving toward a totally abstract world in the tradition of George Herriman's *Krazy Kat* and Garry Trudeau's *Doonesbury* moving into the realistic world of the radical student generation of the last decade.

The earliest comic books were reprint collections of favorite comic strips, such as *The Yellow Kid*, *Mutt and Jeff*, and *Barney Google*, bound in cardboard covers. The comic book as we know it, however, began in 1933 when ten thousand copies of *Funnies on Parade* were printed, with thirty-two pages of Sunday color newspaper reprints within a paper-covered booklet about 7½" by 10" in size and intended to be given away as a premium for using the products of Proctor and Gamble. The give-away comics were so successful that in 1934 Dell Publishing Company, at the instigation of Max C. Gaines, sold through chain stores for ten cents a copy thirty-five thousand issues of *Famous Funnies*, which then became the first monthly comic magazine and reached a circulation peak of nearly one million copies during its twenty-year existence. While other publishers would begin successful imitations of this reprint comic book, such as *Popular Comics*, *Tip Top Comics*, and *King Comics*, a major innovation occurred when in 1935 National Periodical Publications issued *More Fun*, the first comic book to publish original material specifically written and drawn for its unique page size and format.

The same publishers began *Detective Comics* in 1937 (thus the firm's better known initials "D. C."), the first title devoted to a single theme, but it was not until they issued in June 1938 the first number of *Action Comics*, which introduced writer Jerry Siegel's and artist Joe Shuster's creation, Superman, that the comic book truly became a commercial success and spawned thousands of subsequent super-heroes during the 1940s, such as Batman, the Human Torch, Sub-Mariner, Captain Marvel, Wonder Woman, Captain America, Plastic Man, Blackhawk, Daredevil, and Airboy, among others. The industry would not again witness such a proliferation of super-heroes until 1961 when Stan Lee created a popular set of characters beset with human problems and neuroses despite their superior strength, such as Spiderman, the Hulk, Thor, and the Fantastic Four. Parallel with the super-hero titles, publishers also introduced humorous and funny animal books, among the most popular of which were *Archie*, as drawn by Bob Montana and first introduced in *Pep Comics* in 1941; *Walt Disney's Comics and Stories*, with Donald Duck and his Uncle Scrooge as delineated by Carl Barks, beginning in 1942; and in 1945, *Little Lulu*, with art by John Stanley.

A trend in realistic crime stories developed when editor Charles Biro and publisher Lev Gleason initiated *Crime Does Not Pay* in 1942. Eight years later, horror, science fiction, and war became prominent when William M. Gaines, the son of Max C. Gaines who had helped create the comic book, began publication of such titles as *Crypt of Terror*, *The Vault of Horror*, *The Haunt of Fear*, *Weird Science*, *Weird Fantasy*, *Crime Suspenstories*, and *Two-Fisted Tales*, under the "EC" (Entertaining Comics) imprint. These series proved to include some of the best written and most imaginatively drawn stories in American comic book history. Just as the EC team was hitting its stride, however, in 1954, a psychiatrist named Dr. Fredric Wertham published his book, *Seduction of the Innocent*, the culmination of a war against comic books by those who felt they contributed to juvenile delinquency. When a United States Senate Subcommittee on Juvenile Delinquency was established to investigate this charge, the major publishers responded by creating their own Comics Code Authority as a self-censoring agency. Unable to work under the code's stringent guidelines, Gaines changed his successful satiric comic book *Mad* into a magazine in 1955 and thereby continued to provide America with some of its finest satiric humor in this century.

American comic art, in both comic strip and comic book form, faces a most uncertain future. The space allotted to comic strips by newspapers has grown increasingly smaller while syndicate and editorial preference weeds out the most creative and therefore possibly unsettling strips, even though such formerly forbidden topics as homosexuality, premarital sex, and abortion have entered the funnies. The comic book seems impossibly shackled by the economic and editorial strictures which prevail in the industry, even though a few bright moments have occurred in the 1970s with the appearance of such titles as *Conan the Barbarian, The Swamp Thing, The Shadow,* and *Howard the Duck.* The most promising work has been accomplished by artists working for the underground press, many of whose "comix" have made genuine advances in the art form. Yet comic art, a little over eighty years old, has not realized its full potential and promises yet to become a powerful form of humanistic expression.

REFERENCE WORKS

The sound bibliographical and reference work that must precede historical and critical research has not been accomplished yet for the comics, but a few tentative efforts have been made and much good work is in progress. What should be a comprehensive and useful checklist of secondary data—the *International Bibliography of Comics Literature,* by Wolfgang Kempkes—is marred by inaccuracies, incomplete data, and inconvenience. The material is divided into eight general categories, such as histories of the development of comics, structure, readership, etc., and then subdivided by country of origin (Argentina, Australia, Belgium, Brazil, Germany, Finland, France, Great Britain, Italy, Mexico, the Netherlands, Austria, Portugal, Sweden, Switzerland, Spain, South Africa, Czechoslovakia, the USSR, and the United States). A subject cross-index in the first edition was inexplicably deleted in the revised edition, thus making it impossible to locate entries on specific artists or comics, the major use for a checklist. The book is, however, the only convenient source of information on criticism published outside the United States and illustrates the extent to which the most comprehensive study of American comics has taken place abroad, especially in Italy, France, and Germany, rather than on native shores. As always, the most significant creators of American culture appear evident to Europe before we seem to be able to perceive them, from Edgar Allan Poe and William Faulkner to Winsor McCay and George Herriman.

While *The Comic Book Price Guide* by Robert M. Overstreet began in 1970 as a selling price reference for dealers and collectors, it has grown through annual revisions and expansions into the single most important source of information about the history of the comic book. A comprehensive listing of comic book titles from 1933 to the present, dates of first and last issues, publishing companies, and important artists has been supplemented with updated information on comic book collecting, fan publications, comic book conventions, a history of the development of comic books, and other special features. The text is copiously illustrated with comic book covers. Overstreet's *Guide* has also served to stabilize the vigorous market that has grown up around collectors and fandom, a development many view with unease.

A standard source of biographical data on comic book artists and writers is *The Who's Who of American Comic Books* in four volumes, edited by Jerry Bails and Hames Ware. Conscientiously compiled and edited, each entry provides birth and death dates, pen names, art schools attended, major influences, and career data, including major publishers and comic book credits. Most of the information was obtained directly from the artists and writers themselves. At least one comic artist has been given comprehensive bibliographic treatment in Glenn Bray's *The Illustrated Harvey Kurtzman Index: 1939-1975*, which catalogs Kurtzman's innovative work for comic books (he created *Mad*), magazines, newspapers, and films, with some two hundred examples of his art reprinted in an attractive, usefully arranged format. Some 374 members of the National Cartoonists Society are represented by brief autobiographical sketches, portraits, and art samples in the 1972-77 edition of *The National Cartoonists Society Album*, compiled by Mort Walker. Also listed are winners of the several awards made by the society. Biographical sketches of forty-six popular cartoonists, along with portraits and their favorite recipes, are gathered in *The Cartoonist Cookbook*, edited by Theodora Illenberger and Avonne Eyre Keller.

The Encyclopedia of Comic Book Heroes, by Michael L. Fleisher and research assistant Janet Lincoln, when complete in eight volumes, will cover fifteen costumed super-heroes in encyclopedic fashion. The first volume contains over one thousand entries on every major and minor character to appear in the Batman stories, with one hundred pages alone devoted to the life and adventures of Batman himself. The second volume provides similar coverage for the most popular super-heroine, Wonder Woman, with over five hundred entries. Jerry Bails' *The Collector's Guide: The First Heroic Age* is an extensive effort "to list all costumed- and super-heroes strips appearing from 1934 through 1947 in comic books, including reprints of newspaper strips and adaptations of heroes from pulps to radio." Publishers and artists are also listed. Complementing this volume is Howard Keltner's *Index to Golden Age Comic Books*, an alphabetically arranged index to approximately 98 percent of the "golden age" comic books of the 1940s and 1950s, with notes on publication dates, front cover and interior features, and other useful bibliographic data on over eight thousand issues of three hundred titles in the super-hero line.

The Full Edition of the Complete E. C. Checklist (Revised), by Fred von Bernewitz and Joe Vucenic, focuses on the life of one publisher, Entertaining Comics, generally regarded as the producers of the best drawn and most well written comic books published in America during the early 1950s. The contents of all issues are listed with biographical sketches of the main artists and writers who collaborated on the series. An index would have been useful. George Olshevsky's *Marvel Comics Index* is an extensive computerized project which in fourteen projected volumes will catalog all of the super-hero stories published in Marvel comic books since November 1961 (when the first issue of the *Fantastic Four* appeared). The first four of the projected fourteen volumes are devoted to *The Amazing Spider Man, Conan and the Barbarians, Avengers and Captain Marvel*, and *Fantastic Four* (including the Silver Surfer and the Human Torch). A synopsis of each character's history, information on artists and writers, and several cross-indexes are included. A quantity of artist, title, and publisher checklists have been published in full and fragmentary form in scattered fan magazines and separate pamphlets, but no one has undertaken to assemble a guide to this material.

RESEARCH COLLECTIONS

Except for isolated instances, most public and university libraries have made no effort to collect or preserve comic books, comic strips, or related materials. Even the Library of Congress files of comic books were carelessly maintained, and much of the material has disappeared over the years. The best collections, therefore, are found with private collectors, such as the late Woody Gelman of New York, Gordon Campbell of Tennessee, Jim Ivey of Florida, and Murray A. Harris of California, although several of these emphasize original art and artifacts. Such collections are not generally open to the public or are available on an appointment basis only.

A once-private collector, Bill Blackbeard, has turned his excellent collection into a nonprofit, federally funded research center that is open to the public: the San Francisco Academy of Comic Art. The academy can provide reproductions of sequential runs of all comic strips to institutions and researchers at nominal fees. Another extensive collection is found in the Popular Culture Library, a special division of the Bowling Green State University Library, Bowling Green, Ohio, and other large university libraries have begun to develop an interest in this area. Publisher Harry A. Chesler, Jr. gave to Fairleigh Dickinson University Library in Madison, New Jersey, his collection of materials including four thousand pieces of original art, the correspondence and records of the Chesler Syndicate, and a body of secondary literature. Comic artist Roy Crane deposited his scrapbooks and original art at the Syracuse University Library in Syracuse, New York, and some six thousand original cartoons, the published books, and the personal papers of Jay N. "Ding" Darling are housed in the University of Iowa Library in Iowa City. Significant comic book collections are found at Kent State University Library in Ohio, Michigan State University Library in East Lansing, and Northwestern University Library in Evanston, Illinois. Collections devoted to primary and secondary materials in the areas of comic strips and political cartoons are located at Palomar College Library in San Marcos, California, Kenneth Spencer Research Library at the University of Kansas in Lawrence, James Branch Cabell Library at Virginia Commonwealth University in Richmond, and University of Virginia Library at Charlottesville. The best collection of Walt Disney comic books and strips is found in the Disney Studio Archives in Burbank, California (though not open to the public), but the Anaheim Public Library in California also has an impressive body of Disney material. Undoubtedly other collections exist or are being assembled throughout the country, but the lack of an organized, comprehensive material index to library holdings in popular culture prevents access. Most recently the Museum of Cartoon Art was established with the support of the several professional cartoonist and comic artist societies at Comly Avenue, Town of Rye, Port Chester, New York 10573. Mort Walker is founding president and Jack Tippit is the director and curator of what is becoming a major resource and research center.

According to the fourth edition of the *Directory of Special Libraries and Information Centers*, edited by Margaret Labash Young and others, the library of the Comics Magazine Association of America has a collection including one hundred books and five thousand periodicals about comic books, and the library and information center of the Newspaper Comics Council has 350 books and related materials on comic strips. Neither is open to the general public.

At least two efforts have been initiated to record the primary material on microfilm: "The Microfilm Library of Comic Art" (Jerry Bails, 487 Lakewood, Detroit, Michigan 48215), which specializes in comic books of the years 1934-52, and "Comics on Microfilm" (AMS Press), which includes selected runs of weekly and Sunday strips (the currently available titles include such popular strips as *Blondie, Flash Gordon, The Phantom, Popeye,* and *Prince Valiant*). Since most of the microfilming is being done in black and white, this is not a satisfactory way to preserve that material originally published in color, but at least this system makes inaccessible items available for research. The daily strips in the AMS

Press series are shot directly from syndicate proof sheets and, therefore, are very legible and easy to read.

HISTORY AND CRITICISM

It must be noted that because so little of the basic bibliographic and reference work has been completed, as indicated earlier, almost every single book to be discussed in the following pages abounds to one degree or another in errors and mistaken assumptions. Although the Overstreet *Guide* contains extensive data on the beginning and concluding dates of comic book titles, no such reliable list exists for the major or minor comic strips. Many authors assumed that the beginning date for a daily or Sunday strip was the first appearance in their local newspapers, or the first date on which it was syndicated, whereas it may have begun months earlier. The syndicates themselves have kept very few records and even incomplete files of proof sheets for the strips they distribute. The most knowledgeable and meticulous scholar of the comics, Bill Blackbeard, is writing a history for Oxford University Press which will establish for the first time much of this factual information, but until his book appears all of the existing histories must be used with great caution. Omitted from discussion here are the many historical and appreciative studies of American comics published abroad in Europe or South America.

A *History of American Graphic Humor*, by William Murrell, was the first authoritative history of the development of pictorial satire and cartooning in America to include the comics. While he devotes only a few appreciative pages to the comic strip, the work is still valuable as a panorama of the forms of visual art that have influenced the comics. The earliest full-length book entirely devoted to American comic art was Martin Sheridan's *Comics and Their Creators* in 1942. Not actually an organized history, it consisted primarily of biographical sketches and interviews with the artists and writers of over seventy-five of the most popular newspaper comics, copiously illustrated with portraits and reproductions of the strips. It remains a useful resource for some of the primary data on the views and working habits of the cartoonists. The earliest full-scale history was *The Comics*, by Coulton Waugh, a practicing comic artist and devoted scholar of the subject. While many of his facts were faulty, Waugh attempted a comprehensive survey of the important movements and types of comic strips from *The Yellow Kid* through the first decade of the modern comic book. His insights into the reasons for the popularity of certain strips, his comments on the aesthetic principles behind them, and his early effort to define the medium make Waugh's pioneer effort of lasting interest, although he had little appreciation for the comic book as it had developed, and he appeared to accept without question some of the highbrow standards often applied to popular art by the self-appointed guardians of high culture.

The next effort on the part of a single author to chart the history of the medium was Stephen Becker's *Comic Art in America*, although his interests were broader than Waugh's in that he envisioned his book, according to its pretentious subtitle, as "A social history of the funnies, the political cartoons, magazine humor, sporting cartoons, and animated cartoons." Casting his net so broadly led to much superficiality, and his commentary is often derivative, but the volume is a useful storehouse of over 390 illustrations and sample sketches. The text is kept to an absolute minimum and the illustrations are at a maximum in *The Penguin Book of Comics*, by George Perry and Alan Aldridge, aptly described in its subtitle as "a slight history." Originally published in French in conjunction with an exhibition of comic art at the Louvre, and the joint product of six contributors headed by Pierre Couperie, *A History of the Comic Strip* is understandably uneven, yet it contains some of the most provocative comments yet ventured on the aesthetics, structure, symbolism, and themes in comic art. A recent general survey was undertaken by comic artist Jerry Robinson, *The Comics: An Illustrated History of Comic Strip Art*. Robinson provides a readable and interesting text complemented by thirteen original essays by eminent artists about the theories behind their work.

Though assembled as a catalog for an exhibition at the University of Maryland, Judith O'Sullivan's *The Art of the Comic Strip* contains a brief history with emphases on Winsor McCay, George McManus, George Herriman, and Burne Hogarth, a compilation of short biographies and bibliographic references on 120 comic artists, a chronology of important dates, and a bibliography. *Comics: Anatomy of a Mass Medium*, by Reinhold Reitberger and Wolfgang Fuchs, is a broad effort by two German scholars to relate the comics to their social context and developments in other mass media, but faulty secondary sources and inaccessible primary material have led to an inordinate number of factual and other errors, which no one corrected in the process of translation. What appears to be the most ambitious effort yet undertaken to describe the "history of the comic strip" has yielded the first massive volume, *The Early Comic Strip*, by David Kunzle, which reaches the year 1825 before the comic strip as we know it actually begins. Kunzle traces the full development of narrative art in the European broadsheet which he sees as an antecedent to the comic strip as he defines it in the introduction. The complete corpus of reproductions of broadsheets in the over-sized volume makes it of greater interest to art historians than comic scholars, but it will be interesting to see how this research is brought to bear on the American comic strip in the next volume.

The main body of *The World Encyclopedia of Comics*, edited by

Maurice Horn, consists of more than twelve hundred cross-referenced entries arranged alphabetically and devoted either to an artist, a writer, a comic strip's title, or a comic book character, and prepared by an international group of contributors. Additional materials include a short history of the development of comic art, a chronology from the eighteenth century to 1975, an original analytic inquiry into the aesthetics of the comics by the editor, a history of newspaper syndication, a glossary, a selected bibliography, and several appendixes and indexes. Unfortunately, there are an inordinate number of typographical errors in the text, and the critical comments are often idiosyncratic or biased, shortcomings one ordinarily does not expect to find in a reference work of this scope. Nevertheless, with corrections, revisions, and updating, this volume could become a chief authority among historians and critics of the comics. Maurice Horn also explores the comics as art, as literature, and as propaganda in a set of well-produced film strips and cassettes, "The Comics: A Cultural History," issued by the Educational Audio Visual firm of Pleasantville, New York. This set will provide an excellent introduction to the comics for both secondary school and college students. A more specialized study is Horn's *Comics of the American West*, a heavily illustrated historic survey of the major Western comic strips and comic books and their basic symbolic themes.

In *Backstage at the Strips*, Mort Walker provides an engaging insider's tour of the world of comic strip artists, how the strips are created, and who the people are who draw and read them. Ron Goulart's *The Adventurous Decade* is an informal and subjective history of the adventure comic strips during the 1930s when the American funnies came of age. The interviews Goulart conducted with living veterans of the period enrich the volume, which tends to adopt a studied controversial view in its critical judgments of the work of classic artists. In the catalog for the Smithsonian Institution's Bicentennial exhibition, *A Nation of Nations*, edited by Peter Marzio, there is an essay by M. Thomas Inge and Bill Blackbeard on the influences of Europe on the development of the comic strip and the later influences of the fully developed American comic strip and book on the culture of the world at large. An offshoot of interest in the comics is the large market for toys and merchandise based on the more popular characters, such as Mickey Mouse, Buck Rogers, Superman, or Little Orphan Annie. An extensive quantity of these mass-produced artifacts have been photographed and cataloged in Robert Lesser's *A Celebration of Comic Art and Memorabilia*.

If any of the already noted histories pay any attention to the comic book, it is often as a perverse offshoot of the daily comic strip. The first writer to inaugurate what he claims will ultimately be a full-scale history of the comic book is James Steranko, a comic book artist. Volume 1 of

The Steranko History of Comics finds that pulp fiction of the 1930s was the most important source of inspiration to the development of the comic book and then traces the history of the *Superman, Batman, Captain America, Captain Marvel,* and D.C. comic books. Volume 2 continues the coverage of *Captain Marvel* and related Fawcett super-heroes, the *Black-hawks* and other flying heroes, *Plastic Man* and the Quality super-heroes, and Will Eisner's *Spirit.* Four additional volumes are projected. Encyclopedic in detail, there is more information in these volumes than most readers can easily assimilate, but Steranko's contributors have a high regard for the distinctive qualities of the comic book and view it as a part and reflection of the total context of popular culture.

A single-volume history is *Comix: A History of Comic Books in America,* by Les Daniels. Although some disagree with his choice of representative titles and his judgments, Daniels provides a sensible outline of the major developments and reprints over twenty complete stories (rather than the usual excerpts), four of them in color. The final chapter deals with the greatest recent innovation in the comic book—the development of underground comic books, generally called "comix" to distinguish them from the traditional publications. Partly a radical rejection of the stringent Comics Code Authority and partly a natural development of the counter-culture underground press, comix have provided artists with totally unrestricted freedom to write and draw to the limits of their imagination, something seldom possible in comic art. While bad taste and shameless obscenity abound, several striking talents have emerged from the movement and much highly original work has been accomplished. Mark James Estren has attempted to produce *A History of Underground Comics,* which is difficult to accomplish because the publishing centers have ranged among California, New York, and the Midwest, and underground artists are not among the most cooperative people when researchers intrude on their privacy and subject their work to analysis. While much of his commentary is debatable, Estren has assembled an excellent cross-section of representative art by the major artists, many of them are allowed to speak for themselves through interviews and letters, and an excellent checklist of underground comic titles by comix scholar Clay Geerdes concludes the volume. It is an entertaining grab bag of reading matter, especially for the comix freak.

A great deal of information about numerous comic books and comic artists, along with full-color reproductions of forty classic covers, has been gathered in Richard O'Brien's *The Golden Age of Comic Books: 1937-1945.* An oddity is *How to Read Donald Duck: Imperialist Ideology in the Disney Comic,* by Ariel Dorfman and Armand Mattelart. Originally published in South America and translated into English in 1975 by David Kunzle, this tract attempts to demonstrate how Disney comic books were used in Chile before Allende to promote capitalistic ideology. Actually the culprits here were the translators who put words into the mouths of characters not contained in the originals approved by Disney. Another oddity is the only full-scale biography of a comic book character (a Disney creation via Carl Barks), *An Informal Biography of Scrooge McDuck*, by Jack Chalker.

For information about the political cartoon, one can do no better than to turn to *The Ungentlemenly Art: A History of American Political Cartoons*, by Stephen Hess and Milton Kaplan. First issued in 1968 and revised in 1975, the volume is valuable for its historic narrative, the copious reproductions of classic cartoons, the extensive source notes, and the full bibliography which should be consulted for additional works in this area of comic art.

The bookshelf of biographies of major comic artists is practically empty. Most early efforts have taken the form of brief personal memoirs or picture books in which the text is incidental to the illustrations. Illustrative of such promotional books are *Milton Caniff: Rembrandt of the Comic-Strip*, by John Paul Adams, *John McCutcheon's Book*, by John McCutcheon, which includes a biography of McCutcheon by Vincent Starrett, and *Charlie Brown & Charlie Schulz*, by Lee Mendelson. Charles Schulz provided an autobiographical memoir for the twenty-fifth anniversary album, *Peanuts Jubilee: My Life and Art with Charlie Brown and Others*. Also of interest for its autobiographical content is Walt Kelly's anthology, *Ten Ever-lovin' Blue-eyed Years with Pogo*. Peter Marzio's *Rube Goldberg: His Life and Work*, however, is an attempt at a full-scale objective biographical account of Goldberg's highly versatile career and an interpretation of his art. Marzio achieves a sense of Goldberg's personality and character, and other classic cartoonists need similar treatment. Goldberg's autobiography has been incorporated in Clark Kinnaird's edition of *Rube Goldberg vs. the Machine Age*. Another cartoonist who has ventured to tell his own story is John T. McCutcheon in *Drawn from Memory*. Frank Jacobs' *The Mad World of William M. Gaines* is a semi-biography and personal memoir of the publisher responsible for the distinguished E.C. line of comic books and later *Mad* magazine (which began as a comic book).

The first complete book on the comic book was neither a history nor an appreciation. The purpose of *Seduction of the Innocent*, by psychologist Fredric Wertham, in 1954 was to prove that comic books, especially of the crime and horror variety, were a major contributing factor to juvenile delinquency. Although his data was scientifically invalid, Wertham's book upset many parents and teachers groups and added to the general hysteria of the McCarthy era, resulting in a congressional investigation chaired by Estes Kefauver (the proceedings are found in a Greenwood

Press reprint of the government documents, *Juvenile Delinquency*, United States Senate Committee on the Judiciary). Anticipating the investigation, in October 1954, the Comics Magazine Association of America moved to adopt a self-regulating Comics Code Authority with the most stringent code ever applied to any of the mass media. The history and complete text of the code is found in a promotional booklet *Americana in Four Colors*, by John L. Goldwater, president of the association. Before Wertham, Gershon Legman had issued early warnings about the baneful effect of violence in the comics in *Love & Death: A Study in Censorship* in 1949. Also in tune with Wertham, in *The Undergrowth of Literature*, Gillian Freeman fears that costumed super-heroes will inspire fantasies of fetishism and sado-masochism. A chapter of Ron Goulart's *The Assault on Childhood* traces how he feels that the comic book industry "ignored its potential and became preoccupied with murder, torture, sadism and storm-trooper violence."

Throughout the years the popular magazines, newspapers, and journals of commentary have published hundreds of articles and essays on the comics, many worthwhile, others superficial, and still others steeped in disdain for the subject. For example, a comment on the E.C. comic books in *The Village Voice* of January 18, 1973 read: "Clearly this is junk, not harmless junk but sensational sadistic trash (the quality of the artwork is irrelevant: scum that glistens is scum still)." Much of this material is listed in the Kempkes bibliography. A useful anthology of some of the better essays is *The Funnies: An American Idiom*, edited by David Manning White and Robert H. Abel. All of the following anthologies of essays on popular culture and mass media reprint one of more of the periodical pieces: *Mass Culture*, edited by Bernard Rosenberg and David Manning White; *Pop Culture in America*, edited by David Manning White; *Mass Media and the Popular Arts*, edited by Fredric Rissover and David C. Birch; *Mass Culture Revisited*, edited by Bernard Rosenberg and David Manning White; *The Arts Explosion*, edited by Clifford A. Ridley; *The Popular Culture Explosion*, edited by Ray B. Browne and David Madden; *Popular Culture and the Expanding Consciousness*, edited by Ray B. Browne; *Mass Media: The Invisible Environment*, edited by Robert J. Glessing and William P. White; and *The Great Contemporary Issues: Popular Culture*, edited by David Manning White.

Several critics who have undertaken general assessments of popular culture have devoted portions of their studies to comic art. One of the earliest was Gilbert Seldes in his 1924 pioneer survey of the mass media, *The 7 Lively Arts*. Though somewhat apologetically, Seldes found some virtues in "The 'vulgar' comic strip" in one chapter of that title, but his essay on George Herriman and *Krazy Kat* was one of the first partly to define Herriman's unique genius. In *The Astonished Muse*, Reuel Denney finds the comics deeply rooted in the larger conventions and traditions of art and literature, especially naturalism, and Leo Lowenthal calls for more serious study of the comics in *Literature, Popular Culture, and Society*. One chapter of Charles Beaumont's *Remember? Remember?* praises the daily funnies for their beauty, imagination, communication, and general good to the world. Perhaps some of the most fruitful, provocative, and rational comments are found in Alan Gowans' *The Unchanging Arts*. Gowans recognizes the extent to which the popular visual arts play a functional part in the total context of society and finds the comics one of the century's major art forms. A social scientist who has specialized in writing about the subject is Arthur Asa Berger, whose books include *Li'l Abner: A Study in American Satire*, the first book-length study of a single comic strip; *The Comic-Stripped American*, a series of pieces on the way comics reflect our culture; and *Pop Culture*, a collection of essays with three on the comics. Unfortunately all of his books are marred by factual inaccuracies, superficial judgments, and general carelessness.

A special category of interpretive books are the "gospel" studies. Robert L. Short began the trend with *The Gospel According to Peanuts* and followed the phenomenal success of that book with *The Parables of Peanuts*. Then came *The Gospel According to Superman* by John T. Galloway, Jr., *The Gospel According to Andy Capp* by D. P. McGeachy, III and *Good News for Grimy Gulch* by Del Carter (based on Tom K. Ryan's comic strip *Tumbleweeds*). These books basically are sermons or theological disquisitions illustrated by the comics in question and make little commentary of a significant sort on their meaning or value, except insofar as they are all concerned with the problems of human existence. Jeffrey H. Loria's *What's It All About, Charlie Brown?* is a similar kind of book which describes with frequent illustrations the philosophical and psychological meaning of *Peanuts*.

Most serious study of comic art seems to have focused on how it reflects or relates to society and the culture out of which it has grown. Only now are we witnessing the development of a body of writing that attempts to assess the comics on their own terms, by measuring their worth against their own developed standards and aesthetic principles rather than by the irrelevant yardsticks of other related arts. A collection of essays mainly on comic book super-heroes helped initiate this development, *All in Color for a Dime*, edited by Dick Lupoff and Don Thompson. Many of the essays originated in a series of fan magazine articles and still bear the stylistic and judgmental marks of their origin. A second volume, also edited by Thompson and Lupoff, *The Comic-Book Book*, is a marked improvement in this regard. In style and judgment, many of these essays are distinguished. Although most of Maurice Horn's *75 Years of the Comics* is devoted to reprinting sample pages from an exhibition at the New York

Cultural Center, his excellent ten-page introduction is one of the best efforts so far to define comic art as it relates to the other narrative arts and on its own internal principles. In *The Art of Humorous Illustration*, Nick Meglin has assembled appreciative, fully illustrated tributes to twelve illustrators, including comic artists Sergio Aragones, Jack Davis, Mort Drucker, Johnny Hart, and Arnold Roth. The purpose of *Moviemaking Illustrated: The Comicbook Filmbook*, by James Morrow and Murray Suid, is to teach the technical principles of filmmaking, but the textbook utilizes nothing but frames from Marvel comic books and thereby makes many valuable points about the complex sound and visual techniques of comic art. *The Art of the Comic Strip*, edited by Walter Herderg and David Pascal, is noteworthy for its excellent choice of illustrations and the perceptive quality of the brief notes and commentary (originally a special issue of *Graphics* magazine). Also of interest is *The Very Large Book of Comical Funnies*, compiled by the staff of the *National Lampoon* as a good-natured satire on the plethora of historic and appreciative books about the comics but which in its own way displays an appreciative sense of what makes the comics special.

Although primarily designed as a guide on how to create comic strips, editorial cartoons, gag cartoons, and caricatures, Ray Paul Nelson's *Cartooning* provides the most complete survey of cartooning techniques and graphic principles that apply to the art available. It is an essential book for those who would appreciate the art and significance of the modern cartoon. Also helpful in this regard is the introductory essay for *The Art in Cartooning: Seventy-five Years of American Magazine Cartoons*, edited by Edwin Fisher, Mort Gerberg, and Ron Wolin. This selection of 330 humorous drawings and gag cartoons, beginning in the 1880s with Thomas Nast and moving through the best years of *Judge, Life, Saturday Evening Post*, and *The New Yorker*, also provides an engaging progress through the history of the magazine cartoon.

The publication of fan magazines and amateur press publications about comic art began in the 1950s and reemerged in the 1960s as a significant development in the history of American magazines. Much of the pioneer scholarship about the comics first appeared in those pages, and extremely useful biographical and bibliographical information can be found there. A history of their development and a listing of titles would require more space than is available for this entire essay, and it would be almost impossible to assemble a file for back issues on most of them. The comments here will be restricted to a very few of the most professional, informative, and regularly published periodicals to which subscriptions are available.

Alan L. Light is the editor and publisher of *The Buyer's Guide for Comic Fandom*, the most widely circulated tabloid publication for collectors who wish to buy and sell comics and comics-related materials. In addition to advertisements, the semi-monthly publication occasionally includes feature stories and articles. A pioneer and widely read magazine for advertisers is *The Rocket's Blast—Comicollector*, better known simply as *RBCC*, edited and published by G.B. Love through summer 1974 and afterwards by James Van Hise. Recent issues have begun to carry more essays, features, and reprints, and fewer advertisements. Professional cartoonist Jud Hurd edits the quarterly *Cartoonist Profiles*, which specializes in interviews with living comic artists and profiles on classic artists of the past. A wealth of professional and historical data is found in each issue. Another useful publication of this type is *Cartoonews*, edited by cartoonists Jim Ivey and James Sheridan.

The most current news about the comic book publishing world and forthcoming titles is found in *The Comic Reader*, issued monthly and edited by Jerome L. Sinkovec and Michael L. Tiefenbacher. A one-sheet newsletter about the world of underground comic books is *Comix World*, published by Clay Geerdes. Two high-quality and beautifully produced magazines containing well researched and critically stimulating essays are John Benson's *Squa Tront*, which focuses specifically on the E. C. comic book titles, and Bill Spicer's *Fanfare*, which considers the entire range of the visual arts, including television, film, animation, and the comics within its purview.

ANTHOLOGIES AND REPRINTS

From the very beginning of the American comic strip in the 1890s, paperback collections of the most widely read titles were popular publications. Thus *The Yellow Kid, Foxy Grandpa, Buster Brown,* and *Mutt and Jeff* appeared in series of reprints, and in 1933 the first comic book, *Funnies on Parade*, was composed of reprints of Sunday and daily strips in color. Over the years various comics would find their way into paperback anthologies and less often into hardcover collections. Usually considered of ephemeral value, few copies survive and are considered collector's items. One of the first substantial anthologies of American cartoons, complete with historical introductions and annotations, was Thomas Craven's *Cartoon Cavalcade* in 1943. Interspersed among the chronologically arranged examples of political and gag cartoons filling over four hundred pages were selections from all the popular newspaper comic strips.

The one publisher who first initiated a program of reprinting classic comic strips in the most responsible format, in selected complete runs with authoritative introductions, was the late Woody Gelman of Nostalgia Press. Beginning with Alex Raymond's *Flash Gordon* in 1967, Gelman published one or more volumes a year in his series The Golden Age of

Comics. He also issued a series of anthologies of selected daily strips entitled *Nostalgia Comics*. The ultimate result of his program is an extensive bookshelf of handsomely produced collections of the classic comic strips, preserved for convenient reading and future research.

The most ambitious reprint operation undertaken so far is the Classic American Comic Strips series by Hyperion Press of Westport, Connecticut, under the editorship of Bill Blackbeard. Series I contains twenty-two volumes in large format and in hardcover or paperback editions. Drawing on the archives of the San Francisco Academy of Comic Art, each volume contains complete sequential reprints from the first or peak years of selected daily and Sunday strips and an introduction by an authority on the subject of that volume. Future series are planned, and if the program is successful, it may prove to be the most significant scholarly project ever undertaken to preserve American comic art in a usable format.

Several publishers have issued over the years paperback collections of the most popular comic strips. Among them are Simon and Schuster; Holt, Rinehart and Winston; New American Library; Grosset and Dunlap; Ballantine; Fawcett; Bantam; Avon; Dell; and Pyramid Books. For a list of available titles, one should consult their catalogs as the books go in and out of print with unpredictable frequency.

The reprinting of comic book material has occurred with much less frequency than with comic strips, possibly because of the expense of color reproduction which is necessary to do it properly. The first hardcover anthology of selected comic book stories was Jules Feiffer's *The Great Comic Book Heroes* in 1965, a best-selling volume which partly spurred the commercial nostalgia market development. The book is of additional interest for the extensive introduction in which satirical author/cartoonist Feiffer reminisces about his days in the comic book industry and provides his personal commentary on the meaning of the super-hero. One of the major comic book publishers, National Periodical Publications, devoted a special publication, *Famous First Edition*, to over-sized, full-color, facsimile reproductions of valuable first issues: *Action* No. 1, *Detective* No. 27, *Sensation* No. 1, and *Whiz Comics* No. 2, each of which introduced Superman, Batman, Wonder Woman, and Captain Marvel respectively, as well as *Batman* No. 1, *Superman* No. 1, *Wonder Woman* No. 1, *Flash Comics* No. 1, and *All Star Comics* No. 3. A few of these were issued in hardcover editions by Lyle Stuart.

The number of anthologies of reprinted comic strip and comic book stories is so extensive that they cannot be discussed here. Instead, the reader will find a separate checklist of these appended to the list of works cited at the end of this essay. In most cases these books include introductory appreciations, background essays, biographical notes, and other additional material which will be of interest to the reader and researcher.

BIBLIOGRAPHY

BOOKS

Adams, John Paul. *Milton Caniff: Rembrandt of the Comic Strip.* New York: David McKay, 1946.

Bails, Jerry, *The Collector's Guide: The First Heroic Age.* Detroit: Jerry Bails, 1969.

————, and Hames Ware, eds. *The Who's Who of American Comic Books.* 4 vols. Detroit: Jerry Bails, 1973-76.

Beaumont, Charles. *Remember? Remember?* New York: Macmillan, 1963.

Becker, Stephen. *Comic Art in America.* New York: Simon and Schuster, 1959.

Berger, Arthur Asa. *The Comic-Stripped American.* New York: Walker and Co., 1973.

————. *Li'l Abner: A Study in American Satire.* New York: Twayne Publishers, 1970.

————. *Pop Culture.* New York: Pflaum/Standard, 1973.

Bernewitz, Fred von, and Joe Vucenic. *The Full Edition of the Complete E.C. Checklist (Revised).* Los Alamos, N.M.: Wade M. Brothers, 1974.

Bray, Glenn. *The Illustrated Harvey Kurtzman Index: 1939-1975.* Sylmar, Calif.: Glenn Bray, 1976.

Browne, Ray B., ed. *Popular Culture and the Expanding Consciousness.* New York: John Wiley & Sons, 1973.

————, and David Madden, eds. *The Popular Culture Explosion.* Dubuque, Iowa: William C. Brown, 1972.

Carter, Del. *Good News for Grimy Gulch.* Valley Forge, Pa.: Judson Press, 1977.

Chalker, Jack. *An Informal Biography of Scrooge McDuck.* Baltimore: Mirage Press, 1974.

Couperie, Pierre, et al. *A History of the Comic Strip.* Translated by Eileen B. Hennessy. New York: Crown, 1968.

Daniels, Les. *Comix: A History of Comic Books in America.* New York: Outerbridge & Dienstfrey, 1971.

Denney, Reuel. *The Astonished Muse.* Chicago: University of Chicago Press, 1957.

Dorfman, Ariel, and Armand Mattelart. *How to Read Donald Duck: Imperialist Idealogy in the Disney Comic.* Translated by David Kunzle. New York: International General, 1975.

Estren, Mark James. *A History of Underground Comics.* San Francisco: Straight Arrow Books, 1974.

Fisher, Edwin; Mort Gerberg; and Ron Wolin. *The Art in Cartooning: Seventy-Five Years of American Magazine Cartoons.* New York: Charles Scribner's Sons, 1975.

Fleisher, Michael L. *The Encyclopedia of Comic Book Heroes.* Vol. I: *Batman.* Vol. II: *Wonder Woman.* New York: Macmillan, 1976. Eight volumes projected.

Freeman, Gillian. *The Undergrowth of Literature*. London: Thomas Nelson and Sons, 1967.

Galloway, John T., Jr. *The Gospel According to Superman*. Philadelphia: Lippincott-A. J. Holman, 1973.

Glessing, Robert J., and William P. White, eds. *Mass Media: The Invisible Environment*. Chicago: Science Research Associates, 1973.

Goldwater, John L. *Americana in Four Colors*. New York: Comics Magazine Association of America, 1974.

Goulart, Ron. *The Adventurous Decade*. New Rochelle, N.Y.: Arlington House, 1975.

————. *The Assault on Childhood*. Los Angeles: Sherbourne Press, 1969.

Gowans, Alan. *The Unchanging Arts*. Philadelphia: Lippincott, 1971.

Herderg, Walter, and David Pascal, eds. *The Art of the Comic Strip*. Zürich, Switzerland: Graphis Press, 1972.

Hess, Stephen, and Milton Kaplan. *The Ungentlemanly Art: A History of American Political Cartoons*. New York: Macmillan, 1975.

Horn, Maurice. *Comics of the American West*. New York: Winchester Press, 1977.

————. *75 Years of the Comics*. Boston: Boston Book & Art, 1971.

————, ed. *The World Encyclopedia of Comics*. 1 and 2 vol. editions. New York: Chelsea House, 1976.

Illenberger, Theodora, and Avonne Eyre Keller, eds. *The Cartoonist Cookbook*. New York: Hobbs, Dorman & Co., 1966.

Inge, M. Thomas, and Bill Blackbeard. "American Comic Art." In *A Nation of Nations*, edited by Peter Marzio. New York: Harper and Row, 1976.

Jacobs, Frank. *The Mad World of William M. Gaines*. New York: Lyle Stuart, 1972.

Kelly, Walt. *Ten Ever-lovin' Blue-eyed Years with Pogo*. New York: Simon and Schuster, 1959.

Keltner, Howard. *Index to Golden Age Comic Books*. Detroit: Jerry Bails, 1976.

Kempkes, Wolfgang. *International Bibliography of Comics Literature*. Detroit: Gale Research Co., 1971. 2nd rev. ed. New York: R. R. Bowker/Verlag Dokumentation, 1974.

Kinnaird, Clark, ed. *Rube Goldberg vs. the Machine Age*. New York: Hastings House, 1968.

Kunzle, David. *The Early Comic Strip*. Vol. I: *History of the Comic Strip*. Berkeley: University of California Press, 1973.

Legman, Gershon. *Love & Death: A Study in Censorship*. New York: Breaking Point, 1949. Reprint. New York: Hacker Art Books, 1963.

Lesser, Robert. *A Celebration of Comic Art and Memorabilia*. New York: Hawthorne Books, 1975.

Loria, Jeffrey H. *What's It All About, Charlie Brown?* New York: Holt, Rinehart and Winston, 1968.

Lowenthal, Leo. *Literature, Popular Culture, and Society*. Englewood Cliffs, N.J.: Prentice-Hall, 1961. Reprinted. Palo Alto, Calif.: Pacific Books, 1968.

Lupoff, Dick, and Don Thompson, eds. *All in Color for a Dime*. New Rochelle, N.Y.: Arlington House, 1970.

McCutcheon, John T. *Drawn from Memory*. Indianapolis: Bobbs-Merrill, 1950.

————. *John McCutcheon's Book*. Selections by Franklin J. Meine and John Merryweather. New York: Caxton Club, 1948.

McGeachy, D. P., III. *The Gospel According to Andy Capp*. Richmond, Va.: John Knox Press, 1973.

Marzio, Peter C. *Rube Goldberg: His Life and Work*. New York: Harper and Row, 1973.

Meglin, Nick. *The Art of Humorous Illustration*. New York: Watson-Guptill Publications, 1973.

Mendelson, Lee. *Charlie Brown & Charlie Schulz*. New York: World, 1970.

Morrow, James, and Murray Suid. *Moviemaking Illustrated: The Comicbook Filmbook*. New York: Hayden Book Co., 1973.

Murrell, William. *A History of American Graphic Humor*. Vol. I, 1747-1865. New York: Whitney Museum of American Art, 1933. Vol. II, 1865-1938. New York: Macmillan, 1938. Reprinted. New York: Cooper Square, 1967.

National Lampoon. *The Very Large Book of Comical Funnies*. New York: National Lampoon, 1975.

Nelson, Ray Paul. *Cartooning*. Chicago: Henry Regnery, 1975.

O'Brien, Richard. *The Golden Age of Comic Books: 1937-1945*. New York: Ballantine Books, 1977.

Olshevsky, George. *Marvel Comics Index*. Vol. I: *The Amazing Spider-Man*. Vol. II: *Conon and the Barbarians*. Vol. III: *Avengers and Captain Marvel*. Vol. IV: *Fantastic Four*. Toronto, Ontario, Canada: G & T Enterprises, 1976-.

O'Sullivan, Judith. *The Art of the Comic Strip*. College Park: University of Maryland, Department of Art, 1971.

Overstreet, Robert M. *The Comic Book Price Guide*. Cleveland, Tenn.: Robert M. Overstreet, 1970 (and subsequent annual editions).

Perry, George, and Alan Aldridge. *The Penguin Book of Comics*. New York: Penguin Books, 1969. Rev. ed., 1971.

Reitberger, Reinhold, and Wolfgang Fuchs. *Comics: Anatomy of a Mass Medium*. Translated by Nadia Fowler. Boston: Little,Brown, 1972.

Ridley, Clifford A., ed. *The Arts Explosion*. New York: Dow Jones Books, 1972.

Rissover, Fredric, and David C. Birch, eds. *Mass Media and the Popular Arts*. New York: McGraw-Hill, 1971. 2nd ed., 1977.

Robinson, Jerry. *The Comics: An Illustrated History of Comic Strip Art*. New York: G. P. Putnam's Sons, 1974.

Rosenberg, Bernard, and David Manning White, eds. *Mass Culture*. New York: Free Press, 1957.

————. *Mass Culture Revisited*. New York: Van Nostrand Reinhold, 1971.

Schulz, Charles. *Peanuts Jubilee: My Life and Art with Charlie Brown and Others*. New York: Holt, Rinehart, and Winston, 1975.

Seldes, Gilbert. *The 7 Lively Arts*. New York: Harper and Brothers, 1924. Rev. ed. Layton, Utah: Peregrine Smith, Inc./Sagamore Press, 1957.

Sheridan, Martin. *Comics and their Creators*. Boston: Hale, Cushman & Flint,

1942. Reprinted. Brooklyn, N.Y.: Luna Press, 1971. Reprinted. Arcadia, Calif.: Post-Era Books, 1973.

Short, Robert L. *The Gospel According to Peanuts.* Richmond, Va.: John Knox Press, 1964.

Steranko, James. *The Steranko History of Comics.* 2 vols. Wyomissing, Pa.: Supergraphics, 1970-72.

Thompson, Don, and Dick Lupoff, eds. *The Comic-Book Book.* New Rochelle, N.Y.: Arlington House, 1973.

U.S. Congress. Senate Committee on the Judiciary. *Juvenile Delinquency: Comic Books, Motion Pictures, Obscene and Pornographic Materials, Television Programs.* Westport, Conn.: Greenwood Press, 1969.

Walker, Mort, comp. *The National Cartoonists Society Album.* 1972-77 ed. Brooklyn, N.Y.: National Cartoonists Society, 1972.

————. *Backstage at the Strips.* New York: Mason/Charter, 1975.

Waugh, Coulton. *The Comics.* New York: Macmillan, 1947. Reprinted. Brooklyn, N.Y.: Luna Press, 1974.

Wertham, Fredric. *Seduction of the Innocent.* New York: Holt, Rinehart and Winston, 1954. Reprinted. Port Washington, N.Y.: Kennikat Press, 1972.

White, David Manning, ed. *Pop Culture in America.* New York: Quadrangle Books, 1970.

————, ed. *The Great Contemporary Issues: Popular Culture.* New York: The New York Times-Arno Press, 1975.

————, and Robert H. Abel, eds. *The Funnies: An American Idiom.* New York: Free Press, 1963.

White, Edward M., ed. *The Pop Culture Tradition.* New York: W. W. Norton, 1972.

Young, Margaret Labash, Harold Chester Young, and Anthony T. Kzuras, eds. *Directory of Special Libraries and Information Centers.* 4th edition. Detroit: Gale Research Co., 1977.

ANTHOLOGIES AND REPRINTS

This supplementary checklist is selective and includes primarily hardcover and quality paperback volumes. Newsstand paperbacks, fan publications, and limited editions are not listed since they may no longer be in print when this is published.

Barlow, Ron, and Bob Stewart, eds. *Horror Comics of the 1950's.* Franklin Square, N.Y.: Nostalgia Press, 1971.

Batman from the 30's to the 70's. New York: Crown, 1971.

The Best of the Rip Off Press. 2 vols. San Francisco: Rip Off Press, 1973-74.

The Best of Walt Disney Comics. 4 vols. Racine, Wisc.: Western Publishing Co., 1974.

Bizarre Comix. 4 vols. New York: Bélier Press, 1975-76.

Bodé, Vaughn. *Cheech Wizard.* Smithers, British Columbia, Canada: Northern Comfort Communications, 1976.

————. *Deadbone*. Smithers, British Columbia, Canada: Northern Comfort Communications, 1975.

Briggs, Clare. *When a Feller Needs a Friend and other Favorite Cartoons*. New York: Dover Publications, 1975.

Caniff, Milton. *Terry and the Pirates*. Franklin Square, N.Y.: Nostalgia Press, 1970.

————. *Terry and the Pirates Meet Burma*. Franklin Square, N.Y.: Nostalgia Press, 1976.

————. *Terry and the Pirates: Enter the Dragon Lady*. Franklin Square, N.Y.: Nostalgia Press, 1976.

Cobb, Ron. *The Cobb Book*. Sydney, Australia: Wild & Woolley, 1975.

Corben, Richard. *Bloodstar*. Leawood, Kans.: Morning Star Press, 1976.

————. *Richard Corben's Funny Book*. Kansas City, Kans.: Nickelodeon Press, 1976.

Coutts, John Alexander Scott. [John Willie.] *The Adventures of Sweet Gwendoline*. New York: Bélier Press, 1974.

Craven, Thomas, ed. *Cartoon Cavalcade*. New York: Simon and Schuster, 1943.

Crumb, Robert. *Fritz the Cat*. New York: Ballatine Books, 1969.

————. *Head Comix*. New York: Ballantine Books, 1970.

————. *Robert Crumb's Carload o' Comics: An Anthology of Choice Strips and Stories—1968 to 1976*. New York: Bélier Press, 1976.

Dille, Robert C., ed. *The Collected Works of Buck Rogers in the 25th Century*. New York: Chelsea House, 1969. Rev. ed. 1977.

Dirks, Rudolph. *The Katzenjammer Kids*. New York: Dover Publications, 1974.

Donahue, Don, and Susan Goodrick, eds. *The Apex Treasury of Underground Comics*. New York: Quick Fox, 1974.

EC Portfolio. 5 vols. Adel, Iowa: Russ Cochran, 1971-74.

Falk, Lee, and Phil Davis. *Mandrake the Magician*. Franklin Square, N.Y.: Nostalgia Press, 1970.

————, and Ray Moore. *The Phantom*. Franklin Square, N.Y.: Nostalgia Press, 1969.

Feiffer, Jules, ed. *The Great Comic Book Heroes*. New York: Dial Press, 1965.

Fleischer, Max. *Betty Boop*. New York: Avon Books, 1975.

Foster, Hal. *Prince Valiant in the Days of King Arthur*. Franklin Square, N.Y.: Nostalgia Press, 1974.

————. *Prince Valiant Companions in Adventure*. Franklin Square, N.Y.: Nostalgia Press, 1974.

Fox, Fontaine. *Toonerville Trolley*. Edited by Herb Galewitz and Don Winslow. New York: Charles Scribner's Sons, 1972.

Galewitz, Herb, ed. *Great Comics Syndicated by the New York Daily News and Chicago Tribune*. New York: Crown, 1972.

Gilmore, Donald H. (pseud.) *Sex in Comics*. 4 vols. San Diego, Calif.: Greenleaf Classics, 1971.

Gould, Chester. *The Celebrated Cases of Dick Tracy, 1931-1951*. Edited by Herb Galewitz. New York: Chelsea House, 1970.

Gray, Harold. *Arf! The Life and Hard Times of Little Orphan Annie, 1935-1945*. New Rochelle, N.Y.: Arlington House, 1970.

———. *Little Orphan Annie and Little Orphan Annie in Cosmic City.* New York: Dover Publications, 1974.

Griffith, Bill, and Jay Kinney. *The Young Lust Reader.* Berkeley, Calif.: And/Or Press, 1974.

Herriman, George. *Krazy Kat.* New York: Henry Holt, 1946.

———. *Krazy Kat.* New York: Grosset & Dunlap-Madison Square Press, 1969.

Hogarth, Burne. *Jungle Tales of Tarzan.* New York: Watson-Guptill Publications, 1976.

———. *Tarzan of the Apes.* New York: Watson-Guptill Publications, 1972.

Johnson, Crockett. [David Johnson Leisk.] *Barnaby.* New York: Henry Holt, 1943. Reprint. New York: Dover Publications, 1967.

Kurtzman, Harvey, and Will Elder. *Playboy's Little Annie Fanny.* 2 vols. Chicago: Playboy Press, 1966, 1972.

Lee, Stan. *Bring on the Bad Guy: Origins of Marvel Villains.* New York: Simon and Schuster, 1976.

———, ed. *Origins of Marvel Comics.* New York: Simon and Schuster, 1974.

———. *Son of Origins of Marvel Comics.* New York: Simon and Schuster, 1975.

Levine, David. *Artists, Authors, and Others: Drawings by David Levine.* Washington, D.C.: Smithsonian Institution Press, 1976.

Lynch, Jay, ed. *The Best of Bijou Funnies.* New York: Links Books, 1975.

McCay, Winsor. *Dreams of the Rarebit Fiend.* New York: Dover Publications, 1973.

———. *Little Nemo.* Franklin Square, N.Y.: Nostalgia Press, 1972.

———. *Little Nemo—1905-1906.* Franklin Square, N.Y.: Nostalgia Press, 1976.

———. *Little Nemo in the Palace of Ice and Further Adventures.* New York: Dover Publications, 1976.

McManus, George. *Bringing up Father.* Edited by Herb Galewitz. New York: Charles Scribner's Sons, 1973.

Metzger, George. *Beyond Time and Again: A Graphic Novel.* Huntington Beach, Calif.: Kyle and Wheary, 1976.

Moores, Dick. *Gasoline Alley.* New York: Avon Books, 1976.

Nostalgia Comics. 6 vols. Franklin Square, N.Y.: Nostalgia Press, 1971-74.

O'Neil, Dennis, ed. *Secret Origins of the DC Super Heroes.* New York: Crown-Harmony Books, 1976.

Outcault, Richard F. *Buster Brown.* New York: Dover Publications, 1974.

Preiss, Byron, and Ralph Reese. *One Year Affair.* New York: Workman Publishing Co., 1976.

Raymond, Alex. *Flash Gordon.* Franklin Square, N.Y.: Nostalgia Press, 1967.

———. *Flash Gordon in the Planet Mongo.* Franklin Square, N.Y.: Nostalgia Press, 1974.

———. *Flash Gordon in the Underwater World of Mongo.* Franklin Square, N.Y.: Nostalgia Press, 1974.

———. *Flash Gordon into the Water World of Mongo.* Franklin Square, N.Y.: Nostalgia Press, 1971.

Ripley, Robert L. *Ripley's Giant Believe It or Not!* New York: Warren Books, 1976.

Schulz, Charles M. *Peanuts Jubilee: My Life and Art with Charlie Brown and Others.* New York: Holt, Rinehart and Winston, 1975.

————. *Peanuts Treasury.* New York: Holt, Rinehart and Winston, 1968.

————. *The Snoopy Festival.* New York: Holt, Rinehart and Winston, 1974.

Smith, Sidney. *The Gumps.* Edited by Herb Galewitz. New York: Charles Scribner's Sons, 1974.

Superman from the Thirties to the Seventies. New York: Crown, 1971.

Trudeau, G. B. *The Doonesbury Chronicles.* New York: Holt, Rinehart and Winston, 1975.

————, and Nicholas Von Hoffman. *Tales from the Margaret Mead Taproom.* New York: Sheed and Ward, 1976.

Verbeek, Gustave. *The Incredible Upside-downs.* Summit, N.J.: Rajah Press, 1963.

Willard, Frank H. *Moon Mullins: Two Adventures.* New York: Dover Publications, 1976.

Wonder Woman. New York: Holt, Rinehart and Winston, 1972.

PERIODICALS

The Buyer's Guide for Comic Fandom. East Moline, Ill.: 1970-.

Cartoonews. Orlando, Fla., 1975-.

Cartoonist Profiles. Fairfield, Conn., 1969-.

The Comic Reader. Menomonee Falls, Wisc., 1961-.

Comix World. Berkeley, Calif., 1974-.

Fanfare. Los Angeles, 1977-.

RBCC (The Rocket's Blast—Comicollector). Miami, Fla., 1961-.

Squa Tront. New York, 1967-.

Detective and
CHAPTER 5 Mystery Novels
Larry Landrum

Mystery and detective fiction have been among the most popular fictional genres to emerge in Western literature. The roots of mystery fiction have been traced into antiquity, and arguments have been made for the universality of many of its characteristics. Puzzles and narrative riddles are found in the folklore of all cultures, and the investigation of wrongdoing and the search for solutions to problems found in detective fiction reaches beyond recorded history. The particular forms that such interests take are not universal; they emerge in particular cultures at particular times, pass into and come to dominate appropriate modes of expression, and reveal tendencies found in their parent cultures. Detective stories demand keen observation, superior reasoning, and the disciplined imagination of their protagonists. The immediacy of physical danger may require a strong arm, fighting skills, or a quick gun. In any case the narrative must provide a suitable challenge with high enough stakes so that the measures taken by the detective seem appropriate.

Mysteries are less specialized than detective stories and often verge on the gothic. There is often some sense in which the mystery threatens to escape rational explanation. Such uncertainty is expressed in other ways: the narrator is vulnerable, caught in a web of intrigue, or susceptible to the frailties of ordinary people. The central figure of a mystery is usually the narrator, and the weight of suspense allows little distance between the narrator and the reader. In the detective story, distance is established by focusing the reader's attention on detection and often by placing the recorder of the experience, the Watson figure, between the reader and the detective. While many structural similarities suggest a common origin for gothic and mystery fiction, mysteries clearly reflect the growing influence of rational explanations of mysterious causes that marked early nineteenth-century popular literature.

HISTORIC OUTLINE

The origins of the detective story, it is generally agreed, are found in the work of a single writer, Edgar Allan Poe. Though mystery and detection figure in numerous Poe stories, those that most influenced the detective tradition are "The Murders in the Rue Morgue" (1841), "The Mystery of Marie Rôget" (1842-43), and "The Purloined Letter" (1844). Most historians of the genre agree that nearly all the conventions of the classic detective story achieve their earliest coherent form in these tales, though later variations are important to the development of the genre.

Poe's major contribution was the celebration of independent observation and reason in the investigation of the murkier levels of human affairs. In "The Murders in the Rue Morgue," C. Auguste Dupin concludes a friend's train of thought for him by reconstructing the clues to his associative thoughts. In "The Mystery of Marie Rôget" the author attempts to solve a real crime by using only the evidence available to him in the newspapers; and in "The Purloined Letter," Dupin illustrates that imagination is crucial to the solution of problems conceived by intelligent criminals. Poe himself drew in part on the fanciful reminiscences of Francois Eugene Vidocq, a thief who was hired to catch criminals in Paris and who published his memoirs in 1828-29. Poe considered Vidocq only "a good guesser and a persevering man" who often erred because he failed to see the whole as well as the parts.

Numerous writers in subsequent years failed to mark Poe's caution and created a legion of detectives whose solutions relied heavily on luck. Others created police detectives rather than the inspired amateur or private investigator. In the long run, however, policemen were considered competition for the private detective or too dull or compromised or rule-bound for the serious intellectual business of crime detection, unless some special status gave them the freedom and independence to see the whole picture and the leisure to pursue the unusual and bizarre. Throughout much of the rest of the nineteenth century, the narrative form in which the detective appeared remained relatively open. The detective's investigation tended to merge in most novels with themes from gothic fiction, domestic romance, courtroom exposition, exposés, and picaresque adventure stories.

Developments in Europe often appeared in America almost simultaneously. Dickens' works were eagerly awaited and often pirated within a few days of publication. Only his Inspector Bucket in *Bleak House* (1852-53) and the unfinished novel, *The Mystery of Edwin Drood* (1870), have direct influence, but his descriptions of low life and sharply etched characters influenced popular writers on both sides of the Atlantic. Dickens' son-in-law Wilkie Collins came closer to the genre. The first of his books,

A Woman in White (1860), finds a young artist called to a remote country house where mysteries began to build around a beautiful heroine and her stigmatized but brilliant sister. In the story told through witnesses' accounts, the young man is disappointed in love, disappears for a time from the narrative, then in book three returns to conduct an investigation that carries him into old court records and a battle of wits with a master criminal-spy. With the 1868 publication of *The Moonstone,* serialized in America in *Harper's Weekly,* Collins captured many of the conventions and nuances that became formulas in later detective fiction.

However, it was Anna Katherine Green's *The Leavenworth Case* in 1878 that brought the disparate elements together for the classic detective novel. Her portly detective, Ebenezer Gryce, soon became well-known on both sides of the Atlantic. A novel of detection as well as mystery, *The Leavenworth Case* eliminated many of the threads of extraneous genres and created a suspense that kept readers close to the action. In the next decade Green's work was eclipsed by the shadow of Arthur Conan Doyle, whose work was as popular in the United States as it was in England. *A Study in Scarlet* (1886) got off to a slow start, but with the publication of Fergus Hume's *The Mystery of a Hansom Cab* in 1887, British detective fiction achieved a popularity that Doyle led for many years.

The classic story appeared in slick magazines and hardcover novels, making its strongest appeal to the upwardly mobile middle class. By the turn of the century the novel of pure detection and the mystery novel whose central figure was forced into uncertain detection were distinct genres and both were popular. Jacques Futrelle's *The Thinking Machine* (1907) stories featured observation and analysis. His short story, "The Problem of Cell 13," is a classic of its kind. R. Austin Freeman's Dr. Thorndyke, first appearing in *John Thorndyke's Cases* in 1909, was a scientist whose laboratory methods fascinated readers. Thorndyke carried a compact laboratory kit with which he was able to do immediate analysis of physical clues. In *The Singing Bone* (1912), Freeman tells the murderer's story, then allows the reader to follow the detective's investigative procedures, relying on the interest in the method of detection to hold his readers.

The mystery strain developed by Anna Katherine Green is polished to perfection in the mysteries of Mary Roberts Rinehart. Probably best known for her introduction of the "had I but known" element, Rinehart's handling of suspense led to many imitations. *The Circular Staircase* (1908) established her reputation as a mystery writer and subsequent novels made her one of America's highest paid authors. Carolyn Wells' *The Clue* (1909), the first of her Fleming Stone mysteries, led to a formulaic approach that she outlined in *The Technique of the Mystery Story* (1929). Many later mystery and detective writers would attempt to explain the secret of writing the successful mystery novel. The middle-class dream in the classic story is apparent in the novels of Willard Huntington Wright, who wrote under the pen name of S. S. Van Dine. His detective, Philo Vance, first appeared in *The Benson Murder Case* in 1926, a scholarly eccentric who carried out meticulously detailed investigations in a milieu of conspicuous consumption. Rex Stout avoids this tendency, or rather balances his opulent Nero Wolfe with the tough Archie Goodwin, an updated and sophisticated Watson figure. Stout's fiction, beginning with *Fer-de-lance* (1934), represents a masterful balance of entertaining tales and detection.

If the tale of pure detection is expressed most faithfully in the seemingly impossible problem, then its most concise form is the locked room mystery, best expressed in America in the novels of John Dickson Carr, who also writes as Carter Dickson. Beginning with *It Walks by Night* (1929), Carr developed a series of fascinating puzzles for alert readers. In *The Hollow Man* (1935), his detective, Dr. Gideon Fell, launches into a lengthy thesis on types of locked room situations.

In this period, often called the "golden age" of detective fiction, Earl Derr Biggers' *The House Without a Key* (1925) began a series of novels that immortalized Charlie Chan, the Honolulu detective who inverted the image of the Oriental mastermind popularized in the Fu Manchu figure created by Sax Rohmer in the first decade of the twentieth century. Another detective that achieved immortality during this period was detective-author Ellery Queen. Created by Frederic Dannay and Manfred B. Lee in *The Roman Hat Mystery* (1929) and appearing in numerous subsequent stories and novels, Ellery Queen narrated his own novels and was drawn into cases to help his police inspector father. Queen has consistently given the reader a fair chance to solve the mystery, the "fair play" rule for writers, and has kept this tradition alive. Though the tight construction of the more or less pure story of detection continues to the present day, a second strain of detective fiction evolved that reached its peak in the 1930s. It is often seen as burgeoning independently out of the heads of a few key writers, but its roots are actually in the nineteenth century. The form that evolved out of the dime-novel tradition and reached its flowering in well fertilized pages of the pulps is the hardboiled detective story.

The figure of the detective emerged slowly and tentatively in the story papers and dime novels from a vigilante figure of instant justice to a special representative of the government, and from the West to the urban East. The rise of the Eastern detective figure roughly parallels the shift of crime from the West to the East, or as Arthur Schlesinger notes, between the James Brothers' aborted attempt to rob the Northfield, Minnesota, bank on September 7, 1876, and the Jimmy Hope gang's $3,000,000 robbery of the Manhattan Savings Institution in New York on October 27, 1878. The first dime-novel detective is generally agreed to be the Old Sleuth, who first appeared as a serial titled, "Old Sleuth, the detective; or, The Bay Ridge Mystery" in the *New York Fireside Companion* in 1872.

The success of Green's *The Leavenworth Case* may have inspired editors to print translations of Emile Gaboriau's more adventurous French detective stories, and they appeared in quantities in 1879-80 and after. At least eighteen appeared in Munro's *Seaside Library* during these years. By 1883 the *New York Detective Library* and the *Old Cap Collier Library* were both entirely made up of detective stories. In 1885 the *Old Sleuth Library* began by reprinting the 1872 "Bay Ridge Mystery." Early paper libraries featured a variety of detectives of various ages, ethnic origins, occupations, and both sexes. Of these, Old King Brady and Nick Carter became most popular.

Though Old King Brady is now remembered mainly by collectors, over 100 Nick Carter stories have been reprinted recently in paperbacks. *The Nick Carter Weekly* began in 1891 and as late as 1933 there were still 400 paper volumes in print. J. Randolph Cox counted 78 serials and 115 short stories in *Street & Smith's New York Weekly*, 282 issues of the *Nick Carter Detective Library*, 819 issues of the *Nick Carter Weekly*, 160 issues of *Nick Carter Stories*, 127 issues of *Detective Story Magazine* and 40 issues of *Nick Carter Magazine*, as well as scattered stories elsewhere. The detective's exploits were written by various hands and have emerged in radio, film, and television. Nick Carter was a man of breeding, education, and polish who liked an after-dinner cigar and a glass of port, but he was also a tough man of action known for his great strength and courage. In short, he combined the classic attributes of the urban gentleman detective with the Western adventure hero.

Changes in the copyright law, the invention of cheaper wood pulp paper, the rise of yellow journalism and more widespread adult literacy made the pulps possible in the 1890s. Detectives appearing in pulp magazines were at first extensions of those in dime novels, but soon evolved into fully urbanized figures. Dialogue and backgrounds began to be more authentic and Prohibition made the underworld chic. Exposés of city politics and gangster activities, postwar disillusionment, and literary naturalism made conventional adventure heroes seem less believable. Though the relatively genteel puzzle story reached its greatest popularity during the first quarter of the twentieth century, hard-boiled detective fiction began to deal with the feelings and reactions of the lower middle class. Pulp detective stories circumvented the social restrictions of the classic story to reveal the shocking rawness of American materialism. Authenticity seemed to demand a rejection of the social complacency found in the formal story, to require a commitment that went beyond the specific investigation of a case. The metaphorical link that evolved in the 1920s was the contract between an independent detective and a person willing to pay for his services.

It is not surprising that writers should grope for a style to express feelings about the predatory quality of society nor that they should be drawn to follow the lead of writers who successfully captured them. The pattern can be seen in the detective fiction of *Black Mask* (1920-51), a magazine initially financed as a money-making scheme by George Jean Nathan and H. L. Mencken. The stories of Carroll John Daly, who created the detective Race Williams, owed much to the dime novels, but his stories had a grit and cold violence that were rare in earlier fiction. Within a few years the magazine, especially under the editorship of Joseph T. Shaw, had attracted a number of superior writers who refined and fashioned the violence into a style for the 1920s and 1930s. Numerous pulps, such as *Dime Detective, Detective Story, Detective Fiction Weekly,* and others picked up stories in the hard-boiled style. By the late 1940s, however, the pulps were disappearing.

Many of the pulp detective writers were soon forgotten and relatively few saw their work in hardcover editions. Some reached great fame as novelists as well as writers of detective fiction. Dashiell Hammett's work is probably most significant. From his *Red Harvest* (1929), which introduced the Continental Op, through *The Maltese Falcon* (1930) where the Op becomes the private detective Sam Spade, to the mystery, *The Glass Key* (1931), Hammett explored the potentials of the hard-boiled genre. Raymond Chandler wrote numerous stories for *Black Mask* and other pulps and became the spokesman for the hard-boiled school. Beginning with *The Big Sleep* (1939), Chandler's novels capture almost perfectly the balance between the vulnerable mystery narrator in a predatory milieu and the detective who must assert his solution to the crime.

If one of the risks of the classic story is that it becomes too mechanistically concerned with plot, a risk of the hard-boiled story is that the detective becomes an extension of the atmosphere rather than its mediator. Dashiell Hammett's Continental Op in *Red Harvest* feels himself afflicted with the epidemic killing in "Poisonville," and Mickey Spillane's Mike Hammer, in *I, The Jury* (1947) is stricken with the disease. Spillane became identified with the excesses and distortions of McCarthyism, but from 1947 to 1951 his first seven novels were bestsellers and have now sold about forty million copies. Many critics saw this formulaic expression of the hard-boiled world as a dead end, much as earlier critics had seen the puzzle story as the end of the classic detective story. Yet writers continue to produce variations on the puzzle story, and the violence implicit in the hard-boiled form continues to be metaphorically viable.

Erle Stanley Gardner had shown with his first Perry Mason novel, *The*

Case of the Velvet Claws (1932), that the hard-boiled world could be softened by adopting some of the conventions of the classic detective story in the form of a courtroom drama. So successful was this approach that together with his other detective fiction Gardner sold more than one hundred million copies. Ross Macdonald (Kenneth Millar) represents another direction. His early novels are close to the Hammett tradition, but his later novels show a turn to greater subtlety in which his detective, Lew Archer, is an extension of the author's moral sensibilities. His *On Crime Writing* (1973) includes an essay on the writing of *The Galton Case* (1959). Chester Himes's detective fiction is similarly complex and hard-boiled, but while Macdonald compresses much of his violence into metaphor, Himes infuses his police detectives Coffin Ed Johnson and Grave Digger Jones with a picaresque comic spirit. Other contemporary writers have explored the potentials of mystery, as the superb work of Margaret Millar attests, or followed the criminal into the psychology of crime and social concepts of justice found in the work of Patricia Highsmith.

No single writer or school of writers presently dominates detective fiction, possibly because no investigative style can very accurately reflect the turbulent social conditions and attitudes of the times. Fictional detectives do not, as even their nineteenth-century detractors were fond of pointing out, correspond very closely to their real life counterparts. Instead they seem to represent a way of reflecting upon the darker social metaphors of life and the problems in the way to their understanding. Throughout the history of detective fiction, literal investigation has been closely followed by a more metaphorical form. Police memoirs and procedurals have been closely followed by fictional detectives who reestablish human proportions. Over time writers of detective and mystery fiction have evolved conventions that allow readers the opportunity to share in setting proportions right.

REFERENCE WORKS

As in many other areas of popular culture, much of the available reference work has been done by fans, advocates, and collectors. The most useful brief reference source is Chris Steinbrunner and Otto Penzler's *Encyclopedia of Mystery and Detection*, an encyclopedia of information on most aspects of mystery and detective fiction. This illustrated volume is indispensable for its concise, accurate entries on authors, major works, central characters, and a wealth of other relevant information. Jacques Barzun and Wendell Taylor's *A Catalogue of Crime* is an annotated bibliography of novels and collections arranged by author, together with an annotated critical bibliography and varied miscellaneous information.

Each author entry is accompanied by a two- or three-line impression of the work, while the bibliography is most useful for unusual items. Emphasis in this volume is on the classic narrative, and the slight coverage of American hard-boiled fiction, together with the idiosyncratic annotations, weakens a useful source.

Ordean Hagen's *Who Done It?* is the most comprehensive bibliography of detective novels available, though it contains numerous factual errors, an often arbitrary selection of editions, and is not at all comprehensive on nineteenth- and early twentieth-century fiction. Its inclusion of some twenty thousand author items does make it the most extensive list available. Fiction entries are identified as mysteries, detective, or suspense stories. Included in the volume are a subject guide, sections on film adaptations, plays, lists of anthologies and collections, checklists of settings and awards, a character list of some one hundred pages, and a title index. Another volume that should be used with caution is Linda Herman and Beth Stiel's *Corpus Delecti of Mystery Fiction*, which contains biographies and bibliographies for fifty British and American authors, but which also contains a number of significant errors. *Armchair Detective* is currently serializing an author checklist that may prove to be accurate, though it will not claim to be comprehensive.

Melvyn Barnes' *Best Detective Fiction* is a lively annotated bibliography of some 250 authors who have written in "the classic puzzle form" and whose work centers around the "how" or "why" of murder. More of a series of reader's impressions and plot summaries than a formally annotated bibliography, this work is most useful to the casual reader. Another work for the casual reader is Eric Quayle's *The Collector's Book of Detective Fiction*, a beautifully illustrated discussion of first editions of authors and series, including some dime novels. Quayle's notes on American detective fiction are light and sometimes unreliable. In contrast, Tage LaCour and Harald Mogensen's *The Murder Book* is both handsomely illustrated and a useful brief reference tool. The variety of the illustrations and the concise international history in *The Murder Book* make it a worthwhile introductory volume.

For the extensive treatment that should be afforded all dime novels, see Albert Johannsen's *The House of Beadle and Adams*, a carefully researched three-volume listing of the publisher's production together with biographical sketches of the authors. Fiction published by other dime-novel houses is less well-documented, but *The Dime Novel Roundup* has provided much information. For Nick Carter checklists, see J. Randolph Cox's essay and his *Roundup* supplements, *New Nick Carter Weekly*, and *Nick Carter Library*. Old King Brady is discussed in an article by Edward Lerthead in the *American Book Collector*. Charles Bragin's brief *Bibliography of Dime Novels, 1860-1964* is only suggestive.

Short stories in collections are indexed in E. H. Mundell and G. Ray Rausch's *The Detective Short Story*. This volume contains references to seventy-five hundred short stories in fourteen hundred collections and is divided into sections listing espionage stories, problem and puzzle stories, and detective experiences, and includes detective lists and an author index. Francis Lacassin's *Mythologie du Roman Policier* is useful for brief backgrounds on Poe, Biggers, Hammett, Chandler, Brown, Fearing, and Himes and for the appearances of these authors' works in several media.

Memoirs of actual detectives are often noted in the preceding sources, as are descriptions of real crimes that have provided inspiration for fiction. Thomas McDade's *The Annals of Murder* lists books and pamphlets on murders through about 1900. James Sandoe's *Murder: Plain and Fanciful* contains a list of some two hundred short stories and novels based on actual crimes or criminals. Fictional characters in mystery and detective stories have been the subject of many lists, but the most extensive sources are Chris Steinbrunner and others' *Detectionary*, Hagen's list in *Who Done It?*, Howard Haycraft's list in *Murder for Pleasure*, and Allen J. Hubin's list of series characters, "Patterns in Mystery Fiction," in John Ball's anthology, *The Mystery Story*.

Since many writers of detective fiction have written under two or more names, many articles have included references to these, and some of the reference works cited provide such information for a limited number of writers. Lenore Gribbin's *Who's Whodunit* is the single most comprehensive source for this information, though there are many omissions. Reviews of detective fiction are widely available in major newspapers, such as the New York *Times* and London *Times*, as well as such journals as *The Wilson Library Bulletin* and *Library Journal*. Retrospective as well as current reviews can be found in the *Armchair Detective* and *Mystery and Detection Annual*. Recurrent critical bibliography since 1972 can be found in Walter Albert's "A Bibliography of Secondary Sources" beginning in *Armchair Detective* in 1973.

RESEARCH COLLECTIONS

Manuscripts and papers relating to American detective fiction have not yet been adequately collected and identified, though the papers of some authors, such as Ellery Queen, Dashiell Hammett, Rex Stout, Raymond Chandler, John D. MacDonald, Erle Stanley Gardner, and Mary Roberts Rinehart, have been reported. Most of Chandler's manuscripts and papers are located at the University of California libraries at Los Angeles, and a collection of over 250 editions of his works can be found at the Kent State University libraries at Kent, Ohio. Most of John D. MacDonald's papers are located at the University of Florida. Rex Stout's papers are in the University of North Carolina libraries, those of Mary Roberts Rinehart are located at the University of Pittsburgh libraries, and Erle Stanley Gardner's, Dashiell Hammett's, and Ellery Queen's are at the University of Texas.

Listings in Lee Ash's *Subject Collections* (4th ed., 1974) and the *National Union Catalog of Manuscript Collections* suggest that several libraries have strong holdings in the manuscripts of detective writers, but these are not often cataloged or the catalogs are not easily available. The Special Collections Department of the University of Pittsburgh libraries list four hundred cataloged manuscripts, Boston University's Division of Special Collections in the Mugar Memorial Library holds the papers of "more than fifty" authors, Occidental College lists six thousand cataloged manuscripts, and the University of Oregon lists the manuscripts of a number of writers. Other libraries holding manuscripts include the University of Colorado, Indiana University's Lilly Library, Bowling Green State University's Popular Culture Library, and Brigham Young University's James S. Sandoe Collection.

Collections of detective fiction can be found at most large public libraries, and more specialized collections can often be located in university libraries, especially those that have received gifts of large private collections. The Queen Collection at the University of Texas, the Sandoe Collection at Brigham Young University, the University of North Carolina's four thousand volumes of British and American detective fiction, the Popular Culture Collection at Bowling Green State University, and Michigan State University's Special Collections all house large collections of detective and mystery fiction. Most libraries will contain many more volumes than is at first apparent, because the volumes may not be adequately identified in subject catalogs or separated into defined collections.

The media for the development of much popular American mystery and detective fiction—the dime novels and story papers of the nineteenth century and the pulps and paperbacks of the twentieth century—have not until recently been sought by research libraries. Now numerous libraries have attempted to collect such materials and excellent collections are available throughout the United States. Ash calls the Johannsen Collection of eleven hundred volumes at Northern Illinois University's Swen Franklin Parson Library "probably the most extensive collection [of dime novels] there is." The Library of Congress' twenty thousand issues of uncataloged dime novels in 270 series must rank as one of the most comprehensive collections, though it remains in nearly unusable order. Other major repositories of dime novels can be found in the Popular Library Department of the Cleveland Public Library (thirteen hundred issues), the Huntington Library (over two thousand), Yale University libraries, the George H. Hess Collection of forty-one thousand dime novels and other books at the University of Minnesota libraries, the New York Public Libraries' collection identified in 1922 in their *Bulletin,* the Department of Special Collections' eight thousand issues at the New York University libraries, and Oberlin College Library's twenty-two hundred issues of eighty-nine series.

Because pulp magazines date only from about 1895 and were printed on high acid content paper and because they were considered subliterature, collections of them are less accessible than dime-novel collections. Many pulps are in such delicate condition that libraries may refuse to copy them; certainly care should be taken in handling the now brittle and yellowed paper where access is permitted. In some cases publishers records are extant, though I am aware of no extensive checklist of pulps. The University of California at Los Angeles reports 12,500 issues in four hundred titles, Harvard University libraries house an extensive collection, and numerous other libraries have samples or partial collections. The Swen Franklin Parson Library at Northern Illinois University, for example, houses the Western Pulp Magazine Collection of six hundred magazine titles, the David Mullins Library at the University of Arkansas contains the Gerald J. McIntosh Dime Novel Collection, 1879-1969, as well as complete files for Street & Smith's *Tip Top Weekly* and *New Tip Top Weekly* for 1895-1915. The University of Oregon Library has the records of Renown Publications for 1955-72, which published the *Girl from U.N.C.L.E. Magazine* and *The Mike Shayne Mystery Magazine.* The New York Public Library holds records for Street & Smith, Munsey's, and other publishers.

Detective and mystery fiction collected into published editions are far too numerous to list here. One of the best annual publications is *Best Detective Stories of the Year.* This series has been graced with several excellent editors including the late Anthony Boucher (William Anthony Parker White) and Alan Hubin. Since Hubin's editorship the annual has contained a brief bibliographical list of collections, anthologies, criticism, and a list of "best" stories of the year. The volumes also contain a necrology and note awards given by the Mystery Writers of America. Since 1946 the Mystery Writers themselves have collected short fiction under various titles and editors. Several anthologies for the classroom have appeared in the last few years. Two of these, Nancy Ellen Talburt and Lyna Lee Montgomery's *A Mystery Reader* and Saul Schwartz's *The Detective Story* appear oriented to high schools, while Dick Allen and David Chacko's *Detective Fiction* is more clearly a college text.

The nostalgia for the pulps that reached its peak in the early 1970s inspired several collections of pulp fiction. Tony Goodstone compiled *The Pulps*, an illustrated collection of stories, including examples of detective fiction with a very brief introduction. Ron Goulart's *The Hardboiled Dicks* and Herbert Ruhm's *The Hard-Boiled Detective* are more in the tradition of Joseph T. Shaw's *The Hardboiled Omnibus* and are less erratic than Goodstone's collection.

HISTORY AND CRITICISM

Little scholarly attention was paid to the mystery and detective story prior to the turn of the century. Such stories were considered of little consequence and most of the writing done about them was in the form of brief reviews in popular periodicals. Carolyn Wells' study guide, *The Technique of the Mystery Story* for the Home Correspondence School, translated the general features of the British style into American terms, and thus was one of the first attempts to relate formally the conventions of the mystery to aspiring writers. In 1921 E. M. Wrong collected British detective stories under the title *Crime and Detection*, and in 1926 the volume was published in the United States. Wrong is the first to trace the roots of the detective story to ancient texts and to identify some of the salient themes of the classic detective story in his introduction. He admires the action potential of what he calls "the Moriarty theme," the villain who fights back, and he is put off by the avoidance of social retribution; too many stories have the criminal punished by self-imposed or accidental means. Wrong suggests that the rise of an organized police and an attention to external detail were necessary to the emergence of the detective story, an argument that Dorothy Sayers accepts in her introduction to *Omnibus of Crime*. Sayers also sees the detective story as a substitute for the romance and the adventure story in a shrinking world and lists numerous subterfuges used by writers to make the relatively closed form work.

It was Howard Haycraft who wrote the first book-length history of the detective story, *Murder for Pleasure*. This volume is both an appreciation and a history that traces the development of the form from Poe through the late 1930s, though it is partial to the "golden age" from 1918-30. *Murder for Pleasure* contains a readers' list of best fiction which later writers are fond of revising, a trivia quiz for careful readers, and a list of principal characters. The checklist of criticism is entitled "Friends and Foes." Haycraft's observations on American writers are generally sound and can be profitably read today. In *The Art of the Mystery Story*, Haycraft also collected some of the best early impressions and critiques of detective fiction. The book's contents are largely oriented to the classic form with one section devoted to rules for writers, including such curiosities as "The Detective Club Oath," but it also contains such gems as E. M. Wrong's and Dorothy Sayers' introductions already noted. Other important pieces are Joseph Wood Krutch's "Only a Detective Story," Erle Stanley Gardner's "The Case of the Early Beginning," Raymond Chandler's "The Simple Art of Murder," Anthony Boucher's "Trojan Horse Opera" (on spy novels), James Sandoe's "Dagger of the Mind" (on the thriller), John Dickson Carr's locked room essay, Ellery Queen's brief history of the detective short story, and other useful essays. The collection also includes parodies and essays on the differences between fictional and actual practices of detectives and criminals.

Writing about the mystery story proliferated during the 1930s and early 1940s and, as Haycraft's remarks on Dashiell Hammett suggest, by 1930 the hard-boiled genre was understood to have staked out new territory. When Raymond Chandler's famous essay, "The Simple Art of Murder," appeared in the *Atlantic Monthly* in 1944, he was not defining a new departure, but simply summarizing the development of the form over the last twenty years. Joseph T. Shaw had begun editing *Black Mask* in 1926 and within a few years had attracted some of the finest detective fiction available. Nevertheless, Chandler's essay underlined the critical importance of the hard-boiled story, a point which the next major critic overlooked.

Alma Murch's *The Development of the Detective Novel* includes one of the most thorough studies of the literary antecedents of many of the conventions of detective fiction, but it gives little indication of the direction of the fiction after the 1930s. The "golden age" is extended to the 1950s, but it might as well have ended twenty years earlier. Three-fourths of this history is devoted to a pre-Conan Doyle study of backgrounds. The author is anxious to maintain an aesthetic distance from her subject and in so doing tends to attribute too much importance to major writers and hardly anything to the great popular traditions flourishing in France, England, and the United States.

A similar problem of taste confuses Mary Noel's *Villains Galore*, which does deal directly with American story papers and dime novels. Though coverage of detective fiction and mysteries is limited, and the study lacks documentation, this is one of the few available studies on American story-paper literature in the nineteenth century. Quentin Reynolds' *The Fiction Factory* fills in some of the background, but remains too general to more than hint at the needs of most investigators. The pulps are somewhat better covered, primarily through the efforts of publishers and writers themselves. Harold Hersey's *Pulpwood Editor*, an early reminiscence of the pulps by an editor and writer, is representative of the style used by most participants to disclaim any deep commitment to the pulps. Hersey thought his audience unimaginative. Frank Gruber's *The Pulp Jungle* is much more valuable for its insights into the economies of writing for the pulps and for Gruber's thoughts on structuring mysteries. Robert Turner's *Some of My Best Friends are Writers* is another author's view on the pulps, but one that emphasizes the human problems of writing in a disposable medium. It is much easier to see from Turner's insights on writers' agencies that the differences in quality between slick and pulp fiction were not clear and in fact were often whimsical.

The publication of David Madden's collection of essays, *Tough Guy Writers of the Thirties,* marked a higher level of seriousness toward the pulps than any available earlier. Here hard-boiled fiction achieved academic respectability. Madden's introduction places the hard-boiled writer directly in the modern sensibility and the hard-boiled detective is treated from a number of varying perspectives. Essays by Philip Durham, Robert Edenbaum, Irving Malin, Herbert Ruhm, and George Grella are especially useful. Francis Nevins' collection of essays, *The Mystery Writer's Art,* is much more in the Haycraft tradition of an eclectic group of contributors with a common interest in detective fiction. The twenty-one essays in the volume are organized into "Appreciations," "Taxonomy," and "Speculation and Critique," and are concerned with both classic and hard-boiled fiction, with emphasis on appreciation and description.

Julian Symons' *Mortal Consequences* is part history and part analysis, a major attempt to bring the history of detective fiction into the 1970s. As both a novelist and reviewer of detective fiction, Symons has a critical appreciation and broad familiarity with the genre. His observations are usually fresh and perceptive, even of his own fiction. Through the first half of his study beginning with a chapter on why we read detective fiction and a chapter on Poe, Symons balances developments in England and the United States with asides on the major writers of other countries. The second half is less coherent. Here he touches on writers and topics relating to several countries, resulting in something of a patchwork. Fortunately, the book is indexed so that it is possible to explore to a different drummer.

Two recent collections of essays reflect the directions of most of the current work on detective fiction. *Dimensions of Detective Fiction,* edited by Larry N. Landrum, Pat Browne, and Ray B. Browne, contains twenty-three scholarly essays on various aspects of detective fiction. The volume is divided into explorations of the genre, considerations of style, and studies of detective fiction in a larger literary context. Included in the first section are essays associating the genre with myth, history, psychology, society, and literary form; the second section focuses on particular writers; the third part ties the genre to political influence and the detective figure in Faulkner and Ishmael Reed. *The Mystery Story,* edited by John Ball, contains seventeen informal essays, bibliographies, and appreciations on a spectrum of subjects by familiar writers on detective fiction. The bibliographies cover private eye fiction, series characters, and criticism.

Book-length analyses of detective fiction are rare, but the continuing popularity of the genre has brought out several important works. William Ruehlmann's *Saint with a Gun* is an attempt to link the private detective tradition to a broad American longing for vigilante justice. This is a one-dimensional work, but also a provocative investigation of the relationship between fiction and the disparate violence that has marked recent American history. A more sophisticated examination is found in John Cawelti's *Adventure, Mystery, and Romance.* This volume is the most important contribution to the understanding of popular American genres to date. Cawelti examines the structure of both classic and hard-boiled fiction and the relationships between the creator and the reader and relates these to other genres and to the social milieu.

The popularity of detective and mystery fiction in relation to other bestsellers can be found in Frank Luther Mott's *Golden Multitudes,* James D. Hart's *The Popular Book,* and for more recent fiction in Alice Payne Hackett's most recent volumes, *Seventy Years of Best Sellers* and *80 Years of Best Sellers.*

More substantive information is available in periodical publications than ever before. The *Armchair Detective* since 1967 is an especially useful source of bibliography, reviews, articles, information on current research activities, and other material. *The Mystery and Detection Annual* began in 1972 and promises to develop a rich mine of critical articles, reviews, and other information in hardcover format. Similar coverage was provided by *The Mystery Reader's Newsletter* between 1967 and 1974 and files of this publication are still useful. *The Ellery Queen Mystery Magazine* since 1975 has included "The Ellery Queen Mystery Newsletter," yet another source of current information. Standard sources of critical bibliography in American literature should be consulted for scholarly articles, since these are not always included in specialized bibliographies.

BIBLIOGRAPHY

BOOKS AND ARTICLES

Albert, Walter. "A Bibliography of Secondary Sources." *Armchair Detective.* 1973-.
Allen, Dick, and David Chacko, eds. *Detective Fiction: Crime and Compromise.* New York: Harcourt Brace Jovanovich, 1974.
Ball, John, ed. *The Mystery Story.* San Diego, Calif.: University Extension, University of California, in cooperation with Publisher's Inc., 1976.

Barnes, Melvyn. *Best Detective Fiction: A Guide from Godwin to the Present.* Hamden, Conn.: Shoe String, 1975.

Barzun, Jacques, and Wendell Hertig Taylor. *A Catalogue of Crime.* New York: Harper and Row, 1971.

"The Beadle Collection." *Bulletin of the New York Public Library,* 22 (1922), 555-628.

Best Detective Stories of the Year. New York: E. P. Dutton, 1945-   .

Bragin, Charles. *Bibliography of Dime Novels, 1860-1964.* Rev. ed. Brooklyn: Dime Novel Club, 1964.

Cawelti, John G. *Adventure, Mystery, and Romance.* Chicago: University of Chicago Press, 1976.

Chandler, Raymond. "The Simple Art of Murder." *Atlantic Monthly,* 173 (December 1944), 53-59.

Cox, J. Randolph. "Chapters from the Chronicles of Nick Carter." *Dime Novel Roundup,* May 1974, 50-55; June 1974, 62-67.

————. *New Nick Carter Weekly, Bibliographic Listing. Dime Novel Roundup Supplement,* December, 1975.

————. *Nick Carter Library, Bibliographic Listing. Dime Novel Roundup Supplement,* December, 1975.

Goodstone, Tony, ed. *The Pulps: Fifty Years of American Pop Culture.* New York: Bonanza Books, 1971.

Goulart, Ron. *Cheap Thrills: An Informal History of the Pulp Magazines.* New Rochelle, N.Y.: Arlington House, 1972.

————. *The Hardboiled Dicks.* New York: Pocket Books, 1967.

Gribbin, Lenore S. *Who's Whodunit: A List of 3,218 Detective Story Writers and their 1,100 Pseudonyms.* Chapel Hill: University of North Carolina Library, 1968.

Gruber, Frank. *The Pulp Jungle.* Los Angeles: Sherbourne Press, 1967.

Hackett, Alice Payne. *70 Years of Best Sellers, 1895-1965.* New York: R. R. Bowker, 1967.

————, and James Henry. *80 Years of Best Sellers, 1895-1975.* New York: R. R. Bowker, 1977.

Hagen, Ordean A. *Who Done It?: A Guide to Detective, Mystery and Suspense Fiction.* New York: R. R. Bowker, 1969.

Hart, James D. *The Popular Book: A History of America's Literary Taste.* New York: Oxford University Press, 1950.

Haycraft, Howard, ed. *The Art of the Mystery Story: A Collection of Critical Essays.* New York: Simon and Schuster, 1946.

————. *Murder for Pleasure: The Life and Times of the Detective Story.* New York: Appleton-Century, 1941.

Herman, Linda, and Beth Stiel. *Corpus Delicti of Mystery Fiction: A Guide to the Body of the Case.* Metuchen, N.J.: Scarecrow Press, 1974. Bowker, 1977.

Hersey, Harold. *Pulpwood Editor: The Fabulous World of the Thriller Magazines Revealed By A Veteran Editor and Publisher.* New York: Frederick A. Stokes Company, 1937.

Johannsen, Albert. *The House of Beadle and Adams and Its Dime and Nickel Novels.* 3 vols. Norman: University of Oklahoma Press, 1950, 1962.

Lacassin, Francis. *Mythologie du Roman Policier.* 2 vols. Paris: Union Generale d'Editions, 1974.

LaCour, Tage, and Harald Mogensen. *The Murder Book: An Illustrated History of the Detective Story.* London: Allen and Unwin, 1971.

Landrum, Larry N., Pat Browne; and Ray B. Browne, eds. *Dimensions of Detective Fiction.* Bowling Green, Ohio: Bowling Green University Popular Press, 1976.

Lerthead, J. Edward. "The Great Detective Team: Old and Young King Brady." *American Book Collector,* 20 (November-December 1969), 25-31.

McDade, Thomas M. *The Annals of Murder: A Bibliography of Books and Pamphlets on American Murders from Colonial Times to 1900.* Norman: University of Oklahoma Press, 1961.

Macdonald, Ross. *On Crime Writing.* Santa Barbara, Calif.: Capra Press, 1973

Madden, David, ed. *Tough Guy Writers of the Thirties.* Carbondale: Southern Illinois University Press, 1968.

Mott, Frank Luther. *Golden Multitudes: The Story of Best Sellers in the United States.* New York: Macmillan, 1947.

Mundell, E. H., and G. Ray Rausch, comps. *The Detective Short Story: A Bibliography and Index.* Manhattan: Kansas State University Library, 1974.

Murch, Alma Elizabeth. *The Development of the Detective Novel.* Port Washington, N.Y.: Kennikat Press, 1968.

Mystery Writers of America. *The Mystery Writer's Handbook: A Handbook on the Writing of Detective, Suspense, Mystery and Crime Stories.* Edited by Herbert Brean. New York: Harper and Brothers, 1956.

Nevins, Francis N., ed. *The Mystery Writer's Art.* Bowling Green, Ohio: Bowling Green University Popular Press, 1971.

Noel, Mary. *Villains Galore: The Heyday of the Popular Story Weekly.* New York: Macmillan, 1954.

Quayle, Eric. *The Collector's Book of Detective Fiction.* London: Studio Vista, 1972.

Reynolds, Quentin. *The Fiction Factory; or, From Pulp Row to Quality Street: The Story of 100 Years of Publishing at Street & Smith.* New York: Random House, 1955.

Ruehlmann, William. *Saint with a Gun: The Unlawful American Private Eye.* Washington, D.C.: American University Press,1974.

Ruhm, Herbert, ed. *The Hard-Boiled Detective: Stories from Black Mask Magazine, 1920-1951.* New York: Random House-Vintage Books, 1977.

Sandoe, James, ed. *Murder: Plain and Fanciful, with Some Milder Malefactions.* New York: Sheridan House, 1948.

Sayers, Dorothy. "Introduction" to *Omnibus of Crime.* New York: Payson and Clarke, 1929.

Schlesinger, Arthur, Jr. "The Business of Crime." In *The Professional Criminals of America,* edited by Thomas Burns. New York: Chelsea House, 1969.

Schwartz, Saul, ed. *The Detective Story: An Introduction to the Whodunit.* Skokie, Ill.: National Textbook Company, 1975.

Shaw, Joseph T., ed. *The Hardboiled Omnibus: Early Stories from Black Mask.* New York: Simon and Schuster, 1946.

Steinbrunner, Chris, and Otto Penzler. *Detectionary: A Biographical Dictionary of Leading Characters in Detective and Mystery Fiction, Including Famous and Little-Known Sleuths, Their Helpers, Rogues Both Heroic and Sinister, and Some of Their Most Memorable Adventures, as Recounted in Novels, Short Stories, and Films.* Woodstock, N.Y.: Overlook Press, 1977.

———. *Encyclopedia of Mystery and Detection.* New York: McGraw-Hill, 1976.

Symons, Julian. *Mortal Consequences: A History from the Detective Story to the Crime Novel.* New York: Schocken Books, 1973.

Talburt, Nancy Ellen, and Lyna Lee Montgomery. *A Mystery Reader: Stories of Detection, Adventure and Horror.* New York: Charles Scribner's Sons, 1975.

Turner, Robert. *Some of My Best Friends are Writers, But I Wouldn't Want My Daughter to Marry One.* Los Angeles: Sherbourne Press, 1970.

Wells, Carolyn. *The Technique of the Mystery Story.* Springfield, Mass.: Home Correspondence School, 1929.

Wrong, E. M. "Introduction" to *Crime and Detection.* New York: Oxford University Press, 1926.

PERIODICALS

Armchair Detective. Midland, Minn., 1967-.

Dime Novel Roundup. Fall River, Mass., 1931-32, 1933-.

Ellery Queen's Mystery Magazine. New York. 1941-.

Mystery and Detection Annual. Beverly Hills, Calif., 1972-.

Mystery Reader's Newsletter. Melrose, Mass., 1967-74.

CHAPTER 6 Film

Robert A. Armour

Despite the drop in the number of people going to the movies each week, the interest in the study of the history and appreciation of film has increased greatly in the past decade. The first edition of the American Film Institute's (AFI) *Guide to College Courses in Film and Television* in 1974 listed courses in 613 colleges. The new edition, which was published in early 1978, notes that courses are being offered in over one thousand different colleges. The number of books and articles on film has kept pace with the increase in the demand for study at both the secondary school and college levels. The explosion of books on the subject that occurred in the mid-1960s has waned, but the publication of solid—and in some cases, not so solid—books has continued. Now the problem becomes one of wading through the mass of material to find good scholarly help when studying film. Students and others interested in film sometimes have serious problems trying to find film study materials beyond that of reviews in the daily paper or monthly magazine.

As with any other area of popular culture, the books published on film appeal to a wide variety of audiences. Many of these books are intended for the popular audience and are written quickly without much film analysis. This article will focus on the more serious type whose facts and judgments can more generally be considered reliable; occasional reference will be made to more popular books when they have proved to be especially well done or unique. In this brief survey of film study materials, only books have been included. There are, of course, thousands of useful articles, but in this limited space all that can be done is to direct the reader to indexes of journals. The emphasis of this article—by limitation of space and purpose—is on American film and on books readily available in this country in English.

HISTORIC OUTLINE

The date was December 28, 1895. The place was the basement of a cafe in Paris. The audience was the first public one to pay its way to watch movies, paying to be fascinated by moving images of a baby eating his meal, workers leaving a factory, and a train rushing into a station. The scenes were taken from ordinary life, but the experience was far from ordinary. This event was produced by the Lumière brothers, but the technology that led to this moment had been the result of the imagination and persistence of many inventors, both in Europe and America.

Eadweard Muybridge in 1877 had discovered that sequential still photographs of a horse running could be placed in a series and "projected" in such a manner as to make the photographic image of the horse appear to be running. In New Jersey in the late 1880s Thomas Edison and his crew led by William Dickson developed the idea of putting photographs on a single piece of continuous film, and George Eastman supplied the film. For projection Edison decided on the Kinetoscope, a peephole machine through which the film could be shown to one person at a time. Several creative inventors worked on the idea of a projector, but it was finally the Lumière brothers who were able to adapt Edison's ideas and develop the first practical means of allowing many people to view a movie simultaneously. The history of this new art form was then to be written in light.

Once the photographic technology had been developed, the next stage was to decide what to do with it. Obviously audiences could not long be enthralled by shots of a baby eating and would demand more. Both the Lumières and Edison attempted to expand the cinematic subject matter; but it was another Frenchman, George Melies, who first achieved any success at telling a story with film. He was a magician who used the medium as part of his act, but in the process he began to depict plot as well as action. His most famous film was *A Trip to the Moon* (1902) which described a fanciful space voyage.

In order to develop a narrative process for film, the filmmaker had to learn to manipulate both space and time, to change them, and to move characters and action within them much as a novelist does. What Melies had begun, Edison and his new director of production continued. Edwin S. Porter learned how to use dissolves and cuts between shots to indicate changes in time or space, or both; the result was *The Great Train Robbery* (1903). This Western, shot in the wilds of New Jersey, told the complete story of a train robbery, the chase of the bandits, and their eventual defeat in a gunfight with the posse. Cross-cutting allowed Porter to show in sequence activities of both the posse and the bandits that were supposed to take place at the same time.

Businessmen began to realize the financial potential for movies. While movies were first shown as part of other forms of entertainment, they soon became the featured attraction themselves. By 1905 the first nickelodeon had opened in Pittsburgh, where customers each paid a nickel to see a full program of a half dozen short films. The opening of theaters completed the elements necessary for an industry: product, technology, producer, purchaser, and distributor.

In 1907, a would-be playwright came to Edison with a filmscript for sale. Edison did not like the script, but he hired its author, David Wark Griffith, as an actor. Griffith refused to use his real name, which he wanted to save for his true profession of the stage, but he needed money and accepted the job. Thus began the career of the man who would turn this entertainment into an art. He began making films himself shortly. His tastes in plots were melodramatic, but his interests in technique were both innovative and scientific. Guided by his cameraman, Billy Bitzer, he began to experiment with editing and shots, finding many ideas for cinematic technique in the sentimental novels and poems of nineteenth-century literature. Gradually he persuaded both audiences and company bosses to accept the idea of a more complicated plot told in a lengthy movie. The result was the first major, long film. In 1915, after unheard-of amounts of time in production, Griffith released *The Birth of a Nation*, a story of the South during the Civil War and Reconstruction. The racial overtones of the film caused considerable controversy, but the power of the images and the timing of the editing created a work of art whose aesthetic excellence is not questioned. In response to the criticism of his racial views, the next year Griffith directed *Intolerance*, which interwove four stories of intolerance into a single film. Griffith was to continue as one of America's leading directors until audiences began to lose their taste for melodrama, and other directors had learned his methods. He had been responsible for launching the careers of several directors, such as Raoul Walsh, and numerous actors, such as Lillian and Dorothy Gish, Mary Pickford, and H. B. Walthall.

While Griffith was learning how to get the most from screen actors, Thomas Ince was polishing the art of telling a story efficiently. In the early 1900s, he directed a few films (*Civilization*, 1916, is the best known), but he quickly turned his attention to production, leaving the details of directing to others under his close supervision. His talent was for organization, and today he is credited with perfecting the studio system. Film is actually a collaborative art, and Ince learned how to bring the talents of many different people into a system that produced polished films, without the individualizing touches found in those films of Griffith or others who work outside the strict studio system.

One man who learned his trade from Griffith was Mack Sennett. Sennett worked for Griffith for a few years as a director and writer, but his interests were more in comedy than in melodrama. In 1912 he broke away and began to work for an independent company, Keystone. Here he learned to merge the methods of stage slapstick comedy with the techniques of film; the results were the Keystone Cops, Ben Turpin, and Charlie Chaplin. Sennett's films used only the barest plot outline as a frame for comic gags that were improvised and shot quickly. From the Sennett method, Charlie Chaplin developed his own technique and character. He began making shorts under the direction of Sennett, but in 1915 he left and joined with Essenay which agreed to let him write and direct his own films at an unprecedented salary. Here he fleshed out his tramp character; one of his first films for Essenay was *The Tramp* (1915). He continued making films that combined his own comic sense and acrobatic movements with social commentary and along with Mary Pickford became one of the first "stars." Later he made features, such as *The Gold Rush* (1925) and *Modern Times* (1936). Sennett and Chaplin began a period of great film comedy. Buster Keaton combined a deadpan look with remarkable physical ability and timing. He too began making shorts, but soon was directing and starring in features, such as *The General* (1926). Harold Lloyd (*The Freshman*, 1925) and Harry Langdon (*The Strong Man*, 1926) also created comic characters that demonstrated their individuality and imagination.

From these ingredients came the studio system and the star system. The demands of the moviegoing audiences created a need for a great number of films, and small companies were unable to meet the demands. Adolph Zukor at Paramount and Marcus Loew, Louis B. Mayer, and Irvin Thalberg at Metro-Goldwyn-Mayer quickly learned the means of applying American business methods to this new industry. They bought out their competition and eventually controlled film production, distribution, and exhibition. Even the actors and directors got into the act as Chaplin, Griffith, Pickford, and Douglas Fairbanks joined together to create United Artists, intended at first to distribute the various productions of its founders. Later it too became a studio force, along with Columbia, Fox, Warners, and others.

With the studios came the stars. The public hungered for new heroes and new sex objects, and the studios were quick to give the public what it wanted. Along with the stars who had been established in the early 1900s came the new generation of the 1920s: Rudolph Valentino, Gloria Swanson, Clara Bow. The stars soon became the nucleus of American myth, and the public followed the stars' affairs, marriages, and extravagant lives with keen interest. This was the stuff Hollywood was made of. Fortunately there were behind these stars creative directors, such as Cecil B. DeMille, Eric Von Stroheim, and Henry King, who were able to mold the talents of the stars into movies.

During the 1920s American films dominated the worldwide industry, but they were greatly influenced and enhanced by developments and personalities from Europe. The Russians Sergei Eisenstein (*Potemkin*,

1925) and V. I. Pudovkin (*Mother*, 1926) were especially influential in their understanding of montage (the relationship of the images to each other and the meaning that results). American interest in fantasy was influenced both directly and indirectly by *The Cabinet of Dr. Caligari* (1919) directed by the German Robert Wiene and *Destiny* (1921) directed by an Austrian working in Germany, Fritz Lang.

Some Europeans came to America to make films: Ernst Lubitsch, Victor Seastrom, and F. W. Murnau, for examples. The influence on American film of these films and filmmakers was profound; they left their strong impression on what came to be known as the Hollywood movie.

The story surrounding the coming of sound to movies is a complex and complicated one. The idea of connecting sound to the visuals was an old one; Edison had in fact entered the movie business because he was searching for visuals to go with the phonograph he was already marketing. To convert the movie technology to sound was expensive. Despite development of the necessary technology (most notably in this country by Lee de Forest), the industry was reluctant to invest in the change. In the mid-1920s Western Electric developed a method for putting the sound on a disk that could be roughly synchronized with the film. None of the big studios could be convinced to try it, but Warners Brothers was about to be forced out of business by the other, larger companies. It had little to lose and decided to take the risk. For a year Warners distributed a program with short sound films of slight interest, but on October 6, 1927, it premiered *The Jazz Singer* with Al Jolson. Sound was used to help tell the story, and the public loved it. Quickly, Warners established its financial base, and other studios rushed to emulate them; but problems developed. Studios had to reequip themselves. The camera, which had been struggling to free itself and discover new methods of expression, found itself confined to a large box and immobile. Actors had to learn to speak to their audiences, and exhibitors had to invest in sound projectors and speakers. Once the problems were overcome, however, the marriage of sound to the visuals became a natural extension of the art.

The period between the coming of sound and World War II was dominated by the studios. They controlled the production—including story, the role of the directors, and the selection of actors—distribution, and exhibition (they owned their own theaters). In the 1930s America went to the movies; by the end of the decade some eighty million people saw a movie every week. The studios provided them with the means to live out their fantasies, find heroes, and escape from the Depression.

One factor directly affecting the films of the 1930s was censorship. Hollywood movies in the late 1920s and early 1930s had become rather open in their use of sex, and the scandals in the private lives of the stars shocked the public even as it hungered for vicarious living. Fear of government intervention and of the Depression forced the studios to censor themselves. They established the Hays Office under the directorship of Will Hays, former postmaster-general, and this office published a strict moral code for on-screen activities and language. The results stifled creativity, but the new moral tastes of the public were satisfied.

The stars captured the public's imagination as in no other time in American popular culture: Fred Astaire and Ginger Rogers, Jean Harlow, Clark Gable and Vivian Leigh, Edward G. Robinson, and Marlene Dietrich. The comics maintained the traditions of the silent comedians: Charlie Chaplin continued to make movies and was joined by the Marx brothers, Mae West, and W. C. Fields.

At the same time, the directors had to find a path through the maze created by the studios, the Hays Office, and the stars. They had to bring all these divergent elements together and make movies. Men such as John Ford and Howard Hawks created their own visions of America and discovered methods of capturing the American myth on film. Many of the directors of the period were immigrants: Josef von Sternberg, Alfred Hitchcock, Fritz Lang, Otto Preminger, and Frank Capra. Each discovered for himself the essence of this country and its people. Perhaps that essence was most fittingly expressed in a film that came at the end of the prewar period, *Citizen Kane* (1941), the first film Orson Welles directed.

The war changed the industry. Many residents of Hollywood took time off to participate in the war effort. Some like John Ford and Frank Capra made films for the government. Others like Fritz Lang continued to make commercial films, but they were propaganda-oriented and helped build morale. The stars went to the battle areas to entertain the troops. Even studio space was commandeered to produce war documentaries, and war films became a dominant fictional genre.

After the war the rate of change accelerated. Anti-trust suits broke up the large companies and forced them to sell their theaters. And television began to keep the public at home. The movie industry responded with attempts at expanding the medium to attract new interests: 3-D, Cinema-Scope, Technicolor; and it continues to experiment: quadraphonic sound, sensurround, holographic images, and giant leaps in special effects have been tried.

However, in responding to competition from television, the use and type of subject matter has taken precedence over the development of technology. The movie makers have thought it necessary to give the public something that cannot be beamed into private living rooms. The results have been increased depiction of explicitness in sex and violence. Both sex and violence have been staples of the movies since the beginning, but the contemporary cinema has found new methods of enticing the public with them.

As the major Hollywood studios began to lose their domination of the American movie industry and turn their attention to television production, the leadership was taken up by independent producers and directors, making their own films and then distributing them through the networks originally established by the Hollywood companies. Stanley Kubrick, Robert Altman, Arthur Penn, Peter Bogdanovich, and Francis Ford Coppola have provided America with a new group of filmmakers, men who have demonstrated a certain independence of subject and method. Part of the void left by the diminishing importance of Hollywood has been filled by foreign filmmakers whose films have been greeted with enthusiasm by American audiences. Ingmar Bergman, François Truffaut, and Federico Fellini have dominated, but for the first time countries outside of Europe have begun to leave their mark. Japan has been especially productive.

Perhaps, however, the most important change in movies in recent years has been in the audience. By no means the number of people who went to the movies in the late 1930s still do, but those who do go are younger and more knowledgeable about film. They read the books, subscribe to film journals, watch filmed interviews with movie people on television, and read daily reviews. Many in today's audience are college-educated and have taken film courses while in school; they can talk intelligently about montage, jump cuts, and fade outs. It is for this audience that *Scenes from a Marriage* is imported from Europe and *Star Wars* is made.

REFERENCE WORKS

A valuable collection of general reference books that cover a great number of film topics has been published. None is complete in itself and all contain numerous errors, but they can be used for quick and easy reference as long as detailed criticism or analysis is not needed. One of the most useful is *Guidebook to Film*, by Ronald Gottesman and Harry Geduld. Its range of materials is a bit eclectic, even surprising; but it is the type of book the reader may return to frequently. It includes lists of film schools, museums and archives, journals, awards, etc. Its bibliography is not long but is still more extensive than most. One problem with this book is inherent in its nature: it dates quickly.

Three books compete as encyclopedias of film. The oldest is Roger Manvell's *The International Encyclopedia of Film*. It contains brief essays on film directors, important films, significant actors, and recurring cinematic themes. Where possible, a book or two on the entry will be mentioned as bibliography. *The Filmgoer's Companion*, edited by Leslie Halliwell, is updated periodically, but, aside from the occasional brief discussion of a theme, consists almost entirely of filmographies of film figures. The most recent of the encyclopedias is *The Oxford Companion to Film,* edited by Liz-Anne Bawden. Although it is flawed, it can be perceptive and generally accurate. Perhaps its most disappointing feature is in its limited filmographies of the major figures.

One important general reference is the annual *International Film Guide* published in London under the general editorship of Peter Cowie. This book is an odd collection of film information from reviews to lists of film societies to a survey of film production in countries around the world. It is sometimes difficult to find what one is looking for, but the search will be fun because the reader may well find something else he or she was not looking for.

One of the most serious problems in film study is finding the factual data necessary for accuracy. Knowing when a film was released and who deserves credit for it is important, but often the information is hard to uncover. If the film is not available for firsthand checking, the researcher will have to turn to one of the reference guides. Richard Dimmitt began a list called *A Title Guide to the Talkies,* which has been continued by Andrew Aros. These men list title, date, distributor, and source of the story, but little else. In a series of volumes the Library of Congress has published a complete list of all the films that have been copyrighted. These volumes also list the dates, length, and producer. One nice feature of this work is that it includes television commercials and short films, which are often difficult to date from other sources. Eventually this work will be replaced by one coming out under the sponsorship of the AFI, called *The American Film Institute Catalogue of Motion Pictures.* A separate volume will cover each decade and every film produced during the decade will be listed with credits, date, and plot summary. The indexes will be extensive. So far only two volumes of this valuable book have been released (1921-30 and 1961-70), but other volumes are in production and will eventually include short films and newsreels as well as features.

An important aspect of film study is locating the films themselves for rental or purchase. Two books are especially helpful. James Limbacher's *Feature Films on 8mm and 16mm* lists the renter or seller, running time, and brief credits. Kathleen Weaver's *Film Programmer's Guide to 16mm Rentals* contains limited credits, but does include rental prices, which do get out of date quickly these days.

Bibliographies of published material about film are central to film study as they lead the researcher to articles and books on film. Finding magazine articles is one of the most serious problems for the film researcher, but now there are a number of bibliographic guides to help. Unfortunately none is so good or so complete as to make all the rest unnecessary, and they must be cross checked if the researcher wishes to be complete.

Peter Bukalski's *Film Research* is of a general nature. Basically this is a selected, critical bibliography but very useful. Since it tries to do much in a single volume, it obviously cannot be complete.

In 1941 Harold Leonard published *The Film Index* that existed for years as the main bibliography of film articles in English. It covers chiefly the silent period, but it mentions some articles to about 1936. To fill in the gap between Leonard and the present time, three different bibliographies have appeared. Perhaps the most valuable is *The New Film Index*, edited by Richard Dyer MacCann and Edward W. Perry. They have included the articles listed in standard annual journal lists, such as *The Reader's Guide*, and then in addition fully indexed thirty-eight of the major film journals in English. MacCann and Perry have brought their bibliography to 1970 at which point several annual bibliographies have begun. The *Humanities Index* and *Reader's Guide to Periodical Literature* both list numerous articles in film; in each the reader must look under "moving pictures" to find the bulk of the entries. They are especially valuable in locating reviews.

Two major annual indexes to periodical articles are now being published. Vincent Aceto, Jane Graves, and Fred Silva have begun their annual bibliography *Film Literature Index* which fully covers 126 journals and selectively another 150 nonfilm journals. Unfortunately there is no annotation of the entries. Karen Jones is the general editor of the *International Index to Film Periodicals* which covers fewer journals than the *Film Literature Index* but does include a few journals not indexed by the latter. *The International Index's* brief annotations are helpful. The researcher would do well to consult both indexes.

The most convenient guide to the numerous periodicals containing articles on film is a recent publication of the American Film Institute, called *Factfile: Film and Television Periodicals in English*. (It can be purchased by writing to the AFI.) This volume lists eighty-two journals that deal primarily with film, or television, or both, and gives a brief annotation of each. The list includes the scholarly journals, such as *Film Heritage* or *Cinema Journal*, technical ones, such as *American Cinematographer*, and popular ones, such as *American Film*, the organ of the AFI.

The researcher should be aware that while many of the journals are of general interest, others appeal to the special interests of readers. For instance, *Literature/Film Quarterly* devotes its space to articles on feature films that have some connection with works of literature. *Media and Methods* is directed at the secondary school teacher, and *Film Culture* is concerned with the independent filmmaker.

The list in *Factfile* is not complete and does not include the many periodicals that frequently publish articles on film though not primarily film journals, but it contains the basic journals and is an excellent checklist.

Other checklists may be found in the bibliographies mentioned earlier in this essay, but unlike the AFI *Factfile*, they all lack annotation and do not include subscription information.

RESEARCH COLLECTIONS

In dealing with archives that house film materials, the researcher is faced with some libraries that collect films and others that collect film related materials. Locating the film itself may be one of the most difficult problems for the researcher. Most of the early nitrate films have been destroyed for one reason or another, often because the film stock itself is unstable. The researcher can depend on only five centers in this country for major—and expensive—efforts to preserve the early films: The Library of Congress and the American Film Institute in Washington, the Museum of Modern Art in New York, Eastman House in Rochester, and the University of California at Los Angeles Film and Television Archive. Each of these archives is collecting, preserving and holding films and does a first-rate job of maintaining our film heritage, but there are problems. The work is costly and time-consuming. Not all films are held in viewable prints, and the archives have not yet been able to publish an index of their holdings. There are additionally several other libraries with sizable collections of films, and the researcher should not overlook local sources.

Aside from the films themselves, film related material might include film scripts, stills, journals, books, costumes, and fugitive materials, such as letters and posters. All of the archives mentioned with film collections also have some film related material, but the best collections of related material are at the Library and Museum of the Performing Arts (a branch of the New York Public Library at Lincoln Center) and the Theater Arts Library at the University of California at Los Angeles.

Whether the researcher is looking for films or film related materials, he or she would do best to write to the archives to inquire whether they have the necessary material before making the effort to visit the archives themselves. Security is understandably tight at these centers, and the researcher should take proper identification and should be prepared to demonstrate the seriousness of his or her research.

A general guide to the archives can be found in the *North American Film and Video Directory*, by Olga S. Weber. This guide lists the archives and their locations and approximate sizes, but its value is limited. It lists only archives with film collections and does not describe the holdings or distinguish between significant holdings and minor ones.

Finally, it might be noted that while the distributors of films do not maintain research collections, they are usually most helpful to the researcher. Most are happy to work with researchers. Some of their better catalogs (such as those from Janus, Macmillan/Audio-Brandon, and Films, Inc.) are useful sources of information, and the people in charge of collections for the companies are often knowledgeable and helpful.

HISTORY AND CRITICISM

One of the most popular aspects of film study is concerned with the personalities of the people involved in the industry. Perhaps the actors and actresses attract the most attention, but directors and other members of the production team have their devoted followers too. In a guide as short as this one, it is impossible to list individually all the books that have appeared on the personalities. The researcher can consult the card catalog in almost any good library for these books, but there is a sizable list of reference works that pertain to the personalities. These works may well lead the researcher to hard-to-find or obscure data about the personality.

Mel Schuster has written two books, *Motion Picture Performers* and *Motion Picture Directors*, that list magazine and periodical articles. These guides list articles on both the personalities and their cinematic contributions from the turn of the century to the early 1970s.

David Thomson's book, *A Biographical Dictionary of Film*, also covers both directors and actors, but he gives different information. His book consists of short essays on the major figures. Most essays include a filmography, a brief critical comment, and a highly selected bibliography.

Directors are the subjects of several research guides. James Robert Parish and Michael R. Pitts have edited *Film Directors: A Guide to Their American Films*. Included are the feature films, with dates and company, for approximately 520 directors. Georges Sadoul's *Dictionary of Film-makers* is even more inclusive. This book contains about one thousand entries for directors, screenwriters, and others in the production side of the industry, but no actors.

Information about the actors can be found in other works. Richard Dimmitt has edited *An Actor Guide to the Talkies* which covers movies between 1949 and 1964. He surveys some eight thousand features and lists the actors for each, but he does not list the role played by each actor, a serious handicap. Evelyn Mack Truitt has also listed actors in *Who Was Who on Screen*. Arranged by actor rather than by film, this guide gives all of an actor's films and dates.

And finally a reference guide to screenwriters has been published jointly by the Academy of Motion Pictures and the Writers Guild of America. *Who Wrote the Movie and What Else Did He Write?* is extensive for the period 1936 through 1969. Included are both film title and writer's indexes.

In light of the fact that researchers may often be forced to work without a copy of the film easily available, they may have to resort to secondary sources for help in remembering the exact line of dialogue or the name of the minor character appearing in that key scene. The screenplay can provide vast assistance, but of course it is never a substitute for the film itself.

There are now a number of variations of the generic screenplay being published. A shooting script is written before the film is shot and is the outline for what is going to happen. The cutting continuity is the written record of what has been shot and is obviously made after the film is finished. The shooting script tells what the screenwriter felt should be included. The cutting continuity tells what the director and the editor actually left in. And finally a shot analysis is a more detailed cutting continuity. The researcher needs to know which he is dealing with since a shooting script may indicate a scene that was never included in the final film and a cutting continuity may not demonstrate the screenwriter's intentions at all.

There are two checklists of published screenplays in print. Both are needed as neither is inclusive, and neither makes a distinction between shooting scripts, cutting continuities, and shot analysis. Howard Poteet's *Published Radio, Television and Film Scripts: A Bibliography* lists some 668 film scripts (some are different versions of the same film script). Clifford McCarty's *Published Screenplays: A Checklist* lists the scripts for only 388 films, but he gives slightly more information than does Poteet about each entry. McCarty includes production company, date, director, author of the screenplay, original source, and the bibliographical data for the published screenplay. Through both of these sources the researcher can locate most of the screenplays that have so far been published.

There is another variation of the screenplay which is gaining in popularity: the frame blowup continuity. These books give a frame enlargement for every shot in the film and the researcher can almost "read a film." Perhaps the most impressive of these works is *The Complete Greed*, by Herman Weinberg, which combines frame blowups with the screenplay. Universe Books has begun a project to publish a series of the frame blowup continuities, and so far some seven have appeared, including *Casablanca, The General,* and *Ninotchka.*

The definitive history of film is yet to be written, but there are numerous books that contribute to that history, and they do make fascinating reading. Despite the fact that no other art has its history so well-documented, there remains much confusion about many of the details in the early development of film, in part because at the beginning so few people took this new form of entertainment seriously.

One of the earliest attempts at writing the history of the medium came from an Englishman, Paul Rotha, in what is now a respected classic, *The*

Film Till Now. The book first was published in 1930, but in the mid-1960s Richard Griffith brought it up to date. It is thorough, complete, and long; it was written by a man who could write about film critically and theoretically, as well as historically. It is by no means a popular history, but the researcher will find it very useful. Later in the same decade Lewis Jacobs wrote the first general history of real importance to deal primarily with the American cinema. *The Rise of the American Film* emphasizes the industry but manages to cover a great number of films and their makers.

In the post-World War II period, Arthur Knight contributed *The Liveliest Art: A Panoramic History of the Movies*, which first came out in 1957. Though dated now, the book is still readable and reliable. It is valuable but too short to make any claim at completeness.

Most recently there have been several attempts at writing a good general history. Highly regarded and now in its second edition is Gerald Mast's *A Short History of the Movies*. This balanced and perceptive book is perhaps the most useful history on the market so far.

Thomas Bohn and Richard Stromgren have written *Light and Shadows*, which is also a solid general history. In some ways their book is more valuable than Mast's, especially in the modern period on which they have an excellent chapter on the influence of television on movies.

And finally, Eric Rhode's massive book, *A History of the Cinema from its Origins to 1970*, is a large-scale effort at writing a world history of the movies. Both Mast and Bohn and Stromgren devote chapters to the European cinematic contributions and developments, but Rhode's focus is far more international than theirs. The book is not as readable as Mast's, but on the international scene it is unsurpassed.

Then there are books that do not record a general history, but do focus on a particular period, such as the silent era. One of the nicest aspects of the silent era is that its history can still be told by the people who were part of it. Firsthand accounts, such as *When the Movies Were Young*, by Linda Arvidson, who was Mrs. D. W. Griffith, and *The Movies, Mr. Griffith, and Me*, by Lillian Gish, have the natural flaws of any history written by the subjective participants, but the freshness and familiarity make such books excellent places to begin a study of the early days of the art.

Kevin Brownlow's *The Parade's Gone By* makes a similar contribution. In this case a young scholar has interviewed the most important directors of the silent era and has intermingled their remarks with his own deliberate insights. This is oral history interpreted by a scholar without the biases of participation in the events that become that history. While Brownlow intermingled his thoughts with the words of the directors, George Pratt has written his history of the era, *Spellbound in Darkness*, by combining his commentary with reviews of the films as they were seen by critics contemporary with the films. The book is at times hard to follow, but Pratt is a competent scholar, and the reviews chronicle an art form and the culture that spawned it.

Naturally, latter-day scholars are writing histories of the silent era without including the primary material found in Brownlow or Pratt. D. J. Wenden's short book, *The Birth of the Movies*, takes the medium to the coming of sound; and Harry Geduld's *The Birth of the Talkies* is actually a study of the efforts of the industry to develop a sound system. He starts with Edison and takes the reader through the early stages of sound technology that eventually led to "You ain't heard nothing yet."

And last there is a charming and intriguing book sponsored by the American Film Institute called *The American Film Heritage* edited by Tom Shales and others. It includes essays by scholars on films, filmmakers, studios, and themes of the silent era. Often the essay subject is little known to the general public, and the book becomes part of the AFI's effort at rediscovering the lost heritage of the medium.

Naturally other eras in film history have received similar attention. Books such as Andrew Bergman's *We're in the Money*, about the Depression, and Penelope Houston's *The Contemporary Cinema, 1945-1963* devote themselves to particular periods.

Some of the histories concentrate on the role Hollywood has played in the development of American culture. Hortense Powdermaker was one of the first to take an anthropological look at Hollywood in her book *Hollywood: The Dream Factory*. The book is a bit dated now but it has set standards for a particular method of considering the medium. Recently the American Film Institute has sponsored a book by Garth Jowett that is a general history with an emphasis on Hollywood and its impact. Jowett includes much history of the controversies originated by Hollywood and is especially detailed on the problems of censorship. A delightful book for the fan of the popular film has been edited by Todd McCarthy and Charles Flynn and entitled *Kings of the B's*. The focus of the book is on the many minor directors who worked within the Hollywood system to produce countless movies that may be aesthetically insignificant but culturally powerful. In addition to history and criticism, the book includes a valuable filmography for 325 directors who are given scant attention in other histories.

Tino Balio's *The American Film Industry* is an anthology of essays on the industry that made the movies. Some were written by people who were part of the industry during its development and others by scholar historians. It is the best so far of an emerging field of study into the practices of the industry. The book is historically organized around the chronological period of the subject of each essay.

And there is a large group of books concentrating on single studios and their roles within the Hollywood industry. Studies, such as Charles Higham's *Warner Brothers* and Rochelle Larkin's *Hail Columbia*, explore the inner workings of a studio and the escapades of the moguls who made it successful.

The area of film criticism is large, diverse, and eclectic, but perhaps the best critical research tools can be divided into smaller categories. Many of the best can be considered introductions to film. The fact that a book is intended as an introduction to the subject and was published for the many students who may be taking their first film course should not suggest that the book is necessarily superficial. In fact, a number of them delve deeply into the aesthetics of the medium. One of the earliest scholars to publish an introduction was Lewis Jacobs in his anthology, *Introduction to the Art of the Movies*. This book is a collection of essays on image, movement, time and space, color, and sound—standard topics to be covered in an introduction.

During the 1960s a number of introductions came out and several have remained highly regarded. Ernest Lindgren's *The Art of the Film* has sections on mechanics, techniques, and criticism; and *The Film Experience*, by Roy Huss and Norman Silverstein, deals with continuity, rhythm, structure, image, and point of view.

Of the introductions written during the 1970s by single authors, Louis Giannetti's *Understanding Movies* has proved to be most durable. His chapters deal with the picture, movement, editing, sound, drama, literature, and theory. A similar book by Richard Blumenberg, *Critical Focus: An Introduction to Film*, was written by a teacher and scholar with some experience as a filmmaker. After an introduction that defines the medium and relates it to the other arts, Blumenberg devotes sections to the narrative film, the documentary, and the experimental film.

Elements of Film, by Lee R. Bobker, now in its second edition, is perhaps the best of the introductions in the area of technique. None of the others explains the technical side of the art in prose as easy to understand. Of the anthologies that serve as introductions, the best is a large book by Gerald Mast and Marshall Cohen, *Film Theory and Criticism*. They have shown discretion in the authors whose essays they have chosen to reprint, and their categories (reality, language, theory, literature and film, genre, artists, and audience) cover a wide range of film criticism. Not many of the introductions deal with the aesthetics of the short film, but one by David Sohn does. *Film: The Critical Eye* discusses films distributed by Pyramid Films, but its general discussion helps to create understanding of a type of film often overlooked.

Most recently, James Monaco has written *How to Read a Film*. He covers a full range of film studies from technique to history, and the book may prove to be one of the most valuable of the introductions.

These introductions for the most part are based on the work of the film theorists whose work is earlier and more complex. Once the students have passed the need for the introductions, they will find the work of the theorists challenging and fascinating. As early as 1915 the poet Vachel Lindsay published a curious book that was part theory and part encomium on what was then a new art form. In fact his title, *The Art of the Moving Picture*, would have surprised many people who would not have called this entertainment form an art.

Much of the early theory was developed by the Russians, some of whom learned their lessons by watching films made by Americans who wrote little about the theory. Sergei Eisenstein (*The Film Sense, Film Form*, and *Film Essays and a Lecture*) and V. I. Pudovkin (*Film Technique and Film Acting*) were directors who, through their writings, helped to establish the language of film criticism while at the same time coming to an understanding of how film works.

They were followed by the French and Germans. Of the French, Béla Balázs was also a director; his *Theory of Film* was a summary of his thoughts on the use of the camera and editing. André Bazin was not a director but a mentor of the directors who make up the French New Wave and editor of *Cahiers du Cinéma*, the most important French cinema journal. *What is Cinema?* contains a sample of his extensive criticism. Siegfried Kracauer was a German who came to America to escape the Nazis. His book, *Theory of Film*, is basically a general theory with an emphasis on acting, sound, and music. The book, however does range into many areas, including a notable chapter on the film and the novel. Most recently, important film theory has again been coming from France where the theory of semiotics has been developed. The semiotics of film is a linguistic approach to the study of film in which visuals are seen as signs between the sender and viewer. The leading proponent of this theory is Christian Metz, whose book *Film Language* is the easiest of his works to understand, but the beginner should be warned that semiotics is not a simple approach to film.

There are several anthologies of essays that attempt to give an overview of film criticism. Richard Dyer MacCann's *Film: A Montage of Theories* is well-known. His essays are by the best known writers of film theory from Eisenstein to Bergman and cover the nature of film, film and the other arts, the reality of film, and the future of the medium. More recent is *The Major Film Theories*, by Dudley J. Andrew. This book analyzes the work of the major theorists who are broken into three broad groups: the formative tradition, realist film theory, and contemporary French film theory. MacCann covers more theorists, but Andrew is more up-to-date.

One of the types of film criticism that both scholars and film viewers have found most useful is the study of film genre, although there is some debate over the meaning of the word *genre* when applied to film. As far as this essay is concerned *genre* will refer simply to film types, without much regard for the important scholarly debate over definition. It is admitted that "fantasy" may well overlap with "Western" and that "comedy" may not be a genre at all, but there is not space enough here to resolve that controversy.

The guides to the fantasy films, including horror films and science fiction, are numerous. Walt Lee in the *Reference Guide to Fantastic Films* packs a lot of information about horror, science fiction, and fantasy films into a short space. He includes data about the cast, director, running time, source and type of fantasy, and a brief bibliography for each film. Less complete but valuable is a checklist compiled by Donald C. Willis, *Horror and Science Fiction Films*. He has included some forty-four hundred titles and has given a one-sentence plot description, lacking in Lee. Roy Huss and T. J. Ross have concentrated on the horror film alone in their book *Focus on the Horror Film*, an anthology of essays on gothic horror, monster terror, and the psychological thriller. And Carlos Clarens does not overburden the excellent text of *An Illustrated History of the Horror Film* with too many photos. A special type of horror film is covered in James Ursini and Alain Silver's *The Vampire Film*, but *In Search of Dracula*, by Raymond T. McNally and Radu Florescu, is more reliable even though its chief focus is not on films.

The standard book on the Western is by George N. Fenin and William K. Everson and simply titled *The Western*. It traces the history of the genre, discusses the major films and even many of the minor ones, and includes enough photographs to stir memories of Saturday afternoons of long ago—sitting in small theaters, munching popcorn, and watching heroes on beautiful horses. An excellent reference guide to study about the Western is *Western Films: An Annotated Critical Bibliography*, by John G. Nachbar. This book, with both author and subject indexes, includes an intelligent and scholarly introduction and useful annotations.

The most useful guide to the gangster pictures is *The Great Gangster Pictures*, by James Robert Parish and Michael R. Pitts. This book is basically an index to the credits, distributors, and running times of the movies in this genre, but an introductory essay on the history of the genre and brief critical comments about the individual films raises it beyond the level of an index.

John Kobal's *Gotta Sing, Gotta Dance* is a popular history of the musicals; it is a good place to begin the study of that genre.

Comedy is a diverse and complex genre, if in fact it is a genre at all. The books on the movie comedies are numerous, and it is most difficult to select one or two as the point at which one might begin a study. Gerald Mast's *The Comic Mind* is a major study with an emphasis on the silent comedians. As with most of Mast's work, this book is both theoretical and historical. Walter Kerr in *The Silent Clowns* presents a historically oriented study of the greats.

The serials that so many of us remember from those Saturday afternoons of our youth are well remembered and studied in *Continued Next Week: A History of the Moving Picture Serial,* by Kalton C. Lahue. This excellent history is complemented by an extensive appendix that includes the credits and other data about the serials. Ken Weiss and Ed Goodgold have indexed the serials in *To Be Continued.*

The best general study of movie genres is *Beyond Formula,* by Stanley J. Solomon. He devotes a chapter to each of the important genres: Western, musical, horror, crime, detective, and war. Each chapter begins with a general discussion of the genre and definition of the characteristics of it. Then it discusses in depth seven or eight feature-length films of the genre. Also included are a good bibliography and an index to the films mentioned in the book.

The history of work in documentary film is ably recorded in both *Nonfiction Film,* by Richard Meran Barsam, and *Documentary: A History of the Non-fiction Film,* by Erik Barnouw. Both are solid, but the latter especially emphasizes the images and themes of the documentaries rather than the personalities.

Two anthologies have selected essays on the theory of the documentary as well as the history. *The Documentary Tradition,* edited by Lewis Jacobs, contains essays on the leading films and filmmakers from *Nanook* to *Woodstock.* Arranged according to the decades of the films studied, the essays also include general theory. Another of Barsam's books is *Nonfiction Film: Theory and Criticism.* This anthology includes essays on the idea of the documentary, its history, its artists, and its films.

Finally, Roy Levin's *Documentary Explorations* is a series of interviews with the major makers of documentary films. Included are Frederick Wiseman and Richard Leacock and six other Americans as well as a number of Europeans.

One of the most important, but often overlooked, areas of film production is the experimental film. This area is difficult to define, even difficult to name. Whether it goes by the term *experimental film, underground film, independent film,* or whatever, it is concerned with the efforts of the filmmaker to expand the knowledge and technology of the medium. The basic study of the experimental film is by Sheldon Renan, *An Introduction to the American Underground Film.* This important book contains definition, history, and theory as well as studies of the important filmmakers and films. The appendix includes an excellent list of significant experimental films and an all too brief bibliography.

The history of the underground movement is told in two good books:

Underground Film: A Critical History, by Parker Tyler, and *Experimental Cinema,* by David Curtis. The latter book emphasizes the economic aspect of the experimental films, an important subject since these films are rarely shown in big money markets.

Two interesting anthologies of essays on the experimental film have been published. Gregory Battcock edited *The New American Cinema,* which includes essays by critics, such as Andrew Sarris, and filmmakers, such as Stan VanDerBeck and Stan Brakhage; and P. Adams Sitney's *Film Culture Reader* is a collection of the most important essays from the journal that bills itself as "America's Independent Motion Picture Magazine." The essays give history and criticism, but the emphasis is on theory.

The best study of the technology of the experimental film is *Expanded Cinema.* This outstanding book by Gene Youngblood begins with a difficult but sound discussion of the nature of the experimental film and its effect on audiences. The first chapter is as much sociology as film criticism. His second and third chapters deal with the theory and cosmic consciousness of this type of film, and the latter part of the book considers in depth the technology of the major attempts at expanding the limits of the medium.

Much paper and ink are taken up discussing the relationship that exists between film and the other arts—literature, theater, music, dance, even architecture—perhaps because to a large extent, film is a synthesis of the arts. A good general introduction can be found in an anthology edited by T. J. Ross, *Film and the Liberal Arts.* The essays here compare and contrast film with literature, the visual arts, and music. An index to the relationship is *Filmed Books and Plays, 1928-1974* by A. G. S. Enser. The book contains indexes to the authors, films, and changes in original titles. It is by no means complete, but it is a good place to begin the study of the relationship between film and novels and the theater. That relationship between film and the theater is further explored by Nicholas Vardac in *Stage to Screen,* a study of theatrical method from David Garrick to D. W. Griffith; and critics, filmmakers, and playwrights have commented on that relationship in *Focus on Film and Theatre,* edited by James Hurt.

Perhaps the best known of the books dealing with the relationship between literature and film is George Bluestone's *Novels into Film.* He begins with a theoretical essay and then analyzes several major adaptations, such as *The Grapes of Wrath* and *The Ox Bow Incident.* Overall the book provides a good introduction to the relationship, but it is more limited in scope than its title and first chapter suggest. More valuable as introduction because it is more general and more theoretical is Robert Richardson's *Literature and Film.* Richardson has a good background in both media, and the result is a basic resource. His is one of the few books to pay much attention to the relationship between poetry and film, as most books concentrate on fiction or theater. Other studies abound, such as Geoffrey Wagner's thought provoking (at times it is just provoking) *The Novel and the Cinema* and John Harrington's anthology *Literature and/as Film*. There is a series of books dealing with the adaptation of short stories into film under the general editorship of Thomas Erskin and Gerald Barrett. Titles include "An Occurrence at Owl Creek Bridge" and "The Rocking-Horse Winner." Each of the volumes is introduced by a solid essay on the problems and nature of adaptation. Fred Marcus has recently published a book called *Short Story/Short Film* that will become very useful to the researcher working with the shorter material. He gives the story, a story board, and film continuity, as well as analysis.

Recently, as a result of the burgeoning recognition of the rights of minorities and other identifiable groups, much attention has been paid to the role played by minorities in film and their image portrayed by the films. For instance, books analyzing the depicting of women on the screen have been written by Marjorie Rosen (*Popcorn Venus*), Molly Haskell (*From Reverence to Rape*), and Joan Mellon (*Women and Their Sexuality in the New Film*). These books all combine history with criticism. Reference guides to women in film include a valuable book by Sharon Smith, *Women Who Make Movies*. Her brief essay on each woman filmmaker analyzes the woman's career and mentions her most important films. Smith, of course, deals with the better known women filmmakers, such as Elaine May and Eleanor Perry, but she also devotes some space to the women who are just beginning but will be known soon (with a little luck). Bonnie Dawson's book *Women's Films in Print* is an annotated guide to some eight hundred films by women. A brief bibliography for each film is included when possible.

There have also been released solid books on the role of the black in film. Several have been critical histories. Donald Bogle calls his *Toms, Coons, Mullatoes, Mammies, and Blacks* an "interpretative history of blacks in American films." Lindsay Patterson has edited an anthology of essays that considers both the image of the black in film and the black's role in the film industry. His *Black Films and Film-makers* is notable for its contributors as well as its subject. Daniel Leab in *From Sambo to Superspade* demonstrates the progress—or more accurately the lack of progress—of the black screen image from *Birth of a Nation* to *Shaft*. The most scholarly of the critical histories of the black on the screen is by Thomas Cripps. *Slow Fade to Black* is an excellent study of the black in American film from 1900 to 1942. The reference guides to blacks and film, however, are somewhat less satisfactory. Anne Powers has published *Blacks in American Movies: A Selected Bibliography*. This book is fair, but uneven and at times pedestrian. It includes both an author and subject index, as well as an occasional brief annotation. Richard Maynard has written a guide for teachers who wish to use films about blacks in the classroom. *The Black Man On Film: Racial Stereotyping* includes essays and a practical filmography; its chief flaw lies in its brevity.

A popular form of film criticism is the interview; the current expression for this device is *oral history,* history recorded through the actual words of the men and women who made the history. Film and comics are probably the only art forms so far whose entire history can be recorded in this manner. This is the method and virtue of Kevin Brownlow's *The Parade's Gone By,* mentioned in the section of this essay on history. Other interviews with movie people abound, but most often they are published in journals and must be discovered through the various guides to periodicals. Some few have been published in book form.

For some years now the American Film Institute has been publishing the written record of interviews held by the staff and students at the AFI West Coast facility. Many movie makers—directors, actors, others—have talked informally with the students and staff, and the results have been transcribed. The transcriptions were first published separately as *Dialogue on Film;* more recently they have been included as the centerfold of *American Film.* The AFI says that they have an additional three hundred interviews that will not be published, but are on file at their offices on both coasts.

The first important published book of interviews was probably that of Andrew Sarris, *Interviews with Film Directors.* He reprints interviews with forty directors, most of which were conducted by people other than himself. He believes that the results support his theory about the importance of the role of the director in the movie-making process. He has been followed by others interested chiefly in directors. Eric Sherman and Martin Rubin, in *The Director's Event,* interviewed Peter Bogdanovich, Samuel Fuller, Abraham Polonsky, Budd Boetticher, and Arthur Penn. Charles Thomas Samuels interviewed no Americans, but in *Encountering Directors* he has recorded interviews with filmmakers, such as Alfred Hitchcock and Ingmar Bergman, who have been especially influential in this country. And in *The Men Who Made the Movies,* Richard Schickel gives the transcripts of his televised interviews with Frank Capra, George Cukor, Howard Hawks, Alfred Hitchcock, Vincente Minnelli, King Vidor, Raoul Walsh, and William Wellman.

Probably the form of criticism most people see most often is the movie review published in the daily newspaper or monthly magazine. Naturally reviews serve a different purpose than does the in-depth scholarly article, but reviews can provide the researcher with valuable material. It can suggest the public reaction to the film at the time it was released; it can cite needed data about the production of the film. For many films in many libraries the review may be the only printed material available. *Reader's*

Guide and the *Humanities Index* both list reviews under "Moving Picture Plays" for the year in which the review appeared.

Stephen Bowles's *Index to Critical Film Reviews in British and American Film Periodicals* is a three-volume guide to the reviews published in thirty-one journals. It is useful but the list of journals is not complete. The critic, rather than the journal, becomes the emphasis for Richard Heinzkill in *Film Criticism: An Index to Critics' Anthologies.* A number of the better critics, such as Andrew Sarris, Pauline Kael, and John Simon, have had their reviews, originally published in periodicals, collected and published in book form. Heinzkill has indexed the work of twenty-seven such reviewers, and through his list it is possible to begin the study of either films or critics.

There are a few books that reprint reviews from a number of critics. *The New York Times Film Reviews, 1913-1968* is a massive six-volume collection of all the film reviews published in the *Times.* Included are the reviews of Bosley Crowther, Vincent Canby, Frank S. Nugent, and others. The *Film Review Digest Annual* is a single volume collection of the capsule reviews published in that journal. *Film Review Digest* excerpts reviews from twenty-eight periodicals and therefore gives a good idea of the general reception of a film. And Stanley Kauffman has edited two books of reviews: *American Film Criticism* is a collection of one or two reviews of many of the important films from the beginning to *Citizen Kane,* and *American Film Directors* is a collection of excerpted reviews of the important films of major American directors.

This essay is not intended as a how-to guide to making movies, but some knowledge of technique is essential to the critic. The critic must know what each of the persons involved in the process does even if he or she does not want to make a film personally.

First a critic must develop a vocabulary of technical terms. Raymond Spottiswoode's *A Grammar of the Film* discusses the art of film production and helps with definition of the terms. It is now somewhat old and hard to read, but useful. More up-to-date is *An Illustrated Glossary of Film Terms* by Harry Geduld and Ronald Gottesman. The definitions are brief and even complicated matters are not discussed in depth, but as a guide it does what it is supposed to.

The entire process of film production is given an overview in several books. John Quick and Tom La Bare have written a *Handbook to Film Production,* which is an easy method of studying all the work that goes into the production of a film. More ambitious are two volumes sponsored by the American Film Institute. Eric Sherman in *Directing the Film* covers in depth the contribution of the directors, while Donald Chase considers the rest of the collaborators in *Filmmaking: The Collaborative Art.* There are many other books that deal with the individual contributions of members of the production team, but these general guides are a good place to begin.

Some of the best film criticism is that written about a single film, but space here does not permit a list of the books on single films any more than it permits lists of books on individual actors or directors. The researchers should consult the card catalog at the local library or search through the bibliographies mentioned earlier in this essay. The researcher should be aware that there is a large range of types of books about individual films—some are historic, others technical, some analytic.

The range of books on film is large and this bibliographic essay is by necessity highly selective. As the movie-going audience has become better educated, the demand for intelligent books to provide background and interpretation has increased. This list can only point in the direction of the appropriate books and offer the encouragement that many of them can enhance watching the movies themselves.

BIBLIOGRAPHY

BOOKS

Aceto, Vincent J.; Jane Graves; and Fred Silva. *Film Literature Index.* Albany, N.Y.: Filmdex, annual.

The American Film Institute Guide to College Courses in Film and Television. Princeton, N.J.: Peterson's Guides, 1978.

Andrew, J. Dudley. *The Major Film Theories.* New York: Oxford University Press, 1976.

Anobile, Richard J. *Casablanca.* New York: Universe Books, 1974.

———. *The General.* New York: Universe Books, 1975.

Aros, Andrew, *A Title Guide to the Talkies, 1964 through 1974.* Metuchen, N.J.: Scarecrow Press, 1977.

Arvidson, Linda. *When the Movies Were Young.* New York: Benjamin Bloom, 1968.

Balázs, Béla. *Theory of the Film.* New York: Dover Publications, 1970.

Balio, Tino, ed. *The American Film Industry.* Madison: University of Wisconsin Press, 1976.

Barnouw, Erik. *Documentary: A History of the Non-fiction Film.* New York: Oxford University Press, 1974.

Barrett, Gerald R., and Thomas L. Erskine. *From Fiction to Film: D. H. Lawrence's "The Rocking-Horse Winner."* Encino, Calif.: Dickenson, 1974.

———. *From Fiction into Film: Ambrose Bierce's "An Occurrence at Owl Creek Bridge."* Encino, Calif.: Dickenson, 1973.

Barsam, Richard Meran. *Nonfiction Film.* New York: E. P. Dutton, 1973.

———, ed. *Nonfiction Film: Theory and Criticism.* New York: E. P. Dutton, 1976.

Battock, Gregory, ed. *The New American Cinema.* New York: E. P. Dutton, 1967.

Bawden, Liz-Anne. *The Oxford Companion to Film.* New York: Oxford University Press, 1976.

Bazin, André. *What is Cinema?* Berkeley: University of California Press, 1967.

Bergman, Andrew. *We're in the Money.* New York: New York University Press, 1971.

Bluestone, George. *Novels into Film.* Berkeley: University of California Press, 1957.

Blumenberg, Richard. *Critical Focus: An Introduction to Film.* Belmont, Calif.: Wadsworth, 1975.

Bobker, Lee R. *Elements of Film.* New York: Harcourt, Brace and World, 1969, 1974.

Bogle, Donald. *Toms, Coons, Mulattoes, Mammies and Blacks.* New York: Viking, 1973.

Bohn, Thomas W., and Richard L. Stromgren. *Light and Shadows.* Port Washington, N.Y.: Alfred Publishing, 1975.

Bowles, Stephen E. *Index to Critical Film Reviews in British and American Film Periodicals.* 3 vols. New York: Burt Franklin, 1973.

Brownlow, Kevin. *The Parade's Gone By.* New York: Ballantine, 1968.

Brownstone, David, and Irene M. Franck, eds. *Film Review Digest Annual, 1976.* Millwood, N.Y.: KTO Press, 1976.

Bukalski, Peter J. *Film Research: A Critical Bibliography.* Boston: G. K. Hall, 1972.

Catalogue of Copyright Entries: Motion Pictures. 4 vols. Washington, D.C.: Library of Congress, 1951, 1953, 1960, 1971.

Chase, Donald. *Filmmaking: The Collaborative Art.* Boston: Little, Brown, 1975.

Clarens, Carlos. *An Illustrated History of the Horror Film.* New York: Capricorn Books, 1967.

Cowie, Peter, ed. *International Film Guide.* London: Tantivy, annual.

Cripps, Thomas. *Slow Fade to Black.* New York: Oxford University Press, 1977.

Curtis, David. *Experimental Cinema.* New York: Dell, 1971.

Dawson, Bonnie. *Women's Films in Print.* San Francisco: Booklegger Press, 1975.

DeNitto, Dennis, and William Herman. *Film and The Critical Eye.* New York: Macmillan, 1975.

Dickinson, Thorold. *A Discovery of Cinema.* New York: Oxford University Press, 1971.

Dimmitt, Richard Betrand. *An Actor Guide to the Talkies, 1949-1964.* Metuchen, N.J.: Scarecrow Press, 1967-1968.

———. *A Title Guide to the Talkies, 1927-1963,* Metuchen, N.J.: Scarecrow Press, 1965.

Eisenstein, Sergei. *Film Essays and a Lecture.* New York: Praeger, 1970.

———. *Film Forum.* New York: Harcourt, Brace and World, 1949.

———. *The Film Sense.* New York: Harcourt, Brace and World, 1947.

Elsas, Diana. *Factfile: Film and Television Periodicals in English.* Washington, D.C.: American Film Institute, 1977.

Enser, A. G. S. *Filmed Books and Plays, 1928-1974*. London: Andre Deutsch, 1975.

Fell, John L. *Film: An Introduction*. New York: Praeger, 1975.

Fenin, George N., and William K. Everson. *The Western*. New York: Orion, 1962.

Friar, Ralph E., and Natasha A. Friar. *The Only Good Indian . . . The Hollywood Gospel*. New York: Drama Book Specialists, 1972.

Geduld, Harry M. *The Birth of the Talkies*. Bloomington: University of Indiana Press, 1975.

————, and Ronald Gottesman. *An Illustrated Glossary of Film Terms*. New York: Holt, Rinehart and Winston, 1973.

Gessner, Rolent, *The Moving Image*. New York: E. P. Dutton, 1968.

Giannetti, Louis D. *Understanding Movies*. Englewood Cliffs, N.J.: Prentice-Hall, 1976.

Gish, Lillian. *The Movies, Mr. Griffith, and Me*. Englewood Cliffs, N.J.: Prentice-Hall, 1969.

Gottesman, Ronald, and Harry M. Geduld. *Guidebook to Film*. New York: Holt, Rinehart and Winston, 1972.

Halliwell, Leslie. *The Filmgoer's Companion*. New York: Avon Books, 1974.

Harrington, John. *Literature and/as Film*. Englewood Cliffs, N.J.: Prentice-Hall, 1977.

Haskell, Molly. *From Reverence to Rape*. New York: Holt, Rinehart and Winston, 1973, 1974.

Heinzkill, Richard. *Film Criticism: An Index to Critics' Anthologies*. Metuchen, N.J.: Scarecrow Press, 1975.

Higham, Charles. *Warner Brothers*. New York: Charles Scribner's Sons, 1975.

Houston, Penelope. *The Contemporary Cinema, 1945-1963*. Baltimore: Penguin Books, 1963.

Humanities Index. New York: H. W. Wilson, annual.

Hurt, James, ed. *Focus on Film and Theatre*. Englewood Cliffs, N.J.: Prentice-Hall, 1974.

Huss, Roy, and Norman Silverstein. *The Film Experience*. New York: Harper and Row, 1968.

————, and T. J. Ross, eds. *Focus on The Horror Film*. Englewood Cliffs, N.J.: Prentice-Hall, 1972.

Jacobs, Lewis, ed. *The Documentary Tradition*. New York: Hopkinson and Blake, 1971.

————. *Introduction to the Art of the Movies*. New York: Noonday Press, 1960.

————. *The Movies as Medium*. New York: Farrar, Straus and Giroux, 1970.

————. *The Rise of the American Film*. New York: Teachers College Press, 1939, 1968.

Jones, Karen. *International Index to Film Periodicals*. New York: St. Martin's, annual.

Jowett, Garth. *Film: The Democratic Art*. Boston: Little, Brown, 1976.

Katz, John Stuart, ed. *Perspectives on the Study of Film*. Boston: Little, Brown, 1971.

Kauffman, Stanley, ed. *American Film Criticism.* New York: Liveright, 1972.
————. *American Film Directors.* New York: Ungar, 1974.
Kerr, Walter. *The Silent Clowns.* New York: Alfred A. Knopf, 1975.
Knight, Arthur. *The Liveliest Art: A Panoramic History of the Movies.* New York: New American Library, 1957.
Kobal, John. *Gotta Sing, Gotta Dance.* New York: Kamlyn, 1971.
Kracauer, Siegfried. *Theory of Film.* New York: Oxford University Press, 1960.
Krafsur, Richard. *The American Film Institute Catalog of Motion Pictures: Feature Films, 1961-70.* New York: R. R. Bowker, 1976.
Lahue, Kalton C. *Continued Next Week: A History of the Moving Picture Serial.* Norman: University of Oklahoma Press, 1964.
Larkin, Rochelle. *Hail Columbia.* New Rochelle, N.Y.: Arlington House, 1975.
Leab, Daniel J. *From Sambo to Superspade.* Boston: Houghton Mifflin, 1975.
Lee, Walt. *Reference Guide to Fantastic Films: Science Fiction, Fantasy and Horror.* Los Angeles: Chelsea-Lee Books, 1972.
Leonard, Harold. *The Film Index: A Bibliography.* New York: Arno, 1970.
Levin, G. Roy. *Documentary Explorations.* Garden City, N.Y.: Doubleday-Anchor, 1971.
Limbacher, James. *Feature Films on 8mm and 16mm.* New York: R. R. Bowker, 1977.
Lindgren, Ernest. *The Art of the Film.* New York: Macmillan, 1963.
Lindsay, Vachel. *The Art of the Moving Picture.* New York: Liveright, 1970.
MacCann, Richard Dyer, ed. *Film: A Montage of Theories.* New York: E. P. Dutton, 1966.
————, and Edward S. Perry. *The New Film Index.* New York: E. P. Dutton, 1975.
McCarthy, Todd, and Charles Flynn. *Kings of the B's.* New York: E. P. Dutton, 1975.
McCarty, Clifford. *Published Screenplays: A Checklist.* Kent, Ohio: Kent State University Press, 1971.
McNally, Raymond T., and Radu Florescu. *In Search of Dracula.* New York: Galahad Books, 1972.
Manchel, Frank. *Film Study: A Resource Guide.* Rutherford, N.J.: Fairleigh Dickinson University Press, 1973.
Manvell, Roger, ed. *The International Encyclopedia of Film.* New York: Crown, 1972.
Marcus, Fred H. *Short Story/Short Film.* Englewood Cliffs, N.J.: Prentice-Hall, 1977.
Martin, Leonard. *The Great Movie Shorts.* New York: Crown, 1972.
Mast, Gerald. *The Comic Mind.* Indianapolis: Bobbs-Merrill, 1973.
————. *A Short History of the Movies.* New York: Pegasus, 1976.
————, and Marshall Cohen, eds. *Film Theory and Criticism.* New York: Oxford University Press, 1974.
Maynard, Richard. *The Black Man on Film: Racial Stereotyping.* Rochelle Park, N.J.: Hayden, 1974.
————. *The Celluloid Curriculum.* Rochelle Park, N.J.: Hayden, 1971.

Mellon, Joan. *Women and Their Sexuality in the New Film.* New York: Dell, 1973.

Metz, Christian. *Film Language.* New York: Oxford University Press, 1974.

Monaco, James. *How to Read a Film.* New York: Oxford University Press, 1977.

Munden, Kenneth W., ed. *The American Film Institute Catalogue of Motion Pictures Produced in the United States, Feature Films, 1921-1930.* New York: R. R. Bowker, 1971.

Nachbar, John G. *Western Films: An Annotated Critical Bibliography.* New York: Garland Publishing Co., 1975.

The New York Times Film Reviews, 1913-1968. 6 vols. New York: New York Times/Arno Press, 1970.

Niver, Kemp R. *Motion Pictures from the Library of Congress Paper Print Collection, 1894-1912.* Berkeley: University of California Press, 1967.

Parish, James Robert, and Michael R. Pitts. *Film Directors: A Guide to their American Films.* Metuchen, N.J.: Scarecrow Press, 1974.

—————. *The Great Gangster Pictures.* Metuchen, N.J.: Scarecrow Press, 1976.

Patterson, Lindsay, ed. *Black Films and Black Film-makers.* New York: Dodd, Mead, 1975.

Poteet, G. Howard, ed. *The Complete Guide to Film Study.* Urbana, Ill.: National Council of Teachers of English, 1972.

—————. *Published Radio, Television, and Film Scripts: A Bibliography.* Troy, N.Y.: Whitson Publishing, 1975.

Powdermaker, Hortense. *Hollywood: The Dream Factory.* Boston: Little, Brown, 1950.

Powers, Anne. *Blacks in American Movies: A Selected Bibliography.* Metuchen, N.J.: Scarecrow Press, 1974.

Pratt, George C. *Spellbound in Darkness.* Greenwich, Conn.: New York Graphic Sociey, 1973.

Pudovkin, V. I. *Film Technique and Film Acting.* New York: Grove Press, 1970.

Quick, John, and Tom La Bare. *Handbook of Film Productions.* New York: Macmillan, 1972.

Reader's Guide to Periodical Literature. New York: H. W. Wilson, annual.

Renan, Sheldon. *An Introduction to the American Underground Film.* New York: E. P. Dutton, 1967.

Rhode, Eric. *A History of the Cinema from Its Origins to 1970.* New York: Hill and Wang, 1976.

Richardson, Robert. *Literature and Film.* Bloomington: Indiana University Press, 1969.

Rosen, Marjorie. *Popcorn Venus.* New York: Coward, McCann, and Geoghegan, 1973.

Ross, T. J. *Film and the Liberal Arts.* New York: Holt, Rinehart, and Winston, 1970.

Rotha, Paul, with Richard Griffith. *The Film Till Now.* London: Spring Books, 1967.

Sadoul, Georges. *Dictionary of Filmmakers.* Berkeley: University of California Press, 1972.

————. *Dictionary of Films*. Berkeley: University of California Press, 1965, 1972.

Samuels, Charles Thomas. *Encountering Directors*. New York: Capricorn, 1972.

Sarris, Andrew. *Interviews with Film Directors*. New York: Avon, 1967.

Schickel, Richard. *The Men Who Made the Movies*. New York: Atheneum, 1975.

Schuster, Mel. *Motion Picture Directors: A Bibliography of Magazine and Periodical Articles, 1900-1972*. Metuchen, N.J.: Scarecrow Press, 1973.

————. *Motion Picture Performers: A Bibliography of Magazine and Periodical Articles, 1900-1969*. Metuchen, N.J.: Scarecrow Press, 1971.

Shales, Tom, et al. *The American Film Heritage*. Washington, D.C.: Acropolis Books, 1972.

Sherman, Eric. *Directing the Film*. Boston: Little, Brown, 1976.

————, and Martin Rubin. *The Director's Event*. New York: New American Library, 1969.

Sitney, P. Adams, ed. *Film Culture Reader*. New York: Praeger, 1970.

Smith, Sharon. *Women Who Make Movies*. New York: Hopkins and Blake, 1975.

Sohn, David A. *Film: The Critical Eye*. Dayton, Ohio: Pflaum, 1970.

Solomon, Stanley J. *Beyond Formula*. New York: Harcourt Brace Jovanovich, 1976.

Spottiswoode, Raymond. *A Grammar of the Film*. Berkeley: The University of California Press, 1969.

Thomson, David. *A Biographical Dictionary of Film*. New York: William Morrow, 1976.

Truitt, Evelyn Mack. *Who Was Who on Screen*. New York: R. R. Bowker, 1974.

Tyler, Parker. *Underground Film: A Critical History*. New York: Grove Press, 1969.

Ursini, James, and Alain Silver. *The Vampire Film*. Cranbury, N.J.: A. S. Barnes, 1975.

Vardac, A. Nicholas. *Stage to Screen*. New York: Benjamin Blom, 1968.

Wagner, Geoffrey. *The Novel and the Cinema*. Rutherford, N.J.: Fairleigh Dickinson University Press, 1975.

Walls, Howard Lamarr. *Motion Pictures, 1894-1912, Identified from the Records of the U.S. Copyright Office*. Washington, D.C.: Library of Congress, 1953.

Weaver, Kathleen. *Film Programmer's Guide to 16mm Rentals*. Albany, Calif.: Reel Research, 1975.

Weber, Olga S. *North American Film and Video Directory*. New York: R. R. Bowker, 1976.

Weinberg, Herman G. *The Complete Greed*. New York: Arno, 1972.

Weiss, Ken, and Ed Goodgold. *To Be Continued*. New York: Crown, 1972.

Wenden, D. J. *The Birth of the Movies*. New York: E. P. Dutton, 1974.

Who Wrote the Movie and What Else Did He Write? Los Angeles: The Academy of Motion Picture Arts and Sciences and the Writers' Guild of America, 1970.

Willis, Donald C. *Horror and Science Fiction Films: A Checklist*. Metuchen, N.J.: Scarecrow Press, 1972.

Youngblood, Gene. *Expanded Cinema*. New York: E. P. Dutton, 1970.

PERIODICALS

American Cinematographer. Los Angeles, 1919-.
American Film. Washington, D.C., 1975-.
Cinema Journal. Philadelphia, 1961-.
Dialog on Film. Beverly Hills, Calif., 1972-1975.
Film Culture. New York, 1962-.
Film Heritage. Dayton, Ohio, 1965-.
Film Review Digest. Millwood, N.Y., 1975-.
Literature/Film Quarterly. Salisbury, Md., 1973-.
Media and Methods. Philadelphia, 1965-.

CHAPTER 7 Gothic Novels

Kay J. Mussell

The gothic novel had its greatest general popularity in a relatively brief period of literary history, the end of the eighteenth and the beginning of the nineteenth centuries. It was originally an English literary form, although authors and readers in other countries quickly adopted gothic fiction and its conventions for their own. The influence of the gothic in fiction, however, has been much more significant than its relatively short period of great popularity would indicate. Besides its contributions to the detective novel, science fiction, horror stories, the popular melodrama, and the works of such writers as Poe, Hawthorne, Irving, James, and Faulkner, the gothic novel also continued as a form in itself, although much less well defined and less pervasive than it had been in its heyday. The audience for the gothic novel, from the work of Ann Radcliffe in eighteenth-century England to that of Phyllis Whitney in twentieth-century America, is primarily female. Women are attracted to gothic novels by the combination of romance and terror, a blend that has remained relatively constant over the past two hundred years.

Although the gothic novel as a form is capable of containing and exploring sensitive and sophisticated questions in fiction, as shown by the work of such writers as Poe and Hawthorne, in its popular version, it has been a formulaic and predictable kind of fiction. The world view of the gothic novel offers vicarious danger and romantic fantasy of a type that is particularly appealing to female readers. Women are cast as victims in a man's world, but through the demonstration of feminine virtues, the victim proves herself worthy of the love of the hero, who becomes her deliverer from the terrors that beset her. The gothic villain, on the other hand, is capable of manipulating terrifying props and producing fear and danger, but is defeated by true love. The gothic novel over two centuries reaffirms the romantic belief in love as the cure for evil.

HISTORIC OUTLINE

Scholarly consideration of the gothic novel in America is long overdue, but the study has been hampered by a variety of legitimate difficulties beyond the traditional resistance to the study of popular art forms. The term *gothic* does not lend itself to easy definition and has not been consistently applied. In its earliest British form, as written by Horace Walpole, the gothic novel was synonymous with supernatural horror; but almost immediately, in the works of Ann Radcliffe and Clara M. Reeve, among others, the gothic took on more sentimental and romantic characteristics, almost as though the work of Samuel Richardson had been overlaid with gothic props. In Ann Radcliffe's works, the "supernatural" is explained as the manipulations of the gothic villain who threatens the lovers. Clara Reeve's gothic novels were historical romances that used the exotic trappings of medieval chivalry to provide excitement. It was these latter types of the gothic that were most appealing and influential in America.

After the early nineteenth century, the word *gothic* was not consistently applied to formula novels until recently, even though the form flourished between those dates. In the early 1960s, Gerald Gross, an editor at Ace Books, entitled a paperback series of romantic mysteries designed for women *gothics*. The term caught on immediately and is now applied to a wide range of novels, recognized as one of the most active and lucrative areas of publishing. However, the current gothic boom is not dependent upon new material; many of the popular titles were published long ago, and either were never out of print or were returned to print to satisfy the readers. The gothic novel was never out of vogue; it simply was submerged.

Beyond the problem of definition, another impediment to the serious study of gothic fiction is the fact that the audience for the form has been primarily female, relatively inarticulate, and lacking access to the outlets for critical expression. The forms influenced by the gothic, on the other hand, have been much more thoroughly documented and studied. When the original gothic novels lost their vitality for readers, the tradition splintered in a number of directions. Gothics influenced detective fiction, science fiction, and the Western, especially in the works of James Fenimore Cooper. In Europe, although not in America, they were influential in the development of horror stories, such as *Frankenstein* and *Dracula*. Their influence on serious American writers has been well-documented.

The gothic novel might be best defined as a story with a characteristic world view supported by a particular set of conventions. It consists of a story set in a remote place or a remote time in which a usually improbable and terrifying mystery is completely intertwined with a successful love story. Unlike the detective story, gothic novels do not provide a logical solution to the mystery; to the contrary, the mystery and the love story are so coincidentally interconnected that it is virtually impossible to separate them. The solution of the mystery usually removes the impediments to the successful conclusion of the romance. Women are doubly victimized by their finding themselves in a situation (castle, monastery, crumbling mansion) where a gothic villain can threaten them. The novels depend upon a setting in which the social structure is hierarchical; the conventions of gothic fiction, such as mysterious inheritances, hidden identities, lost wills, family secrets, inherited curses, incest and illegitimacy, require a world in which social mobility takes place through family identity and marriage rather than individual worth. The novels also depend upon the audience's belief that the successful courtship and marriage of the characters is the most satisfactory conclusion of the plot, thus elevating the place of family formation through love to a supreme position.

For the late eighteenth and early nineteenth centuries, as well as for the mid-twentieth century, there is relatively firm agreement upon what a gothic novel is. However, the definitions from the two periods are not entirely congruent, and for the century and a half between them there is no such agreement. The first gothic novels, those of Horace Walpole, Ann Radcliffe, Clara M. Reeve, "Monk" Lewis, and others, were read in America and influenced American fiction. The rise of the novel in America coincided with the peak popularity of gothic fiction in Britain, and since American fiction was very derivative of British models, much early American fiction was strongly influenced by gothic novels. Critics of gothic novels have traditionally divided them into several categories, sentimental-gothic, terror-gothic, and historical-gothic, although there are also some subcategories of lesser significance. Sentimental-gothic novels usually focused upon the love story and used supernatural terrors that had rational explanations. The primary writer of this type in Britain was Radcliffe, and her work was most influential upon American fiction. Terror-gothic novels, like those of Walpole and Lewis, emphasized the supernatural, often using depraved monks or nuns as villains. Their influence was most marked upon serious writers in America, but the terror-gothic tradition never developed fully in this country. The historical-gothic was much more influential in America for its method of romanticizing the past, usually with anachronistic elements, using the strangeness of the past as part of the atmosphere of terror.

Although the gothic was influential in America, there are several reasons why it never developed fully here. The most important reason was that the American society and landscape did not provide the necessary moldering castles, sinister monasteries, and hierarchical social structure so necessary to the novels. A second reason was the American antipathy to novels as "not true" and "not instructive." A third was that, in the absence of international copyright laws, it was simple and cheap for American printers to pirate the works of British popular authors. Even today, the most popular gothic writers are usually British, and American authors are not only derivative but also use British settings to a large extent. In American fiction, then, the sentimental-gothic and historical-gothic modes flourished, especially in terms of their more sensational elements. The supernatural only developed in the works of serious authors. The popular audience was much more interested in terrors with rational explanations than in explorations of the irrational or the psychological. Alexander Cowie suggests that the gothic in America was a matter of using gothic conventions in a frame of sentimental romance.

Charles Brockden Brown was the first major American writer to use the gothic in his fiction, although he was much more skillful than most of his contemporaries. His novels, including *Wieland* (1798), *Ormond* (1799), and *Edgar Huntly* (1799), use American settings. Brown provided rational explanations for his apparently supernatural effects and was interested in exploring psychological states and experiments more than in exploiting the possibilities of terrorizing material.

A lesser contemporary of Brown was Isaac Mitchell, the author of one of the most popular novels of the period, *The Asylum, or Alonzo and Melissa* (1804), a gothic romance hinging upon the opposition of a father to his daughter's proposed marriage. Mitchell went so far as to place a medieval castle on Long Island Sound, from which Alonzo rescues Melissa after a series of gothic adventures. On the other hand, Sally Wood's *Julia, or the Illuminated Baron*, another novel that is very close to British models, is set in eighteenth-century France. The book, published in 1800, has a plot that depends upon the hidden identity of Julia and her suitor, who endure many dangers before being united. In the end, both are revealed to be aristocrats, but in deference to American democratic sentiment they renounce their titles. Many traditional gothic elements are present, including a dangerous chateau, visits to tombs, kidnappings, and an attempted rape. Other novels by Wood, similar in type, are *Dorval, or the Speculator* (1801), *Amelia; or the Influence of Virtue: an Old Man's Story* (1802?), and *Ferdinand and Elmira: a Russian Story* (1804).

Other novelists of the period, some anonymous, who wrote gothic fiction include Ann Eliza Bleecker, and the women who used the pseudonyms "A Lady of Massachusetts," and "A Lady of Philadelphia." *Laura* (1809) by "A Lady of Philadelphia" is about a nun who comes to America and endures many terrors in a yellow fever epidemic. Chapbooks and magazines were also filled with gothic fiction. George Lippard's *The Quaker City, or The Monks of Monk's Hall* (1844) used many gothic conventions.

After the heyday of the gothic novel in Britain and America, the tradition splintered in a number of directions. Poe was influenced by the gothic in both his stories of detection and his stories of horror. Science fiction was also indebted to gothic fiction for its premise of the seemingly super-natural (or strange) explained by rational means. The melodrama often resembled gothic novels in world view as well as conventions. Some critics have even suggested that the Western was influenced by the gothic, especially in its use of Indians and the dangers of the wilderness as a form of American gothic terror. However, all of these uses of the gothic go beyond the imaginative world posited by the original gothic novelists.

Because the American democratic and practical mind was never quite comfortable with the gothic novel of terror, the true heirs of the gothic novels can be found in the women's novels of the nineteenth and twentieth centuries. Many writers of sentimental romances wrote novels that today would be called *gothics*, novels that are dependent upon the models of Radcliffe or the Brontës for their plot and their world view. Even at their tamest, the domestic and sentimental novelists often relied upon gothic conventions for suspense.

Probably the most important of these writers was E.D.E.N. Southworth, whose novels were written over a good part of the nineteenth century. In books like *The Hidden Hand* (1859) and *The Curse of Clifton* (1852), she used many gothic conventions (lost heirs, evil villains, virtuous maid-ens, nobles, and castles in foreign settings) within novels that accurately reflected the world view of gothic fiction. That world by the mid-nine-teenth century could be defined as one in which life itself was precarious, but especially for young women. There was always someone, a villain or a jealous woman, willing to jeopardize the romantic happiness of the young girl by the use of various gothic trappings.

Another important writer of the period was "Bertha M. Clay," the pseudonym for a group of writers, beginning with Charlotte M. Breame, who wrote women's novels in the gothic mode for Street and Smith's dime-novel series. The popularity of the gothic is further demonstrated in this period by the fact that one of the major dime-novel publishers, Nor-man Munro, once published Walpole's *Castle of Otranto* in a story paper without acknowledging the source by either author or title.

Gothic novels of this period, however, were not novels of the super-natural, although they used many gothic conventions and techniques. Most were very long, written in a highly romantic style, and full of coincidences in plot and anachronisms in setting. They were usually written very quickly, in order to satisfy the voracious appetite of their large audience.

The turn of the century saw a great increase in the interest in historical romances, many of which were gothic in type. Some followed the tradition of Clara M. Reeve and others in Britain, mining the past ages of Europe for romantic and strange material. But, by the end of the nineteenth century, most historical gothics no longer were set in the Middle Ages. Colonial America and the Revolutionary period, as well as the Civil War, were also appropriate settings. Mary Johnston, the Virginia author, wrote several novels in this form. Her *To Have and To Hold* (1900), one of the most popular historical romances in American publishing, is the tale of a young aristocratic woman who falls upon hard times in Britain and comes to Jamestown in a ship full of potential brides in order to escape a villainous suitor. In America she is purchased by a young settler who, after surviving a number of dangers with her, saves her from her pursuer and falls in love with her. Much of the novel uses gothic conventions, better adapted than most to the American landscape.

Authors of the early twentieth century who use gothic material in romances include Mary Roberts Rinehart, Mignon Eberhart (both better known as detective and mystery writers), Kathleen Norris, Emilie Loring, and Kathleen Winsor. These authors, and others who use gothic material, have never been studied with consistency; but their popularity is attested to by the fact that all of them have books written long ago that are still in print in paperback. The demand for Rinehart and Loring is especially insatiable.

Gothic novels began to receive attention again early in the 1960s. However, the roots of the current gothic boom were evident at least as early as the 1930s, with the publication and immense popularity of Daphne du Maurier's *Rebecca* (1938) in England. The current group of major gothic novelists includes two Americans, Phyllis Whitney and Anya Seton, who published books in the 1940s and are still writing and publishing today. It is impossible, in this period, however, to ignore the influence of British writers on the American formula.

In 1960, the first novel by Victoria Holt (a pseudonym of Eleanor Burford Hibbert) was published in America. *Mistress of Mellyn,* a novel with a close relationship to *Jane Eyre,* sparked the interest in gothic fiction in America in two ways, by creating a renewed market for the writings of popular British writers (Mary Stewart, Barbara Cartland, Dorothy Eden, and Hibbert herself under her various pseudonyms) and also by increasing the market for such American writers as Phyllis Whitney, Anya Seton, Daoma Winston, and a variety of pulp writers like Dorothy Daniels (Norman Daniels), Marilyn Ross (Dan Ross), and Edwina Noone (Michael Avallone). These novels fall into several related categories. Some are gothic novels with contemporary settings in which the strange and terrifying events come from the exotic nature of the setting; an example is Phyllis Whitney's *Black Amber* (1964), which takes place in Turkey. Others are classic gothic stories in which a young woman (governess, new bride) endures the terrors of an old house with ancient legends, superstitions, and family secrets; an example is Anya Seton's *Dragonwyck* (1944). Others are novels about historical figures, cast in gothic terms; two of the most popular of these are Anya Seton's *Devil Water* (1962) and *Katherine* (1954).

Very recently, a new type of gothic fiction has been gaining popularity, as indicated by advertisements and displays in bookstores. Novels by such new authors as Rosemary Rogers, Kathleen Woodiwiss, Claire Lorimer, and Lolah Burford are original paperback gothics, but much longer than those published a few years ago. Rogers' *Wicked, Loving Lies* (1976) is set in the eighteenth and nineteenth centuries in Spain, England, France, Tripoli, Louisiana, and Texas. The heroine is raped innumerable times, always by the same man in different situations (he is, of course, the hero). She is, for a time, Napoleon's mistress, a prisoner in a harem, a British noblewoman, a quadroon slave in the American South, and an heiress. These books are much more sexually explicit than many of the earlier gothics, but the world view in them is still the same, indicating that the twentieth-century audience is becoming more tolerant of sexual deviation but still wishes its romance to take much the same form.

Contemporary gothics rarely reach the bestseller lists; however, their sales figures and continuing availability show their popularity among their primarily female audience. Although there has been some change, the value system of gothic novels has remained relatively stable over the years. The stories still occur in a world in which marriage is seen as the best of all possible states for women and in a world which, because women have very little control over their lives, is especially precarious for them. Despite the irrationality of gothic dangers in a twentieth-century context, these books are still full of old houses, corrupt aristocrats, supernatural effects rationally explained, and melodramatic reconciliations.

It is clear that there is much more research and study to be done on gothic novels, for their continued popularity over the last two centuries shows that they are significant cultural indicators of the interests, tastes, tensions, and values of their primarily feminine audience. All of the other inheritors of the original gothics (mysteries, science fiction, melodrama, and Westerns) have gone on to become the subjects of full-scale studies of their own. Only the gothic novel for women has been neglected, and it is clearly deserving of the same full-scale treatment in its own right.

REFERENCE WORKS

Because the study of American popular gothic fiction is still so new, there are no specific reference tools that are generally useful. There are, however, a number of reference works in related areas that can yield significant information. Much more is available on the gothic in Britain than in America, so that researchers must often read between the lines of reference works in searching out materials.

A useful source book, although almost entirely devoted to eighteenth-century British gothic fiction, is Dan J. McNutt's *The Eighteenth-Century Gothic Novel: An Annotated Bibliography of Criticism and Selected Texts.* The book provides brief annotations of bibliographies and secondary sources, including background materials, specialized studies, and other items of interest. It is current through 1971. A companion volume on the gothic after the eighteenth century is in progress. Although the focus in this volume, as in so many others, is on British manifestations of the form and the serious literary consideration of such works rather than the popular culture aspects of the gothic, it is still indispensable.

The only other specialized bibliography of the gothic is less useful. Montague Summers' *A Gothic Bibliography* is a listing of primary gothic works to 1916. Annotations are sketchy. McNutt says: "An essential book, yet one to be used with caution."

Many general books on early American fiction provide titles, authors, and publishing information about gothic novels written in America. Among the best of these are Lyle Wright's *American Fiction 1774-1850* and *American Fiction 1774-1900.* The volumes are listings of American fiction included in major collections in the United States. Books are listed by author (if known) or titles (if not). Entries show place, date of publication or the printer, if known, along with locating copies. Some books have descriptive annotations, thus providing information for researchers looking for gothic fiction. There is also an index of unexamined titles, as well as a title index. Although much of the listed material is not gothic, the volumes are well worth consulting.

Arthur Hobson Quinn's *American Fiction: An Historical and Critical Survey* includes a great number of plot summaries, and is thus useful for finding many forgotten novels with gothic elements. Similarly useful is Frank Luther Mott's *Golden Multitudes,* a history of the bestseller in America, as well as Ernest A. Baker's *A Guide to the Best Fiction in English* for books published prior to 1911.

Less useful but worth consulting are John Williams Tebbel's *A History of Book Publishing in the United States* for information on publishers, bestsellers, and copyright laws, and the *Author Catalog and Title Catalog* of the Microbook Library of American Civilization, which includes some early American novels. Both the Microbook and the Lyle Wright volumes are primarily useful because books listed are available more readily than those in most other listings.

For Charles Brockden Brown, whose gothic fiction has popular elements, two bibliographical tools are available: S. J. Krause and Jane

Nilset's "A Census of the Works" and Robert Hemenway and D. H. Keller's "A Checklist of Biography and Criticism."

Much of the fiction of the mid- to late nineteenth century that has gothic elements was published in dime novels, story papers, and women's sentimental novels. There is no comprehensive guide to such material and some of the best collections are uncataloged. However, there are a few good places to start.

Quentin Reynolds' *The Fiction Factory* is a history of the publications of Street and Smith and thus provides much solid information on authors, titles, and bibliographic data. The book is marred by the lack of a good annotated bibliography and information on the location of primary source material. A better bibliographical guide is Albert Johannsen's *The House of Beadle and Adams.* Although neither of these books is devoted exclusively, or even primarily, to gothic material, both contain enough information about particular authors and series that they can be of help. For example, Bertha M. Clay was a pseudonym used by Street and Smith authors of a particular kind of women's novel with strong gothic characteristics. Reynolds' book provides information on the series and its various authors. Unfortunately, given the current state of dime-novel and story-paper bibliography, the only effective way to discover what gothic material was published by a given source is to go to the collections and search. In an uncataloged collection, the task can be immense.

Several specialized volumes are also of use in searching for gothic material in American fiction. Because most gothic novels are set in the past, information on historical fiction often turns up titles and authors. Especially useful is A. T. Dickinson, Jr.'s *American Historical Fiction,* a briefly annotated checklist by period of history. The book includes author-title and subject indexes, and the annotations are extensive enough to suggest whether the book is a gothic novel. Ernest E. Leisy's study, *The American Historical Novel,* is an excellent guide to titles and authors.

A less useful, because unannotated, listing is Everett F. Bleiler's *The Checklist of Fantastic Literature: A Bibliography of Fantasy, Weird and Science Fiction Books Published in the English Language.* A researcher might find useful information in this volume, but only for the most supernatural manifestations of the gothic and only if the author's name were previously known.

Ordean A. Hagen's *Who Done It? A Guide to Detective, Mystery, and Suspense Fiction* includes many modern gothic authors and titles and is relatively accurate for the major authors. The book usually categorizes the gothic under suspense. A final useful volume is Alice Payne Hackett's *Eighty Years of Best Sellers.* Again, it is most helpful when a particular author is known in advance, but its lists of mystery and detective fiction include some gothic fiction as well.

RESEARCH COLLECTIONS

American popular gothic fiction is found in great profusion in research collections in the United States, although it is rarely identified or cataloged as such. Because the rise of fiction in America coincided with the peak influence of the gothic on popular fiction, many collections of early American fiction are fruitful sources for the researcher. The Lee Ash guide, *Subject Collections*, lists major collections of early American fiction at the American Antiquarian Society, New York University, the Athenaeum of Philadelphia, and the University of Pittsburgh, which has the Hervey Allen Collection of two thousand volumes and related manuscripts in American historical fiction. The most extensive collection of books and manuscripts is at the New York Public Library, which contains over two million volumes. Many libraries, including the Library of Congress, have volumes listed in Lyle H. Wright's bibliographies of early American fiction; efforts to publish on microfiche many of the books listed in Wright's *American Fiction 1774-1900* continue.

Dime-novel and paperback fiction collections are another useful source of popular gothic fiction. The Library of Congress's uncataloged collection of dime novels includes twenty thousand titles. Many of the series contained there consist of gothic romances, including books by Bertha M. Clay and Mrs. E. D. E. N. Southworth, two of the major formula writers using gothic elements in nineteenth-century fiction. Street and Smith's Bertha Clay Library is available there. Ash lists other collections of dime novels at the University of California at Los Angeles, Yale University, the New York Public Library, and New York University. Northern Illinois University, DeKalb, has the Albert Johannsen Collection of eleven hundred cataloged volumes and some related material; the University of Alberta, Canada, has a collection that is especially strong in "penny dreadfuls" and gothics. Both Oberlin College and the Cleveland Public Library have collections; Cleveland is especially good in nineteenth-century romances. Charles Bragin in *Bibliography: Dime Novels, 1860-1964* lists his own collection as the largest private one (1525 W. 12th St., Brooklyn) and adds the University of Minnesota collection.

Major collections of gothic novels, although not mainly American, include the Sadleir-Black Gothic Collection at the University of Virginia (two thousand volumes—see Robert Kerr Black, *The Sadleir-Black Gothic Collection*), the Yale University Library, and the University of California at Los Angeles (three hundred volumes). Two brief published collections that contain American material and are worth noting are edited by Peter Haining (*Gothic Tales of Terror*) and Robert Donald Spector (*Seven Masterpieces of Gothic Horror*). A collection of facsimile reprints (*Gothic Novels*), edited by Devendra Varma, is in progress by Arno Press. One other library collection of interest is the Barnard College Library collection of manuscripts and volumes by American women authors (Bertha Van Riper Overbury Gift). The New York Public Library also contains catalogs of lending libraries and booksellers in the eighteenth and nineteenth centuries.

The Library of Congress Manuscript Division contains the Ernest E. Leisy Collection on the American historical novel. The collection is composed of manuscripts and related material c. 1923-50 (450 items) from work on his published study, *The American Historical Novel.*

Major authors of gothic popular fiction in America are rarely taken seriously enough to have their papers and manuscripts collected by a library. However, the papers of E. D. E. N. Southworth are in the Duke University Library, those of Mary Johnston can be seen at the University of Virginia, and those of Mary Roberts Rinehart (who wrote a few gothics as well as mysteries) are at the University of Pittsburgh.

Because so much fiction of the nineteenth century was serialized, another valuable, although uncataloged, source is nineteenth-century newspapers and story papers. Southworth, for example, wrote for the *New York Ledger,* the *National Era,* the *Saturday Evening Post,* the *New York Weekly* (Street and Smith), and the *Baltimore Saturday Visiter.* For modern gothic novels, the best source for current titles (besides *Publisher's Weekly*) is a mass market bookstore; for novels since the current publishing boom began in 1960, the public library.

The most pressing needs currently in the study of American popular gothic fiction is for finders' guides and bibliographies of dime-novel collections and the collection of papers of the major authors.

HISTORY AND CRITICISM

Most of the relevant critical consideration of gothic novels in America occurs in articles and books on more general or related topics. Only a few authors directly confront the subject, although there is much valuable critical consideration in standard and specialized volumes. Both *The Book in America,* by H. Lehman-Haupt, L. D. Wroth, and Rollo Silver, and *Cheap Book Production in the United States 1870-1891,* by Raymond H. Shove, provide important information about the publishing of popular novels in America. Shove's book is especially valuable for its discussion of the economics of pirating and the impact of the International Copyright Law of 1891 on American book publishing.

General studies on popular literature that include criticism of the gothic and related literature include James D. Hart's *The Popular Book: A History of America's Literary Taste,* a chronological study of popular publishing, a book that is less analytical than it is complete. A better critical survey is contained in Russel Nye's *The Unembarrassed Muse.* The methodology suggested by John G. Cawelti in *Adventure, Mystery, Romance* is particularly fruitful for the study of formulaic literature, the gothic novel included.

For the eighteenth-century gothic novel, there is much critical work available; unfortunately, most of it is of use in the study of American popular gothic material only by way of providing background. If American authors are considered, they are invariably Poe and Hawthorne, not the popular authors of whom Hawthorne complained so eloquently that if "that damned mob of scribbling women" did not lose its hold on the public, his work would never be appreciated.

The chapter "Literary Influences," in Kenneth Clark's *The Gothic Revival: An Essay in the History of Taste,* links the Graveyard Poets and the gothic novelists with the gothic revival in architecture in England. Three specialized studies of the gothic novel in England are Eino Railo's *The Haunted Castle,* Montague Summers' *The Gothic Quest,* and Devendra P. Varma's *The Gothic Flame.* Railo is especially good in his descriptions of the various strains of the gothic in England. Summers is far too much the ideologue and bibliophile for the book to be of critical use; he is interested in "spreading the faith" rather than analysis. Varma, on the other hand, provides a lucid discussion of the gothic novel in England, but is particularly useful because he suggests the various ways that the gothic was diffused in other forms of literature after its heyday. An appendix analyzes the influence of the gothic on the detective novel and his bibliography is extensive. Varma defines the term *gothic* very broadly, unlike Summers.

Edith Birkhead's *The Tale of Terror* is excellent on the supernatural in English gothic fiction, but traces the gothic in America only through Charles Brockden Brown, Poe, Hawthorne, and Irving; she is more interested in the influence of the gothic on serious literature than upon popular culture. Michael Sadleir's "'All Horrid?': Jane Austen and the Gothic Romance" is a fascinating essay describing the novels Austen satirized in *Northanger Abbey.* Two specialized early studies provide background information only. William W. Watt's *Shilling Shockers of the Gothic School: A Study of Chapbook Gothic Romances* is only about British fiction but explains much of the way in which serious gothic literature became watered-down for the pulp audience. Dorothy Blakey's *The Minerva Press 1790-1820* is a basic study of one of the popular publishers in Britain that put out gothic material. Unfortunately, no similar study has been done of an American publisher.

Worthy of note is Lowry Nelson, Jr.'s "Night Thoughts on the Gothic Novel," especially for its suggestive discussion of the gothic hero/villain.

Of little use in the study of popular gothic fiction is Robert D. Hume and Robert L. Platzner's exchange on the gothic in *PMLA*.

Much more to the point than any of the preceding studies of the gothic, for purposes of analysis of popular novels, is a quasi-serious short article by Clell T. Peterson, "Spotting the Gothic Novel," in *Graduate Student of English*. Peterson lists sixteen characteristics of the gothic novel, most of which are applicable to modern gothic fiction as well as earlier versions.

General studies of American literature that are especially good on the gothic include Alexander Cowie's *The Rise of the American Novel*. Cowie says that the American novel never really developed a gothic tradition (a debatable assumption), but his analysis of Charles Brockden Brown, Lippard's *The Quaker City*, and Mitchell's *Alonzo and Melissa* is particularly fine. Cowie also suggests that Indians and the dangers of the West substitute in American fiction for gothic castles and villains. Edward Wagenknecht in *Cavalcade of the American Novel* has an excellent chapter on women novelists, emphasizing their use of sensational material, although he does not call it specifically *gothic*. He has a section on the novels of Mary Johnston, which he expanded in an essay in *Sewanee Review*, "The World and Mary Johnston." Two studies of the early American novel are also interesting. Lily D. Loshe's 1907 book, *The Early American Novel*, covers the period from 1789 to 1830. It is sketchy, but was only superseded by Henri Petter's *The Early American Novel* in 1971. Petter is a German scholar who analyzes American uses of gothic conventions in his chapter "Mystery and Terror." He is also suggestive when he writes about the general attack on novel reading in the period, which often was an attack on women's novels in general and the gothic in particular. Most of the attack was focused upon novels as a "waste of time" and "not true," although the supposed pernicious influence of such fiction on suggestible young female minds also came in for its share of criticism.

Leslie Fiedler's *Love and Death in the American Novel* deals more directly with gothic novels than with any of the others, although he draws his definitions too narrowly. Most suggestive is his theory of the connection between death and the orgasm, with the approach of danger in the gothic representing a strong sexual urge toward death. Since in most gothic fiction, the culmination of the love story and the salvation from danger are simultaneous, his argument seems relevant.

Other studies are variously useful. Oral Sumner Coad's "The Gothic Element in American Literature Before 1835" is an influential analytical survey. George L. Phillips' "The Gothic Element in the American Novel Before 1830" is similarly useful. O. W. Long's "Werther in America" traces the influence of Goethe on American fiction, while Jane Lundblad's *Nathaniel Hawthorne and the Tradition of the Gothic Romance* shows how Hawthorne adapted gothic elements in his own work. Neither is especially relevant to the study of popular fiction, although both should be consulted for definitions of the gothic. G. H. Orians' "Censure of Fiction in American Magazines and Romances 1789-1810" is not directly relevant, either, but provides useful background on American attitudes toward the novel. Since the gothic did not develop a full-fledged tradition in America, at least partly because of the American preference for literal and didactic literature, the thesis is interesting.

Of specific value in the study of early American gothic fiction is Sister Mary Mauritia Redden's *The Gothic Fiction in the American Magazines (1765-1800)*. She includes both definitions of the characteristics of British and American gothic fiction and plot summaries of gothic fiction in American magazines. She says that the gothic first appeared in American magazines in 1785; almost all of the stories in the period were anonymous imitations of Ann Radcliffe. The appendices include magazine lists, bibliography, and a chronological listing of stories.

On the dime novels and the "scribbling women," there are several good critical studies, although Fred L. Pattee's *The Feminine Fifties* is far too sketchy and lacks a bibliography. Much better is Herbert Ross Brown's classic study *The Sentimental Novel in America 1789-1860*. Brown never cites gothic novels as such, but his analytical study deals with gothic novelists and conventions in a general survey of sentimental fiction. Brown indicates his aim is "to trace in popular fiction some manifestations of the sentimental mind." He succeeds; the study is constantly cited and has never been superseded. Helen Waite Papashvily's *All the Happy Endings* covers the same ground, although she is probably too breezy and her strong feminist slant sometimes gets in the way of objective analysis. Her argument that women's escape fiction in the period was a way of getting back at a male society seems too facile. The bibliography of secondary sources is good up to 1954 but is not annotated. The book also lacks a good list of primary material. An essay-length study of similar usefulness is Alexander Cowie's "The Vogue of the Domestic Novel."

On periodical literature of the type, the most comprehensive work is Mary Noel's *Villains Galore: The Heyday of the Popular Story Weekly*. The book is useful on publishers and publications, but it is superficial and lacks a bibliography. It has no system for analysis of plot and type of story. The same criticism might be leveled at Harry B. Weiss's *A Book About Chapbooks: The People's Literature of Bygone Times*. However, his chapter on American chapbooks is interesting.

Three studies in related areas are of much more interest as critical analysis, even if not directly on gothic fiction. Katharine West's *Chapter of Governesses: A Study of the Governess in English Fiction 1800-1949* is especially relevant since so many gothic novels have governesses as protagonists. She suggests that a governess is an appropriate heroine for novels about women as victims because of her anomalous place in the household (usually a house that lends itself to gothic horror) and her ability to find a family of her own through vicarious involvement in her employer's family. The prevalence of governesses as heroines from Brontë through James to the modern gothic novels indicates the usefulness of her argument. Barbara Welter's "The Cult of True Womanhood" delin-eates the feminine ideal for the nineteenth century and, in the process, indicates how certain types of escape fiction might have filled feminine psychological needs. Chapter eight of David Grimsted's *Melodrama Un-veiled* is the best single analysis of the place of the love story in gothic fiction, because the romantic world view of the nineteenth-century melo-drama was very close to that of the gothic at many points.

For individual authors, very few specialized studies exist. An exception is Regis Louise Boyle's *Mrs. E. D. E. N. Southworth*. The only full-length study of this author or of any of her contemporaries, it is especially fine on bibliographic material. Boyle notes that contemporary reviewers of Southworth compared her work to that of Currer Bell (Charlotte Brontë).

Analysis of modern gothic novels is confined almost entirely to jour-nalistic sources. Phyllis Whitney's "Writing the Gothic Novel" defines what she means by the kind of writing she does and castigates exploiters of the formula; she insists that the male pulp writers of gothics who use feminine pseudonyms are not true gothic writers. *Time* and *Newsweek* have both discussed the revival of the form and some of its authors in "Extricating Emily" and "On the Road to Manderley" in *Time* and "Heath-cliff: Cliff-Hangers" in *Newsweek*. A satirical piece in the *New York Times Book Review* by Gary Jennings, "Heathcliff Doesn't Smoke L and M's," is a humorous male view of the excesses of women's gothic fiction. A side-bar by Lewis Nichols, "The Gothic Story," cites figures and facts about gothic publication in 1969. Good sources of reviews are Anthony Boucher in the New York *Times* and Lenore Glen Offord in the San Francisco *Chronicle* during the 1960s. *Publisher's Weekly* since the early 1960s has contained many advertisements for gothic novels. And there is much to indicate that gothic novel publishers are searching for a wider audience with the expensive advertising now being given to the new erotic and historical gothics of such writers as Lolah Burford, Rosemary Rogers, and Kathleen Woodiwiss. (A new fragrance has been developed to aid in the marketing of Burford's *Alyx*.) "Beautiful and Damned: The Sexual Woman in Modern Gothic Fiction," by Kay Mussell, is a brief analysis of the part played by the beautiful woman in contemporary gothics. Two unpublished doctoral dissertations deal with women and the gothic: Raymond Winfield Mise, "The Gothic Heroine and the Nature of the Gothic Novel," and Kay J. Mussell, "The World of Modern Gothic Fiction: American Women and Their Social Myths."

It is evident that critical consideration of gothic fiction in America has merely scratched the surface. Much remains to be done, but comprehensive critical analysis of the formula must wait for the basic bibliographic work that would serve to define and locate the material for the researcher.

BIBLIOGRAPHY

Ash, Lee. *Subject Collections. A Guide to Special Book Collections and Subject Emphases as Reported by University, College, Public, and Special Libraries and Museums in the United States and Canada.* 4th ed. New York: R. R. Bowker, 1974.

————, and Dennis Lorenz. *Subject Collections. A Guide to Special Book Collections and Subject Emphases as Reported by University, College, Public, and Special Libraries in the United States and Canada.* 3rd ed. New York: R. R. Bowker, 1967.

Baker, Ernest A. *A Guide to the Best Fiction in English.* London: George Routledge, 1913.

Birkhead, Edith. *The Tale of Terror.* New York: E. P. Dutton, 1921. Reprint. New York: Russell and Russell, 1963.

Black, Robert Kerr. "The Sadlier-Black Gothic Collection." An Address Before the Bibliographic Society of the University of Virginia, University of Virginia Library. Charlottesville: University Press of Virginia, 1949.

Blakey, Dorothy. *The Minerva Press 1790-1820.* London: Oxford University Press, 1939.

Bleiler, Everett F. *The Checklist of Fantastic Literature: A Bibliography of Fantasy, Weird and Science Fiction Books Published in the English Language.* Chicago: Shasta, 1948.

Boyle, Regis Louise. *Mrs. E. D. E. N. Southworth, Novelist.* Washington, D. C.: Catholic University Press, 1939.

Bragin, Charles. *Bibliography: Dime Novels, 1860-1964.* Rev. ed. Brooklyn, N.Y.: Dime Novel Club, 1964.

Brown, Herbert Ross. *The Sentimental Novel in America 1789-1860.* Durham, N.C.: Duke University Press, 1940; Reprint. New York: Octagon Books, 1975.

Cawelti, John G. *Adventure, Mystery, and Romance: Formula Stories as Art and Popular Culture.* Chicago: University of Chicago Press, 1976.

Clark, Kenneth. *The Gothic Revival: An Essay in the History of Taste.* London: Constable, 1928, 1950; Murray, 1962; New York: Holt, Rinehart and Winston, 1962; Humanities Press, 1970.

Coad, Oral Sumner. "The Gothic Element in American Literature Before 1835." *Journal of English and Germanic Philology,* 24 (January 1925), 72-93.

Cowie, Alexander. *The Rise of the American Novel.* New York: American Book Co., 1948, 1951.

———. "The Vogue of the Domestic Novel," *South Atlantic Quarterly,* 41 (October 1942), 416-25.

Dickinson, A. T., Jr. *American Historical Fiction,* 3rd ed. Metuchen, N.J.: Scarecrow Press, 1971.

Duffy, Martha. "On the Road to Manderley," *Time,* 97 (April 12, 1971), 95-96.

"Extricating Emily," *Time,* 87 (April 22, 1966), 88.

Fiedler, Leslie A. *Love and Death in the American Novel.* New York: Criterion, 1960. Reprint. New York: Dell, 1966.

Grimsted, David. *Melodrama Unveiled.* Chicago: University of Chicago Press, 1968.

Hackett, Alice Payne. *Eighty Years of Best Sellers.* New York: R. R. Bowker, 1977.

Hagen, Ordean A. *Who Done It? A Guide to Detective, Mystery, and Suspense Fiction.* New York: R. R. Bowker, 1969.

Haining, Peter, comp. *Gothic Tales of Terror.* 2 vols. Baltimore: Penguin Books, 1972.

Hart, James D. *The Popular Book: A History of America's Literary Taste.* New York: Oxford University Press, 1950. Reprint. Westport, Conn.: Greenwood, 1976.

"Heathcliff: Cliffhangers," *Newsweek* (April 24, 1966), 101-02.

Hemenway, Robert, and D. H. Keller. "A Checklist of Biography and Criticism." *Papers of the Bibliographic Society of America* 60 (July-September 1966), 349-62.

Hume, Robert D. "Gothic Versus Romantic: A Revaluation of the Gothic Novel." *PMLA,* 84 (March 1969), 282-90; see also Hume and Robert L. Platzner. "Gothic v. Romantic: A Rejoinder." *PMLA,* 86 (March 1971), 266-74.

Jennings, Gary. "Heathcliff Doesn't Smoke L and M's." *New York Times Book Review,* July 27, 1969, pp. 4-5, 24-25.

Johannsen, Albert. *The House of Beadle and Adams.* Norman: University of Oklahoma Press, 1950, 1962.

Krause, S. J., and Jane Nilset. "A Census of the Works." *Serif,* 3 (December 1966), 27-57.

Lehman-Haupt, H.; L. C. Wroth; and Rollo Silver. *The Book in America.* New York: R. R. Bowker, 1952.

Leisy, Ernest E. *The American Historical Novel.* Norman: University of Oklahoma Press, 1950.

Long, O. W. "Werther in America." In *Studies in Honor of John Albrecht Walz.* Lancaster, Pa.: Lancaster Press, 1941; Reprint, Freeport, N.Y.: Books for Libraries Press (Essay Index Reprint Series), 1968.

Loshe, Lily D. *The Early American Novel, 1789-1830.* New York: Columbia University Press, 1907. Reprint. New York: Ungar, 1966.

Lundblad, Jane. *Nathaniel Hawthorne and the Tradition of the Gothic Romance.* Cambridge, Mass.: Harvard University Press, 1946. Reprint. New York: Haskell House, 1964.

McNutt, Dan J. *The Eighteenth-Century Gothic Novel: An Annotated Bibliog-*

raphy of Criticism and Selected Texts. New York: Garland Publishing Co., 1975.

Microbook Library of American Civilization. *Author Catalog and Title Catalog,* edited by Herman C. Bernick. Chicago: Library Resources, 1972.

Mise, Raymond Winfield. "The Gothic Heroine and the Nature of the Gothic Novel." Ph.D. dissertation, University of Washington, 1970.

Mott, Frank Luther. *Golden Multitudes.* New York: Macmillan, 1947.

Mussell, Kay J. "Beautiful and Damned: The Sexual Woman in Modern Gothic Fiction." *Journal of Popular Culture,* 9 (Summer 1975), 84-89.

———. "The World of Modern Gothic Fiction: American Women and Their Social Myths." Ph.D. dissertation, University of Iowa, 1973.

Nelson, Lowry, Jr. "Night Thoughts on the Gothic Novel." *Yale Review,* 52 (December 1962), 236-57.

Nichols, Lewis. "The Gothic Story." *New York Times Book Review,* July 27, 1969, p. 25.

Noel, Mary. *Villains Galore: The Heyday of the Popular Story Weekly.* New York: Macmillan, 1954.

Nye, Russel. *The Unembarrassed Muse.* New York: Dial, 1970.

Orians, G. H. "Censure of Fiction in American Magazines and Romances 1789-1810." *PMLA,* 52 (March 1937), 195-214.

Papashvily, Helen Waite. *All the Happy Endings.* New York: Harper, 1956. Reprint. Port Washington, N.Y.: Kennikat, 1972.

Pattee, F. L. *The Feminine Fifties.* New York: Appleton-Century, 1940.

Pearson, Edmund. *Dime Novels.* Boston: Little, Brown, 1929. Reprint. Port Washington, N.Y.: Kennikat, 1968.

Peterson, Clell T. "Spotting the Gothic Novel." *Graduate Student of English,* 1 (1957), 14-15.

Petter, Henri. *The Early American Novel.* Columbus: Ohio State University Press, 1971.

Phillips, George L. "The Gothic Element in the American Novel Before 1830." *West Virginia University Bulletin: Philological Studies,* 3 (September 1939), 37-45.

Quinn, Arthur Hobson. *American Fiction: An Historical and Critical Survey.* New York: Appleton-Century Crofts, 1936, 1964.

Railo, Eino. *The Haunted Castle.* London: George Routledge, 1927. Reprint. New York: Gordon Press, 1974.

Redden, Sister Mary Mauritia. *The Gothic Fiction in the American Magazines (1765-1800).* Washington, D.C.: Catholic University Press, 1939.

Reynolds, Quentin. *The Fiction Factory.* New York: Random House, 1955.

Sadleir, Michael. " 'All Horrid?': Jane Austen and the Gothic Romance." In *Things Past.* London: Constable, 1944.

Shove, Raymond H. *Cheap Book Production in the United States, 1870-1891.* Urbana: University of Illinois Press, 1937.

Smith, Warren Hunting. "Recent Acquisitions in Gothic Fiction." *Yale University Library Gazette,* 8 (1934), 109-11.

Spector, Robert Donald, ed. *Seven Masterpieces of Gothic Horror.* New York: Bantam, 1963.

Summers, Montague. *A Gothic Bibliography*. London: Fortune, 1941, 1969. Reprint. New York: Russell and Russell, 1964.

————. *The Gothic Quest*. London: Fortune, 1938; New York: Russell and Russell, 1964.

Tebbel, John W. *A History of Book Publishing in the United States*. New York: R. R. Bowker, 1972.

Varma, Devendra P. *The Gothic Flame*. New York: Russell and Russell, 1957, 1966.

————, ed. *Gothic Novels*, 40 vols. New York: New York Times/Arno, 1971-.

Wagenknecht, Edward. *Cavalcade of the American Novel*. New York: Holt, Rinehart and Winston, 1952.

————. "The World and Mary Johnston." *Sewanee Review*, 44 (April-June 1936), 188-206.

Watt, William W. *Shilling Shockers of the Gothic School: A Study of Chapbook Gothic Romances*. Cambridge, Mass.: Harvard University Press, 1932. Reprint. New York: Russell and Russell, 1967.

Weiss, Harry B. *A Book About Chapbooks: The People's Literature of Bygone Times*. Ann Arbor, Mich.: Edwards Brothers, 1942. Reprint. Hatboro, Pa.: Folklore Associates, 1969.

Welter, Barbara. "The Cult of True Womanhood." *American Quarterly*, 18 (Summer 1966), 151-74.

West, Katharine. *Chapter of Governesses: A Study of the Governess in English Fiction 1800-1949*. London: Cohen and West, 1949.

Whitney, Phyllis A. "Writing the Gothic Novel." *The Writer*, 80 (February 1967), 9-13, 42-43.

Wright, Lyle H. *American Fiction 1774-1850*. San Marino, Calif.: Huntington Library, 1939.

————. *American Fiction 1774-1900*. Louisville, Ky.: Lost Cause Press, 1970.

CHAPTER 8 Popular Music
Mark W. Booth

The idea that popular music deserves serious attention is recent but already widespread. Increasing acceptance of the idea is shown by the growing bulk of writing devoted to popular music, both in the forms and places implying an audience of scholars and in books for the general reading public. Some of these trade books, especially those directed to fans of recent or current popular music, reflect the results and methods of academic study: they present themselves as history, discography, collective or individual biography, or encyclopedic reference. The study, or at least the display, of popular culture is itself becoming a form of popular culture.

Within this proliferation of writing there is a body of careful and useful study of American popular music of the present and past; most of it has been written in the last two decades. The recent date of many of the books that will be mentioned here reflects an early stage of respectability and maturity reached by popular music studies. Essential discographic and other scholarly tools are emerging. A great deal of data has been assembled, and fundamental history and analysis have begun. The challenge remains of what best use to make of the tools for the purpose of coming to terms with what is being recognized and rediscovered. Much careful attention and much intelligence have been invested in the study of popular music. More history is yet to be written, more sociological analysis, more musicological description and more critical study of lyrics. Yet if popular music studies are treated only by the separate methods of the scholarly disciplines, as if they were only more fine art or more social behavior, the results will not be fully satisfactory. The array of tools that has been assembled suggests that new questions and new methods or combinations of methods are needed for the next stage of maturity.

HISTORIC OUTLINE

While thoughtful attention to popular music is relatively new, the music itself has been vigorously alive in this country for a long time. Some of the music brought to the New World by the colonists was serious academic music; some was what we now call *folk music*, belonging to the community by tradition and freely. Some, however, was popular music, printed and sold in broadsides and song books or performed by professional entertainers to paying audiences. The source of this popular music was the mother countries of the new Americans, chiefly England. The same ballads sold in the streets of London were sold in the colonial American cities and towns; the same ballad operas and other musical entertainments were heard in English and American theaters.

During the eighteenth century an increasing amount of this popular music was written in the colonies for colonists. During the years of the Revolution, the sentiments of Americans were expressed in anti-British broadsides that could hardly have been imported, but a significant number of these broadsides were specific parodies of British songs. They set anti-British words to British music. As such they remained, however rebellious, colonial popular music. The forms of the lyrics as well as of the music were indebted to the model brought over from England.

To decide, then, where we can mark the beginning of American popular music, it is necessary to find the stage in the developing history of music that has been enjoyed by Americans where not only the actual writing, printing, and selling of the music take place on American ground, but where the product itself has an American quality—some flavor that is not borrowed or inherited.

English music remained in the American marketplace throughout the nineteenth century, but it gradually became mixed with, then edged by, popular music that is distinctly native. Where this genuine American popular music really began cannot be said for certain. A sign of the beginning can be located in 1827. Among the few scattered relics of the music sold or professionally performed a century and a half ago that we know were hits of the day, two songs suggest in retrospect that that year marks a turning point. In *Variety Music Cavalcade 1620-1969*, Julius Mattfeld, the editor, lists four prominent songs for 1827 and of the four, two, "My Long-Tail Blue" and "The Coal-Black Rose," were popularized by the minstrel singer George Washington Dixon. Dixon, whom Mattfeld calls "a Negro minstrel," was a white man performing in blackface. He was neither the first nor the most successful performer in that masquerade tradition, which was still alive more than a century later, but he can be taken to represent with these two hits an emblem, or a portent, of the course of American popular music. The native American note we are looking for was struck in the meeting of Afro-American and Euro-American styles.

Most popular songs in the years after 1827 continued to be the work of English writers or indistinguishable from English work; tunes continued to be borrowed, as the tunes of "Yankee Doodle" and "The Star-Spangled Banner" had been borrowed, from English songs, but a new way had been opened. The music that slaves brought with them from west Africa evolved into an Afro-American folk music and then evolved into a variety of styles of professional performance for black audiences. In themselves these styles are an American popular music. Throughout their history, in all their forms, they have also exerted an influence on the shaping of the rest of American popular music.

Alec Wilder argues that the first truly native American popular songs are those a generation after George Washington Dixon, at the next stage of interaction between black and white music, the songs of Stephen Foster. Foster was influenced not only by the minstrel mimicry of slave music but also by Negro church music. After Foster's death in 1864, Wilder contends, the disruption of the Civil War and Reconstruction in the lives and culture of black men and women kept black music away from the ears of white Americans, and popular music entered a recession that ended in the 1890s when the sounds of ragtime played by young black pianists began to be heard by a white public. The distinctively American feeling that derived from ragtime rhythm enters the mainstream of those major songwriters of the twentieth century whose work Wilder traces. Often very remote from ragtime—or from the successors of ragtime, blues and jazz—American music continued to show the rhythmic and harmonic signs of inspiration from the black tradition, from Tin Pan Alley to swing bands to rock, with a contribution by the way to country and western.

Popular music is a marketplace art. American popular music was the commercial extension of the eighteenth-century publishing and theater business as it had evolved in London and been imitated in New York. This publishing and theater system, in nineteenth-century American cities and towns, met with an American buying public and gradually learned to offer that public music flavored by American folk music styles, most distinctively black music. The evolution came slowly, and when something clearly American predominated at the end of the nineteenth century, it was the product both of American musicians and of the American genius for commercial promotion. (An entertaining account of this evolution is given in the first chapter of Ian Whitcomb's *After the Ball*.) A massive market was sought out, or built, by promoters and salesmen for shows, for sheet music, and for pianos to play the music. Some of the sold entertainment still had, at the turn of the century, the prestige of being European, but the booming American music business drew on a growing body of native writers and performers and sold to a public gaining in cultural self-confidence in spite of itself.

Thomas Edison built the first phonograph in 1877, but for half a century phonograph records would be only a smaller or larger minority of popular music sales. Joseph Murrells, in his *Book of Golden Discs*, supplies the lore of successful recordings: the first to sell a million in 1902 and a couple of dozen of them by the 1920s for home phonographs and juke boxes.

At the opening of the twentieth century the decisive influence of the ragtime pianists fell on white audiences tiring of the minstrel show and willing to pay to hear black performers. At the same time the American band was being heard everywhere, promoted by John Philip Sousa, the most successful musician of his time, and testifying among other things to pugnacious nationalism. Both phenomena would modulate into dance bands playing vigorous dance music. Burgeoning displays of sheet music in neighborhood stores, often music calling itself *rag*, attracted a diverse public, much of which never heard the concerts of the creators of ragtime. Modest as well as prosperous homes had a keyboard, either a piano or the less expensive reed organ: the industry built 107,000 harmoniums a year in 1900, and 177,000 pianos. By 1909, the figure was 364,000 pianos. Piano music was available beyond the proportion of the population that could play: by 1925, more than half the pianos produced were automatics, using player rolls for current hits (see Cyril Ehrlich, *The Piano: a History*). Such instruments, giving out more and better sound than the evolving phonograph had yet mastered, tuned the audience more closely than ever before to the latest fad in music.

A boom in social dancing began during the second decade of the twentieth century, along with the first recognition of music called *jazz*. Nat Shapiro quotes *Variety* as estimating that in the mid-1920s there were 60,000 dance bands playing on the dance floors of jazz age America. Beginning in 1920, radio broadcasting brought recorded and live music into homes, posing an economic challenge to pianos and combining with the Depression in 1929 to decimate record and phonograph sales. The music that America absorbed through these media came mostly from New York, from Tin Pan Alley publishing houses and from the flourishing Broadway stage, reproduced also in vaudeville houses across the country. When in the middle of the 1920s recording engineers developed microphones to replace recording horns, a new softer "crooning" performance became possible and stylish on records and over the radio.

Al Jolson's songs on screen in 1927 opened another medium. When the Depression crippled the New York musical theater, Hollywood studios became the patrons of much of professional songwriting, for the movies that were the country's largest entertainment indulgence during the 1930s. The record industry struggled back late in the decade, dominated by the big swing bands and their vocalists. As the war overtook the United States, a significant economic struggle surfaced in musical entertainment. The American Society of Composers, Authors, and Publishers (ASCAP) had been formed in 1914 to collect performance royalties for the owners of song copyrights. By 1939 it held monopoly power over popular music performance, and a contract dispute with radio broadcasters led to the formation of Broadcast Music Incorporated (BMI) as a rival guild. Following a ten-month interval in 1941 during which no ASCAP music could be played on the radio, causing a boom in classical, folk, and public domain music generally, ASCAP entered into a new broadcast contract, but BMI continued and grew. BMI, growing out of the dispute where its rival stood for established interests, came to represent popular music from outside the New York-Hollywood establishment, and local markets compared with the network emphasis of ASCAP. An institution had appeared to reflect the regional, rural, and minority interests in the music world that would gain great audience support after the war.

When the war ended, the entertainment industry responded to the ready money of a new public, more urbanized, but less in touch with Broadway sophistication, and with expanding young families preparing to be the next generation of popular music consumers—raised with unprecedented pocket money and leisure time and with an unsuspected susceptibility to the energies of rock and roll they would first hear in 1954. Carl Belz describes the recording industry in the years after the war as dividing its market in the interest of stability and consequently producing for the general market dull, or at least highly controlled and predictable, music. Small independent record companies sold to the country and Western and rhythm and blues markets, while the major companies guided the music of the largest pop market down a narrow channel, with a slow succession of new songs and much repetitive recording by competing stars.

Rock and roll, which the industry learned to ride to a staggering new sales volume, also jarred that industry into new patterns: new companies, new small-group recording economics, new audience definitions, and new relationships to radio broadcasting. Some of the story can be told in terms of technical innovations. Television as the surging home entertainment medium turned radio stations toward the disc jockey format of record programming. New sizes, speeds, and materials for the records themselves may have had wide implications. Belz makes an interesting analysis of the cultural meaning of the shift from 78 to 45 rpm records, as streamlining the experience of recorded music toward casualness, especially for young audiences, while their parents bought the more substantial 33 long-playing records that emerged at the same time in the early 1950s. The later movement of rock and its audience into long-playing records reflects the triumphing cultural and economic power of the same young generation, along with a growing seriousness and self-confidence of the makers of rock music.

The relationship of popular culture to ideology in the 1960s and into the 1970s has become of interest to academic sociology, although the alarmed interest of politicians has given way to accommodation. The relationship of the entertainment favored by highly visible classes of teenagers and young adults to the behavior of that audience, and especially its use of drugs, is probably now still too current an issue for full perspective and confident judgment. The history of popular music suggests that it is very unlikely that musical entertainment can induce new behavior, or even introduce new ideas to the audience it must court in order to sell itself. Though popular music has been blamed in the past for undermining community standards or otherwise damaging society, it is a new phenomenon for popular music to have the pervasive presence that prosperity and the portable radio and tape deck have given it lately, and for such conspicuous economic power to be vested in a youth audience. The history of popular music that is now happening cannot be fully schematized and managed by the patterns of earlier popular music. Its development has always been contingent, surprising, and even discontinuous except when we rationalize it with hindsight, and it is continuing that unpredictable development now.

As rock has evolved in the last quarter of a century and brought, among other things, self-conscious seriousness to popular music, it has prompted an immense volume of reportage and analysis, much of it empty but some perceptive and judicious. The attention that rock has demanded has occasioned the first widespread, serious critical attention to the popular arts in general. Nostalgia, publicity promotion, and the university environment of a part of the proprietary audience of rock have contributed to the growing critical and scholarly interest in popular music of the past as well as the present. We are in the process of discovering a heritage; it is certain to contribute to the understanding of our own culture.

REFERENCE WORKS

While the careful study of popular culture is recent and spotty, music history is an established discipline, and the apparatus of music bibliography and discography has been extended with energy and professional rigor to order the new field of study. The most useful device for managing the rest of the apparatus is now David Horn's *Literature of American Music in Books and Folk Music Collections: A Fully Annotated Bibliography*, which is generously inclusive and carefully descriptive of popular music materials. Also useful is the much more selective listing, often deftly evaluative, in Richard Jackson's *United States Music: Sources of Bibliography and Collective Biography*. Some listings relevant to popular music are also given in the second and third editions of Vincent Duckles' standard

Music Reference and Research Materials: An Annotated Bibliography. Much less useful is the *Chicorel Bibliography to Books on Music and Musicians,* edited by Marietta Chicorel, volume 10 of a general bibliographical series that gives trade information on books in print. The Chicorel series is processed by an apparently quirky computer, and not well proofread. A few specialized studies are listed by Rita H. Mead, *Doctoral Dissertations in American Music: a Classified Bibliography.* Review-like commentary is given to a few significant books in the *Guide to the Study of the United States of America: Representative Books Reflecting the Development of American Life and Thought,* by Donald H. Mugridge and Blanche P. McCrum, published by the Library of Congress, although even its new supplement covers only books published through 1965. New books are listed, and significant new books are reviewed, in *Notes: the Quarterly Journal of the Music Library Association.* Reviews in this journal, by authoritative scholars of music history, often offer useful perspectives on current studies; in the last decade coverage of works on popular music has increased. Books in the border areas between popular music and folklore are reviewed in the *JEMF Quarterly.* Books on black music are listed and reviewed in *Black Perspective in Music.*

A succession of directories have been compiled to provide access to songs printed in books by means of a master index. These works, covering a range of song collections that might be expected to be found in a large public library, locate the text and tune of a song when the title is known. The first of them grew out of a project of the American Library Association for assisting reference librarians in answering queries. It was the *Song Index,* published in 1926 by Minnie Sears. A *Supplement* followed in 1934. Robert Leigh's *Index to Song Books* in 1964 is a continuation; *Songs in Collections, an Index,* by Desiree De Charms and Paul F. Breed, is a fuller continuation. The most recent, for song books published between 1940 and 1972, is the *Popular Song Index,* by Patricia Pate Havlice. They are best considered as a set and used with the awareness that their reference lists are quite different, and what is not in one may be in the other.

These library tools for tracking down a song that may be printed in a book are eclectic: Havlice, for example, indexes such books as *Korea Sings* and the *Pooh Song Book* along with compilations of Broadway lyrics and pop hits. They give no information about a song except where to find it. The song book in which a song is listed must be evaluated for accuracy if accuracy of text or tune transcription is relevant to the inquiry.

Distinct from the indexes are the various lists and chronologies of popular songs at large, defined as popular and included whether available in a book or not. Nat Shapiro has edited six volumes of *Popular Music: an Annotated Index of American Popular Songs.* Volume numbers do not line up with periods covered in sequence: Volume I, 1950-1959; Volume II,

1940-1949; Volume III, 1960-1964; Volume IV, 1930-1939; Volume V, 1920-1929; Volume VI, 1965-1969. In each volume Shapiro selects popular and otherwise significant songs and ranges them by year, giving writers, composers, and principal performers identified with a given song. His set is the widest general inventory of popular songs for the years it covers. Fewer songs, selected from a longer span of years, are cataloged in another work that began its life as a librarian's locator file, Julius Mattfeld's *Variety Music Cavalcade, 1620-1969: a Chronology of Vocal and Instrumental Music Popular in the United States.* (At an intermediate stage it was serialized in *Variety* magazine.) Although Mattfeld's title indicates sweeping coverage, the years before 1800 are covered in less than nine pages of history. Still his coverage is extensive for a century before Shapiro's listings begin. Both Shapiro and Mattfeld include material valuable for understanding the context of the songs they list. Mattfeld concludes the listing for each year in the nineteenth and twentieth centuries with a compilation of miscellaneous historical notes, including both major historical events and suggestive trivia. Shapiro includes in every volume but the first an essay on the development of popular music during the period covered, and together his introductions make an excellent brief history of the subject in the twentieth century.

Fuller for its field than either Shapiro or Mattfeld is Richard Lewine and Alfred Simon's *Songs of the American Theater: a Comprehensive Listing of More than 12,000 Songs, including Selected Titles from Film and Television Productions.* Lewine and Simon cover the years from 1925 through 1971, and they marshal more than twice as many titles as in all of Mattfeld. John H. Chipman's *Index to Top-Hit Tunes (1900-1950)* selects some three thousand songs by sales success. David Ewen, the most prolific popular historian of popular music, has compiled *American Popular Songs from the Revolutionary War to the Present* with anecdotal commentary. The *Index of American Popular Music,* by Jack Burton, is a cross-reference index to three volumes he has edited: *Blue Book of Tin Pan Alley: a Human Interest Encyclopedia of American Popular Music, Blue Book of Broadway Musicals,* and *Blue Book of Hollywood Musicals.* Together, the set provides a substantial body of information, especially on songs by major writers. Reviewers have cautioned of errors and omissions, and more recent works may be preferred.

A large listing makes up volume one, *Music Year by Year 1900-1950,* in the four-volume set of the *Complete Encyclopedia of Popular Music and Jazz 1900-1950,* edited by Roger D. Kinkle. Two of the other volumes collect biographical articles that also inventory the works of writers and artists, and the fourth volume contains indexes and various kinds of supplemental lists. For the years it covers, Kinkle's work is the most massive treasury of information on popular music gathered under a single title.

Where it is most comprehensive, it is not always fullest. The other works listed, except Chipman, define areas not entirely taken in by Kinkle's range (which is itself very wide since it aims to incorporate jazz).

Finally among the general inventories of popular songs the *Stecheson Classified Song Directory*, calculated "for the use of the music industry," groups a similarly huge repertory of songs by the supposed subject of the lyric. "If you wanted to compile a program of songs about the skies," as the editor suggests, or about numbers, nurses, or nuts, or anything else, this is the right book. It is probably less valuable for its designed purpose to scholars than to disc jockeys, but it has another value as a survey of what the subjects of popular songs have been.

RESEARCH COLLECTIONS

Archives where printed and recorded popular music are collected are widely scattered. (Note the availability of a great variety of filmed musical performances through film rental agencies.) While most public libraries maintain some collection of popular music on record, few have assembled really large inventories, which are likelier to be in the possession of radio stations. There are, of course, many private enthusiasts who have assembled large personal collections of records; for rock and modern pop, these collectors are mostly too young to have passed their collections on to public institutions. The largest collection of recorded music is in the Rodgers and Hammerstein Archives of Recorded Sound of the New York Public Library, located at the Performing Arts Research Center in Lincoln Center.

More numerous significant collections exist of music on paper. Libraries with such holdings can be located through the R. R. Bowker Company's book *Subject Collections: a Guide to Special Book Collections and Subject Emphases as Reported by University, College, Public, and Special Libraries and Museums in the United States and Canada*, compiled by Lee Ash; and less easily, by reference to particular libraries or by state groupings under "music" in the index, in the *Directory of Special Libraries and Information Centers*, edited by Margaret Labash Young and others.

The greatest single collection of sheet music is in the Americana Collection of the Music Division, New York Public Library, also housed at the Performing Arts Research Center. Other collections of early sheet music are located at Brown University in Providence, Rhode Island; the Kean Archives in Philadelphia; the Buffalo and Erie County Public Library; the Minneapolis Public Library; and the Harmony Foundation in Kenosha, Wisconsin. Many other public libraries report some accumulation of sheet music.

Special song indexes to holdings are provided by the public libraries of

New York City, Newark, San Diego, Cleveland, Detroit, and perhaps other cities. Collections of song books are reported by the library of the University of California, Los Angeles; the Berkshire Athenaeum in Pittsfield, Massachusetts; the American Antiquarian Society in Worcester, Massachusetts; the New York Historical Society in New York City; and the Free Library of Philadelphia.

The great Archive of Folk Song at the Library of Congress is primarily a repository of field recordings and a center of folklore research, but its materials may be sometimes relevant to the study of popular music. Among the bibliographies provided by the archive on request are those on Charles Edward "Chuck" Berry; Blues; Country and Western Music; Bob Dylan; Folksong Revival; and "She Is More to be Pitied than Censured."

Collections of black music are located at the State University of New York at Buffalo; Indiana University School of Music (Indiana University also has a Black Music Center); the Rutgers Institute of Jazz Studies in Newark; and at the William Hogan Archives of New Orleans Jazz at Tulane University. The Free Library of Philadelphia also has a jazz collection.

Nashville has the Country Music Foundation Library and Media Center.

There are two major collections of Broadway materials: the Institute of the American Musical, Incorporated, in New York City; and the Collection of the Literature of the American Musical Theater at Yale University, New Haven, Connecticut.

HISTORY AND CRITICISM

Midway between listings of songs and narrative histories are two books by James J. Fuld, *American Popular Music (Reference Book) 1857-1950* and the larger *Book of World-Famous Music: Classical, Popular and Folk.* The first is, compared to the books mentioned earlier, highly selective, but rigorously thorough in its descriptive bibliography of first editions of sheet music for some 250 songs. The second builds on this scholarship to construct historical accounts of the birth and adventures of well-known tunes, including popular songs along with classical themes and familiar folk songs.

The participation of popular music in the general history of music in America was first taken seriously and treated in the context of other American musical styles by Gilbert Chase in *America's Music: from the Pilgrims to the Present* in 1955, though even in revision in 1966 he does not include rock. (Chase has been a prominent reviewer of books on popular music in *Notes* and elsewhere.) Wilfrid Mellers devotes the second half of *Music in a New Found Land: Themes and Developments in the History of American Music* to popular forms.

Two extended chronicles, as opposed to analytical histories, of popular music in itself are Sigmund Spaeth's *History of Popular Music In America* (in 1948, an early book, although Spaeth was writing, with some jocularity, about popular music as early as the 1920s), and David Ewen's newer but less reliable *History of Popular Music*. Ewen has constructed several other books with similar anecdotal material which cover the history to some extent, including *Great Men of American Popular Song*, composed of chatty biographies. Two recent books by participants in the popular music world are valuable histories in very different styles. Alec Wilder's *American Popular Song, the Great Innovators, 1900-1950* gives the music of songs of his period, especially theater songs, a loving and subtle critical examination; Ian Whitcomb's *After the Ball: Pop Music from Rag to Rock* provides an intelligent historical context for Whitcomb's own quick career as a rock star. A careful analysis of the art of the performing artists is *Great American Popular Singers*, by Henry Pleasants.

FOLK MUSIC IN THE BACKGROUND

The infusion of folk music, white and black, into American popular music is what has made it more than a provincial echo of British ballad opera, broadside and music hall music, and Viennese operetta. Whether or not, as Carl Belz claims, rock music of the 1950s was actually a folk music itself, that music certainly drew on the white country and Western and black rhythm and blues styles, both of which have clear folk roots. Folk forms lurk behind popular music forms in America from Stephen Foster on, occasionally taking a turn on stage with little costuming and occasionally honored by impersonation. Even the enlivening invasion of the American market by the Beatles and succeeding British rock bands brought in nothing so much as the blues sounds and the rhythms derived from the Afro-American folk tradition.

Folklore study relevant to popular song can begin with Bruno Nettl's brief *Introduction to Folk Music in the United States*; a new edition has been revised and expanded by Helen Myers. Such study must refer for guidance to Charles Haywood's *Bibliography of North American Folklore and Folksong*, volume 1, *American People North of Mexico, including Canada*. G. Malcolm Laws, in *Native American Balladry: a Descriptive Study and a Bibliographical Syllabus*, inventories the specifically American branch of ballad folk song. A broad catalog of information and of sources of information is assembled in the *Folk Music Sourcebook*, by

Larry Sandberg and Dick Weissman. Ray M. Lawless, in *Folksingers and Folksong in America: a Handbook, Biography, Bibliography, and Discography*, makes a survey of the recent and current at the time world of folk artists and their songs. Kristin Baggelaar and Donald Minton, in *Folk Music: More than a Song*, present the folk-derived section of commercial music, as it verges into country and Western.

Study of "those forms of American folk music disseminated by commercial media" including "music referred to as cowboy, western, country and western, old time, hillbilly, bluegrass, mountain, country, cajun, sacred, gospel, race, blues, rhythm and blues, soul, and folk rock" is the object of the John Edwards Memorial Foundation at UCLA, which publishes a journal, *JEMF Quarterly*.

(For work in the history of the Afro-American folk tradition, see pp. 183-84.)

BEGINNINGS

The early American music that has survived in printed form was cataloged by Oscar G. T. Sonneck and his successor William Treat Upton in the *Bibliography of Early American Secular Music (18th Century)*, which like other grand standard research instruments has assumed its authors' names and is usually referred to as Sonneck-Upton. A successor work, larger than the original because of the swelling bulk of materials produced and surviving with each succeeding decade, is Richard Wolfe's *Secular Music in America, 1801-1825: a Bibliography*. A less full though wider range (religious music as well as secular is included) is presented by Donald L. Hixon in *Music in Early America: a Bibliography of Music in Evans* (Evans being Charles Evans' immense *American Bibliography*). The materials in Evans, and hence in Hixon, are progressively being made available on microfilm. The Hixon list includes only works with printed musical notation: some of these are popular songs. After the period covered by Wolfe there is no comparable inventory, although Marjorie Lyle Crandall and others have a sampling of music printed in the South under the Confederacy in *Confederate Imprints: A Check List Based Principally on the Collection of the Boston Athenaeum*, volume 2, *Unofficial Publications*.

Norm Cohen writing in a review in *JEMF Quarterly* describes work still undone in gathering and assessing the varieties of music printed in the nineteenth century. Despite the surveys of sheet music hits in Mattfeld and in Spaeth's history, the territory is mostly wild. (Books have been written by and for dealers and collectors, from Harry Dichter and Elliott Shapiro's *Early American Sheet Music, Its Lure and Lore, 1768-1880* in 1941 to several current glossy productions, but there is nothing systematic.) Even less well charted than sheet music is the area of "cheap print"—

broadsides and songsters, and small specialty periodicals. Little clearings have been made by Edwin Wolf, II, *American Song Sheets, Slip Ballads, and Poetical Broadsides 1850-1870*, cataloging a single collection, and by Philip S. Foner, *American Labor Songs of the Nineteenth Century*.

A sampling of sheet music itself is available in Richard Jackson's *Popular Songs of Nineteenth-Century America: Complete Original Sheet Music for 64 Songs*. Sigmund Spaeth printed texts, mostly from the nineteenth century, in *Read 'em and Weep* and *Weep Some More, My Lady*.

BLACK TRADITIONS

A scholarly overview is provided in *Music of Black Americans: a History*, by Eileen Southern. The rural folk music underlying other styles and developments is studied in Harold Courlander's *Negro Folk Music, USA*. Important essays and introductions that presented black music to the readers of books from 1867 to 1939 are collected in *Social Implications of Early Negro Music in the United States*, edited by Bernard Katz.

Ragtime

The first serious study of ragtime artists and their work was Rudi Blesh and Harriet Janis' *They All Played Ragtime*. Musical analysis is undertaken by William J. Schafer and Johannes Riedel in *Art of Ragtime: Form and Meaning of an Original Black American Art*. A good introduction and history is *This Is Ragtime*, by pianist Terry Waldo. A discography, *Recorded Ragtime, 1897-1958*, has been assembled by David Jasen.

Blues

Three books by an English writer, Paul Oliver, offer good history and good analysis of the forms called *blues*: *Aspects of the Blues Tradition*, first published as *Screening the Blues*; *Story of the Blues*, an illustrated history; and *Meaning of the Blues* (originally *Blues Fell this Morning*), which sympathetically re-creates the social context of what is said in blues words. Harry Oster's *Living Country Blues* also gives texts, and some tunes, from the folk blues tradition.

A sumptuous anthology, which looks calculated for the coffee table and so seems sharply incongruous with its contents, is *Blues Line: a Collection of Blues Lyrics*, compiled by Eric Sackheim. A real virtue of this lavish production is that with page space to squander, the editor is able to space and position lines and line fragments to suggest spatially the delivery of the lines in song. He thus avoids some of the deflation that befalls almost all printings of song lyrics not spaced by musical notation—which has its own drawbacks as an environment for printed words. A discography of early blues is *Blues and Gospel Records, 1902-1942*, by Robert Dixon and John Godrich.

Blues as the popular music of urban black listeners is traced in successive phases in two books: *Urban Blues* in 1966 by Charles Keil, and *Right On: from Blues to Soul in Black America* in 1975 by Michael Haralambos. A discography of postwar blues is Mike Leadbitter and Neal Slaven, *Blues Records, 1943-1966.*

Jazz

Jazz emerged from ragtime and blues in the second decade of this century. Growing out of black musical styles, it attracted white musicians as well, early and late, and became the Afro-American, black-white music most distinctive of the new world. It was first respected as serious art and artistry by European critics, and it is now widely judged to be the major contribution that America has made to the arts it shares with Europe. Such interest and esteem has been raised by jazz that it is now treated in a very large literature. *A Bibliography of Jazz* was prepared by Alan P. Merriam in 1954. In 1959 Robert G. Reisner published *Literature of Jazz: a Selected Bibliography.* The newer *Literature of Jazz*, by Donald Kennington, is less satisfactory; it lists only books and not periodical writing.

There has also been considerable scholarship invested in discographies of recorded jazz. A key to it is the second half of David Edwin Cooper's *International Bibliography of Discographies: Classical Music and Jazz & Blues.* The fundamental work in the field is Brian Rust's *Jazz Records, 1897-1942* (first published, in England, as *Jazz Records A-Z*) and the same editor's two-volume *American Dance Band Discography, 1917-1942.* A selective discography for the period from 1945 to 1970 is *Modern Jazz: the Essential Records*, by five English critics (Max Harrison, Alun Morgan, Ronald Atkins, Michael James, and Jack Cooke), listing their choices of the two hundred most significant long-playing records of the period.

A general reference work on jazz, including historical and analytical essays but principally devoted to biographies of jazz figures, is Leonard Feather's *New Encyclopedia of Jazz: Completely Revised and Brought Up to Date* (1960), which was followed by his *Encyclopedia of Jazz in the Sixties* in 1966 and *Encyclopedia of Jazz in the Seventies* in 1976, the last with the collaboration of Ira Gitler. A specialized directory is *Jazz: New Orleans 1885-1963, an Index to the Negro Musicians of New Orleans*, by Samuel B. Charters. The first full history was *Story of Jazz*, by Marshall Stearns. Gunther Schuller's *Early Jazz: Its Roots and Musical Development* is a musicologist's history, published as the first of a projected two-volume work. A collection of studies edited by Martin T. Williams is *Art of Jazz: Essays on the Nature and Development of Jazz.*

STAGE AND SCREEN

The immensely popular minstrel show was the distinctively American stage musical entertainment of the nineteenth century. Its history is given in *Dan Emmett and the Rise of Early Negro Minstrelsy*, by Hans Nathan, and in *Blacking Up: the Minstrel Show in Nineteenth-Century America*, by Robert C. Toll.

The facts of the history of Broadway are assembled in another book by David Ewen, the *New Complete Book of the American Musical Theater*. Somewhat less extensive treatment of shows, their makers, and their performers is given by Stanley Green in his *Encyclopedia of the Musical Theatre*, which also embraces the London musical. Green has also written a connected history, *World of Musical Comedy: the Story of the American Musical Stage as Told Through the Careers of Its Foremost Composers and Lyricists*. A history and analysis by Lehman Engel is *American Musical Theater: a Consideration*. Jack Burton's reference books on Broadway and Hollywood have been mentioned earlier, as has Lewine and Simon's song inventory, and Alec Wilder's study of the musical history made by the Broadway composers. Lehman Engel's *Their Words Are Music: the Great Theatre Lyricists and Their Lyrics* is an anthology of the tradition of sophisticated wit and romance in the songs of Broadway musicals.

The songs themselves are often conspicuously unavailable for study. Engel in his introduction lists the few samplings of lyrics that have been published (of these, Wilder notices that the Simon and Schuster edition of Jerome Kern songs has many errors or alterations). Wilder's book struggles valiantly with the commercial security that invests the music: some composers, and some publishers in defiance of their composers, refuse all permission to print even bars of music for analysis. All apparently refuse publication of any whole chorus of a song, for fear of a loss of potential sheet music sales.

A discography of recordings by a grand roster of entertainers, including "minstrel pioneers, vaudevillians, film stars and radio personalities" is the *Complete Entertainment Discography from the Mid-1890's to 1942*, again by Brian Rust, with the assistance of Allen Debus.

A history and encyclopedia of musical productions on film is *Hollywood Musical*, by John Russell Taylor and Arthur Jackson. Songs from films are cataloged in *Songs from Hollywood Musical Comedies, 1927 to the Present: a Dictionary*, by Allen L. Woll. Many of the films in which these songs are preserved in their native environment are available for rental, including remade Broadway shows (often with new songs), display events for individual singing stars or pairs of stars, and the curious large genre of pseudo-biographies of songwriters. For access to these films, see James L. Limbacher, *Feature Films on 8 mm and 16 mm*, or Kathleen

Weaver, *Film Programmer's Guide to 16 mm Rentals.* See also the essay on films by Robert A. Armour in this volume.

COUNTRY AND WESTERN

Country Music USA, by Bill C. Malone, is the principal history. A more recent account is Douglas B. Green's *Country Roots: the Origins of Country Music.* Linnell Gentry gathered important reference materials that underlie the work of writers since the subject has become more fashionable in *History and Encyclopedia of Country, Western, and Gospel Music.* More recent and more widely available is Irwin Stambler and Greg Landon's *Encyclopedia of Folk, Country, and Western Music*; see also the work of Baggelaar and Minton listed in the folk music section, on p. 181. Melvin Shestack's *Country Music Encyclopedia* promotes contemporary performers and adds little to the earlier reference works.

Dorothy Horstman, in *Sing Your Heart Out, Country Boy*, prints a selection of lyrics with anecdotes she solicited from the writers about how they happened to write the songs. The anecdotes are amusing, in some cases, showing mainly that the writers in question have the traditional poet's knack for evading impertinent questions, or that they could use it.

POP AND ROCK

General reference concerning the current world of popular music is better pursued in Irwin Stambler's *Encyclopedia of Pop, Rock, and Soul* or in the *Rolling Stone Illustrated History of Rock and Roll*, edited by Jim Miller, than in Lillian Roxon's popular *Rock Encyclopedia.* The newest such reference book at this writing is the *Illustrated Encyclopedia of Rock*, compiled by Nick Logan and Bob Woffinden. The paperback marketing of these works, and their nearly annual proliferation, suggests that they marry the function of fan magazine to that of library reference. The space devoted to graphics and publicity photographs grows steadily; the best use of photographs is in the *Rolling Stone* book. The fan audience will not readily accept inaccuracy or capricious choice of artists covered; on the other hand it may not demand much judicious perspective.

Chronicles of hit songs of the rock era are Joel Whitburn's *Top Pop Records, 1955-72* and Peter E. Berry's *"And the Hits Just Keep On Comin'."* Partial discography for the period has been produced for hobbyists in Jerry Osborne's *Record Collector's Price Guide.* There is a full discography for the Beatles: *All Together Now: The First Complete Beatles Discography, 1961-1975*, by Harry Castleman and Walter Podrazik.

Current writing about popular music is monitored in the *Popular Music Periodicals Index*, annually from 1973, by Dean Tudor and Nancy Tudor, then by Dean Tudor and Andrew D. Armitage. The trade magazines *Billboard* and *Cash Box* are essential sources of information about the vast flux of recorded music. Two studies of the music industry that produces the records are C. A. Schicke's history, *Revolution in Sound: a Biography of the Recording Industry*, and R. Serge Denisoff's *Solid Gold: the Popular Record Industry*.

The early history of rock and roll is studied by Carl Belz in *Story of Rock*, and by Charles Gillett in *Sound of the City: the Rise of Rock and Roll*. A great deal of journalistic analysis and commentary has been devoted to rock. Jonathon Eisen collected two volumes of it, *Age of Rock* and *Age of Rock 2*. Greil Marcus assembled another, by Berkeley area writers, in *Rock and Roll Will Stand*. One of the best critics of the music as it has appeared has been Robert Christgau, who has collected some of his writings in *Any Old Way You Choose It: Rock and Other Pop Music, 1967-1973*.

The tabloid *Rolling Stone*, a primary document of the counterculture and its entertainment, has published a large number of interviews with principals of rock, and two volumes of them have been collected as the *Rolling Stone Interviews*. Extensive analysis of the rock phenomenon has been undertaken by David Laing, *Sound of Our Time*, and by Richard Meltzer, *Aesthetics of Rock*. The latter is a highly subjective performance. Sociological analysis has been published since 1971 in the journal *Popular Music and Society*; articles here often have references that locate writing about popular music in other academic sociological journals. An exercise in musicological analysis is Wilfrid Mellers' *Twilight of the Gods: the Music of the Beatles*.

Literary analysis has been brought to bear on the lyrics of some rock songs. Richard Goldstein's editorial comments in his anthology, *Poetry of Rock*, are perceptive though extremely brief. Michael Gray's *Song and Dance Man: the Art of Bob Dylan* assumes that the poetical tradition taught in literature courses is a loftier thing than songwriting, and that Dylan belongs to it. No very striking success has been achieved by sustained literary criticism of rock lyrics, which has yet to find a mode between polemics and patronization. Dylan's lyrics up to 1973 have been published as a collected anthology, *Writings and Drawings by Bob Dylan*, and there is an anthology of *Beatles Lyrics Illustrated* (updated, in a small paperback, without the flamboyant graphics of the earlier *Beatles Illustrated Lyrics*).

BIBLIOGRAPHY

BOOKS

Ash, Lee. *Subject Collections: a Guide to Special Book Collections and Subject Emphases as Reported by University, College, Public, and Special Libraries and Museums in the United States and Canada*. 4th ed. New York: R. R. Bowker, 1974.

Baggelaar, Kristin, and Donald Minton. *Folk Music: More than a Song*. New York: Thomas Y. Crowell, 1976.

Beatles Illustrated Lyrics. 2 vols. London: Macdonald Unit 75, 1969.

Beatles Lyrics Illustrated. New York: Dell, 1975.

Belz, Carl. *Story of Rock*. New York: Oxford University Press, 1969.

Berry, Peter E. *"And the Hits Just Keep On Comin'."* Syracuse, N.Y.: Syracuse University Press, 1977.

Billboard International Buyer's Guide. Los Angeles: Billboard Publications, 1955-.

Blesh, Rudi, and Harriet Janis. *They All Played Ragtime*. New York: Alfred A. Knopf, 1950. Reprint. New York: Grove Press, 1959.

Burton, Jack. *Blue Book of Broadway Musicals*. Watkins Glen, N.Y.: Century House, 1969.

———. *Blue Book of Hollywood Musicals*. Watkins Glen, N.Y.: Century House, 1953.

———. *Blue Book of Tin Pan Alley: a Human Interest Encyclopedia of American Popular Music*. 2 vols. Watkins Glen, N.Y.: Century House, 1962.

———. *Index of American Popular Music: Thousands of Titles Cross-Referenced to Our Basic Anthologies of Popular Song*. Watkins Glen, N.Y.: Century House, 1957.

Castleman, Harry, and Walter J. Podrazik. *All Together Now: The First Complete Beatles Discography, 1961-1975*. New York: Ballantine, 1976.

Charters, Samuel B. *Jazz: New Orleans, 1885-1963, an Index to the Negro Musicians of New Orleans*. New York: Oak Publications, 1963.

Chase, Gilbert. *America's Music: from the Pilgrims to the Present*. New York: McGraw-Hill, 1966.

Chicorel, Marietta, ed. *Chicorel Bibliography to Books on Music and Musicians*. New York: Chicorel Library Publishing Corp., 1974.

Chipman, John H. *Index to Top-Hit Tunes (1900-1950)*. Boston: Bruce Humphries, 1962.

Christgau, Robert. *Any Old Way You Choose It: Rock and Other Pop Music, 1967-1973*. Baltimore: Penguin Books, 1973.

Cohen, Norm. "Review of *American Labor Songs of the Nineteenth Century*, by Philip S. Foner," *JEMF Quarterly*, 39 (Autumn 1975), 162-63.

Cooper, David Edwin. *International Bibliography of Discographies: Classical Music and Jazz & Blues*. Littleton, Colo.: Libraries Unlimited, 1975.

Courlander, Harold. *Negro Folk Music, USA*. New York: Columbia University Press, 1963.

Crandall, Marjorie Lyle. *Confederate Imprints: A Check List Based Principally on the Collection of the Boston Atheneum.* Vol. II: *Unofficial Publications.* Boston: Boston Atheneum, 1955.

De Charms, Desiree, and Paul F. Breed. *Songs in Collections, an Index.* Detroit: Information Service, Inc., 1966.

Denisoff, R. Serge. *Solid Gold: the Popular Record Industry.* New Brunswick, N.J.: Transaction Books, 1975.

Dichter, Harry, and Elliott Shapiro. *Early American Sheet Music, Its Lure and Lore, 1768-1880.* New York: R. R. Bowker, 1941.

Dixon, Robert, and John Godrich. *Blues and Gospel Records 1902-1942.* New York: Stein and Day, 1970.

Duckles, Vincent, comp. *Music Reference and Research Materials: An Annotated Bibliography.* 3rd ed. New York: Free Press, 1974.

Dylan, Bob. *Writings and Drawings by Bob Dylan.* New York: Alfred A. Knopf, 1973.

Ehrlich, Cyril. *The Piano: a History.* London: Dent, 1976.

Eisen, Jonathan. *Age of Rock.* New York: Random House, 1969.

———. *Age of Rock 2.* New York: Random House, 1970.

Engel, Lehman. *American Musical Theater: a Consideration.* New York: Columbia Broadcasting Systems, 1967. Rev. ed. (without subtitle). New York: Macmillan, 1975.

———. *Their Words Are Music: the Great Theatre Lyricists and Their Lyrics.* New York: Crown, 1975.

Ewen, David. *American Popular Songs from the Revolutionary War to the Present.* New York: Random House, 1966.

———. *Great Men of American Popular Song.* Rev. ed. Englewood Cliffs, N.J.: Prentice-Hall, 1972.

———. *History of Popular Music.* New York: Barnes and Noble, 1961.

———. *New Complete Book of the American Musical Theater.* New York: Holt, Rinehart and Winston, 1970.

Feather, Leonard. *Encyclopedia of Jazz in the Sixties.* New York: Horizon, 1966.

———. *New Edition of the Encyclopedia of Jazz: Completely Revised, Enlarged and Brought up to Date.* New York: Horizon, 1960.

———, and Ira Gitler. *Encyclopedia of Jazz in the Seventies.* New York: Horizon, 1976.

Foner, Philip S. *American Labor Songs of the Nineteenth Century.* Urbana: University of Illinois Press, 1975.

Fuld, James J. *American Popular Music (Reference Book) 1875-1950.* Philadelphia: Musical Americana, 1955.

———. *Book of World-Famous Music: Classical, Popular and Folk.* New York: Crown, 1971.

Gentry, Linnell. *History and Encyclopedia of Country, Western, and Gospel Music.* Nashville, Tenn.: McQuiddy Press, 1961.

Gillett, Charles. *Sound of the City: the Rise of Rock and Roll.* New York: Outerbridge and Dienstfrey, 1970.

Goldstein, Richard, ed. *Poetry of Rock*. New York: Bantam, 1969.

Gray, Michael. *Song and Dance Man: The Art of Bob Dylan*. New York: E. P. Dutton, 1972.

Green, Douglas B. *Country Roots: the Origins of Country Music*. New York: Hawthorn, 1976.

Green, Stanley. *Encyclopedia of the Musical Theatre*. New York: Dodd, Mead, 1976.

————. *World of Musical Comedy: the Story of the American Musical Stage as Told through the Careers of Its Foremost Composers and Lyricists*. Cranbury, N.J.: A. S. Barnes, 1974.

Haralambos, Michael. *Right On: from Blues to Soul in Black America*. New York: Drake, 1975.

Harrison, Max; Alun Morgan; Ronald Atkins; Michael James; and Jack Cooke, comps. *Modern Jazz: the Essential Records*. London: Aquarius, 1975.

Havlice, Patricia Pate. *Popular Song Index*. Metuchen, N.J.: Scarecrow Press, 1975.

Haywood, Charles. *Bibliography of North American Folklore and Folksong*. 2 vols. Vol. 1: *American People North of Mexico, including Canada*. New York: Dover Publications, 1961.

Hixon, Donald L. *Music in Early America: a Bibliography of Music in Evans*. Metuchen, N.J.: Scarecrow Press, 1970.

Horn, David. *Literature of American Music in Books and Folk Music Collection: A Fully Annotated Bibliography*. Metuchen, N.J.: Scarecrow Press, 1977.

Horstman, Dorothy. *Sing Your Heart Out, Country Boy*. New York: E. P. Dutton, 1975.

Jackson, Richard. *Popular Songs of Nineteenth-Century America: Complete Original Sheet Music for 64 Songs*. New York: Dover Publications, 1976.

————. *United States Music: Sources of Bibliography and Collective Biography*. Brooklyn, N.Y.: Institute for Studies in American Music, 1973.

Jasen, David A. *Recorded Ragtime, 1897-1958*. Hamden, Conn.: Archon, 1973.

Katz, Bernard, ed. *Social Implications of Early Negro Music in the United States*. New York: New York Times/Arno, 1969.

Keil, Charles. *Urban Blues*. Chicago: University of Chicago Press, 1966.

Kennington, Donald. *Literature of Jazz*. Chicago: American Library Association, 1971.

Kinkle, Roger D. *Complete Encyclopedia of Popular Music and Jazz, 1900-1950*. 4 vols. New Rochelle, N.Y.: Arlington House, 1974.

Laing, David. *Sound of Our Time*. Chicago: Quadrangle, 1970.

Lawless, Ray M. *Folksingers and Folksong in America: a Handbook, Biography, Bibliography and Discography*. New York: Meredith, 1965.

Laws, G. Malcolm. *Native American Balladry: a Descriptive Study and a Bibliographical Syllabus*. Philadelphia: American Folklore Society, 1964.

Leadbitter, Mike, and Neal Slaven. *Blues Records, 1943-1966*. New York: Oak, 1968.

Leigh, Robert. *Index to Song Books: a Title Index to over 11,000 Copies of almost 6,800 Songs in 111 Song Books Published between 1933 and 1962.* Stockton, Calif.: Robert Leigh, 1964.

Lewine, Richard, and Alfred Simon. *Songs of the American Theater: a Comprehensive Listing of More than 12,000 Songs, including Selected Titles from Film and Television Productions.* New York: Dodd, Mead, 1973.

Limbacher, James L., comp. *Feature Films on 8mm and 16mm.* New York: R. R. Bowker, 1977.

Logan, Nick, and Bob Woffinden. *Illustrated Encyclopedia of Rock.* New York: Harmony, 1977.

Malone, Bill C. *Country Music USA.* Austin, Tex.: American Folklore Society, 1968.

Marcus, Greil, ed. *Rock and Roll Will Stand.* Boston: Beacon, 1969.

Mattfeld, Julius. *Variety Music Cavalcade, 1620-1969: a Chronology of Vocal and Instrumental Music Popular in the United States.* Third ed. Englewood Cliffs, N.J.: Prentice-Hall, 1971.

Mead, Rita H. *Doctoral Dissertations in American Music: a Classified Bibliography.* Brooklyn, N.Y.: Institute for Studies in American Music, 1974.

Mellers, Wilfrid. *Music in a New Found Land: Themes and Developments in the History of American Music.* New York: Alfred A. Knopf, 1965.

————. *Twilight of the Gods: the Music of the Beatles.* New York: Viking, 1973.

Meltzer, Richard. *Aesthetics of Rock.* New York: Something Else, 1970.

Merriam, Alan P. *A Bibliography of Jazz.* Philadelphia: American Folklore Society, 1954.

Miller, Jim, ed. *Rolling Stone Illustrated History of Rock and Roll.* New York: Rolling Stone, 1976.

Mugridge, Donald H., and Blanche P. McCrum. *Guide to the Study of the United States of America: Representative Books Reflecting the Development of American Life and Thought.* Washington, D.C.: Library of Congress, 1960. *Supplement*, ed. Oliver H. Orr, Jr., et al., 1976.

Murrells, Joseph, comp. *Book of Golden Discs.* London: Barrie and Jenkins, 1974.

Nathan, Hans. *Dan Emmett and the Rise of Early Negro Minstrelsy.* Norman: University of Oklahoma Press, 1962.

Nettl, Bruno. *Introduction to Folk Music in the United States,* 3rd ed. revised and expanded by Helen Myers. Detroit: Wayne State University Press, 1976.

Oliver, Paul. *Aspects of the Blues Tradition.* New York: Oak, 1970.

————. *Meaning of the Blues.* New York: Collier, 1972.

————. *Story of the Blues.* Philadelphia: Chilton, 1969.

Osborne, Jerry. *Record Collector's Price Guide.* Edited by Bruce Hamilton. Phoenix, Ariz.: O'Sullivan, Woodside, 1976.

Oster, Harry. *Living Country Blues.* Detroit: Folklore Associates, 1969.

Pleasants, Henry. *Great American Popular Singers.* New York: Simon and Schuster, 1974.

Reisner, Robert G. *Literature of Jazz*. New York: New York Public Library, 1959.

Rolling Stone Interviews, Volume 1. New York: Warner, 1971.

Rolling Stone Interviews, Volume 2. New York: Warner, 1973.

Roxon, Lillian. *Rock Encyclopedia*. New York: Grosset and Dunlap, 1969.

Rust, Brian. *American Dance Band Discography, 1917-1942*. 2 vols. New Rochelle, New York: Arlington House, 1975.

———. *Jazz Records, 1897-1942*. 2 vols. London: Storyville, 1970.

———, with Allen G. Debus. *Complete Entertainment Discography from the Mid-1890's to1942*. New Rochelle, New York: Arlington House, 1973.

Sackheim, Eric, comp. *Blues Line: a Collection of Blues Lyrics*. New York: Grossman, 1969.

Sandberg, Larry, and Dick Weissman. *Folk Music Sourcebook*. New York: Alfred A. Knopf, 1976.

Schafer, William J., and Johannes Riedel. *Art of Ragtime: Form and Meaning of an Original Black American Art*. Baton Rouge: Louisiana State University Press, 1973.

Schicke, C. A. *Revolution in Sound: a Biography of the Recording Industry*. Boston: Little, Brown, 1974.

Schuller, Gunther. *Early Jazz: Its Roots and Musical Development*. New York: Oxford University Press, 1968.

Sears, Minnie E. *Song Index: an Index to more than 12,000 Songs in 177 Song Collections*. New York: H. W. Wilson, 1926.

———. *Supplement: an Index to More than 7,000 Songs in 104 Collections*. New York: H. W. Wilson, 1934.

Shapiro, Nat, ed. *Popular Music: an Annotated Index of American Popular Songs*. 6 vols. New York: Adrian Press, 1967.

Shestack, Melvin. *Country Music Encyclopedia*. New York: Thomas Y. Crowell, 1974.

Sonneck, Oscar G. T., and William Treat Upton. *Bibliography of Early Secular American Music (18th Century)*. Washington, D.C.: Library of Congress, Music Division, 1945. Reprint. New York: Da Capo, 1964.

Southern, Eileen. *Music of Black Americans: a History*. New York: W. W. Norton, 1971.

Spaeth, Sigmund. *History of Popular Music in America*. New York: Random House, 1948.

———. *Read 'em and Weep: the Songs You Forgot to Remember*. New York: Doubleday, Page, 1926.

———. *Weep Some More, My Lady*. Garden City, N.Y.: Doubleday, Page, 1927.

Stambler, Irwin. *Encylopedia of Pop, Rock, and Soul*. New York: St. Martin's, 1974.

———, and Greg Landon. *Encyclopedia of Folk, Country, and Western Music*. New York: St. Martin's, 1969.

Stearns, Marshall. *Story of Jazz*. New York: Oxford University Press, 1956.

Stecheson, Anthony, and Anne Stecheson. *Stecheson Classified Song Directory.* Hollywood, Calif.: Music Industry Press, 1961.

Taylor, John Russell, and Arthur Jackson, *Hollywood Musical.* New York: McGraw-Hill, 1971.

Toll, Robert C. *Blacking Up: the Minstrel Show in Nineteenth-Century America.* New York: Oxford University Press, 1974.

Tudor, Dean, and Nancy Tudor. *Popular Music Periodicals Index, 1973.* Methuchen, N.J.: Scarecrow Press, 1974.

————, and Andrew D. Armitage. *Popular Music Periodicals Index: 1974.* Metuchen, N.J.: Scarecrow, Press, 1975.

————. *Popular Music Periodicals Index: 1975.* Metuchen, N.J.: Scarecrow, 1976.

Waldo, Terry. *This Is Ragtime.* New York: Hawthorn, 1976.

Weaver, Kathleen, ed. *Film Programmer's Guide to 16mm Rentals.* Berkeley, Calif.: Reel Research, 1975.

Whitburn, Joel. *Top Pop Records, 1955-72.* Menomonee Falls, Wisc.: Record Research, 1973.

Whitcomb, Ian. *After the Ball: Pop Music from Rag to Rock.* New York: Simon and Schuster, 1972. Reprint. New York: Penguin, 1974.

Wilder, Alec. *American Popular Song, the Great Innovators, 1900-1950.* New York: Oxford University Press, 1972.

Williams, Martin T., ed. *Art of Jazz: Essays on the Nature and Development of Jazz.* New York: Oxford University Press, 1959.

Wolf, Edwin, II. *American Song Sheets, Slip Ballads, and Poetical Broadsides, 1850-1870.* New York: Kraus Reprint, 1963.

Wolfe, Richard J. *Secular Music in America, 1801-1825. A Bibliography.* 3 vols. New York: New York Public Library, 1964.

Woll, Allen L. *Songs from Hollywood Musical Comedies, 1927 to the Present: a Dictionary.* New York: Garland Publishing Co., 1976.

Young, Margaret Labash; Harold Chester Young; and Anthony T. Kruzas. *Directory of Special Libraries and Information Centers.* Detroit: Gale, 1977.

PERIODICALS

Billboard. Los Angeles, 1894-.

Black Perspective in Music. Cambria Heights, New York: 1973-.

Cash Box. New York, 1942-.

JEMF Quarterly. Los Angeles, 1965-.

Notes: The Quarterly Journal of the Music Library Association. Ann Arbor, Mich., 1934-.

Popular Music and Society. Bowling Green, Ohio, 1972-.

Rolling Stone. San Francisco, 1967-.

CHAPTER 9 The Pulps
Bill Blackbeard

HISTORIC OUTLINE

Until about twenty years ago, the terms *pulp, pulp magazine,* and *pulp fiction* were writers' and publishers' trade terms, little known to or used by the general public. Readers who bought such magazines as *Dime Detective, Argosy, Blue Book,* and *Weird Tales* in the 1930s and 1940s did not think of these popular titles as pulps, but just as fiction magazines, or more generically, according to subject matter, as detective story magazines, adventure story magazines, fantasy magazines, etc. Infrequent and casual articles in such magazines as *Esquire* and *Vanity Fair* dealing with the phenomenon of the popular fiction magazines did, of course, use the term *pulp,* but it did not gain broad usage. From the point of view of the general reader, who once absorbed reams of pulp fiction as he does hours of television today, the paper on which his reading matter was printed was simply irrelevant. A Western novel serialized in the slick paper magazine *Saturday Evening Post* could, in his eyes, be quite as entertaining as another printed in pulp paper *Wild West Weekly.* He read the latter magazine largely because the more eclectic *Post* did not publish enough Western fiction to satisfy his specialized cravings over a given period of time.

To the magazine publisher and his potential advertisers, however, the quality of paper used was a vital concern. So-called slick paper, made of rag content stock, afforded a highly desirable surface for the reproduction of advertisements, particularly those involving a lavish use of color. Unfortunately, slick paper was a costly item and was economically feasible only for very large circulation magazines, such as the *Saturday Evening Post, Collier's,* or *Life,* of low newsstand cost supported in large part by their advertising revenue or for more highly priced "quality" magazines, such as *Esquire, The New Yorker,* or *Vanity Fair,* with an "elite" appeal, again substantially supported by their advertisements. Pulp paper, on the other hand, prepared from a wood-fiber base and also called *newsprint,* largely in newspaper publishing circles, was much cheaper than slick or coated paper, and its use made it possible for publishers so inclined to reach a mass reading market at low prices without any substantial financial aid from its advertisers. (For this reason, "radical" political journals, that tended to alienate advertisers *per se*, almost always appeared on the cheapest kind of pulp paper stock, generally called *butcher paper* by its left-wing users of the time.)

Many different kinds of magazines with low advertising content utilized pulp paper: the early color comic strip magazines (or comic books); political and cultural journals of all sorts (some of which, like *Harper's* and *The Atlantic*, used a high grade of wood-based paper, called *book paper* in the publishing field); newspaper book review and entertainment supplements; scholastic, library, and book trade publications, etc. However, only the popular fiction or all-fiction magazine acquired the name pulp from its writers and editors in the decades following the turn of the present century, and it is, of course, with this widely circulated, enormously varied body of publications that we are concerned here.

In referring to the pulp fiction magazine in these pages, we are speaking of a specific, readily defined kind of periodical, found only in six sizes and forms, all of which share in common wood-pulp paper and a two-column text. The most frequently encountered form of pulp magazine is a sheaf of several octavo signatures, stapled together at two equidistant points near the spine, enclosed with a slick paper cover attached with glue over the flat area of the spine, and usually featuring interior illustrations, as well as color printing on the outside of the cover. This basic form of pulp magazine is found in three sizes: the large "flat" of about 8½″ × 11″, usually about ¼ to 1 inch thick with trimmed page edges, and composed of three to four signatures (or, very occasionally, perfectly bound, with or without staples); the median, standard size (representing the vast majority of all pulps) of 10″ × 7″ untrimmed, or about 9″ × 6½″ trimmed, averaging ⅛ to ½ inch in thickness (some exceptional pulps of this size can go to two inches or more of thickness), made up of six to twelve signatures (or again, in rare instances, dozens of signatures); and the "digest" size, of about 7½″ × 5″, ¼ to ½ inch thick (with some rare titles reaching an inch or more), almost always trimmed, and involving six to eight signatures (or perfectly bound, with or without staples). A much less frequent form of pulp magazine is the saddle-stitched, single signature variety. The standard form for the nickel thriller and the comic book, it is most often encountered in pulps with the under-the-counter sex story magazines of the 1920s and 1930s. It can also range in size from the flat to the digest form, although the latter is extremely rare in this form, and the median of 9″ × 6½″ is standard.

The all-fiction magazine, by its nature, emphasized a basic broad appeal in its writing and narrative content. Here and there, especially in its later, closing years, the pulp magazine might chance a "difficult," experimental piece of fiction, because of real editorial enthusiasm and a feeling that one such item in a given issue would not alienate finicky readers provided with a half dozen other standard pieces of fiction. Even in such work some kind of straightforward narrative progress had to be in evidence, so that while as bizarre a writer as H. P. Lovecraft or Joel Townsley Rogers could (and did) appear regularly in pulps, a post-*Dubliners* James Joyce or a contemporary equivalent of John Barth probably would not. Basically, the all-fiction magazines provided a market for genre fiction that, often because of peculiar editorial biases as much as any real lack of intrinsic merit, failed to sell to the very limited but higher-paying slick paper magazine markets. While much of the pulp magazine content was, understandably, a mass-produced, stereotyped product seized upon by editors desperate to fill the endless pages of twenty or more titles a month in publishing house after publishing house, virtually all of the fine fiction written in America between the turn of the century and the close of the 1940s found print in these magazines if it could not find it in the slicks or literary journals. Much worthwhile material is still being uncovered today and reprinted to critical applause; indeed, in the case of some long-neglected writers, separate publishing houses with a largely academic clientele have been founded essentially to republish the works of such authors complete in successive, highly priced volumes.

The popular, all-fiction magazine and pulp paper were not, of course, always linked. The American and English predecessors of the American pulp magazine, appearing early in the nineteenth century, generally were printed on the then much cheaper rag content paper. The American "story papers" of the 1850s and later tabloid size nickel weekly journals were crammed inky cheek to jowl with six to eight pages of sensational fiction by such worthies as Nick Carter, Horatio Alger, and Ned Buntline. Their enormous cover illustrations, replete with blood and thunder, were matched by those of the English "penny dreadfuls" of the same period, which carried endless grisly narratives. These were illustrated penny serial parts, 8 pages long, 7 inches x 10 inches, carrying the title of the continued story each featured until slumping sales or author fatigue finally forced a pause before the launching of a new group of continuing narratives, usually penned by the same small group of ferociously productive authors, the most notorious of whom were the prolific G. W. M. Reynolds and Thomas Pecket Prest. Pulp paper first entered the scene with the development of the American weekly novel series of the 1870s in an 8 inches by 11 inches format of sixteen to twenty-four pages, which became as classic during the next few decades as the infamous dime novel. (In fact, the original and definitive dime novels were paperbacked, pocket-sized publications manufactured by Beadle and Adams primarily for Civil War troop use in the 1860s while the later and larger pulp paper thrillers of turn-of-the-century notoriety generally sold for five cents.) These nickel thrillers, an endless series of short novels about such juvenile favorites as Nick Carter, Diamond Dick, Buffalo Bill, Old Sleuth, King Brady, and Old Cap Collier, were the effective forerunners of the publications the next generation of writers called *pulps*. With their lurid, full-color covers (which did not fully supplant the earlier black and white covers until the 1890s), double columns of narrative text, wholehearted focus on sensational fiction, recurrent characters in series novels, pulp paper pages, and regularity of newsstand appearance, these dime novels of the 1870s-1910s lacked only the general dimensions of the definitive pulp magazines of the succeeding period: the popular 7 inches by 10 inches quarto, one hundred page or more in length in which virtually all pulps appeared until the introduction of the pocket-sized or digest-sized pulps of the 1940s.

In moving from the nickel thrillers of the nineteenth century to the pulps of the twentieth, we are, of course, passing from fiction of minimal literacy aimed almost entirely at juvenile readers, or the most naïve of uneducated adults, to a narrative prose intended for a mature mass readership not satisfied by the relatviely small amount of genre fiction available in quality or general content magazines, or in inexpensive paperback book reprints. Interestingly, the first periodical to establish the profitable existence of such a mature mass readership (initially in England rather than America) was not printed on pulp paper at all, nor was it an all-fiction publication. This was the widely famed, slick paper magazine of George Newnes, *The Strand*, in which such fictional figures as Sherlock Holmes and Bulldog Drummond appeared in series after series of novelettes and novels, together with sensational adventure and mystery fiction of all kinds, all profusely illustrated, often with color plates in holiday issues. Sandwiched in was a respectable (though peripheral) stock of nonfiction pieces on prominent personalities, exotic places, pets, and patriotism, so that despite its bounty of popular fiction, parlors that had previously accepted only such dull slick paper periodicals as *Blackwood's*, *Good Words*, and *The Leisure Hour* now received *The Strand*.

Ambitious imitators of *The Strand* appeared almost at once in England, all bounteously illustrated (at the rate of about one cut for every two pages) and replete with thrilling action or detective fiction written by such masters as H. Rider Haggard, R. Austin Freeman, Guy Boothby, E. Phillips Oppenheim, and many others; among these new and sensationally popular magazines were *The Windsor Magazine*, *Pearson's*, *Cassell's*, *Harmworth's* (later *The London Magazine*), and *The Idler*. Many of these published American editions to protect their copyrights in the United States, and their popular impact was much the same here as in England, although direct American imitations were not at all immediately evident (the earliest, possibly, being the *The Cosmopolitan* after 1905, when it was purchased by William Randolph Hearst and immediately took an engaging turn toward broadly popular fiction in great and well-illustrated quantity). American publishers of general magazines, dominated by the images of the more serious *Harper's* and *Scribner's* magazines at the close of the century, seemed to eschew the kind of fun-and-games fiction featured in the new group of British publications, and certainly they avoided any broad body of it in their pages at all times. Even the popularly oriented weekly slick paper magazines of wide dimensions, such as *Collier's* and *Saturday Evening Post* of the 1890s and 1900s, in which the Sherlock Holmes and Raffles stories were reprinted for American consumption, ran only one or two pieces of fiction per issue, with but one or two illustrations apiece, and placed their heavier editorial emphasis on journalistic nonfiction and illustrations of various kinds.

The would-be American consumer of quantitatively published popular action fiction was thus frustrated on two fronts: the imported British magazines, such as *The Strand* and *Pearson's*, were too highly priced for the mass reading public's budget even in American reprint form, while the cheaper popular American magazines, such as *Collier's* and *Saturday Evening Post*, ran about a single evening's worth of engaging fiction per week between them. The stage was thus set in the United States for the emergence of what was to be the single most successful medium for the merchandising of cheap fiction to a mass audience in the history of publishing: the pulps. It was an idea whose time had come, and if one publisher had not developed the concept, another would have in short order. At it happened, however, the man who published the first definitive pulp fiction magazine in 1896, *The Argosy*, did so only as one more step to save a foundering magazine, not as a calculated move in opening a new publishing frontier. Frank Andrew Munsey, who first converted his feebly conceived children's weekly of 1882, *The Golden Argosy*, into a boy's adventure story paper called simply *The Argosy* in 1888, then into a general illustrated monthly magazine of the same name in 1894, finally tried making it a monthly all-fiction adult adventure story magazine companion to his previously successful, general, illustrated *Munsey's Magazine* of 1891. By printing his new 1896 version of *The Argosy* on pulp paper and omitting all illustrative art, Munsey found he could provide a fat bundle of reading matter for a dime, well below the quarter charged at the time by slick paper magazines of similar bulk, such as *Harper's* or *The Century*. Moreover, a great deal of the normal editorial content of such general magazines was pictorial, while in their fastidious prose, nonfiction usually had a marked edge in pages over fiction. On the average, it would be safe to say that a single monthly issue of *The Argosy* of 1896 held more fiction than any six of the leading general monthlies of the time—and it was virtually *all* sensational adventure and mystery fiction of reasonably mature quality.

That this kind of magazine was exactly what the mass adult reading public of the 1890s wanted was at once evidenced by the steep increase in *The Argosy's* circulation. From a rock-bottom low of nine thousand in 1894, the new *Argosy's* sales figures quickly soared to eighty thousand, gradually ascending to a peak of half a million by 1907, a mere decade from its start. *The Argosy* was not long alone in its pulp paper splendor, but it was some time before its burgeoning imitators equalled or surpassed it in overall story quality. The inspired early editorial work in the post-1895 *Argosy* was not that of Munsey, who was much more involved in *Munsey's Magazine* and other projects by that time, but that of Matthew White, Jr., who had joined the Munsey staff in 1886 (and who was later closely aided by Robert "Bob" Davis, a Munsey editor hired in 1904). That White's judgment was sound is indicated by the impressive roster of writers whose early work was printed in *The Argosy* between 1896 and 1910: James Branch Cabell, Upton Sinclair, Mary Roberts Rinehart, Sidney Porter (later "O. Henry"), Susan Glaspell, George Allen England, Albert Payson Terhune, Joseph Louis Vance, Frank L. Packard, William MacLeod Raine, and Ellis Parker Butler, many of whom became regular contributors to the prestigious *Saturday Evening Post* of the upcoming century.

Among the earliest of *The Argosy's* technical rivals were two other Munsey adventure fiction pulps, *The All-Story* of 1905 (later *All-Story Weekly*) and *The Cavalier* of 1908. Both monthlies and both essentially duplicate *Argosies* with interchangeable authors and cover artists, these two new publications in effect put an over 220-page, all-fiction Munsey magazine on the newsstands three times a month; and when *All-Story* combined with *Cavalier* and went weekly in 1913, there were *five* Munsey adventure pulps for sale every month—and they all sold, voluminously. There seemed to be plenty of people able to devour twelve hundred closely printed pages of Munsey fiction per month—and more, if the sales of other publishers' action fiction pulps are added to those of the Munsey magazines. It must be kept in mind that ten cents in the 1900s would buy about what a dollar will buy today, at a time when most actual incomes were smaller in real purchasing power. It can accordingly be assumed that most buyers of the early pulps rarely bought on impulse or just to read one or two stories by favorite authors; they read their money's worth out of every magazine purchased. A persistent point made in letters to the editors at this time and later is that the readers read every story in every issue; many even rated them in terms of enjoyment derived. Contemporary authors can only weep for that once vast reading public, a public that sustained the pulps for fifty years.

Among the early and most substantial imitators of *The Argosy* were such other 7 inch by 10 inch quarto pulp magazines containing roughly 150 to 200 pages of adventure and action fiction as Street & Smith's *Popular Magazine* of 1904, which reached a quarter million in circulation by 1905; *Gunter's Magazine*, also of 1904, another Street & Smith response to *The Argosy* (with a leavening of romantic fiction in an attempt to appeal to some female readers), which became *The New Magazine* under another publisher in 1910, then returned to Street & Smith as *New Story Magazine* in 1912; *People's Magazine*, a third Street & Smith undertaking of 1906 with an early emphasis on detective fiction rather than straight adventure; *The Top-Notch* of 1910, a final Street & Smith effort in the general action story field issued in an initial dime-novel format, with a bias toward the sports fiction story; *The Blue Book* of 1907 (originally titled *The Monthly Story* Magazine in its 1905 inauguration), a companion magazine to the women-oriented *Red Book* and the later, theater-slanted *Green Book* of the same period; *Short Stories* of 1910, previously an all-fiction reprint magazine of high price and slick paper; and *Adventure* of 1910, the first issue of which actually appeared on slick paper, apparently for promotional reasons. Some of these newcomers carried a fifteen-cent price, justifying it by a modicum of interior illustrations, while the early *Top-Notch*, the smallest in length of the lot, tried for a nickel, but none ever surpassed the enormous circulation lead attained by *The Argosy* or attempted to emulate the weekly publication of *All-Story* (later merged with *The Argosy* into a single Munsey pulp adventure fiction weekly in 1920, after *The Argosy* itself had been a weekly since 1917), although *Popular, Short Stories, Adventure,* and *Top-Notch* eventually went to twice a month publication for varying periods of time.

It soon became evident to some of these pulp fiction entrepreneurs that the needs of their newly tapped reading public might not be wholly met by action fiction in bulk, and that many readers, as indicated by a growing demand in libraries and bookstores, wanted to read rather narrowly along one line of popular fiction, most notably in the 1910s that of detective and mystery narrative, although a spreading interest in Western fiction was not far behind. Street & Smith, of course, had earlier noted this phenomenon in their nineteenth-century nickel library series, where tens of thousands of copies of the weekly *Nick Carter* detective and *Buffalo Bill* Western thrillers vanished off the newsstands every seven days. Munsey, however, was the first to investigate specialized fiction interests when he launched *The Rail-road Man's Magazine* in 1906. A monthly pulp, this publication featured much more nonfiction than the other men's adventure magazines and was actually more of a fraternal journal for railroad employees and locomotive buffs than anythng else; it lasted until 1919 and was revived by Munsey in 1929. More typical of the specialized fiction pulp was a second Munsey effort in this direction, *The Ocean* of 1907.

Here, although there was considerable nonfiction, sea stories predominated, with as many as four serials running every month. Munsey's estimate of the public's interest in salt water narratives was misguided, however (in fact, there was never to be a really successful sea story pulp at any time), and he was forced to fold the venture after only a year.

Street & Smith, experimenting a little later in the game, had much better luck. In 1915, they decided to convert the old *Nick Carter* nickel thriller into a new ten-cent semi-monthly pulp magazine of detective fiction, called *Detective Story Magazine*. Nick Carter stories, often serialized, were still featured, but the bulk of the new magazine's contents were purchased from the same freelance authors then supplying the other pulps. Initially only a slim 128 pages, *Detective Story Magazine* quickly fattened to 160 pages, then switched to a weekly schedule at 144 pages with a steadily mounting circulation through the 1920s. Encouraged by their initial success, Street & Smith proceeded in 1919 to alter their successful *Buffalo Bill* weekly nickel thriller into another specialized pulp, this one called *Western Story Magazine*. Like *Detective Story Magazine*, *Western Story Magazine* was launched as a semi-monthly ten-cent publication of 128 pages. By 1920, however, circulation had swelled to such an extent that *Western Story Magazine*, like its predecessor, became a 144-page dime weekly. Then at 300,000 circulation, it later reached a half million in sales in the mid-1920s when the extraordinarily popular fiction of the hyper-prolific Max Brand (Frederick Faust) began to run in its pages at the rate of two or three serials at a time. A third Street & Smith attempt at a specialized fiction magazine, the fabled *Thrill Book* of 1919, failed because of a lack of courageous editorial direction. Clearly meant to be a magazine emphasizing the weird, bizarre, and fantastic in popular fiction (material which had already proven its wide popularity through its repeated appearance in *Argosy*, where writers famed for fantastic narratives, such as Edgar Rice Burroughs, Abraham Merritt, George Allen England, J. U. Geisy, Francis Stevens, and many others, were acclaimed headliners), *Thrill Book* lacked the nerve to limit its contents to science fiction and fantasy and, by actually taking on the amorphous shape of just another general action pulp, failed to attract the steadfast band of followers who were later to adhere faithfully to such undiluted exponents of fantastic fiction as the *Weird Tales* of 1923 and *Amazing Stories* of 1926. The *Thrill Book* did run some unusual and memorable fantasy—notably Francis Stevens' "The Heads of Cerebus"—but not enough to catch the notice of the multitude of readers who were regularly buying *Argosy* and *All-Story* for the same thing.

Street & Smith continued with their pioneering creation of specialized genre fiction pulps in the 1920s and introduced the long-lived and vastly popular *Love Story Magazine* in 1921 as a 144-page, fifteen-cent weekly—

and as a cheaper companion to two older Street & Smith romantic fiction monthlies, *Smith's Magazine* and *Ainslee's Magazine,* once aspiring slicks, but now down-at-the-heel twenty-cent pulps. The following year, Street & Smith made their own attempt at a salt spray magazine with *Sea Stories* (which had to be abandoned by 1930 and converted to a mystery-adventure pulp called *Excitement*); they also introduced the nation's first magazine of collegiate fiction in *College Stories,* anticipating the later peak success in that field of *College Humor. Sport Story* was first published in 1923, as a companion to the sports-oriented *Top-Notch,* while by 1927 another long-established nickel-thriller weekly (actually then selling at seven cents), Harry E. Wolff's *Wild West Weekly,* with its feature novels about Young Wild West, was taken over by Street & Smith as a straight Western fiction weekly with the same name.

In the meantime, other publishers had been busy, particularly in the detective and Western fiction fields. H. L. Mencken and George Jean Nathan, engaged in developing their famed *Smart Set Magazine,* merrily launched three deliberate potboiler magazines in the 1910s to bring in supportive funds for *Smart Set.* The first two of these "louse" magazines, as Mencken and Nathan called them, were routine spicy story pulps of the innocent sort prefigured by Street & Smith's *Live Stories* of 1913 or their earlier *Yellow Book* of 1897, the kind of magazine which sold well in wartime; and Mencken and Nathan's *Parisienne* of 1915 and *Saucy Stories* of 1916 were specifically created with the young, war-excited American in mind. Both were immediate hits, with the second giving the leading naughty story magazine of the time, *Snappy Stories,* strong competition for its position. (It might be mentioned at this point that some variety of risqué pulp fiction was always on sale under dozens of different titles from the turn of the century through the 1950s, many published and distributed in legally *sub rosa* operations. Notable titles in the 1920s and 1930s were *La Paree Stories, Bedtime Stories, 10-Story Book, Saucy Movie Stories, Vice Squad Detective, Spicy Mystery Stories,* and *Hollywood Detective.* There were dozens of other titles, and none ever failed financially; every last one was, in fact, ultimately suppressed only by the authorities.) Mencken and Nathan's third "louse" magazine, however, proved to be quite a different matter from the first two; in fact, its reputation eventually overshadowed that of *Smart Set* itself.

Created several years later in 1920, this new monthly action pulp was titled *Black Mask,* and its initial orientation was toward stories of crime, horror, and the quasi-supernatural. Deliberately sensational in title and content, the feisty magazine was intended to attract readers who wanted more fearsome fare than they could find in the relatively sedate *Detective Story Magazine* and *Mystery Magazine* (the latter being a Frank Tousey venture of 1919, a thirty-two-page, 8 inches by 11 inches dime publication featuring cheaply acquired fiction by minor writers). A pitch was made for women readers by the early subtitle wording, "A Magazine of Mystery, Romance, and Adventure," but there was little of the boy-girl romancing that packed the pages of *Ainslee's* or *Love Story Magazine* of the following year; indeed, the cover of the October 1920 issue depicted a young woman cowering from a hot branding iron that has *already* branded her cheek with a livid, smoking image. Although there were a number of generally straightforward detective problem stories in the early issues, these probably reflected the kind of rejects from *Detective Story Magazine* the editors were initially forced to buy, and the obviously desired theme was powerfully rendered in blood and thunder. There was, needless to say, little hint of the restrained, coldly realistic, well-paced fiction that *Black Mask* was later to personify in the writing of Dashiell Hammett, Raymond Chandler, Paul Cain, Raoul Whitfield, and others. Indeed, *Black Mask*, for all of its fame as a pioneering hard-boiled detective story magazine in the 1920s, was in fact a long time in finding its real focus. For most of the 1920s, *Black Mask* was described in its cover subtitle variously as a magazine of air, Western, adventure, and he-man fiction, as well as of detective fiction, and its contents reflected that description. Such later noted writers of tough crime fiction as Whitfield and Horace McCoy initially wrote little but air and Western stories for *Black Mask*. It was not, in fact, until the public impact and circulation rise of the very late 1920s that accompanied the major Hammett serials, such as *Red Harvest* and *The Maltese Falcon*, that *Black Mask* became wholly a magazine of tough detective fiction. In the meantime, there was little influence exerted on other pulp magazines, and the first out-and-out *Black Mask* imitator, *Black Aces*, did not appear until 1931, while such strong and lasting parallel crime fiction magazines as *Dime Detective* and *Detective Tales* did not reach their peaks of quality until the middle 1930s.

In the 1920s, following the advent of *Black Mask* and the minor curiosity called *Mystery Magazine*, the only notable introductions in detective story magazines were Munsey's first move into the field in 1924 with the weekly *Flynn's* (later *Flynn's Weekly Detective Fiction* and finally *Flynn's Detective Fiction Weekly*), starting out with two hundred pages for a dime; Edwin Baird's somewhat earlier *Detective Tales* of 1923, an oddly old-fashioned magazine which quickly jumped to an 8½ inches by 11¼ inches format (the size of the "true" detective and "confession" slicks of the period), but retained its pulp paper as its title changed to a twenty-five cent *Real Detective Tales & Mystery Stories* in 1924; the Priscilla Company's *Mystery Stories* of 1925, a quality twenty-five cent magazine of 160 pages, emphasizing true crime accounts and crime action fiction; W. M. Clayton's *Clues: A Magazine of Detective Stories* of 1926, which directly paralleled *Detective Story Magazine* and ran twice a month for a while in the late 1920s at fifteen cents; Dell's short-lived *Crime Mysteries* of 1927, a fifteen-cent, 120-page monthly which featured much of the interest in the horrific and grisly which characterized the early *Black Mask*; and Harold Hersey's *Dragnet Magazine* of 1928, a twenty-cent, 128-page monthly which was later (in 1931) to become the famed *Ten Detective Aces*, in which such top pulp writers as Lester Dent and Norvell Page wrote monthly novelettes about continuing feature characters in deliberately fantastic and gruesome adventures. The great bulk of the pulps jamming the newsstands of the 1920s were adventures and Westerns, with detectives a slim third, and a random spotting of other early genre pulps, such as *Ghost Stories, Weird Tales, Amazing Stories, Secret Service Stories, Sky Birds,* and the like. The earlier adventure pulps had been augmented by such 1920s titles as *The Danger Trail, Complete Stories, Five-Novels Monthly, Tropical Adventures, Thrills, Romance, Ace-High Magazine,* etc., while the Western fiction deluge inaugurated by *Western Story Magazine* counted among its 1920s arrivals *The Frontier, Lariat, Cowboy Stories, West, Rangeland Stories, Western Trails,* and many others.

It was at the close of the 1920s, however, that the real torrent of new pulps (and fresh varieties of pulps) took place. Suddenly, by 1929, all sorts of new kinds of pulp magazines were appearing—World War I action fiction, in such titles as *War Stories* (actually dating from 1926), *Submarine Stories, Navy Stories, Triple-X Magazine, War Novels, Over the Top,* and a sub-genre which quickly outgrew its parent: air war fiction, featuring *Airplane Stories, Wings, Sky Birds, Aces, Air Stories, Eagles of the Air, Sky Riders, Zeppelin Stories*; gangster fiction, typified by such new titles as *Racketeer Stories, Gun Molls, Speakeasy Stories, Gang World, Gangster Stories, Gangland Stories, The Underworld*; and science fiction, reflected by *Amazing Stories, Science Wonder Stories, Air Wonder Stories, Scientific Detective Monthly,* and (just around the corner in 1930) *Astounding Stories of Super-Science.* The quality of pulp fiction had become speedier and breezier, too, with a general dumping of the kind of prolix description and circumlocution which had filled many of those earlier, endless pages in *The Argosy* and *Detective Story Magazine,* and reflected the general tenor of turn of the century fiction. Those writers who had anticipated the looser, swifter style, such as Edgar Rice Burroughs, Max Brand, Dashiell Hammett, Robert E. Howard, Erle Stanley Gardner, continued to flourish in the decade ahead, while many others stodgily prominent in the 1910s and 1920s, vanished completely from the fast-action pulps of the 1930s, much as certain silent film idols, such as John Gilbert and Ramon Navarro, had essentially slipped from view with their own passing medium.

The rising tide of new pulp variations surged into the 1930s, seeing the birth of such minor one-pulp genres as *Prison Stories, New York Stories,*

Courtroom Stories, Fire Fighters, Jungle Stories, Northwest Stories, Front Page Stories, and similar titles as well as the introduction of many F. B. I. pulps, such as *Federal Agent, Public Enemy, G-Men, G-Men Detective, Ace G-Man Stories, The Feds;* the formal mixing of genre themes and risqué fiction in such mid-1930s magazines as *Spicy Mystery Stories, Spicy Detective Stories, Spicy Adventure Stories, Spicy Western Stories, Saucy Detective, Saucy Movie Tales, Scarlet Adventures, Hollywood Detective;* the unleashing of a number of sadistic horror fiction magazines, such as *Dime Mystery Magazine, Horror Stories, Terror Tales, Uncanny Tales, Eerie Stories, Thrilling Mystery, Ace Mystery Magazine;* plus even more new detective pulp titles—*Popular Detective, Thrilling Detective, Dime Detective, Detective Tales, New Detective, Crime Busters, Private Detective Stories, Black Book Detective, Double Detective, Strange Detective Mysteries;* Westerns—*Western Aces, Mavericks, 10-Story Western, Popular Western, Dime Western Magazine, All Western Magazine, Nickel Western, Thrilling Western, Thrilling Ranch Stories;* adventures—*Action Stories, Thrilling Adventures, All-American Fiction, Dynamic Adventures, Excitement, Northwest Stories, Golden Fleece, Oriental Stories, Magic Carpet;* air war—*Air War, Dare-Devil Aces, Sky Aces, Battle Birds, War Birds, Sky Fighters, Sky Devils, George Bruce's Contact, George Bruce's Squadron;* and science fiction—*Miracle Science and Fantasy Stories, Thrilling Wonder Stories, Startling Stories, Marvel Science Stories, Dynamic Stories, Planet Stories.*

Many of the multitude of new magazines were the product of freshly formed pulp chain publishers who carried as many as thirty or more pulp titles apiece; others were the releases of older publishers attracted to the market by the sizable and rising profits in an economic recession (for a nation out of work had little choice but to drink or read, and with bootleg whisky at a quarter a shot, many chose to read cheap fiction much of the time). Among the major publishers who flooded the newsstands with pulps in the wake of Munsey and Street & Smith were Dell Publishing Co., Fiction House, the Hersey Magazines, Clayton Magazines, Popular Publications, Thrilling Publications, Culture Publications, Standard Publications (later Better Publications), the A. A. Wynn magazines, and others, including spinoffs or front publishers set up by established houses to bring out yet more strings of pulps, such as Fictioneers, Inc., backed by Popular Publications, or Trojan Publishing Co., established by Culture Publications, Inc. At the helms of many of the pulps fielded by these publishers, sometimes editing as many as a dozen or more at once, were a number of talented and canny men, such as the much acclaimed Joseph T. "Cap" Shaw of the later *Black Mask;* Harold Brainerd Hersey of *Thrill Book, Ace-High Magazine, The Danger Trail, Clues-Detective,* and *Dragnet;* John W. Campbell, Jr. of *Astounding Science Fiction* and *Unknown*

Worlds; John L. Nanovic of numerous Street & Smith titles; Ken White of *Dime Detective*; Farnsworth Wright of *Weird Tales* and *Oriental Stories*; Leo Margulies of the Thrilling chain, who shone in his handling of *Thrilling Wonder Stories* and *Startling Stories*; Henry Steeger of Popular, who supervised almost three dozen titles from *Horror Stories* to *Glamorous Love Stories*; Rogers Terrill, direct editor of all Popular titles under Steeger; Hugo Gernsback of *Amazing Stories* and *Wonder Stories*; Daisy Bacon of *Love Story Magazine*; F. Orlin Tremaine of *Top-Notch* and *Astounding Stories*; A. A. Wynn of *Ten Detective Aces*; Donald Kennicott of *Blue Book*; and others of equal capacity and accomplishment.

Probably the most notable and memorable achievement of the large pulp chain publishers and their editors in the 1930s was the fostering of the rebirth of the hero novel, once so central to the prosperity of the nickel thriller magazines of the 1890s. The first of these new monthly pulps was Gilbert Patten's little known *Swift Story Magazine* of November 1930, which, aside from its twenty-cent price and digest pulp size, itself unusual and innovative for the time, anticipated the content and format of the other hero pulps that followed in every detail: 128-page length, a recurrent hero in a monthly feature novel dominating the magazine—Derek Dane, Sky Sleuth in this case—several illustrations in the lead novel, a group of short stories in the closing pages, a department for the readers, and a lurid cover featuring the hero. Next, five months later, was Street & Smith's *Shadow Magazine* of April 1931, which introduced the dual identity outlaw crime fighter to the hero pulps; then came Standard Publications' *Phantom Detective* of February 1933, a *Shadow* imitation; Street & Smith's *Doc Savage* and *Nick Carter* of March 1933, covering the themes of exotic, fantastic adventure and the private detective respectively; Standard's *Lone Eagle* of September 1933, featuring a World War I air ace; Popular's *Spider* and *G-8 and His Battle Aces* of October 1933, presenting yet another masked crime fighter (the best of the lot) and a second World War I air ace *cum* spy respectively; Street & Smith's *Pete Rice* of November 1933, showcasing the first cowpoke sheriff in the hero pulps; Rose Wyn's *Secret Agent "X"* of February 1934, carrying the fourth hidden identity avenger of crime; Street & Smith's *Bill Barnes*, also of February 1934, a pulp with a contemporary aviation hero like Derek Dane; Popular's *Operator #5* of April 1934, introducing an American master spy facing contemporary enemy operations and foreign invasions; Popular's *Dusty Ayres and His Battle Birds* of July 1934, the first science fiction hero pulp, featuring a future interplanetary war; Popular's *Secret Six* of October 1934, multiplying the dual identity crime fighter by six; Ranger Publications' *Masked Rider* Western of December 1934, starring an imitation of the Lone Ranger of radio; Dell's *Doctor Death* of February 1935, introducing the first criminal lead character, *à la* Fu Manchu, in a hero pulp; and Fawcett Publications' *Terence X, O'Leary's War Birds* of March 1935, a second science fiction air war hero pulp.

The astonishing average was one new hero pulp every two months between January 1933 and April 1935, most of which kept going for the remainder of the decade. Nor did the pace slacken; these seventeen stalwart openers of the heroic way were followed by as many more over the next few years: *Wu Fang, Dr. Yen Sin, G-Men, Public Enemy* (later *Federal Agent*), *The Whisperer, The Skipper, Captain Satan, Captain Hazzard, Captain Combat, Captain Danger, Mavericks, Jungle Stories, Ka-Zar, The Lone Ranger, The Masked Detective, The Ghost* (later *The Green Ghost Detective*), *The Octopus, The Scorpion, The Wizard,* and others, including three short-lived newspaper comic strip adaptations: *Flash Gordon, Dan Dunn,* and *Tailspin Tommy.* Only the paper shortages of World War II reduced the tide, but even after the war, in the increasing ebb that ultimately foundered almost all the pulps, a few more hero pulps were expectantly launched, such as *Hopalong Cassiday, Captain Zero,* and *Sheena, Queen of the Jungle,* a comic book adaption. The last hero pulp to succumb was the third to be created, *The Phantom Detective* of 1933, which expired with its 170th, quarterly issue in the summer of 1953. In number of issues, however, it was surpassed by *Doc Savage,* with 181 numbers to the summer of 1949, and the twice-a-month *Shadow,* with 325 issues to the same date. The magazine that pioneered the pulp hero concept and format, *Swift Story Magazine* of 1930, curiously, lasted just one issue.

Illustrating the hero pulps, as well as the pulp chain titles in general, was nearly as important for sales by the 1930s as the lurid covers of nickel thrillers had been for their prosperity at the turn of the century. While the earliest pulps (the Munsey titles, *The Popular, Short Stories,* etc.) were chary of interior illustrations when they carried them at all and generally garbed themselves in thematic covers featuring adventurous or sporting males in static poses with little or no relation to specific stories within, the number and quality of interior drawings increased sharply through competition in the 1920s, while direct story delineation on covers—initiated by the Munsey magazines in the 1910s—gradually became the norm. While a very few well budgeted pulps ran virtually an illustration to a page by the mid-1920s and 1930s (notably the stunning *Blue Book Magazine,* which also ran many illustrations in colored ink, *Real Detective Tales,* and the Spicy chain) and a number of others tried to continue with a minimal number of illustrations or none at all (*Best Detective, Great Detective Stories, Scotland Yard, Dragnet,* and *War Stories* were typical), the vast majority carried at least one lead illustration for every story (very short stories were usually excepted) and between two to four for novelettes and novels, plus continuing department heads. Supplying this considerable quantity of artwork was the task of a few dozen well worked professional ink, watercolor, and oil artists, who varied in quality and reputation from the dreariest kind of scrawlers and daubers who worked for Desperation Row (as the skin-of-their-teeth pulp houses were called) to a number of fine artists of international fame who did occasional or regular pulp magazine illustration for bread-and-butter money. Most, of course, were journeymen artists of reasonable competence and occasional flairs of real genius. Among the renowned artists who did a notable amount of pulp cover or interior work were N. C. Wyeth, Rockwell Kent, John Newton Howitt, J. Allen St. John, Gordon Grant, John R. Neill, Jonn Clymer, Austin Briggs, Nick Eggenhoffer, J. C. Leydendecker, and Herbert Morton Stoops; while the most outstanding and popular of the journeymen numbered such memorable talents as Hubert Rogers, Walter M. Baumhofer, Jerome Rozen, Virgil Finlay, Paul Orban, John Fleming Gould, Frederick Blakeslee, Hannes Bok, Elliot Dold, Edd Cartier, Joseph Doolin, Frank R. Paul, H. W. Wesso, R. G. Harris, Norman Saunders, H. W. Scott, Rudolph Belarski, William Parkhurst, Frank Tinsley, Harold S. DeLay, and Margaret Brundage. Some indifferent comic strip art was introduced experimentally into a few pulps in the 1930s and later, but never with a notable effect on sales or lingering impact, with the possible exception of the classically silly *Sally the Sleuth* in *Spicy Detective Stories.*

The writers, of course—the kids just in from the prairies with their heavy office typewriters in cardboard boxes unloaded on wooden tables in shabby Manhattan furnished rooms, the wealthy top-wordage pulp kings writing from their estates around the world, the five-thousand-words-a-day steady producers in their suburban homes on Long Island or in southern California—these were the mainstay of the whole pulp operation. Following on the early group of pioneer pulp writers in the old Munsey magazines already mentioned, and writing in the 1940s or before, were such gifted and entertaining fictioneers as Edgar Rice Burroughs, whose highly contagious visions of Tarzan and Mars first overwhelmed the mass reading public in Munsey's *All-Story* between January and November 1912; Zane Grey, many of whose best known novels ran in *The Popular, Argosy,* and *All-Story;* Max Brand, who galloped to fame in virtually every early pulp, from *Argosy* and *Blue Book* through *Black Mask* and *Ace High* to *Western Story* and *The Railroad Man's Magazine;* Frank L. Packard, who introduced the dual identity outlaw crime fighter to detective fiction in his Jimmie Dale series for *People's Magazine* and later *Detective Fiction Weekly;* Abraham Merritt, who gripped two generations of readers with his splendid fantasy adventures, such as *The Moon Pool* and *The Ship of Ishtar,* in the Munsey titles; Joel Townsley Rogers, one of the most bizarre writers of suspense prose in American fiction, who wrote both aviation and crime fiction for such disparate magazines as

Wings, Adventure, and *New Detective;* George Bruce, the finest author of air war fiction in the pulps, who was the first writer to have a pulp named for his work—and not just one pulp, but three (*George Bruce's Aces,* 1930; *George Bruce's Squadron,* 1933; and *George Bruce's Contact,* 1933); Howard Phillips Lovecraft, the finest American writer of macabre fiction since Poe, whose stories had enormous reader impact in *Weird Tales* and *Astounding Stories* and now constitute the base of a small publishing industry; Lester Dent, who wrote most of the *Doc Savage* hero pulps, of which over one hundred have been reprinted in top-selling paperback editions in the 1970s; Dashiell Hammett, who introduced his Continental Op, Sam Spade, and other characters in fresh, hard-bitten prose through the pages of *Black Mask, Brief Stories,* and *Argosy-All-Story;* Carroll John Daly, who created the lone private eye concept in *Black Mask* and augmented it through *Dime Detective, Detective Story, Detective Fiction Weekly,* and a dozen other pulps; Robert E. Howard, the freshest writer of adventure prose since Jack London, who wrote for an endless number of pulps from *Weird Tales* to *Argosy,* and whose work is being avidly reprinted here and abroad in over a hundred hardcover and paperback books; Norvell Page, creator of the *Spider* hero pulp, most powerful and memorable of the hero pulp writers and a regular contributor to many other pulps from *Unknown* to *Dime Mystery Magazine;* Raymond Chandler, who added his own bittersweet cachet to crime fiction in *Black Mask* and *Dime Detective* and even experimented with fantasy in *Unknown;* Ray Bradbury, one of the most noted contemporary American authors, who wrote much of his best fiction for *Weird Tales, Startling Stories, Detective Tales,* and other pulps; Walter B. Gibson, creator of *The Shadow* hero pulp and the indefatigable author of over three hundred novels about his cloaked hero, now in active reprint, as well as of other pulp hero series for such magazines as *Crime Busters* and *Mystery Magazine;* and a host of others of almost equal worth and importance: Robert A. Heinlein, Clark Ashton Smith, Steve Fisher, Frank Gruber, John D. MacDonald, Frederick C. Davis, Raoul Whitfield, Paul Cain, Henry S. Whitehead, Clifford D. Simak, Fritz Leiber, Robert Bloch, Luke Short, H. Bedford Jones, Victor Rousseau, Malcolm Jameson, C. L. Moore, Henry Kuttner, Ted Copp, Vincent Starrett, Erle Stanley Gardner, Frederick Nebel, William J. Makin, Cornell Woolrich, Norbert Davis, Donald Wandrei, Howard Wandrei, Harry Sinclair Drago, Fred MacIsaac, Theodore Tinsley, Theodore Sturgeon, John W. Campbell, Jr., Emile C. Tepperman, Cyril Kornbluth, Eric Temple Bell, David H. Keller, Robert J. Hogan, Paul Ernst, J. J. des Ormeaux, Clarence E. Mulford, Walt Coburn, Paul Chadwick, Huge B. Cave, Jack Kofoed, E. E. Smith, Rex Stout, A. E. Van Vogt, Isaac Asimov—a heady roster of famous names (and some no longer so famous), but one that literally cuts away only some of the cream of the pulps' exciting literary fraternity. There are at least fifty more names as well-known or representing as competent a body a work as any on the preceding list. Some—particularly the writers in the science fiction field and the *Black Mask* school—will be mentioned in other essays in this volume; others will have to wait for a longer study to be properly cited.

As can be seen from the authors noted, almost every area of popular American literature was blanketed by the pulps, and nearly always the involvement was both intimate and massive, leaving a major and permanent impression behind. There never was a time before or since that more good, engaging prose fiction (with, admittedly, a sizable, perhaps essential admixture of rubbish) has been available as cheaply to so many people. It lasted more than half a century, but when it entered its decline, the end came quickly. Many pulp readers of the time could see it coming, although the bulk of the editors and publishers in those later years did not seem so prescient. Since it was, by and large, their new policies and approaches to the fiction they were packaging that hastened the ruin of the pulps, this is perhaps not too surprising.

What happened is that the war years of the 1940s not only led to a reduction in the size of the pulps, their frequency of publication, their abundance of titles, and their very sturdiness (many issues had to be published with only one staple to conserve metal), but to the dismemberment of much of the established editorial staffs as well, with many going into the armed forces or war work. In most cases, these veterans of the great pulp boom of the 1930s, often with little formal schooling and sharing many of the tastes and needs of their readers, were replaced by young, draft-exempt people direct from college with liberal arts degrees in hand, who had rarely had the time or inclination to open a pulp for four or more years previously. Instead of feeling that they were the new, fortunate custodians of a marvelously varied treasure house of ongoing accomplishments and exciting possibilities, most seemed to believe that they had been put in charge of horrendously lowbrow products in antiquated packaging, badly in need of immediate improvement. The improvement they felt necessary, unfortunately, was the discarding of the lurid, raffish veneer, which attracted the bulk of their readership, and supplanting it with a neat, trimmed, proper, respectable, "distinguished" look which would permit the pulp editors to hold their heads up along Publishers Row in the future. The most extreme steps along this line were taken at what had become the economic mainstay of the shortage-racked pulp chains, Street & Smith, and when the prosperous flagship threw the Jolly Roger and the cutlasses overboard and broke out the doilies and teacups, it was really all over for the pulps. Through the 1940s, they were improved to death; in the 1950s, the corpses were interred.

The tragedy was compounded by the fact that, while the Street & Smith pulp packages were being upgraded to invisibility so far as the public was concerned, and their contents made increasingly unpalatable (the editorship of the classic *Detective Story Magazine* was taken over in the 1940s by Daisy Bacon, whose whole previous experience and orientation had been derived from her decades with *Love Story Magazine*), the general level of pulp writing elsewhere was improving enormously. A fresh generation of fine young pulp writers, who had cut their creative eye-teeth on the pulps as kids, was entering the field: Frederic Brown, John D. MacDonald, David Goodis, John McPartland, David Karp, Jack Vance, Philip K. Dick, Harlan Ellison, Evan Hunter, James Causey, Robert Turner, Day Keene, Richard S. Prather, Louis L'Amour, and a great many others. Their beautifully written, highly imaginative and innovative stories filled many of the surviving pulps, notably those of the hardily conservative Popular chain, as well as most of the burgeoning science fiction pulps. It was to no avail; as the sales of the top-selling Street & Smith chain tumbled in the wake of the deadly new garb of neat propriety imposed on its pulps, national magazine distributors grew more nervous and reluctant about carrying any pulps at all. Individual dealers gave over more news-stand space to the proliferating comic books and cut back on that afforded the slower-selling pulps, often stacking them in odd corners rather than giving them cover display. What people did not see, or did not see well, they were less inclined to look for and buy. (It must be kept in mind, too, that the hard-core, devoted purchasers of particular pulp titles were always in a minority among the largely impulsive pulp public. If *Argosy*, say, was prominently displayed, it sold to some extent through familiarity with the title and the look of the cover; hidden from immediate sight, it was not sought out enough to sustain anything like the previous level of sales.) Basically, the public simply wanted light entertainment. If comic books and the exploding new field of paperback fiction (which demanded less space from dealers than pulps) were more visible than the pulps, the public's money was largely spent in these areas. When one of the two major national distributors of magazines refused to carry pulps any more in the early 1950s, it was all over for the chain publishers. A colorful hand-ful of pulps survived, largely because of strong specialized markets (such as *Ranch Romances*' healthy newsstand pull in the Midwest and North-west, and the tendency of devoted science fiction fans to buy all of the titles in their field as if they were one publication), but almost all had to adopt the digest pulp size to get even a hope of display at the newsstands. One or two, such as *Argosy* and *Blue Book*, gave up their pulp format and contents altogether and began fresh careers as general slick magazines with male appeal.

Although the bulk of their outlets were gone by the mid-1950s, the new writers remained. Those turning out science fiction had no real problem, for most of their old markets kept publishing, often as the only pulp titles left in the reorganized chains, but other writers had to find fresh sources of income. One of two new digest-size pulps were created with some success to carry some of this material in the crime, detective, and Western fiction fields, notably in Flying Eagle's *Manhunt, Murder! Alfred Hitchcock's Mystery Magazine,* and *Gunsmoke,* but by and large the more adaptable writers turned to the brand new markets for original paperback book fiction, such as Fawcett's Gold Medal Books, Atlas News's Lion Books, and similar title lines at Signet and Dell. These markets were almost exclusively for book-length novels, but paid very well in contrast to the penny-a-word rate still prevailing with most pulps at their demise. A few old-line pulp writers tried these new outlets, as well as the field of hardcover publishing to which most went. Lester Dent of *Doc Savage* tried both, for example, but generally speaking, it was the postwar group of newcomers, such as Day Keene, John D. MacDonald, and David Goodis, who flourished handsomely in the original paperback field.

Still, the pulps as they had been known in their heyday had irrevocably passed from the land. The sight, feel, and smell of them is no more, apart from the shelves of collectors, rare book dealers, and institutions. Only the living heart of their contents beats healthily in the myriad of briskly selling reprints that continue to be unearthed in great quantity from their yellowing pages both here and abroad where—notably in France and Japan—a youthful cabal of interest has sprung up in recent years. The pulps are dead, but at no time has literary and critical awareness of them been livelier than today.

RESEARCH COLLECTIONS

Larry Landrum's listing of major library research collections of pulps and dime novels in his essay on detective and mystery novels in this volume has well anticipated any similar listing that I might make, and although I will augment his listing here, there is no point in my repeating it. Primarily, I will use this space to discuss briefly certain problems likely to be encountered in making use of institutional pulp collections.

The State Historical Society of Wisconsin at Madison holds the August Derleth pulp collection, largely comprising fantasy and science fiction pulps, some in incomplete runs, together with many detective and other genre pulps to which the prolific Derleth contributed material; some of these latter items are relatively rare.

The Literature Department stacks at the San Francisco Public Library house a complete collection of all the science fiction pulps covered in the Donald B. Day *Index to the Science Fiction Magazines: 1926-1950,* extending the runs to the present date.

The San Francisco Academy of Comic Art contains what has been described as the finest cross-genre collection of pulps and dime novels in any public institution, holding key or first issue examples of virtually every pulp, as well as many complete runs of titles in all pulp areas. The academy also provides the researcher with the unique opportunity to study pulps in close conjunction with large special collections in *all* other areas of the popular narrative arts, from comic strips through hardcover and paperback detective, Western, adventure, and science fiction, children's books, comic books, films, drama, general fiction, story papers, general periodicals in all areas, extensive bound newspaper runs, Sherlockiana, Dickensiana, etc., all housed and indexed for efficient cross reference. The academy can provide a perfect, bound facsimile of any pulp on high quality paper, including reproductions of the original color covers, for any fellow institution or serious researcher, at about $12 an issue.

The researcher interested in examining detective, Western, science fiction, or other genre pulps in the institutional collections listed here and elsewhere in this volume should bear the following information in mind.

1. No comprehensive pulp collection exists (although that at the San Francisco Academy of Comic Art comes closest in breadth of material represented); all suffer frequent and wide gaps in various areas. The researcher may well have to go to a number of widely separated institutions in order to locate a given group of titles and dates, and even then there may be some he will not be able to find. Science fiction pulp collections tend to be the most complete, however, due to the assiduity of the private collectors whose files have now entered public institutions.

2. Pulp collections are in varying degrees of accessibility. The Library of Congress pulps, once they are ferreted out, can be one or two days in reaching the Main Library from the warehouse where they are stored, and they are also in dangerously bad condition. The pulps in Special Collections at the University of California at Los Angeles are usually brought promptly, but they are kept in a large number of boxes and often filed out of logical genre or title sequence in these boxes, so that the researcher, usually limited to one box at a time, can spend much time going through successive boxes if he wishes to examine any considerable number of pulps. It would be wise, accordingly, to discuss accessibility factors with the institutions prior to visiting them, in order to have a reasonable idea of how much time will have to be expended. It is quite likely to be more than one would spend in looking at an equivalent number of hardcover books from the stacks of most institutions.

3. The readability condition of pulps will usually vary greatly within the confines of each collection. Few institutions, unfortunately, have the budgets or the inclination to replace poor copies of pulps received as parts of donated collections with better ones, so that these poor copies steadily

deteriorate to the degree that they are used and according to the conditions under which they are stored. The researcher and librarian may well find that a pulp vital to the former's concerns is so browned and brittle with age that it literally cannot be further used without falling to pieces, so that the researcher will have to find another copy at some other institution—if he can. The librarian, meanwhile, will remove the pulp from the stacks and put it away to await restoration or duplication, but will rarely check the collection further to locate similarly aged pulps, which will accordingly continue to stay on the institution's actively accessible list until they also are discovered at the worst possible time. One rarely will be able to learn about the condition of pulps in advance of a visit (many of these collections are not used by anyone for years at a time), so that this is a hazard to be met at any institution.

4. Since study time is understandably limited at most institutions, one will frequently want to leave pulps with stories marked for reproduction by the library. Since reproductive equipment can vary greatly in quality from place to place, it will be wise to sample this by making some few copies of pulp material on the premises, although more and more institutions are acquiring fine reproductive equipment which will provide stunning copies.

5. If one hopes to conduct pulp research with the concurrent aid of critical and historical texts, it would be advisable either to bring along copies of these works or check the institution's general reference stacks prior to arrival. The fact that a library holds a large, donated pulp collection (almost no institution has actually built its own collection from scratch) is no guarantee it will own many specialized reference books in the field—or, indeed, that any of the institution staff will themselves have much knowledge of, or interest in, their pulp holdings.

HISTORY AND CRITICISM

This essay is concerned with the pulps as a publishing phenomenon, rather than with specific works or even bodies of work which appeared in the pulps. Accordingly, these notes reflect that concern and deal only with those texts that relate in some substantial way to the history of pulps or of some variety of pulps. Texts largely concentrating on single writers who happened to appear in the pulps, or on extant popular literary forms which of necessity were represented by pulp genre titles, are not discussed, although a number of such works are covered by other pieces in this volume.

Very little of consequence has been written about the pulps as a publishing form in books from the major trade or academic publishers, either in the past or present. A good deal more has been done in limited edition texts, often in paper wrappers, from small publishers, while a small number of relevant and informative pieces do appear from time to time in a few academic and amateur press periodicals devoted to various aspects of the popular arts.

As a display case of pulp covers, Chelsea House's large volume simply titled *The Pulps*, edited by Tony Goodstone, has considerable merit. Limited in its referential scope and in the representative value of the individual covers reproduced (all in full color) to the resources of the editor's small collection, the book nevertheless provides a reasonably good visual introduction to the newsstand impact and appeal of the pulps over much of their existence. The book's greatest flaw lies in its concentration on the pulp covers of the 1930s (the area of the editor's personal interest), its slighting of the pulps of the 1920s and earlier, and its all but total ignoring of the pulps of the 1940s and later. In its accompanying textual pages, a very abbreviated and inept "history" of the pulps is set forth, together with a largely unimaginative selection of pulp fiction and interior art over the decades. The emphasis in the latter often seems to be on "name" authors regardless of the worth of the material selected (where shortness seems to be a primary factor); for example, a dreadfully bad early piece by Tennessee Williams from *Weird Tales* is included, apparently just because it is by Williams. Similarly, bad to poor pieces by such fine writers as H. P. Lovecraft, Robert E. Howard, Dashiell Hammett, Ray Bradbury, Max Brand, and others are included; on the other hand, relatively good stories by Edgar Rice Burroughs, Clark Ashton Smith, Malcom Jameson, and others are to be found. The interior art selected runs the gamut from fine to dreadful, with much more of the latter than the former, while the reproduction is uniformly poor.

Another pulp text from a major trade publisher is Quentin Reynolds' history of Street & Smith, *The Fiction Factory, or From Pulp Row to Quality Street*. Chiefly of use for its interesting, though not very thoughtful or selective, series of pulp cover reproductions in color and black and white, this volume is primarily a puff job, bought and paid for by Street & Smith. The general thrust of the Reynolds text, as implied in the subtitle, is that Street & Smith has "made it" into big-time publishing by shucking its dismal old line of pulps and developing such paragons of periodical excellence as *Mademoiselle*, *Charm*, and *Living For Young Homemakers*. (Nevertheless, Random House was astute enough, in trying to find *some* sales for the prefinanced vanity job, to splash plenty of pulp covers on the glossy wraparound jacket.) Reynolds' history is dull, circumspect, often misinformed, and obviously the result of a few weeks' cramming before the writing. It does, however, represent the only extant history of any real length covering a major pulp publisher as such, aside from the three generally unsatisfactory texts dealing with the Munsey Company.

The first of these is an autobiographical work by Munsey himself, *The*

Founding of the Munsey Publishing House, which is colorful and lively with regard to Munsey's vicissitudes and triumphs in the publishing business through 1906, but of little use with regard to the texts and art of the Munsey magazines themselves. The same is largely true of George Britt's posthumous study of Munsey, *Forty Years, Forty Millions,* where references to the Munsey pulps—the book is basically concerned with Munsey's newspaper activity—are primarily for background color and anecdote, rather than celebration or critical concern. Neither book has much to offer in the way of illustrative data on the Munsey pulps. The same is unfortunately true of Frank Luther Mott's account of the Munsey Company in his generally exhaustive, five-volume *History of American Magazines.* Mott, as in most of his lengthy pieces on major American magazines, is much more concerned with the relatively trivial data of financing and the musical chair ins and outs of editors and publishers than with the physical contents from year to year of the magazines he is discussing. In personal taste, he is not overly interested in fiction and not at all in pulp fiction; accordingly, he slights even those occasional pulp titles published by the slick paper magazine companies with which his work is primarily concerned. His piece on Munsey in volume four of his set represents his work's only coverage of a pulp publisher, and even here his emphasis is on Munsey's one major slick, the relatively feeble *Munsey's Magazine.* The bulk of the data in the piece is derived from the Munsey and Britt works cited, and it too is largely valid for reference to the limited extent it deals with the Munsey pulps at all.

Excellent as anecdotal color relevant to the creative lives and commerce of the pulp writers in the 1930s and 1940s are two fine works: Frank Gruber, *The Pulp Jungle,* and Robert Turner, *Some of My Best Friends Are Writers, But I Wouldn't Want My Daughter to Marry One.* Turner, however, is much more reliable in areas of strict fact than Gruber, wherein anecdotes are often attributed to the wrong writers or editors or to the wrong time and place. There is a good deal of interesting critical commentary on many of the pulps in both books, although Turner is, again, more astute here than Gruber. Neither book, unfortunately, carries an index or illustrations, although Gruber has a nice display of pulp covers in its wraparound jacket. Harold Hersey's *Pulpwood Editor* is rather superficial and a bit confused in its relatively brief attempt to blanket what was obviously a very complex and exciting career in pulp editing that involved over fifty pulps, but nevertheless of great value in illustrating the capacity and intelligence necessarily involved in mass pulp editing. (Hersey's later, long article in *Golden Atom* for 1953, "Looking Backward Into the Future," which emphasizes his science fiction and fantasy pulp work, is much more precise and interesting than his formal hardcover book.) The book is well indexed, although unillustrated, and has a partial listing of Hersey's pulps.

An interesting but unfortunately latter-day look at the work of pulp agents (the focus is almost wholly on sales to Gold Medal Books and other paperback replacements of the pulps) is to be found in Donald McCampbell's *Don't Step on It—It Might Be a Writer*. Again, there are no illustrations, but there is a useful index. In a class by itself is the only serious study of a single pulp magazine issued by a major publisher, Philip José Farmer's *Doc Savage: His Apocalyptic Life*. It has no index or illustrations, but contains a series of highly informative appendices.

Among formal instructional texts on pulp and general fiction writing between 1900 and 1930, few provide much worthwhile data on pulps *per se*, aside from the transient editorial requirements prevailing at the time of the book's publication. (While a study of such requirements can obviously be very informative, they are much better researched in the numerous writers' magazines of the period on a month-to-month basis than by leapfrogging among the various how-to-write texts.) The handful of writing manuals that do contain a good bit of information about the pulp magazines and pulp writers as such are: *This Fiction Business*, by H. Bedford Jones; *The Fiction Factory*, by John Milton Edwards (pseudonym for William Wallace Cook); *Love Story Writer*, by Daisy Bacon; and *Science Fiction Handbook*, by L. Sprague de Camp.

Book-length studies of detective fiction or collections of shorter studies rarely mention any pulps other than *Black Mask*, and they are usually misinformed about even that title, thinking it was wholly a detective fiction magazine from the start. A partial exception is David Madden's anthology of articles by various writers, *Tough Guy Writers of the Thirties*, in which *Black Mask* nominally receives a long and separate discussion by Philip Durham. Durham is aware of *Black Mask's* early multi-genre aspect and mentions it, but too quickly becomes involved in an exegesis on his King Charles' Heads, Dashiell Hammett and Raymond Chandler (despite the assignment of special articles—all the studies in the book were written to order—on Hammett and Chandler to other hands), to say much of interest about the magazine itself. (Even in discussing Chandler, Durham seems unaware that the best of Chandler's pulp detective fiction appeared in *Dime Detective*—which he does not mention—rather than in *Black Mask*.) Otherwise, despite the book's assumed focus on the style of writing that prevailed in the detective pulps from 1930 on, there is no other discussion of pulps in any of the articles in the volume; there is not even an entry for "pulps" or "pulp magazines" in the index.

The few books to deal seriously with Western fiction neglect the pulps similarly, excepting only John G. Cawelti's *The Six-Gun Mystique*, in which the importance of Western pulps is at least acknowledged, and a number of major pulp titles are listed (oddly including *Doc Savage*), but little informative comment about the pulps themselves is made in the text.

Similarly, Max Brand's and Zane Grey's pulp sales are duly noted in books on the authors (the two best are *Max Brand: The Big Westerner,* by Robert Easton, and *Zane Grey,* by Frank Gruber), but little or nothing is said about the pulps involved, not even such relevant matters as the kind and amount of illustrative art given to major pulp works by the writers discussed. In the area of science fiction, on the other hand, an abundance of talented and scholarly minded "fans," who literally grew up with the pulps of that genre, have seen to it that the central relevance of the pulps to the development of science fiction in the twentieth century has received its just dues in a vast number of amateur, small press, and generally published titles. In fact, there is virtually no text on science fiction as a genre in which the pulps are not discussed in often intimate and highly informative length. (Since a great number of these will doubtless be analyzed and listed in the essay on science fiction in this volume, I will avoid extensive repetition here, mentioning only a few titles in the forthcoming passages dealing with small press publications on the pulps.) Aside from texts on detective fiction, Western fiction, science fiction, and fantasy, little has appeared from general or academic publishers in book form covering fictional genres prominent in the pulps (there has been no study, for example, of adventure fiction as such, or of popular war fiction, etc.), so that the relevant pulp facets here remain as unexamined on this level as in detective and Western fiction.

Some of the very few texts which touch knowledgeably on the fields of periodical popular fiction which preceded the pulps might advantageously be mentioned here. These would include, certainly, the monumental study of the first dime-novel publishing house, *The House of Beadle and Adams and Its Dime and Nickel Novels,* by Albert Johanssen; *Dime Novels,* by Edmund Pearson; *Books in Black and Red,* by Edmund Pearson; *Villains Galore,* by Mary Noel; *Virgin Land,* by Henry Nash Smith; *Bang! Bang!,* by George Ade; *Penrod Jashber,* by Booth Tarkington; and (largely for impressionistic humor) *A Plea for Old Cap Collier,* by Irvin S. Cobb.

In the small press area, several works of direct and important relevance to the pulp fiction magazine field have appeared in recent years, while more will apparently continue to appear, thanks to the development over the past decade of a new, concentrated body of interest among bibliophiles in the contents, sequences, and fine points of differentiation to be found in the pulps. This growth of interest has been augmented by the appearance in recent years of several small journals devoted wholly to the pulps, their contents, and collection. Prominent among the small press works which serve this interest is a fine impressionistic study of several pulp genres, with no pretense to formal history, popular fiction writer Ron Goulart's engaging *Cheap Thrills.* Goulart quickly covers most of the major pulp genres with an engaging gloss and includes a number of black

and white pages of pulp cover and interior art. Some very pertinent in-
mation about pulp writing and editing can be found in the several pages
of direct quotes obtained by Goulart from surviving pulp writers which
close this book. More informative in the sense of its organized emphasis
on a single pulp subject is Robert Kenneth Jones' *The Shudder Pulps* from
a mail order book business, Fax Collector's Editions. This data- and
quotation-packed text deals wholly with the sex-and-sadism pulps of the
1930s, includes a great many reduced black and white pulp cover and
interior art cuts, and is meticulously indexed (although, curiously, no
checklist of the pulps covered is included). In *The Weird Tales Story*,
also from Fax, Robert Weinberg similarly focuses on a single pulp subject,
the development of the famed fantasy magazine between 1923 and 1973.
Although this work lacks the fine index of the Jones title, it includes a
large number of black and white photos and reproductions of covers and
interior art from *Weird Tales*. As with the Goulart books, a number of
short but worthwhile quotations from writers and artists associated with
the magazine are included. Alva Rogers' *A Requiem for Astounding*, from
Advent Publishers, a mail-order house developed within science fiction
fandom in the 1950s, deals engagingly with the history of the central
science fiction pulp, *Astounding Stories*, through all of its literary and
titular permutations, and includes both a detailed index and an excellent
selection of cover and interior art in black and white reproduction.

The foregoing small press titles are hardcover in the original editions.
Among paperback (and generally smaller) texts from this source, one of
the most notable works is Lohr McKinstrey and Robert Weinberg's *The
Hero Pulp Index*. This painstaking and nearly inclusive compilation by
story title and date of all the issues of all the hero pulps in the 1930s and
later has been a vital reference guide to research in this important area of
pulp publishing. Included are a number of black and white pulp cover
reproductions, and summaries of the themes of each pulp covered. Some
separate (and generally well done) studies of individual hero pulps are
The Man Behind Doc Savage, by Robert Weinberg; *America's Secret
Service Ace*, by Nick Carr, which deals with *Operator #5; Gangland's
Doom*, by Frank Eisgruber, Jr., covering *The Shadow;* and *The Many
Faces of the Whisperer*, by Will Murray. None of these texts, published
by Weinberg with no separate press name, has indexes, but all are well
and appropriately illustrated with black and white cuts from the pulps
covered and contain full lists of the issues discussed. Forthcoming texts in
this series from Weinberg will include studies of *The Spider* and *G-8 and
His Battle Aces*.

Among the small reprint publishers almost wholly devoted to hardcover
republication of important works from the pulps (many of which are often
reprinted profitably by major paperback houses in several editions) are

Arkham House of Wisconsin, founded in 1939 and the forerunner of all such publishers, with nearly one hundred titles to its credit, and largely concerned with pulp material from *Weird Tales* and the science fiction and fantasy pulps (particularly the work of H. P. Lovecraft, Clark Ashton Smith, and August Derleth); Donald M. Grant of Rhode Island, who has published over twenty-four titles to date that are largely involved with the pulp works of Robert E. Howard; Fax Collector's Editions, which reprints memorable fiction from the broad range of pulps in a myriad of hardcover and paperback volumes; and Carcosa of North Carolina, which specializes in large, definitive anthologies of the pulp work of major writers in all genres. The science fiction field fostered a number of such pulp reprint publishers in the postwar decades, notably Gnome Press, Fantasy Press, Shasta Publishers, and Hadley Publishing (later Grant-Hadley, now Donald M. Grant), but all but the last are now moribund, the large paperback houses having taken over science fiction and fantasy pulp reprinting directly.

Of important contemporary periodicals concerned in whole or in part with the study of pulps (excluding science fiction fan publications, which are a highly specialized field of their own), it is necessary to mention Nils Hardin's *Xenophile*, Will Murray's *Duende*, Ray B. Browne's *The Journal of Popular Culture*, Robert Weinberg's *Weird Tales Collector*, Allen J. Hubin's *The Armchair Detective*, J. Randolph Cox's *The Dime Novel Round-up*, and Donald Halpern's *Antaeus*. All are firmly established, long-lived publications worth consulting in previous and forthcoming issues.

BIBLIOGRAPHY

BOOKS

Ade, George. *Bang! Bang!* New York: J. H. Sears, 1928.

Bacon, Daisy. *Love Story Writer.* New York: Hermitage House, 1954.

Bedford-Jones, Henry. *This Fiction Business.* New York: Covici-Freide, 1929.

Britt, George. *Forty Years, Forty Millions: The Career of Frank A. Munsey.* New York: n. p., 1935.

Carr, Nick. *America's Secret Service Ace.* Pulp Classics 7. Oak Lawn, Ill.: n. p., 1974.

Cawelti, John G. *The Six-Gun Mystique.* Bowling Green, Ohio: Bowling Green University Popular Press, 1970.

Cobb, Irvin S. *A Plea For Old Cap Collier.* New York: George H. Doran, 1921.

Cook, William Wallace (John Milton Edwards). *The Fiction Factory.* Ridgewood, N.J.: The Editor Co., 1912.

Day, Donald B. *Index to the Science Fiction Magazines: 1926-1950.* Portland, Oregon: Perri Press, 1952.

De Camp, L(yon) Sprague. *Science Fiction Handbook.* New York: Hermitage House, 1953. Reprint. Rev. ed. Philadelphia: Owlswick Press, 1975.

Easton, Robert. *Max Brand: The Big Westerner.* Norman: University of Oklahoma Press, 1970.

Eisgruber, Frank, Jr. *Gangland's Doom: The Shadow of the Pulps.* Oak Lawn, Ill.: n. p., 1974.

Farmer, Philip José. *Doc Savage: His Apocalyptic Life.* Garden City, N.Y.: Doubleday, 1973.

Farsace, Larry. *Golden Atom.* New York: Golden Atom Publications, 1955.

Goodstone, Tony, ed. *The Pulps.* New York: Chelsea House, 1970.

Goulart Ron. *Cheap Thrills: An Informal History of the Pulp Magazines.* New Rochelle N.Y.: Arlington House, 1972.

Gruber, Frank. *The Pulp Jungle.* Los Angeles: Sherbourne Press, 1967.

———. *Zane Grey.* Cleveland, Ohio: World, 1970.

Hersey, Harold. *Pulpwood Editor.* New York: Frederick A. Stokes, 1937.

———. "Looking Backward Into the Future." *Golden Atom,* 1953, 45-68.

Johanssen, Albert. *The House of Beadle and Adams and Its Dime and Nickel Novels.* Norman: University of Oklahoma Press, 1950. Supplement, 1962.

Jones, H. Bedford. *This Fiction Business.* New York: Covici-Fried, 1929.

Jones, Robert Kenneth. *The Shudder Pulps: A History of the Weird Menace Magazines of the 1930s.* West Linn, Oreg.: Fax Collector's Editions, 1975.

McCampbell, Donald. *Don't Step On It—It Might Be a Writer: Reminiscences of a Literary Agent.* Los Angeles: Sherbourne Press, 1972.

McKinstrey, Lohr, and Robert Weinberg. *The Hero Pulp Index.* Evergreen, Colo.: Opar Press, 1971.

Madden, David, ed. *Tough Guy Writers of the Thirties.* Carbondale: Southern Illinois University Press, 1968.

Mott, Frank Luther. *A History of American Magazines. Volume IV.* Cambridge, Mass.: Harvard University Press, 1957.

Munsey, Frank. *The Founding of the Munsey Publishing House.* New York: Munsey, 1907.

Murray, Will. *The Many Faces of the Whisperer.* Pulp 7. Oak Lawn, Ill.: n. p., 1975.

Noel, Mary. *Villains Galore: The Heyday of the Popular Story Weekly.* New York: Macmillan, 1954.

Pearson, Edmund. *Books in Black and Red.* New York: Macmillan, 1923.

———. *Dime Novels.* Boston: Little, Brown, 1929.

Reynolds, Quenton. *The Fiction Factory, or, From Pulp Row to Quality Street.* New York: Random House, 1955.

Rogers, Alva. *A Requiem For Astounding.* Chicago: Advent, 1964.

Smith, Henry Nash. *Virgin Land.* Cambridge, Mass.: Harvard University Press, 1950.

Tarkington, Booth. *Penrod Jashber.* Garden City, N.Y.: Doubleday, 1929.

Turner, Robert. *Some of My Best Friends Are Writers, But I Wouldn't Want My Daughter to Marry One!* Los Angeles: Sherbourne Press, 1970.

Weinberg, Robert. *The Man Behind Doc Savage: A Tribute to Lester Dent.* Oak Lawn, Ill.: n. p., 1974.

———. *The Weird Tales Story.* West Linn, Ore.: Fax Collector's Editions, 1977.

PERIODICALS

Antaeus. New York. Issues undated.
The Armchair Detective. Del Mar, Calif., 1967-.
The Dime Novel Round-Up. Lawrence, Kans. 1913-.
Duende. North Quincy, Mass., 1977-.
The Journal of Popular Culture. Bowling Green, Ohio, 1977-.
Weird Tales Collector. Chicago, 1977-.
Xenophile. St. Louis, Mo., 1974-.

CHAPTER 10 Radio

Nicholas A. Sharp

Since its earliest days, radio has been widely recognized as a tremendously potent force in American culture. Educators were among the medium's first and most enthusiastic exploiters (see S. E. Frost, Jr., *Education's Own Stations: The History of Broadcast Licenses Issued to Educational Institutions*), and the earliest "broadcast pioneers"—Guglielmo Marconi, Lee De Forest, Reginald Fessenden, David Sarnoff—felt strongly that radio would improve the level of American taste by offering every citizen the finest of the world's music, poetry, and drama. In 1910, for instance, De Forest broadcast Caruso and the entire Metropolitan Opera Company as a demonstration of radio's ability to spread Culture (with a capital "C") throughout the land. Less than four years after Fessenden had first used a microphone, the medium's artistic potential was being recognized.

Not surprisingly, therefore, the literature of radio is copious and virtually co-natal with the medium itself. Even excluding the technical and engineering literature (which dates back to Hertz and other pre-Marconi experimenters), a thorough bibliographer will find newspaper and magazine speculations about "wireless telephony"—even television—scattered here and there throughout the last decade of the nineteenth century. The legal and bureaucratic literature of litigation and regulation dates to Marconi's patent documents in 1896, and by World War I these writings had already assumed huge proportions; moreover, their importance in gauging radio's effect on popular culture cannot be ignored. If the United States Navy, for instance, had been allowed to retain full control of radio's development after 1918, as seemed to be a real possibility at the time (see *History of Communications-Electronics in the United States Navy*, prepared by Captain S. L. Howeth, USN), there would never have been a Herbert Hoover to cooperate with the major broadcasters in the development of commercial program patterns.

In this chapter, however, the concentration is on neither the educational, technical, nor bureaucratic aspects of radio. Rather, the focus is on the programming and the personalities connected with radio's development as an entertainment medium. Though an occasional nod is bent toward the international setting within which radio has developed, primary attention is given to the American scene, particularly to comedy, drama, and variety show broadcasting. Inevitably, some attention is given to news, sports, and and "high culture" broadcasting—all of which are at least partially entertainment. Moreover, much of the material reviewed here concerns history, not the contemporary scene. Radio's "golden age," the years of its most obvious and dominating impact on the culture of everyday Americans, came in the 1930s and 1940s.

Even in this comparatively limited field, however, it is not possible to attempt a comprehensive bibliography within the confines of this article. The first issue of *Radio Broadcast* appeared in 1922, and by 1950 there were literally scores of daily, weekly, monthly, and quarterly publications devoted exclusively or primarily to radio programming. Every newspaper and general interest magazine of the 1930s and 1940s had regular columnists assigned to cover radio, and the most popular programs generated dozens of "spin-off" book publications every year—Gertrude Berg's *The Rise of the Goldbergs* and Phillips H. Lord's *Seth Parker's Sunday Evening Meeting: An Entertainment in One Act* are just two examples.

HISTORIC OUTLINE

It is not easy to summarize the history of radio. In its early days, the medium grew so rapidly and in such diverse ways that time still has not fully clarified what things were important and what were merely interesting. One thing, however, is obvious. Radio in America has gone through three developmental stages—the "pioneer" period from the 1890s through the mid-1920s, the "golden age" of network programs in the 1930s and 1940s, and the "television age" which began in the late 1940s and is still in progress. From the viewpoint of the "old-time radio" fans, this pattern is almost tragic, representing periods of adventurous youth, glorious maturity, and senile decay. From a less partisan position, however, the pattern looks better. It shows a medium that went through a period of early technological and commercial development, then through a boom period of unstable and rapid growth, and finally achieved a stable place in the structure of American business and culture.

The pioneer years can be traced to Heinrich Hertz and the other pre-Marconi investigators of the nineteenth century. For our purposes, however, radio really began in 1895 when the young Italian inventor, Guglielmo Marconi, took his wireless telegraph to England. Customs inspectors smashed his prototype (they thought it was a bomb), but he rebuilt it, obtained British patents, and soon had commercial backers. Before the turn of the century, he had used Morse code to broadcast the results of the

America's Cup yacht race, and virtually all of the major Western powers were investigating wireless for military and naval communication.

During the next decade, Reginald Fessenden, Lee de Forest, and scores of other inventors and enthusiasts developed technical improvements—the microphone, the vacuum tube, various crystal receivers—which made radio both inexpensive and exciting.

During World War I, the United States Navy took over almost exclusive control of American radio. It severely limited the use of the medium but made rapid technological progress. Then, in 1919, radio stations again became independent, and the mass production of commercial radio equipment became profitable. General Electric formed the Radio Corporation of America, which took over Marconi's original American company with the idea that the big profits would lie in the production of radio parts. They were not really thinking of broadcasting as anything but a marketing device to help sell radio receivers. The other big electrical companies like Westinghouse and American Telephone and Telegraph had similar ideas. Each of them set up broadcasting stations in order to put interesting things on the air, believing (rightly) that they could sell more receivers that way.

Many other people, however, were also interested in broadcasting. Amateurs broadcast from their garages and basements for the pure joy of contacting people in distant places. Newspapers set up stations to broadcast election results, sporting events, and other notable occurences because they hoped to sell more newspapers by whetting the public's interest. By the early 1920s, dance bands and Broadway plays were being broadcast live from the cramped, ill-equipped studios of pioneer stations, such as WJZ and KDKA, and many stations were beginning to broadcast on regular schedules. Meanwhile, performers were beginning to agitate for payment when they performed on radio.

By 1925, the American Society of Composers, Artists, and Performers (ASCAP) was insisting on pay scales for radio performances. The National Association of Broadcasters had been formed to protect the interests of station owners, and local stations were using telephone lines to achieve multi-station broadcasts of major events. In Chicago, Detroit, Pittsburgh, and other areas, not to mention New York, stations had established their own regular programs of drama, comedy, and vaudeville, many of them with commercial sponsors. Broadcasting had become a business of its own.

In 1926, the General Electric Corporation, Westinghouse, and the Radio Corporation of America formed the National Broadcasting Company. The network system was born. Within a year, the Columbia Broadcasting System was also operating. NBC contracted to supply each local station with a certain number of programs, most of which originated in New York. Local stations still had considerable time at their own disposal, but they had to carry the programs which NBC sent them. NBC, in turn, sold air time to sponsors. The sponsors were to supply the programs; the network simply used its facilities to broadcast whatever program the sponsors wanted. Sponsors, in turn, wanted to use air time to sell products, and they turned to advertising agencies to produce shows that would sell their wares. The result was that certain advertising agencies became the major employers of actors, singers, directors, writers, and all the other show business professions. Only Hollywood and Broadway could compete as a talent market. Vaudeville died, but radio grew and grew.

Programming patterns on the networks developed rapidly. At first, comedy-variety shows dominated, and sponsored programs were heard largely at night. In 1929, when Freeman Gosden and Charles Correll took their local Chicago program to New York, "Amos 'n Andy" became radio's first nationwide phenomenon. Soon, other shows with a continued story line and consistent characters became standard nightime fare, though the variety show performers like Eddie Cantor, Ed Wynn, and Al Jolson continued to be the biggest crowd pleasers.

In a relatively short time, the "Amos 'n Andy" concept was metamorphosed into a form designed for daytime listeners, mainly housewives. The daily, fifteen-minute soap opera was born, and within a few years it became almost the only thing that the networks could carry during the day. There were always sponsors for a soap opera.

During the middle and late 1930s, the networks began to discover that they had programming capabilities of their own. They did not have to rely on advertising firms for programs. All of the networks had certain time periods which no sponsor was using, and the networks had to sustain their programming with fillers. So they began using that time for programs, such as the "Columbia Workshop," which were showcases for experimentation. Archibald MacLeish's verse-drama, "The Fall of the City," for instance, was written for and performed as a part of sustaining-time programming. Programs stressing new, dynamic approaches to history, current events, and the arts were developed, and in some cases they became hits. In turn, they stimulated sponsors, such as *Time* magazine, to develop programs, such as "The March of Time," which recreated current events through dramatization.

During the later 1930s two more networks were formed. The American Broadcasting Company was formed when anti-trust actions forced RCA to give up NBC, and NBC was forced to become one network rather than two; ABC had formerly been the NBC "blue" network which supplemented the larger, more popular "red" network. Also, the Mutual Broadcasting System was formed as a more-or-less cooperative venture among stations which wanted more independence than they would be allowed as part of NBC or CBS and yet needed the greater range of programming and services which only a network could provide.

By 1940, the basic programming patterns were set, and they continued through World War II with very little major change. But in the late 1940s, commercial television became a reality. By 1950, television was cutting heavily into radio's market. Network radio tried to respond with some new, creative concepts, such as "Monitor," a weekend program of interviews, satire, and news features. Basically, the entertainment role that network radio programs had filled for two decades was being thoroughly assumed by television. Radio programming, except for news, reverted primarily to the owners of individual stations. Pioneer stations became "Top-40" stations just to survive.

Today, radio programming is still basically a local station phenomenon, though more and more stations find they must turn to prepackaged models ("beautiful music," "adult rock," etc.) to compete for advertising dollars. The networks sponsor a few shows (CBS's "Mystery Theater" is one example), but radio is again a local medium.

Radio is no longer the big business that it was in 1940. It is, however, still a vital, important factor in our society. Like its budgets, radio's pretentions and ambitions have become smaller. Yet it continues to be a medium of essential communication, especially at the local level. Its broadcasts of community events, its occasionally fiery talk shows featuring local luminaries, and its constant barrage of local advertisements make it an integral part of most people's lives. Radio fills a crucial need in our society, and as long as it does, it will continue to be a major part of America's popular culture.

REFERENCE WORKS

There is no such thing as an authoritative or comprehensive bibliography of radio broadcasting; perhaps such a thing is impossible with our current data bases and programming capacities. There are, however, a number of useful bibliographic sources for the study of radio, and some of them are almost indispensable.

Eleanor Blum's *Basic Books in the Mass Media: An Annotated, Selected Booklist Covering General Communications, Book Publishing, Broadcasting, Film, Magazines, Newspapers, Advertising, Indexes, and Scholarly and Professional Periodicals* is exactly what it claims to be. The third chapter includes 123 entries on broadcasting, many of them exclusively on radio, and all entries give broad, general treatment to various aspects of the subject. Her annotations are succinct, thorough, and useful. The exact canons governing her selections of material are admittedly vague, and her concern is almost entirely with book-length materials, but for a generalist's overview of the whole field, her selections of histories, handbooks, and bibliographies provide an excellent starting point. She includes subject and author-title indexes.

For the person with a specific interest in the "golden age," Oscar Rose's *Radio Broadcasting and Television: An Annotated Bibliography* offers a useful starting point for works produced during the 1930s and 1940s. It is far from an ideal starting point, to be sure. He ignores any number of important works, such as Arnheim's critical study of radio as a formal aesthetic mode (noted in History and Criticism), and he displays a remarkable blindness toward some performers and programs, especially those connected with variety shows. On the other hand, he includes items that might well escape a modern person's thinking; he devotes a subsection of his list to novels and plays with radio backgrounds, for instance, and since many of them are by noted radio personalities (for example, Fielden Farrington's *The Big Noise*, and Mary Margaret McBride's *Tune in for Elizabeth: Career Story of a Radio Interviewer*), they add a significant viewpoint to the study of the medium. Rose's subject headings are practical and useful, and his inclusion of an index and of annotations for each item makes his work quite useful.

G. Howard Poteet's *Published Radio, Television, and Film Scripts* devotes 125 pages to radio dramas available in printed form. Scripts are cataloged alphabetically by title of the program on which they were aired. He analyzes anthologies and lists their contents by title or program of the individual work. It seems to be a thorough piece of work for published scripts and is an important tool for anyone with an aesthetic or critical bent.

Two substantial works have recently appeared that should prove to be of real utility to those who seek recorded versions of radio programming. Michael R. Pitts' *Radio Soundtracks: A Reference Guide* is the closest thing to a comprehensive guide which has yet appeared. Even so, it is far from complete, as Pitts himself points out. It is, however, a reasonably thorough treatment of commercially available tapes and records of radio shows, including both the generally available materials and those which circulate more exclusively among collectors and enthusiasts. It does not attempt to cover the recordings available in research libraries only. Though it is small, the booklet is relatively complex and takes some getting used to; the complexities of the field seem to require relatively subtle classification. The index, however, is thorough, and the introduction is clear and informative, both about the book itself and about the legal and technical pitfalls awaiting those who venture into soundtracks. The prolific Marietta Chicorel has produced a huge three-volume set (Numbers 7, 7a, and 7b of the *Chicorel Index* series) entitled *Chicorel Index to the Spoken Arts on*

Discs, Tapes, and Cassettes. Though the focus of the work is broadly on drama and oratory, she has included numerous radio programs among the materials, and she has covered several items which are not mentioned by Pitts. This set of interlocking bibliographies is complex and requires a good deal of effort to use, but it is of real value for students of poetry and drama on radio.

Though its British focus puts it beyond the pale of this essay, the British Broadcasting Corporation's *British Broadcasting 1922-1972: A Selective Bibliography*, edited by John Houle, is worth mentioning as a highly selected listing of interesting readings. It is the third of the BBC's bibliographies on broadcasting (the earlier ones appeared in 1948 and 1958) and is in some ways a model of how an introductory bibliography can be both thorough and brief. Such a work would be useful in America.

Before looking at serial bibliographies, we should also note one important fact regarding book-length publications. Some of the most valuable bibliographies for radio are available only as appendices to scholarly studies in the area of mass communication. The nearest thing America has yet produced to a bibliography of the history of broadcasting is the set of bibliographies at the end of each volume of Erik Barnouw's three-volume *History of Broadcasting in the United States*. The shortest of them lists over two hundred major items, both published and unpublished, and they are a major starting point for any historical item-hunting that a person might wish to do. Similarly, the bibliography in David Holbrook Culbert's *News for Everyman: Radio and Foreign Affairs in Thirties America* constitutes a major resource for any investigation into the history of news broadcasting. This work started as a dissertation (which explains some of its quirks of style and organization), but the thoroughness of the research bore real fruit in the bibliographic essays which constitute part three of the bibliography. The bibliographies included in some other books are also of real value, and until someone produces a truly sophisticated bibliography in the field, they will continue to serve as major resources.

A number of periodicals have published bibliographic information which is important to the study of radio. Kenneth Harwood compiled the "World Bibliography of Selected Periodicals on Broadcasting (Revised)," in the Association for Professional Broadcasting Education's official quarterly, *Journal of Broadcasting*. This article revises the original 1961 "World Bibliography" which listed more than five hundred periodicals, and it both updated the listing and made it more useful. It includes more than seventy periodicals published in the United States, and while it gives only the most limited information about each of them, it is useful because of its clear concern with professional and scholarly, not just popular and "fan," publications.

The *Journal of Broadcasting* is useful also for its regular inclusion of a

"Books Received" feature which amounts to a bibliography of serious items on broadcasting published during each quarter of the year.

An extremely useful publication is the mimeographically reproduced *Mass Media Booknotes* which Christopher H. Sterling releases on a monthly basis from Temple University's Department of Radio-TV-Film. Begun in 1969 as *Broadcast Bibliophile's Booknotes,* it changed names in 1974, but it has continually provided excellent brief reviews and synopses of publications in the whole broadcasting field, including radio.

Other bibliographies, of course, are available, but with the items cited, it should be possible to get a good start on almost any bibliographic problem in the field of radio and popular culture.

Aside from bibliographies and standard reference works (encyclopedias, biographical dictionaries, etc., many of which include substantial articles on radio and radio personalities), there are a number of publications which offer general information on radio programming. *Broadcasting Yearbook,* for instance, has been published annually since 1935 by *Broadcasting,* the monthly magazine published in Washington, D.C., by the National Association of Broadcasters. Each issue includes directories of radio stations, both commercial and educational, and brief histories of ownership, licensure, etc. for each station. Virtually an almanac of information about broadcasting companies, organizations, and networks, each issue includes a bibliography of the year's outstanding books in the field and numerous pieces of statistical information. Feature articles on items of topical interest are included, too.

Another important reference publication is *Radio Annual,* which was put out by *Radio Daily* of New York from 1938 to 1964. Typically, much of the information in each issue of this handbook concerns names and addresses of key personnel at networks, advertising agencies, and radio stations in the major markets. Also, listings of programming information, statistical data on radio listeners, and numerous short articles on current topics of interest are included in each issue.

For the late 1930s, the *Radio Directory,* issued by *Variety,* is a primary source. Edited by Edgar Grunwald, it appeared four times between 1937 and 1941, but did not reappear after World War II. Like the other annuals, it is a compendium of varied information, but its emphasis is especially on advertisers, producers, and artists. When it is remembered that during these years the bulk of commercially successful programs were produced entirely by advertising agencies (the networks themselves produced only the shows that used unsponsored or sustaining time), the interest in advertising personnel becomes understandable. Most importantly, the *Variety Radio Directory* includes brief entries about hundreds of radio performers, writers, and directors, giving primary attention to their achievements in entertainment aspects of the medium.

Other useful reference books are also available. Sydney Head's *Broadcasting in America: A Survey of Radio and Television* is a thorough, carefully researched treatment of the technological, historical, and economic structure of American broadcasting. It pays special attention to the place of radio and television in the total spectrum of the mass media, and it is especially concerned with the effects of advertising. The second edition (1971) is more up-to-date, but the earlier (1956) edition will also be of interest to students concerned with radio history.

A similar work, but with an international focus, is Walter B. Emery's *National and International Systems of Broadcasting: Their History, Operation, and Control.* Organized by continent, then subclassified into regions and finally, nations, the work surveys the entire world. Each nation is considered in terms of the history, regulation, and current status of its national broadcast system.

Two works in the H. W. Wilson "Reference Shelf" series deserve mention in this category. Poyntz Tyler edited *Television and Radio* and Herbert L. Marx, Jr. edited *Television and Radio in American Life.* Each draws from the general circulation periodicals of its day to anthologize approximately twenty articles on the "state of the art" of broadcasting. Each includes a brief bibliography as well. Surprisingly, the Tyler book is the more useful to radio scholars because it includes several pieces on the final demise of network radio drama, but each offers an interesting view of informal public opinion in its day.

Within the last few years, the "nostalgia market" has prepared the way for three extremely important reference volumes concerning "golden age" radio. The most comprehensive of these is John Dunning's *Tune In Yesterday: The Ultimate Encyclopedia of Old Time Radio 1925-1976.* This large, illustrated volume focuses on drama, comedy, and variety programs carried by the major networks during the 1930s and 1940s. It pays attention to bandleaders, newscasters, and local programs only to the extent that they became prominent on a national level. Though the preface specifically disclaims any intention of being complete, Dunning's work is remarkably thorough. His entries, organized alphabetically by program title, range from ten lines to five pages, and they include good brief coverage of all aspects of the programs. He wisely chose to include an index.

While Dunning's is the largest and newest encyclopedia for old radio, Frank Buxton and Bill Owen can claim the first. Their *The Big Broadcast 1920-1950* is a revised, expanded, and polished edition of their earlier *Radio's Golden Age: The Programs and the Personalities.* Their system of listing programs by exact title has established itself as the norm (that is, "The Romance of Helen Trent" is cataloged among the "R's," not the "H's" or "T's"), and their effort was a truly pioneering achievement. On the other hand, their work reveals some idiosyncrasies. Some programs listed include the program title, the type of program (mystery, variety, etc.), the announcer's standard opening, and nothing else. Amount and type of information vary drastically from entry to entry, and crucial pieces of information, such as dates, network changes, and sponsor shifts, are not always included. On the other hand, the revised edition includes substantial articles on "announcers," "cowboys," and other topical entries, and these are excellent supplements to some of the briefer entries. They include an index and a bibliography.

Dunning and Buxton and Owen are the primary encyclopedias for old network programs, but Ron Lackmann's *Remember Radio* deserves mention in this category, too. Though it was obviously intended for the coffee tables of nostalgia buffs, not the library shelves of scholars, it does include some useful information. Primarily, it is a scrapbook of news and publicity photographs of major network radio figures, but it also includes examples of other radioana—program notes, news stories, etc.—and since it has a moderately thorough index, it is of some real utility.

Also along historical lines, Harrison B. Summers' *A Thirty Year History of Programs Carried on National Radio Networks in the United States 1926-1956* is an excellent chronological analysis of network programs. It includes every program carried by the four major networks (NBC, CBS, ABC, and MBS) and analyzes them into a fairly complex set of categories and sub-categories. Drama, for instance, is subdivided into numerous headings, such as "thriller drama" and "detective drama." Then, in a year-by-year analysis, each program is set down in tabular form giving title, sponsors, seasons on the air, network, length, day and hour, and ratings. The work is not, in fact, a history; it is a chronological log involving virtually no narrative; but it is a crucial source of information, and its reprinting by Arno Press as part of the Arno-New York Times series *History of Broadcasting: Radio to Television* has made it readily available.

A work with a more contemporary value is the *Radio Programming Profile*. Published by BF Communications Service in Glen Head, N.Y., it appeared originally in 1967 and has been revised quarterly since then. Focusing on the one hundred top markets in the United States, it offers hour-by-hour analyses of stations' programming and identifies their type of programming, primary audience, and policies and practices. Though intended for advertisers, it is useful for scholars interested in the impact of radio programming in modern society.

A similarly useful publication is the annual booklet put out by the National Association of Broadcasters, *Dimensions of Radio*. Essentially a statistical handbook, it analyzes station revenues, audience patterns, buying trends, and similar information of interest to station owners and operators.

A work of more tightly defined interest is Bernard E. Garnett's *How*

Soulful is Soul Radio?. Looking specifically at programming patterns among stations with a substantially black audience, it is a logical starting point for anyone concerned with radio's relationship to Afro-American culture.

Finally, some mention should be made of the large number of books, many of them college textbooks, on the subject of radio station management, including programming. These works examine radio from a station operator's viewpoint, and they are probably the easiest way for most non-professionals to get a sense of how and why programming patterns take the shapes they do. J. Raleigh Gaines's *Modern Radio Programming* is a commercial radio operator's "how to" book, and it is especially useful because of its glossary of broadcast terms and its index. Another useful book of this sort is *Radio Broadcasting: An Introduction to the Sound Medium*, edited by Robert L. Hilliard. The chapter on "Producing and Directing" (by Earl R. Wynne) gives excellent treatment of the constraints and conventions of modern radio performance. *Modern Radio Station Practices*, by Joseph S. Johnson and Kenneth K. Jones, includes a bibliography, a glossary, the complete Radio Code, and profiles of fourteen commercial stations as well as the usual chapters on operation. There are dozens of other works with a similar purpose, the earliest of them dating to the 1930s, and each has its own unique value in explaining how and why radio functions the way it does.

There are, to be sure, scores of other publications that would merit extensive mention in a longer work on general references for radio, but the works cited here should be enough to get anyone started on a project connected with radio and popular culture.

RESEARCH COLLECTIONS

Radio is blessed with numerous excellent research collections, both public and private. Not surprisingly, these tend to be clustered in California, the northern Midwest, and the Boston to Washington, D.C., section of the Eastern seaboard. There are exceptions, of course, as a look at Lee Ash's fourth edition of *Subject Collections: A Guide to Special Book Collections and Subject Emphases as Reported by University, College, Public, and Special Libraries and Museums in the United States of America and Canada* or the fourth edition of the *Directory of Special Libraries and Information Centers*, edited by Margaret Labash Young, Harold Chester Young, and Anthony T. Kruzas, will reveal. For the most part, however, research opportunities in the South, the Southwest, and the Great Plains are comparatively limited. Private collectors and enthusiasts, of course, are to be found throughout the country, and their resources, especially their collections of recorded radio shows, are not to be dismissed lightly.

These sources are, however, relatively difficult to track down and not easy to assess without actually making a trip to see the materials. A crucial resource for this field is, therefore, Paul T. Jackson's *Collector's Contact Guide 1975* which is Number three in the Record Collectors' Sourcebook Series. This booklet offers names and addresses of clubs, collectors, and dealers in records, including radio recordings, as well as bibliographies of the limited circulation directories, handbooks, and magazines that make the rounds among enthusiasts in the field.

The Washington, D.C., area has three collections of special note. From a bibliographer's viewpoint the most important of these is the Broadcast Pioneer's Library (BPL) in the National Association of Broadcasters' building at 18th and N Streets. While the BPL contains a substantial collection of primary material, especially of clippings and industry records (the "Hedges files"), its more important role is to serve as a clearinghouse and reference center for materials of all sorts connected with radio broadcasting. It features a very sophisticated data retrieval system, and it has a substantial staff devoted full-time to researching in the area of broadcast history.

The Smithsonian is obviously a primary research center, especially the Clark Collection of Radioana in the Museum of History and Technology Branch Library. The Clark Collection is especially strong on very early radio developments. The Manuscript Division of the Library of Congress also has substantial radio materials, including the Eric Sevareid papers.

Just outside Washington, in Fairfax, Virginia, George Mason University houses the Federal Theatre Project Research Center, which has a huge collection of scripts and research materials prepared by the radio branch of Roosevelt's WPA sponsored Federal Theatre Project.

In New York, the Theater Collection of the New York Public Library has a large collection relating to all aspects of the radio industry. ABC, NBC, and CBS have their official libraries in New York, including indexes of program offerings as well as a variety of other information. The Oral History Project at Columbia University has hundreds of pages of material relating to early radio. The Radio Advertising Bureau maintains a library devoted to radio advertising and marketing on Madison Avenue. The holdings include thousands of taped commercials and printed advertisements by major radio advertisers, as well as books and periodicals.

The David Sarnoff Library in Princeton, New Jersey, is a major source of information on the business aspect of radio, and in Philadelphia, Temple University Library houses a substantial collection of scripts and other radioana.

In the Midwest, the most important research center is the Wisconsin State Historical Society's Library in Madison. Their Division of Archives and Manuscripts contains a collection of several thousand recordings (discs) of network radio shows, and the library also has the National Association of Broadcasters' papers as well as other substantial holdings in the form of private and corporate papers of various radio personalities and organizations.

In California, the most important collections are at UCLA's libraries. UCLA has the National Academy of Television Arts and Sciences Television Library which includes, among many other things, a Jack Benny Collection. Also, UCLA's Theater Arts Library has a collection of over fifteen hundred radio scripts and a major collection of books and periodicals. Also in California the North American Radio Archives Library is located in San Francisco. The archives include tapes of fifteen thousand radio programs and substantial slide, script, and book holdings.

In addition to public research centers, there are hundreds, perhaps thousands, of private collectors who are willing to share their enthusiasm and resources, and many of them belong to various organizations, such as the Pacific Broadcast Pioneers and the Society to Preserve and Encourage Radio, Drama, Variety, and Comedy. The best way of breaking into these groups is to use Jackson's *Collector's Contact Guide* and to avoid being shy.

HISTORY AND CRITICISM

Histories of broadcasting are so many and so varied that a good sized bibliography could be devoted exclusively to this one type of literature. They come in a variety of types ranging from the ponderously academic and scholarly to the breezily informal and anecdotal, and when biography, autobiography, and memoir are included, as they should be, the number of works legitimately identifiable as radio history swells to the hundreds. Obviously, this essay will not attempt comprehensive treatment, but a representative selection should indicate the nature of the field.

The premier work on radio history is certainly Erik Barnouw's three-volume *History of Broadcasting in the United States*. Volume I, entitled *A Tower in Babel*, appeared in 1966 and covers the period from Marconi's first experiments to 1933. Volume II, *The Golden Web*, covers the "golden age" and the rise of television up to 1953. Volume III focuses primarily on television but covers the decline of network radio as well; entitled *The Image Empire*, it also covers the experiments and efforts made by local stations and small groups through the mid-1960s. Barnouw writes well, and his volumes are enlivened by many of the more remarkable anecdotes and stories about radio personalities and programs, but his real concern is with the development of the total broadcast system. His analyses of the development of regulatory policies, corporate structures, technical developments, and dominating personalities are remarkably thorough and lucid.

His concern with programming, however, develops entirely from his interest in the larger pattern. With the exception of occasional digressions on such crucially significant phenomena as the popularity of "Amos 'n Andy" or the rise of news broadcasting during the late 1930s, he seldom offers more than summary analyses of programming patterns during any given period of time, and even then he is concerned primarily with the effects of programming developments in the larger patterns of radio's relationship to society. Barnouw's scholarly thoroughness, however, makes him indispensable, and his inclusion of bibliographies, indexes, chronological tables, and summaries of regulations and laws makes his volumes absolutely central to any inquiry into radio's history.

Though actually outside the scope of this paper, another history of broadcasting deserves some mention since it has some of the same concerns as Barnouw and is equally excellent in its own field. Asa Briggs' *History of Broadcasting in the United Kingdom* includes three volumes of a projected four-volume set which will cover the history of British radio and television in the same way that Barnouw has covered American. Less readable than Barnouw, the work is even more mammothly thorough in coverage and magisterial in its authority.

Barnouw's work stands at the end of a long line of radio histories, each of them unique in its own way. Among the most important of these are Gleason L. Archer's *History of Radio to 1926* and *Big Business and Radio*. Archer's concern, like Barnouw's, is essentially an academic interest in the development of the total broadcasting spectrum, especially in the roles of RCA and NBC. A more enjoyable, more "popular" approach is that of Francis Chase, Jr. His *Sound and Fury: An Informal History of Broadcasting* concentrates heavily on the development of programming and the effects of personalities on radio shows. Since his book was intended for popular consumption during radio's heyday, he has few negative remarks to make about anyone. But he is an excellent raconteur, and his retelling of stories, such as the reason that "Grand Ole Opry" became a four-hour show (in order to give "Uncle Jimmy" Thompson time to get his fiddle warmed up) cannot be found in any other source.

Abel Green and Joe Laurie, Jr. also produced an excellent light history of radio based on *Variety*'s coverage of the medium. *Show Biz: from Vaude to Video* covers the whole spectrum of the entertainment field during the first half of the twentieth century, but much of its attention is fixed on radio. It stresses the most sensational events of the time such as Mae West's "lewd" Adam and Eve sketch during the "Chase and Sanborn Hour" in 1937, but it gives decade-by-decade attention to the development of the medium from the performers' viewpoints, and there is no other book-length work which offers a similar approach.

Another popular book, really a folio-sized coffee-table book, is Lowell

Thomas's *Magic Dials: The Story of Radio and Television.* Though the book is filled with impressive but meaningless color photographs, the text is a brief, no-nonsense history of the medium, written in Thomas's characteristic style. Though uncritical in its assumption that the American system of broadcasting is perfect, it is a better piece of writing than its format would lead one to expect.

Irving Settel's *A Pictorial History of Radio* is another coffee-table book. More than anything else, it is a conglomeration of old publicity photos and news shots, but the text is readable, and it is reasonably thorough in its coverage of radio personalities from the 1930s and 1940s.

One of the best popular histories is Sam J. Slate and Joe Cook's collaboration called *It Sounds Impossible.* Both Slate and Cook were active in radio during the 1930s, 1940s, and 1950s, and they frequently include firsthand reminiscences about programs and personalities. Their primary concern, however, is to present a topical history of radio programming. They include chapters on soap opera, comedy, and so on, each one emphasizing the pioneer developers in the form. Their real usefulness is the detail with which they analyze program patterns. For instance, they include one of the few substantial essays on pathos programming ("Queen for a Day," etc.), and their close involvement with various announcers, directors, and writers gives them a tremendous fund of anecdotal material.

More recently, nostalgia has influenced some of the popular histories. Jim Harmon, for instance, has written *The Great Radio Heroes* and *The Great Radio Comedians*, both of which are prefaced with an unabashed appeal to the reader's yearning for the good ol' days. Nevertheless, Harmon does a good job of pulling together interesting facts about the actors, writers, sponsors, and distributors of "Gangbusters," "Inner Sanctum," "The Shadow," etc. He seems to have an endless store of plot summaries, and his critical sense is quite acute. His approach is idiosyncratic and personal, but it is not dilettantish, and the books rank as serious contributions to the field. Similarly, nostalgia (or at least the urge to exploit the nostalgia market) seems to have been the starting point for Madeleine Edmondson and David Round's book, *The Soaps: Daytime Serials of Radio and TV.* Actually, the book is a serious study of the aesthetic and historical development of soap operas, the first 120 pages of which focus on radio. The tone, however, is light, and the appeal is clearly to the reader's fond memories of happier times (such as the Depression, World War II, and the Korean war). The book offers information on the kingpins of radio soap opera (Irma Phillips, Elaine Carrington, and Frank and Anne Hummert) and the various developments in their formulae. It also offers interesting critical hypotheses for the various successes and failures in the form.

Similar but more scholarly (though that may be too strong a term) is

Raymond William Stedman's *Serials: Suspense and Drama by Installment.* Stedman's real concern in this large, illustrated volume is the whole pop aesthetic of the "cliff-hanger" from its first transmutation out of the serialized novel into pulp, film, radio, comic books, and television. Much of his attention goes to radio programs, however, and he takes a scholar's interest in such questions as the history of the writers, for example, "The Shadow." He includes a substantial bibliography, indexes, and an appendix listing daytime network serial dramas.

Within the general field of popular history, two more works deserve some mention. Lloyd R. Morris's *Not So Long Ago* and Robert Campbell's *The Golden Years of Broadcasting: A Celebration of the First 50 Years of Radio and TV on NBC* are both useful works in their own ways. Morris is a general account of radio and is useful as such. Campbell's work is, as the title indicates, unremittingly celebratory of the virtues and accomplishments of the National Broadcasting Company. Large and heavily illustrated, it is filled with minor facts and details about the growth of NBC and, despite its frothiness, is a useful book.

Some of the most serious historical work in the field of radio has focused less on national and network developments than on individual stations. Actually, this is a reasonable way for things to have gone. Radio stations are relatively concrete, stable phenomena with clear histories and a distinctly real existence. Networks, on the other hand, are essentially corporate entities made up of legal contacts and cable linkages. Conceptually and historically, networks are much more difficult to deal with than are actual broadcasting stations. Moreover, since many stations had established themselves as creative, vital programming entities long before RCA created NBC, it is not surprising that many stations are proudly conscious of their histories as separate entities from any network.

Probably the best known work on an individual station is William Peck Banning's *Commercial Broadcasting Pioneer: The WEAF Experiment 1922-1926.* WEAF was AT&T's broadcast outlet in the early 1920s and was deeply involved in the development of both the "toll" broadcasting concept and early multi-station hookups using cables. Banning's study is a scholarly and thorough analysis of early attempts to commercialize radio.

A number of other station histories have been written from a more partisan viewpoint, frequently by principals in a station's development. Elliott M. Sanger, for instance, wrote *Rebel in Radio: The Story of WQXR.* Sanger was general manager of "the radio station of the New York Times" for nearly thirty years, and his tracing of the station's development from a garage-based hobby to the best known classical music station in the country is told with some understandable bias. Similarly, Steve Post's *Playing in the FM Band: A Personal Account of Free Radio* tells the story of listener-sponsored Pacifica radio's New York station from the viewpoint of an advocate and primary participant in the "underground" or "counterculture" programming for which the station became widely known. More commercial but no less biased is Dick Perry's *Not Just A Sound: The Story of WLW*. This strange book offers a laudatory history of "the nation's station," the huge 500,000 watt WLW (which broadcast during the 1920s and 1930s from its Cincinnati tower with ten times the power of any other station in the country) and "fan" oriented biographies of AVCO Broadcasting's six most popular television personalities. The first part of the book, up to page 120, is of real interest to radio fans. The latter part is not.

Other books of interest for their concern with individual radio stations are James F. Evan's *Prairie Farmer and WLS: The Burridge D. Butler Years* and Gerald Carson's *The Roguish World of Dr. Brinkley*, each of which treats the development of a remarkable Midwestern broadcasting enterprise.

For the development of radio news there is really one primary source from which almost any inquiry can be launched. David Holbrook Culbert's *News For Everyman: Radio and Foreign Affairs in Thirties America* is a book of limited scope, focusing on the careers of six news commentators who came to prominence during the last years of the 1930s. The twenty-page bibiliographic essay which he includes with the volume, however, is so current and so thorough that it amounts to a guidebook for research into the historical development of newscasting. Although most of the networks seem to have published promotional pieces, such as NBC's *The Fourth Chime*, which tells a glorified version of NBC's news operation from the 1930s through World War II and includes biographies of various newsmen, Culbert's sane evaluation of various sources is the most reliable guide to information sources on the news.

Biography and autobiography are a major form of historical information about radio, and scores of works have been produced about the "stars" of network shows. Frequently, as with Charles J. Correl and Freeman Gosden's *All About Amos 'n Andy*, biography is not only romanticized but also confounded with the fictional biography of radio characters associated with performers. Also, many of the biographical works produced during radio's heyday are manifestly unreliable, being designed more to tell the fans what they wanted to hear than to convey significant information. Robert Eichberg's *Radio Stars of Today: Behind the Scenes in Broadcasting* is an example of such a work.

On the other hand, first rate biographical materials are becoming more readily available. Two books on David Sarnoff, for instance, open real channels of understanding about this incredibly influential man. Eugene Lyon's *David Sarnoff: A Biography* is a thorough and sympathetic study of the outlines of Sarnoff's career, and the anthology of Sarnoff's own writings—speeches, memoranda, reports, etc.—collected in *Looking Ahead: The Papers of David Sarnoff* constitutes a major addition to biographical studies.

Autobiography and memoirs are also excellent sources of history, provided they be taken with the appropriate dosage of salt, and they have always been popular with publishers. Fred Allen's *Treadmill to Oblivion*, for instance, includes not only "inside" information about radio techniques but also some really penetrating criticism of the medium and its personalities. Allen's comments on the way that Ed Wynne and Eddie Cantor used visual comedy to become stars of an aural medium, for instance, shed real light on the aesthetics of early variety programs and comedy.

Frequently, the reminiscences of "behind-the-scenes" people shed more light than the memoirs of the better known personalities. Carroll Carroll's *None of Your Business or My Life with J. Walter Thompson (Confessions of a Renegade Radio Writer)* gives some real insight into what it was like to work in program production during the years when advertising agencies were the primary producers of commercially successful shows. Though he later became a radio columnist, Carroll speaks with authority about how the interplay of sponsor, star, agency, network, and audience shaped the creation of a successful program in the 1930s. Similarly, Ben Gross's *I Looked and I Listened: Informal Recollections of Radio and Television* offers a journalist's view of how programs and personalities took their unique shapes, especially during the 1920s and 1930s. Joseph Julian's *This Was Radio: A Personal Memoir* offers a lucid and rancorless account of radio from an actor's point of view, and he is particularly enlightening about how the networks responded to Joseph McCarthy's efforts to "clean up" the media in the early 1950s. A truly singular book about the creation of one of radio's most spectacular programs is Kenneth Koch's *The Panic Broadcast: Portrait of an Event*, which tells about the "Mercury Theater on the Air" production of H. G. Wells's *War of the Worlds*, narrated by Orson Welles. Koch wrote the script (which is included in the book), and his account of the preparation and aftermath of the production makes fascinating reading for anyone concerned with this famous broadcast's genesis.

Announcers are a phenomenon unique to radio and television, and their memoirs give a very special perspective on the medium. Ubiquitous as they are, announcers become involved in wider ranges of programming—sports, news, quiz shows, drama—than almost any other persons who are actually heard on the air. Red Barber, for instance, concentrates on sports announcers in his *The Broadcasters*, but his memoirs touch upon a wide range of figures prominent in radio history. Ted Husing's *Ten Years Before the Mike* has a similarly wide ranging set of interests, especially if read in conjunction with the rather maudlin biography called *My Eyes Are in My Heart*, which was based on the "This Is Your Life" television show done after Husing lost his sight due to a brain tumor.

A few contemporary radio personalities have produced interesting books about themselves and their medium. Gene Klavan's *We Die at Dawn: The True Life Story of America's No. 1 Radio Team, or No. 2, or No. 3, Klavan and Finch* is of interest as an example of how the relatively low prestige position of disc jockey can become a springboard to creative, popular broadcasting. Similarly, Herman Weiskopf's *On Three: Inside the Sports Huddle* offers some good insights as to how an essentially local program can achieve a wide following through a dynamic approach.

While radio is long on historical account, however, it is rather short on criticism. Surprisingly few book-length works have ever been published with the intention of explaining, analyzing, or improving the artistic dimensions of the medium, and the majority of those critical studies exhibit surprisingly naive notions about the medium. In a way, this dearth of criticism is hard to explain. The foundations for an effective, sophisticated aesthetic of radio were set down in the 1930s by the art critic Rudolf Arnheim, and the importance of his work was clearly recognized within the intellectual community, if not by professional broadcasters. No less a personage than Herbert Read collaborated with Margaret Ludwig in translating Arnheim's *Radio* for the English-speaking world. Admittedly, Arnheim's formalist aesthetic depends too much on analogy to the perceptual processes of vision, but Arnheim was onto a potentially enlightening approach to the art of radio, and his aesthetic theories still offer a profoundly intelligent means of understanding the beauty in such creations as the "pure" noise of Fibber McGee's closet or the Great Gildersleeve's giggle. Yet no one seems to have read Arnheim, or if they did, they avoided letting any influence show.

Much more representative of most radio criticism is Erik Barnouw's *Mass Communications: Television, Radio, Film, Press; The Media and Their Practice in the United States of America.* Insightful and intelligent, Barnouw offers some extremely useful points for understanding how radio functions and its proper nature as both an aesthetic form and a communications medium. He points to its unique ability to serve an active audience, for instance, and its inherent leaning toward narrative rather than dramatic presentations. For an understanding of the craftsmanship of radio and the processes by which programs are brought into being, he is unsurpassed as a critic; but he is basically uninterested in the more philosophical questions raised by an aesthetician such as Arnheim. Various other critics have also written good, intelligent books about radio as seen from a non-academic viewpoint. Journalists have been among the best. John Crosby, for instance, was the New York *Herald's* radio critic after

World War II, and his *Out of the Blue: A Book about Radio and Television* collects some of his most provocative and enjoyable comments. A sort of William Hazlitt of the airways, he wrote well, and his comments on such productions as the Maurice Evans and Dorothy McGuire broadcast of *Romeo and Juliet* and the annual Easter parade in New York City are examples of truly acute critical sense combined with a real enthusiasm for the medium. Similarly, Albert N. Williams' *Listening: A Collection of Critical Articles on Radio* collects columns and articles originally written for the *Saturday Review of Literature*. Unlike Crosby, Williams is at his best when he looks at the principles and policies governing network program patterns rather than individual shows or persons, and his commentary sheds real light on the character and style of various network programming policies.

Gilbert Seldes wrote two excellent books concerning radio, and he brings to his trenchant criticisms both the bite of the satirist and the affection of a practitioner. In *The Great Audience*, Seldes is heavily concerned with radio, and he scourges the medium for such things as its penchant to write scripts "in order to be forgotten" (so that the audience will tune in for the next show). On the other hand, Seldes was one of the first people to argue seriously that soap opera was an original and serious literary form, and his praise of Rhymer's "Vic and Sade" reveals his fundamental optimism about radio as an artistic medium. In *The Public Arts*, Seldes treats radio along with all the other mass entertainment media, but he notices such important facts as that radio was the turning point at which Americans began to regard entertainment not as a privilege of leisure but as a right to which they were entitled.

No treatment of criticism would be complete without some mention of Marshall McLuhan. A listing of all the works published on, by, and about Marshall McLuhan would require a substantial bibliography in itself, so we can restrict our attention to *The Gutenburg Galaxy* and *Understanding Media: The Extensions of Man*. In these two works, McLuhan lays out his vision of man's extension and definition of himself through his communications media. In *Understanding Media* he sheds constant light, punctuated by occasional shadows of obscurity, on the essential natures of all the electronic media, and his chapter on radio looks harder at the whole medium than anything since Arnheim. To be sure, his vision of radio as "tribal drums" carrying the electrical impulses of the social nervous system was not so totally unprecedented as some have thought it; but it was new and radical enough to influence substantially the thinking of even so seasoned a critic as Raymond Swing (see, for example, Swing's essay on "Radio: the Languishing Giant," *Saturday Review*, August 12, 1967, reprinted in William M. Hammel's *The Popular Arts in America: A Reader*). Having once read McLuhan, no one will ever again see radio in quite the same way, and his comments are certainly among the most influential remarks ever made by a critic.

Besides this essentially artistic and academic criticism, there is also a large and important body of criticism produced by social scientists. Much of this material is of relatively little concern to students of popular culture, being slanted toward marketing and advertising interests of the narrowest variety. Much of it, however, attacks broad social and psychological questions of real importance to historians and critics. Two names of paramount importance in this field are Hadley Cantril and Paul F. Lazarsfeld. Cantril and Gordon W. Allport, for instance, wrote *The Psychology of Radio*, which was the first major attempt to analyze the psychological process by which listeners respond to radio. Cantril also published (with Hazel Gaudet and Herta Herzog) *The Invasion from Mars: A Study in the Psychology of Panic*, which was merely the first of a long list of scholarly and critical publications about Orson Welles's phenomenal Halloween prank. Cantril is best known as a public opinion researcher, of course, and he was among the earliest people to develop scientific methodologies for dealing with radio audiences.

Even more prolific than Cantril, Paul F. Lazarsfeld was probably the most assiduous sociological researcher of the "golden age." In *Radio and the Printed Page*, subtitled *An Introduction to the Study of Radio and Its Role in the Communication of Ideas*, he discussed the nature of the complex interplay between the aural medium and the visual media of books and newspapers. Vitiated by the lack of a sophisticated concept of information as a measurable substance, Lazarsfeld's study is yet interesting for its attempt to see radio as a medium of exchange and change in opinion. Lazarsfeld also worked with Frank N. Stanton to edit two volumes of *Radio Research*, which attempted to digest developments in the field, and he later worked on two studies of public opinion about radio. With Harry Field he produced a report of an extensive survey of public opinion on radio entitled *The People Look at Radio*. Two years later he worked with Patricia Kendall to produce a follow-up study entitled *Radio Listening in America: The People Look at Radio—Again*. In both studies, he was primarily interested in both the content of programming and the nature of public response to programs and advertisement. Characteristically, he was also interested in the effect of criticism on public response.

Since the late 1940s, social scientists have tended to focus their attention on television as the primary grounds for research, and in this trend they are typical of all criticism. With the exception of occasional anomalies, more criticism today subsumes radio within a larger concern with television and, thus, the field of radio criticism is a relatively dead issue with most periodicals and publishers.

Research into the effects of radio on American popular culture will always be complicated. The interplay of business, government, technology, and art, for instance, causes part of the creative tension within which radio has always existed, and this is an extremely difficult interplay to understand. To what extent, for instance, did the combined development of transistor technology and low import taxes for Japanese products influence the direction of radio programming in the 1950s? Perhaps no one will ever answer such questions, yet they are of real importance in our understanding of American civilization, and it is to be hoped that as bibliography in the field becomes more sophisticated, scholars will become increasingly able to find the information they need in order to get closer to the answers.

BIBLIOGRAPHY

BOOKS AND ARTICLES

Allen, Fred. *Treadmill to Oblivion*. Boston: Little, Brown, 1954.

Archer, Gleason L. *Big Business and Radio*. New York: American Historical Society, 1939.

———. *History of Radio to 1926*. New York: American Historical Society, 1938.

Arnheim, Rudolf. *Radio*. Translated by Margaret Ludwig and Herbert Read. London: Faber & Faber, 1936.

Ash, Lee. *Subject Collections: A Guide to Special Book Collections and Subject Emphases as Reported by University, College, Public and Special Libraries and Museums in the United States of America and Canada*. 4th ed. New York: R. R. Bowker, 1974.

Banning, William Peck. *Commercial Broadcasting Pioneer: The WEAF Experiment 1922-1926*. Cambridge, Mass.: Harvard University Press, 1946.

Barber, Walter L. ("Red"). *The Broadcasters*. New York: Dial Press, 1970.

Barnouw, Erik. *History of Broadcasting in the United States*. 3 vols. New York: Oxford University Press, 1966-70.

———. *Mass Communications: Television, Radio, Film, Press; The Media and Their Practice in the United States of America*. New York: Rinehart, 1956.

Berg, Gertrude. *The Rise of the Goldbergs*. New York: Barse and Co., 1931.

Blum, Eleanor. *Basic Books in the Mass Media: An Annotated, Selected Booklist Covering General Communications, Book Publishing, Broadcasting, Film, Magazines, Newspapers, Advertising, Indexes, and Scholarly and Professional Periodicals*. Urbana: University of Illinois Press, 1972.

Briggs, Asa. *History of Broadcasting in the United Kingdom*. 3 vols. London: Oxford University Press, 1961-70.

Buxton, Frank, and Bill Owen. *The Big Broadcast 1920-1950*. New York: Viking, 1972.

———. *Radio's Golden Age: The Programs and the Personalities*. New York: Easton Valley Press, 1966.

Campbell, Robert. *The Golden Years of Broadcasting: A Celebration of the First 50 Years of Radio and TV on NBC.* New York: Charles Scribner's Sons, 1972.

Cantril, Hadley, and Gordon W. Allport. *The Psychology of Radio.* New York: Harper and Brothers, 1935.

Cantril, Hadley; Hazel Gaudet; and Herta Herzog. *The Invasion from Mars: A Study in the Psychology of Panic.* Princeton, N.J.: Princeton University Press, 1940.

Carroll, Carroll. *None of Your Business or My Life With J. Walter Thompson (Confessions of a Renegade Radio Writer).* New York: Cowles Book Co., 1970.

Carson, Gerald. *The Roguish World of Dr. Brinkley.* New York: Holt, Rinehart and Winston, 1960.

Chase, Francis, Jr. *Sound and Fury: An Informal History of Broadcasting.* New York: Harper and Brothers, 1942.

Chicorel, Marietta, ed. *Chicorel Index to the Spoken Arts on Discs, Tapes, and Cassettes.* 3 vols. Chicorel Index Series, vols. 7, 7a, 7b. New York: Chicorel Library Publishing Corp., 1973-74.

Correl, Charles J., and Freeman Gosden. *All About Amos 'n Andy.* New York: Rand McNally, 1929.

Crosby, John. *Out of the Blue: A Book About Radio and Television.* New York: Simon and Schuster, 1952.

Culbert, David H. *News for Everyman: Radio and Foreign Affairs in Thirties America.* Westport, Conn.: Greenwood Press, 1976.

Dunning, John. *Tune In Yesterday: The Ultimate Encyclopedia of Old Time Radio 1925-1976.* Englewood Cliffs, N.J.: Prentice-Hall, 1976.

Edmondson, Madeleine, and David Round. *The Soaps: Daytime Serials of Radio and TV.* New York: Stein and Day, 1973.

Eichberg, Robert. *Radio Stars of Today: or Behind the Scenes in Broadcasting.* Boston: L. C. Page, 1937.

Emery, Walter B. *National and International Systems of Broadcasting: Their History, Operation, and Control.* East Lansing: Michigan State University Press, 1969.

Evans, James F. *Prairie Farmer and WLS: The Burridge D. Butler Years.* Urbana: University of Illinois Press, 1969.

Farrington, Fielden. *The Big Noise.* New York: Crown, 1946.

Frost, S. E., Jr. *Education's Own Stations: The History of Broadcast Licenses Issued to Educational Institutions.* Chicago: University of Chicago Press, 1937.

Gaines, J. Raleigh. *Modern Radio Programming.* Blue Ridge Summit, Pa.: TAB Books, 1973.

Garnett, Bernard E. *How Soulful Is Soul Radio?* Nashville, Tenn.: Race Relations Institute, 1970.

Green, Abel, and Joe Laurie, Jr. *Show Biz: from Vaude to Video.* New York: Henry Holt, 1951.

Gross, Ben. *I Looked and I Listened: Informal Recollections of Radio and Television.* New York: Random House, 1954.

Harmon, Jim. *The Great Radio Comedians*. Garden City, N.Y.: Doubleday, 1970.

――――. *The Great Radio Heroes*. Garden City, N.Y.: Doubleday, 1967.

Harwood, Kenneth. "World Bibliography of Selected Periodicals on Broadcasting (Revised)." *Journal of Broadcasting*, 16 (1972), 131-46.

Head, Sydney. *Broadcasting in America: A Survey of Radio and Television*. 2nd ed. Boston: Houghton Mifflin, 1971.

Hilliard, Robert L., ed. *Radio Broadcasting: An Introduction to the Sound Medium*. New York: Hastings House, 1967.

Houle, John, ed. *British Broadcasting 1922-1972: A Selective Bibliography*. London: British Broadcasting Corporation, 1972.

Howeth, S. L. *History of Communications-Electronics in the United States Navy*. Washington, D.C.: U.S. Government Printing Office, 1963.

Husing, Ted. *Ten Years Before the Mike*. New York: Farrar and Rinehart, 1935.

Jackson, Paul T. *Collector's Contact Guide 1975*. Record Collectors' Sourcebook Series, No. 3. Peoria, Ill.: Recorded Sound Reserch, 1975.

Johnson, Joseph S., and Kenneth K. Jones. *Modern Radio Station Practices*. Belmont, Calif.: Wadsworth, 1972.

Julian, Joseph. *This Was Radio: A Personal Memoir*. New York: Viking, 1975.

Klavan, Gene. *We Die at Dawn: The True Life Story of America's No. 1 Radio Team, or No. 2, or No. 3, Klavan and Finch*. Garden City, N.Y.: Doubleday, 1964.

Koch, Kenneth. *The Panic Broadcast: Portrait of an Event*. Boston: Little, Brown, 1970.

Lackmann, Ron. *Remember Radio*. New York: G. P. Putnam's Sons, 1970.

Lazarsfeld, Paul F. *Radio and the Printed Page: An Introduction to the Study of Radio and Its Role in the Communication of Ideas*. New York: Duell & Sloan, 1940.

――――, and Harry Field. *The People Look at Radio*. Chapel Hill: University of North Carolina Press, 1946.

――――, and Patricia L. Kendall. *Radio Listening in America: The People Look at Radio Again*. Englewood Cliffs, N.J.: Prentice-Hall, 1948.

――――, and Frank N. Stanton, eds. *Radio Research 1941*. New York: Duell, Sloan and Pearce, 1942.

――――. *Radio Research 1942-43*. New York: Duell, Sloan and Pearce, 1944.

Lord, Phillips H. *Seth Parker's Sunday Evening Meeting: An Entertainment in One Act*. New York: Samuel French, 1930.

Lyons, Eugene. *David Sarnoff: A Biography*. New York: Harper and Row, 1966.

McBride, Mary Margaret. *Tune in for Elizabeth: Career Story of a Radio Interviewer*. New York: Dodd, Mead, 1945.

McLuhan, Marshall. *The Gutenberg Galaxy: The Making of Typographic Man*. Toronto: University of Toronto Press, 1965.

――――. *Understanding Media: The Extensions of Man*. New York: McGraw-Hill, 1964.

Marx, Herbert Lewis, ed. *Television and Radio in American Life*. The Reference Shelf. Vol. 25, No. 2. New York: H. W. Wilson, 1953.

Morris, Lloyd R. *Not So Long Ago*. New York: Random House, 1949.

My Eyes Are in My Heart. New York: Bernard Geis, 1959.

National Broadcasting Company. *The Fourth Chime.* New York: National Broadcasting Company, 1944.

Perry, Dick. *Not Just a Sound: The Story of WLW.* Englewood Cliffs, N.J.: Prentice-Hall, 1971.

Pitts, Michael R. *Radio Soundtracks: A Reference Guide.* Metuchen, N.J.: Scarecrow Press, 1976.

Post, Steve. *Playing in the FM Band: A Personal Account of Free Radio.* New York: Viking, 1974.

Poteet, G. Howard. *Published Radio, Television, and Film Scripts.* Troy, N.Y.: Whitston, 1975.

Rose, Oscar. *Radio Broadcasting and Television: An Annotated Bibliography.* New York: H. W. Wilson, 1947.

Sanger, Elliott M. *Rebel in Radio: The Story of WQXR.* New York: Hastings House, 1973.

Sarnoff, David. *Looking Ahead: The Papers of David Sarnoff.* New York: McGraw-Hill, 1968.

Seldes, Gilbert. *The Great Audience.* Reprint. Westport, Conn.: Greenwood Press, 1970.

————. *The Public Arts.* New York: Simon and Schuster, 1956.

Settel, Irving. *A Pictorial History of Radio.* New York: Grosset and Dunlap, 1960.

Slate, Sam J., and Joe Cook. *It Sounds Impossible.* New York: Macmillan, 1963.

Stedman, Raymond William. *Serials: Suspense and Drama by Installment.* Norman: University of Oklahoma Press, 1971.

Summers, Harrison B. *A Thirty Year History of Programs Carried on National Networks in the United States 1926-1956.* Columbus: Ohio State University Press, 1958.

Swing, Raymond. "Radio: the Languishing Giant." In *The Popular Arts in America: A Reader.* Edited by William M. Hammel. New York: Harcourt Brace Jovanovich, 1972. Pp. 238-45.

Thomas, Lowell. *Magic Dials: The Story of Radio and Television.* New York: Lee Furman, 1939.

Tyler, Poyntz, ed. *Television and Radio.* The Reference Shelf, Vol. 36, No. 2. New York: H. W. Wilson, 1961.

Weiskopf, Herman. *On Three: Inside the Sports Huddle.* Boston: Little, Brown, 1975.

Williams, Albert N. *Listening: A Collection of Critical Articles on Radio.* Reprint. Freeport, N.Y.: Books for Libraries Press, 1968.

Young, Margaret Labash; Harold Chester Young; and Anthony T. Kruzas, eds. *Directory of Special Libraries and Information Centers.* 4th ed. Detroit: Gale, 1977.

PERIODICALS

Broadcast Bibliophile's Booknotes. Philadelphia, 1969-1974.

Broadcasting. Washington, D.C., 1931-.

Broadcasting Yearbook. Washington, D.C., 1935-.
Dimensions of Radio. Washington, D.C., 1960-.
Journal of Broadcasting. Philadelphia, 1956-.
Mass Media Booknotes (originally *Broadcast Bibliophiles Booknotes*). Philadel-
    phia, 1974-.
Radio Annual. New York, 1938-1964.
Radio Broadcast. New York, 1922-1930.
Radio Daily. New York, 1937-1964.
Radio Directory. New York, 1938-1941.
Radio Programming Profile. Glen Head, N.Y., 1968-1974.

CHAPTER 11 Science Fiction
Marshall B. Tymn

During the past decade in the United States, science fiction has emerged not only as a highly popular genre of literature but also as a respectable discipline receiving both critical and academic acceptance. The emergence of science fiction from its exile began in the late 1950s with three significant events: in 1958, Scott Osborne of Mississippi State University organized the first Conference on Science Fiction at the Modern Language Association annual meeting in New York; a year later the first academic journal in the field, *Extrapolation,* was founded by Thomas D. Clareson at the College of Wooster; and "at Princeton, Kingsley Amis, a recognized English poet and author, presented a series of lectures for the Christian Gauss Seminar in Criticism in the spring of 1959, and in the lectures he proclaimed his long-time admiration for science fiction. A year later the lectures appeared as *New Maps of Hell,* and various surprised popular media, reviewing the book, began to reconsider their own policy of consistently ignoring or denigrating the science fiction which had somehow reached their desks."[1]

The genre was given further impetus when the Science Fiction Research Association was established in 1970 to serve as an international clearinghouse for all those concerned with some phase of the study of science fiction. The widespread nature of this new interest in science fiction is evident in the proliferation of course offerings on the subject and in the increase in publication of works of criticism and reference to meet the demands of the scholar and teacher.[2]

At least two national conferences have been established to disseminate materials and methods on teaching science fiction,[3] and an international organization, Instructors of Science Fiction in Higher Education, was founded to establish a forum for teachers of this specialized literature.[4] Special sections on science fiction are regular features on the programs of the Modern Language Association, the National Council of Teachers of English, the American Studies Association, and the Popular Culture Association. Scholarly journals have published special science fiction issues.[5]

Scores of conventions on local, regional, and national levels are held each year in this country at which fans, writers, collectors, book dealers, teachers, and scholars assemble. Science fiction art and movies have become big business. The field is frantic with activity.

Some say this is just the beginning for science fiction. One thing, however, is clear. "After a long exile to the comic strips and the pulp magazines and the late late movies, [science fiction] is suddenly winning recognition as a more or less respectable academic subject"[6] and has become the most popular form of the specialized literary genres published in the United States today.

Beginning with a brief historical summary of the development of science fiction, this essay outlines the current state of science fiction scholarship for those who may wish to pursue research in the field.

HISTORIC OUTLINE

Brian W. Aldiss, the noted British writer and critic, contends that science fiction "was born in the heart of the English Romantic movement with Mary Shelley's *Frankenstein*" (*Billion Year Spree*, 1973). When Shelley wrote her novel in 1818, she started a trend that left behind the supernatural elements of the Gothic horror tale and introduced "science" as an ingredient of fiction. It is probably true that science fiction could not have existed before the creation of a new world by invention and technology, and as the Industrial Revolution burst upon the Victorian world people began to write fantastic tales based upon the possibilities of scientific discovery.[7]

The machine age had been inaugurated and its imprint on fiction was immeasurable. Popular magazines, such as *Century, Cosmopolitan, Harper's, Atlantic,* and *Saturday Evening Post,* along with vehicles like the dime novel, kept the public interest keen with stories featuring new mechanical devices, while at the same time supplying this entertainment at a price affordable to the masses. Nearly every major writer in America and many in Europe experimented with writing science fiction stories, but Jules Verne (1828-1905) was the first to devote full-time effort to the task.

Verne's success helped pioneer a genre. His blend of science and invention in his "voyages extraordinaire" insured the survival of science fiction, and his fertile imagination made it exciting. Verne was not a great innovator of science fiction ideas, but he captured the optimistic spirit of the nineteenth century when he made technological achievements a subject for fiction. Thus science fiction gained its own identity and a measure of respectability as defined by Verne's prolific and highly profitable output. Verne's worlds seem limited, though, when compared with the work of another nineteenth-century writer, H. G. Wells.

With his background as scientist, teacher, and journalist, Wells (1866-1946) published his first "scientific romance," *The Time Machine,* in 1895. This novel is historically significant for two reasons. For the first time in fiction, a mechanical device built by man, a machine which utilized "scientific" principles, became the vehicle for an extraordinary journey. And more important, the novel contained social commentary. Through a variety of motifs and new perspectives Wells made startling insinuations about the insignificance of man in the universe. With Wells science fiction began to take form and direction. It became more a medium of ideas than a variety of adventure, and the ideas that he incorporated into his stories and novels created whole new thematic lineages down to the present.

Although the gadget and invention stories popularized by Verne and others constitute the early core of science fiction, other themes had emerged by the turn of the century. Some endured, some faded, some evolved. The future war motif characterized by George Chesney's *The Battle of Dorking* (1871) established imaginary warfare as a viable theme for science fiction writers, but eventually the warring nations depicted in Chesney's tale were replaced by alien invaders. The interplanetary voyage motif began as a mystical, then a romantic, vehicle before adopting the more technological orientation that remains a staple of modern science fiction. Utopias typically were concerned with the social issues of the day, making only peripheral use of science and technology. Even castastrophes evolved from threats of world destruction by alien invaders as portrayed in Wells' *The War of the Worlds* (1897) to an Earth devastated by atomic warfare, overpopulation, or pollution, as revealed in the post-World War II writings. By far the most popular of the early motifs on both sides of the Atlantic was the lost race. If H. Rider Haggard was the most important writer in this motif, Edgar Rice Burroughs was the most popular.

Burroughs was a master storyteller whose works were packed with solid entertainment and whose Tarzan series made him the most widely read author in the English language. He also wrote a series of novels set on Mars, Venus, the Moon, and the center of the Earth—some seventy books in all. His adventures were light, his characterizations superficial, and his science almost nonexistent. Although Burroughs was criticized for being a formula writer, his exotic settings offered readers an escape from the gloom of industrialized cities and the realities of World War I. A greedy audience, and the inclination of pulp magazine editors to publish stories written for the sake of the story, not only enhanced Burroughs' reputation but also gave science fiction another popular outlet.

It was not until Hugo Gernsback began publishing a succession of electrical magazines which regularly included science fiction stories that the contemporary label *science fiction* evolved. In April 1926, Gernsback placed the first issue of *Amazing Stories* on the stands. The magazine was devoted exclusively to science fiction (*scientifiction*, as Gernsback first termed it), and it was an instant success. Gernsback steadfastly promoted science fiction, as he filled his issues with reprints of classic tales and with a resurrected motif—the gadget story.

These gadget stories were another brand of escape fiction. The wild technological advances dreamed up by the writers were created more for fun than plausibility, and most of the fiction published in *Amazing Stories* emphasized the wonders of science. Other pulp adventure magazines of the 1930s and 1940s published stories with the recurring themes of space exploration, robots, catastrophes, and alien encounters. Like Verne and Burroughs before them, these writers leaned heavily on romance and adventure, exotic settings, indestructible heroes, and super-villains, now interacting on a galactic scale. One of the most famous writers of the Gernsback era was Edward E. "Doc" Smith, whose Skylark series popularized the term *space opera*.

In 1952 Gernsback was the guest of honor at the World Science Fiction Convention in Chicago. Beginning with the 1953 convention in Philadelphia, popular works of fiction were awarded silver rockets named *Hugos*, in honor of the man who invented the term *science fiction* and encouraged the development of new writers in the field.

Science fiction began to change shape and direction when, in 1937, John W. Campbell, Jr. assumed the editorship of *Astounding Stories*. Campbell recruited writers with science backgrounds and demanded from them greater sophistication of style and technique. Under his tutelage, science fiction altered, matured, and entered its "golden age," during which time (roughly 1938-50) writers refined their plots and characters, while emphasizing human relationships, and were encouraged to tap psychological, philosophical, political, and other areas of "social" concern. Among the new writers to appear in the pages of *Astounding* during the early years of Campbell's editorship were A. E. Van Vogt, Robert A. Heinlein, Arthur C. Clarke, and Theodore Sturgeon.

The "golden age" endured until 1950, when the field broadened and improved as *Galaxy, The Magazine of Fantasy and Science Fiction,* and other magazines appeared, and as science fiction spilled over into the paperbacks. But even in the post-World War II period, science fiction experienced a new direction of growth while preserving its romantic-escape and hard-science orientations. The social sciences became important subjects as writers in the 1950s and 1960s came to examine the human consequences of technology, overpopulation, ecology, governmental abuse of power, and racial conflict. Science fiction's response to this new set of problems came largely, at first, from a group of young writers, such as Harlan Ellison, J. G. Ballard, Brian Aldiss, Samuel Delany, and Tom

Disch. The *New Wave* writers, as they came to be called, warned of the chaos and despair threatened by the potential for war and internal corruption in a technological society.

REFERENCE WORKS

Many of the early attempts at indexing and classifying science fiction materials were undertaken by enthusiasts for their own use or enjoyment and were published in severely limited editions now difficult to locate. Robert E. Briney and Edward Wood's *SF Bibliographies* was the first attempt to publish information on early bibliographic work in the field. This book lists and annotates approximately one hundred bibliographies, indexes, and checklists published as separate books or pamphlets; no attempt was made to include materials printed in the professional and amateur science fiction magazines. Entries are organized into four categories: magazine indexes, individual author bibliographies, general indexes and checklists, and foreign language bibliographies. Advent Publishing reports that an enlarged edition of this work is in preparation.

The pioneer bibliography of science fiction and fantasy primary works is Everett F. Bleiler's *The Checklist of Fantastic Literature.* Bleiler lists approximately fifty-three hundred prose titles published in the United States and Great Britain from Walpole's *The Castle of Otranto* (1764) through 1947. Emphasis is on hardcover titles, but an occasional paperback book is listed. The result of over seven years of research, this volume remains the most comprehensive checklist of the science fiction and fantasy genres.

The Bleiler checklist was updated with the publication of Bradford M. Day's *The Supplemental Checklist of Fantastic Literature,* which contains about three thousand titles and extends the coverage of both American and British imprints through 1963. Day also published a survey of paperback titles. His *The Checklist of Fantastic Literature in Paperbound Books* remains the only attempt at a complete survey of the field in paperback books and is of great value for identifying material from the nineteenth and early twentieth centuries. This work complements the Bleiler and Day indexes, which included a few titles bound in paper. Another attempt to update the Bleiler list is my own forthcoming two-volume work, *American Fantasy and Science Fiction.* Volume 1 will cover the period 1820-1947 and will add several thousand American titles to Bleiler's listing; volume 2 covers the period 1948-73 and will also include only American imprints.

One of the most important recent science fiction checklists is Robert Reginald's *Stella Nova,* later reprinted as *Contemporary Science Fiction Authors.* The earlier edition was not widely advertised, and most copies were sold to public and institutional libraries. The second edition contains some corrections and amendments, but remains essentially the same as the original edition. The work includes 483 bibliographies of authors active during the period 1960-68. Each entry provides a checklist of the author's science fiction and fantasy books listed in chronological order according to their sequence of publication. There are biographies of 308 of the authors indexed which often incorporate comments by the writers responding to the compiler's questionnaire. This volume is an absolutely essential reference tool for access to modern works.

The only other attempt at a comprehensive bibliography of primary works is Donald H. Tuck's projected three-volume *The Encyclopedia of Science Fiction and Fantasy Through 1968*. As of this writing the first two volumes, covering authors A through Z, have appeared. The third will include data on magazines, paperbacks, pseudonyms, connected stories, series and sequels, as well as details on publishers, films, amateur magazines, and other general information. Author bibliographies and checklists will comprise the principal portion of the *Encyclopedia*. Full listings of the contents of short story collections and anthologies are an important feature; 1,550 single author collections and 950 anthologies (from the 1890s through 1968) are listed. Tuck stresses in his introduction that this compilation complements the 1948 Bleiler checklist, and "can be considered as a sort of continuation to that book." Although the checklists are now ten years out of date, the scope of this compilation is immense, and it is likely to remain an important science fiction reference tool for many years.

Additional attempts to publish checklists of science fiction and fantasy continue. Most are amateur efforts and are narrow in scope: for example, Richard C. Spelman's *Science Fiction and Fantasy Published by Ace Books (1953-1968)* and his *A Preliminary Checklist of Science Fiction and Fantasy Published by Ballantine Books (1953-1974)*. The most recent professional effort is Neil Barron's *Anatomy of Wonder*, an annotated listing of over 1,150 works of science fiction, organized into literary periods, and intended for libraries, scholars, and serious fans.

Most of the works cited overlap each other to some extent and are more or less limited in their coverage. What the field needs is a master checklist of titles published in the English language which could include selected nineteenth-century titles but would emphasize twentieth-century works to the present.

Science fiction magazines have been well indexed since the publication of Donald B. Day's pioneering effort, *Index to the Science-Fiction Magazines 1926-1950*. This volume indexes the contents of fifty-eight science fiction magazines from their first issues through December 1950. Only English language magazines are covered, and with the exception of three

British titles (*Fantasy, New Worlds,* and *Tales of Wonder*), all are American publications. Day's work remains the standard index for science fiction magazines of the period. The 1951-65 period is covered by two very similar indexes. The first to appear was Erwin S. Strauss's *The MIT Science Fiction Society's Index to the S-F Magazines, 1951-1965,* which indexes the contents of one hundred English language magazines chronologically by magazine issue and alphabetically by author and title. Entries were arranged by computer and the volume is photo-offset from the printout. Two years later Norm Metcalf published *The Index of Science Fiction Magazines 1951-1965,* which is organized along the same lines as the Strauss index. The New England Science Fiction Association subsequently issued a five-year index compiled by Anthony Lewis, *Index to the Science Fiction Magazines 1966-1970,* which includes all of the American and British magazines published during the period. This volume was intended as a continuation of the Strauss compilation and follows a triple listing format (by magazine, by story title, and by author). Commencing with the 1971-72 supplement, coverage was extended to include original anthologies. The NESFA has issued annual volumes each year since 1972.

Supplementing the magazine indexes are the only two existing indexes to science fiction anthologies. Walter R. Cole's *A Checklist of Science-Fiction Anthologies* lists approximately 260 English language anthologies of fantasy and science fiction appearing between 1927 and 1963. Entries are indexed alphabetically by anthology title, by editor, by story title, and by contributing author. This is still the basic source for anthologized fantasy and science fiction, although updates are in progress. William G. Contento's forthcoming *An Index to Science Fiction Anthologies and Collections* will list approximately nineteen hundred anthologies and single author collections published through June 1977 and will supersede the Cole *Checklist.* Also in preparation is a special *Index to Thematic Anthologies of Science Fiction,* compiled by Marshall B. Tymn, Martin H. Greenberg, L. W. Currey, and Joseph D. Olander. The second existing index to anthologies is Frederick Siemon's *Science Fiction Story Index: 1950-1968,* a listing of about thirty-four hundred stories, indexed by author and title and keyed to the anthologies and collections in which they appear. It is an incomplete work that is difficult to use and often provides unreliable information.

Although there is a great need for a systemataic approach to individual author bibliographies, some notable single works have been published. The earliest comprehensive author bibliography, Henry Hardy Heins' *A Golden Anniversary Bibliography of Edgar Rice Burroughs,* is still the standard bibliography of the writings of the man who created Tarzan. Marjorie M. Miller's *Isaac Asimov: A Checklist . . . ,* published as part of the Kent State University Press Serif Series, is currently the most comprehen-

sive Asimov bibliography. The most complete checklist of writings by
H. P. Lovecraft is *The Revised H. P. Lovecraft Bibliography*, compiled by
Mark Owings and Jack L. Chalker. Leslie Kay Swigart's *Harlan Ellison:
A Bibliographical Checklist* is a thorough and professional work and is a
model which many science fiction bibliographies would do well to emulate.
Other excellent author bibliographies are William F. Nolan's *The Ray
Bradbury Companion* and Asa Pieratt and Jerome Klinkowitz's *Kurt
Vonnegut, Jr.: A Descriptive Bibliography and Annotated Secondary
Checklist*.

Dozens of amateur author bibliographies have been published in recent
years, mostly through fan outlets; the quality of these amateur efforts
varies, and the best that can be said for most of them is that they are incomplete and lack a unified format. An effort to bring some kind of order
to the current haphazard publication of author bibliographies is a new
reference series, to be launched by G. K. Hall in 1978 under Marshall B.
Tymn's general editorship. Masters of Science Fiction and Fantasy will
consist of a series of volumes, each dealing with an author's total output
of English language fiction and nonfiction. Also included will be a comprehensive, annotated listing of criticism on the subject author. The volumes will conform to a unified series format.

The area of film has been thoroughly documented by science fiction researchers. The single most valuable index to the fantastic cinema is Walt
Lee's *Reference Guide to Fantastic Films*. This three-volume work lists
twenty thousand titles, covering every science fiction, horror, fantasy, animated, and border-line film to which Lee could find reference. Each entry
provides technical information, including director and cast, a summary of
content, and references to reviews. The volumes cover films produced in
approximately fifty countries over a seventy-five year period. Donald C.
Willis's *Horror and Science Fiction Films: A Checklist* lists some forty-four
hundred titles. Comprehensive production data, full credits, and a lively
synopsis and commentary are provided for the obscure and the well-known,
and for the worst as well as the best of horror and science fiction films.

Neil Barron points out in an article written for *Choice* magazine that
"the biggest single deficiency in the literature of science fiction is the
absence of a comprehensive, current critical bibliography listing the outstanding books in the field."[8] He does not mention Thomas D. Clareson's
Science Fiction Criticism: An Annotated Checklist, perhaps because the
volume was not yet available to Barron. The Clareson volume is a comprehensive guide to the critical literature on the science fiction genre published in English language books and periodicals prior to 1972. It contains
approximately eight hundred entries arranged into nine different sections.

A chronological continuation of Clareson's *Science Fiction Criticism* is
an ongoing series, "The Year's Scholarship in Science Fiction and Fantasy,"

compiled and edited by Roger C. Schlobin and Marshall B. Tymn. This project was created to fulfill the pressing need for an annual secondary bibliography on science fiction and fantasy and is published annually in *Extrapolation*. "The Year's Scholarship" covers all American scholarship, selected British scholarship, and important criticism from major established fanzines. It includes books, monographs, articles, Ph.D. dissertations, published M.A. theses, reprints of major criticism that have been out of print for a significant period, and scholarly or instructional visual media that are informative rather than descriptive. It is expected that this series will relieve the scholar, teacher, and fan of the arduous and sometimes frustrating search for scholarly materials and sources among the array of critical and reference tools that appear each year.

The current summary of science fiction scholarship in pamphlet and book form is *A Research Guide to Science Fiction Studies*, compiled by Marshall B. Tymn, Roger C. Schlobin, and L. W. Currey. This bibliography confronts the problem of where to locate the scholarly materials in the field that have appeared since World War II. The volume contains over seven hundred entries, four hundred of which are fully annotated, covering both general and specialized sources that span the entire range of science fiction scholarship, including general surveys, histories, genre studies, author studies, bibliographies and indexes, book reviews, and Ph.D. dissertations. *A Research Guide* is designed as a handbook for those who wish to pursue research in science fiction studies.

RESEARCH COLLECTIONS

The recent proliferation of science fiction research activity and the popular interest in the field as a whole has prompted academic libraries to develop systematic science fiction collections. Hal Hall lists such collections in his chapter on "Library Collections of Science Fiction and Fantasy" in *Anatomy of Wonder*, edited by Neil Barron. Although Hall cites forty-seven American and five Canadian collections, his listing is still incomplete, for many more collections exist. For a more complete description the researcher is advised to consult Elizabeth Cummins Cogell's "Science Fiction and Fantasy Collections in U.S. and Canadian Libraries," in *The Science Fiction Reference Book*, edited by Marshall B. Tymn. This inventory lists nearly one hundred significant collections, the majority of which are in college and university libraries, although a few city libraries are noted. The purpose of the listing is to guide scholars in locating and using not only the major author and thematic collections but also the several collections within a given geographical area. Therefore, detailed information is furnished for small (at least two hundred books), medium, and large collections. Each entry includes general information about the library and its collection, followed by a specific analysis of both primary and secondary books, magazines, and manuscripts.

Two professional organizations should be acknowledged for their support of library science fiction collections. The Science Fiction Research Association, through its annual meetings and its monthly newsletter, has helped disseminate information; and *Extrapolation*, a scholarly journal which serves SFRA, has published several articles on library research collections. Science Fiction Writers of America has established a Regional Depository System whereby publisher donated books are made available to libraries in selected geographic areas. According to H. W. Hall, "the libraries agree to house the books in closed research collections to support the study and teaching of science fiction, and to make the books available to SFWA members who may need them. Libraries are chosen to give wide geographical coverage of the United States and Canada. The following libraries are currently active members of the SFWA Regional Depository System: California State Library, Fullerton; University of Southern Mississippi; Eastern New Mexico University; Brigham Young University; University of Kansas; University of Tennessee; Michigan State University; University of Dayton; University of New Brunswick; Texas A&M University; and the Imperial College of Science and Technology, London."[9]

Although public libraries, as a rule, do not possess the resources to develop extensive science fiction research collections, mention should be made of the Spaced-Out Library of the Toronto Public Library system. Established in 1970 on the base of a personal collection of approximately five thousand items donated by science fiction writer and editor Judith Merril, the rapidly growing collection comprises more than thirteen thousand items, including novels, short story collections and anthologies, plays, poetry, critical works, art work, tapes, and a large collection of both professional and amateur periodicals.[10] Other significant public library collections are located at the San Diego Public Library, San Francisco Public Library, Santa Ana Public Library, Denver Public Library, Chicago Public Library, City of Bowling Green (Ohio) Public Library, New York Public Library, Library Association of Portland, and the Central Research Library of the Dallas Public Libraries.

The largest collections remain in the hands of private individuals, although the number of these collections is dwindling as they are purchased by research libraries and science fiction book dealers. One of the world's most complete collections is owned by Forrest J. Ackerman, a noted science fiction fan, literary agent, film consultant, editor, and bookseller. In 1934 he helped organize the Los Angeles Science Fantasy Society, the oldest existing fan organization in the world. His two hundred thousand piece collection is housed in a special Fantascience Museum in Hollywood, California.

Because of the historical importance of the early science fiction pulp magazines and their general inaccessibility to scholars and researchers, Greenwood Press has gathered together many of the seminal titles of this genre on 35mm microfilm. The program, entitled "Science Fiction Periodicals, 1926-1945," is being developed under the general editorship of Thomas D. Clareson. Titles in the first series (a second series is in the planning stage) are: *Amazing Stories, Amazing Stories Annal, Amazing Stories Quarterly, Comet, Cosmic Stories, Dynamic Science Stories, Fantastic Adventures, Miracle Stories, Planet Stories, Science Fiction, Science Fiction Quarterly, Science Wonder Stories/Wonder Stories, Science Wonder Quarterly/Wonder Stories Quarterly, Stirring Science Stories,* and *Extrapolation,* a scholarly journal.

A recent development in the collecting and preserving of science fiction research materials has been the formation of the Science Fiction Oral History Association at Eastern Michigan University. This organization has begun to collect, transcribe, and catalog recorded materials so that they may be preserved and made available to fans and scholars in the field.[11]

HISTORY AND CRITICISM

Neil Barron, a librarian and science fiction researcher, has commented that "until the past few years, little in the way of systematic history and criticism of modern (post-1920) science fiction had been published. . . . Amateur publications (fanzines) had published a fair number of studies of varying merit, most rather brief, some occasionally finding their way into more permanent book form. Far too much of what was and is published by and for science fiction readers had and has an inbred, defensive and/or cultish quality, long on adulation and short on balanced appraisals informed by a wider knowledge of literature, to say nothing of science."[12]

The situation, as Barron has outlined it, is essentially accurate, although a few noteworthy early efforts should be mentioned. The first scholarly and comprehensive background study was J. O. Bailey's *Pilgrims Through Space and Time*, a pioneer critical survey of the scientific and utopian romance in English, emphasizing fiction published prior to 1914. Though published in 1947, *Pilgrims* is still a standard work. Another essential background work is W. H. G. Armytage's *Yesterday's Tomorrows*, a major study of a rapidly expanding field of scholarly inquiry, planning for the future. Copious notes and references to hundreds of titles enhance the value of this study. H. Bruce Franklin's *Future Perfect: American Science Fiction of the Nineteenth Century*, an anthology with extensive critical commentary by the editor, remains the most perceptive and provocative study of science fiction by American literary figures of the period. Kingsley

Amis's *New Maps of Hell*, mentioned in the introduction, was the first full-length study of the genre by a critic from outside the science fiction community. The study "gave direction to current criticism of science fiction by emphasizing its role 'as an instrument of social diagnosis and warning' " (Thomas D. Clareson, *SF Criticism*).

The pioneer efforts of Amis, Bailey, Armytage, Franklin, and others have been continued by Robert M. Philmus, whose *Into the Unknown: The Evolution of Science Fiction from Francis Godwin to H. G. Wells* surveys English science fiction of the eighteenth and nineteenth centuries. An important landmark in historical criticism was the publication of Brian W. Aldiss's *Billion Year Spree*, a general critical survey of the genre from its nineteenth-century beginnings through contemporary writings of the 1950s and 1960s. The book's eleven chapters are divided equally between the nineteenth and twentieth centuries, with a single chapter devoted to the precursors of science fiction. In *Alternate Worlds*, James Gunn has provided an informed study of the scientific, social, and philosophical climate that brought forth and shaped science fiction from its early beginnings to the present. Gunn reminds us that science fiction is a popular literature whose origins lie in the complex socioeconomic and intellectual milieu of the Industrial Revolution. Gunn devoted many years to gathering the illustrations and rare photographs of science fiction writers, editors, critics, and fans, which complement the highly readable text. It is certainly the most ambitious of the published histories of science fiction to date.

Two important recent scholarly studies should be mentioned, as they represent a growing interest in theoretical criticism of science fiction. David Ketterer's *New Worlds for Old* is an attempt to place the literature of science fiction within the broader category of the "apocalyptic"—literature that concerns itself with the "destruction of an old world and the coming of a new order." Ketterer maintains that "because of a common apocalyptic quality and a common grounding in the romance, science fiction and mainstream American literature share many significant features." This is an important scholarly study and the first book-length treatment of science fiction to give sustained explication of contemporary texts. Robert Scholes' *Structural Fabulation* is based on four lectures delivered at the University of Notre Dame in 1974. It is a critical and theoretical study of science fiction relating the genre to the literary traditions and to modern intellectual history, arguing for the seriousness of science fiction and its value as literature.

In the light of the increasing popularity of fantasy literature, more critical works are appearing devoted exclusively to this genre. Two early studies of supernatural fiction were H. P. Lovecraft's *Supernatural Horror in Literature* and Peter Penzoldt's *The Supernatural in Fiction*. The only historical survey of modern heroic fantasy is Lin Carter's *Imaginary*

Worlds, which includes coverage of the major genre authors and analyzes their contribution to and influence on the genre. More recent studies include W. R. Irwin's *The Game of the Impossible*, an examination of the common characteristics of fantasies written between 1880 and 1957; L. Sprague de Camp's *Literary Swordsmen and Sorcerers*, which discusses the evolution of sword and sorcery fiction through biographical sketches of its leading practitioners whose works were central to the growth of the genre; and Eric S. Rabkin's *The Fantastic in Literature*, an exploration of the nature and uses of the fantastic following from the recognition that it is not the unreal that is fantastic, but the unreal in a particular context. Each chapter develops this view, using examples from fairy tales, detective fiction, science fiction, utopian fiction, Gothic, and traditional literature.

One of the earliest comprehensive symposiums on modern science fiction was *Modern Science Fiction*, edited by Reginald Bretnor. While partially dated, the eleven essays by writers, critics, and editors comprise an important document on science fiction's "golden age." Bretnor has since compiled *Science Fiction, Today and Tomorrow*, an anthology of essays by science fiction writers about the nature of their genre, art, and craft.

More than any other individual, Thomas D. Clareson has been responsible for bringing together a multitude of critical viewpoints on the literature of science fiction. A pioneer anthology in the field is his *SF: The Other Side of Realism*, which illustrates the many ways in which the study of science fiction may be approached. Clareson's *Many Futures, Many Worlds* integrates recent views on the study of science fiction from starting points as diverse as philosophy, mythology, theology, and technology.

Until recently, the full-length critical study of individual authors has been a neglected area of science fiction scholarship. The earliest attempts at author coverage were two works by historian Sam Moskowitz: *Explorers of the Infinite*, with chapters on pre-World War II writers who influenced the developing genre; and *Seekers of Tomorrow*, with chapters on twenty-one modern writers. The tradition established by Moskowitz has been continued by Thomas Clareson, with his Voices for the Future series, the first volume of which was published in 1976. Volume 1 is a collection by various academics of critical essays concerning writers whose careers had begun by the end of World War II. A second new series, Writers of the 21st Century, edited by Joseph D. Olander and Martin Harry Greenberg, will devote entire volumes to individual authors and will be an important landmark in science fiction author studies. The first two volumes in the series, collections of essays on Isaac Asimov and Arthur C. Clarke, were published in 1977. Studies of science fiction writers are appearing with increasing frequency; the next few years should see a number of book-length studies that will complement the work now being done in science fiction genre studies.

Although the area has not been completely neglected by science fiction historians, more critical-historical studies of the pulp magazine have to be written. Two pioneering works, both by Sam Moskowitz, are *Science Fiction by Gaslight: A History and Anthology of Science Fiction in the Popular Magazines, 1891-1911* and *Under the Moons of Mars: A History and Anthology of "The Scientific Romance" in the Munsey Magazines, 1912-1920*. The thirty-six page introduction to *Science Fiction by Gaslight* is one of Moskowitz's most important contributions to the study of science fiction history. He charts the early development of the mass circulation, general interest English language magazine and, through his historical survey and representative fiction selections, examines the themes and extent of a popular literary form of the period. *Under the Moons of Mars* is, in part, a continuation of *Gaslight*, though here the study is restricted to American periodicals with emphasis on the Munsey group. In a valuable 154-page historical survey, Moskowitz traces the influence of Edgar Rice Burroughs, whose scientific romances sacrificed verisimilitude for romantic adventure. The scientific romance was a dominant literary form during this transitional period and the popular fiction magazine was the major vehicle for this type of fiction.

The New English Library has issued the first three volumes of a projected five-volume series edited by Michael Ashley. Each volume in *The History of the Science Fiction Magazine* will examine a decade of the science fiction magazine from 1926 to 1976 and will feature ten selections from the magazines, prefaced by historical commentary by the editor. The series will provide the first balanced compact historical overview of the development of this specialized magazine genre and will be especially valuable for data on British publications.

Several recent critical studies of the science fiction film are worth noting. John Baxter's *Science Fiction in the Cinema* outlines the history of the science fiction film from 1895 to 1968. The coverage is broad and informed, especially for the period 1900 to 1940. William Johnson's *Focus on the Science Fiction Film* contains essays by American, British, and European critics on the science fiction film covering three historical periods: 1895-1940, the 1950s, and the 1960s. The most comprehensive study of the fantasy film is Jeff Rovin's *The Fabulous Fantasy Films*, which includes discussion of over six hundred films arranged by thematic content, plus chapters on fantasy animation, fantasy film anthologies, and television fantasy. According to Peter Nicholls, writing in *Foundation* magazine, Philip Strick's *Science Fiction Movies* is "the best book so far on SF and the cinema . . . and makes for an excellent balance between word and picture. . . . Although Strick does not flaunt his research work, it must have been very considerable. He lists many more films than any previous work in the field (except, of course, for Walt Lee's extraordinarily thorough three-volume filmography), and gives the impression of having seen most of them."[13]

Science fiction and fantasy periodicals come in three distinct types: fanzines, professional magazines, and scholarly journals. The first American appearance of a fan magazine devoted exclusively to science fiction was the May 1930 number of *The Comet*, the official organ of the newly formed Science Correspondence Club. Many of the big names of the day were regular contributors, including the then unknown German fan Willy Ley, who wrote a column on rockets and space. Fanzines, as they are commonly referred to in science fiction circles, have been published in countless numbers by scores of science fiction clubs and amateur organizations for several decades, and the phenomenon shows no sign of abating. As Elizabeth Calkins and Barry McGhan point out in *Teaching Tomorrow*:

The creation and publication of amateur SF magazines . . . consume a great deal of the time, energy, and money of the more avid science fiction readers. Although most fanzines cost their publishers more than sales bring in, they continue to spew out of basement ditto machines, Mimeographs, and off-set presses in bewildering numbers. Most often, a publication appears on the scene for a while and then disappears just as suddenly, when the publisher/editor runs out of money, time, things to say, or whatever.

The content of these little magazines (some of which are lavishly done, with printed copy, art work, and photos) include articles about authors and their works, debates about trends within the field, extensive letter columns, news items, stories, poetry, and drawings. Many professional writers saw their first work printed in a fanzine.[14]

Most fanzines eventually fade away after a few issues; some, however, manage to stay in print for several years, becoming relatively permanent fixtures in the field. The following fanzines have endured the test of time and can be recommended for their overall fine quality and excellent coverage of the science fiction and fantasy genres: *Luna*, edited by Ann F. Dietz; *Orcrist: A Journal of Fantasy in the Arts*, edited by Richard West; *Riverside Quarterly*, edited by Leland Sapiro; *The Science-Fiction Collector*, edited by J. Grant Thiessen; *SF Commentary*, edited by Bruce Gillespie; *Xenophile*, edited by Nils Hardin; *Science Fiction Review*, edited by Richard E. Geis; *Amra*, edited by George Scithers; *CSL: The Bulletin of the New York C. S. Lewis Society*, edited by Eugene McGovern; *Mythlore: A Journal of J. R. R. Tolkien, C. S. Lewis and Charles Williams*, edited by Glen H. Goodknight; and *Whispers*, edited by Stuart David Schiff.

A small number of science fiction and fantasy periodicals can be classified as professional magazines. Although some overlapping does occur between fanzines and the professional magazines, the latter have at least six distinguishing features: 1) a large circulation; 2) newsstand and/or book dealer distribution; 3) profit-making; 4) upgraded content; 5) upgraded format; and 6) not associated with a science fiction organization. The following five professional magazines are important publications, serving a variety of needs within the field: *Algol: The Magazine about Science Fiction*, edited by Andrew Porter; *Locus: The Newspaper of the Science Fiction Field*, edited by Charles N. and Dena Brown; *Ariel*, edited by Thomas Durwood; *Delap's F & SF Review*, edited by Richard Delap; and *Cinefantastique*, edited by Frederick S. Clarke.

The first academic journal for scholars and teachers of science fiction was *Extrapolation*, established in December 1959 as the newsletter of the Modern Language Association Seminar on Science Fiction; it also publishes papers derived from the annual meeting. Under the editorship of Thomas D. Clareson, *Extrapolation* has achieved a worldwide circulation and has established itself as one of our major scholarly journals. *Extrapolation* is published semi-annually at The College of Wooster in Ohio. *Science-Fiction Studies* was established in 1973 by editors R. D. Mullen and Darko Suvin. This important international journal publishes articles that are critical, theoretical, and bibliographical in nature. An anthology of fifty essays selected from *Science-Fiction Studies* has recently been published by Gregg Press as *Science-Fiction Studies: Selected Articles on Science Fiction 1973-1975*. This journal is published three times a year at Indiana State University. The major scholarly journal published outside of the United States is *Foundation: The Review of Science Fiction*, edited by Peter Nicholls and issued three times a year by the [British] Science Fiction Foundation. *Foundation* is noteworthy for its scholarly reviews of new books and its series on the craft of science fiction by science fiction authors.

REPRINTS

Publishing companies, long aware that a viable market exists not only for current science fiction, but for older, historically important, works have responded by reprinting science fiction and fantasy "classics" for school and library collections.[15]

Hyperion Press took the first step in 1974 with its 23 Classics of Science Fiction series, edited by Sam Moskowitz. The Hyperion series was the first attempt by a publisher to view science fiction in its historical perspective and present it in terms of a coherent and visible past. Though hardly definitive, the collection was the pioneering effort that provided a ready-made and successful model for other reprinters to emulate, which they did, if not from the same angle of vision. Seven of the titles have never before had an American edition, and the others have long been unobtainable. Most buffs will recognize such works as Ray Cummings's *The Girl in the Golden Atom*, David H. Keller's *Life Everlasting and Other Tales of Science, Fantasy and Horror*, A. Merritt's *The Metal Monster*, Stanley G. Weinbaum's *A Martian Odyssey*, and Philip Wylie's *The Gladiator*. Other works, such as William H. Rhodes's *Caxton's Book*, George Griffith's *Olga Romanoff*, or Gustavus W. Pope's *Journey to Mars*, will be known only to a selected group of serious students and science fiction historians. The selections are all the more valuable for their range and appeal to a wide audience. The series as a whole, which spans a period of over two hundred years, is of unquestioned historical importance, highlighting as it does the early development of science fiction in the United States and England.

The Arno Press Science Fiction series of sixty-one volumes was published in 1975. In the words of the editors, R. Reginald and Douglas Menville, "the books included in this series may not be the best-known publications from the period [1751-1934], but we do think they provide the researcher with a broad overview of the field's origins and beginnings, its major and minor writers and writings, and the root themes of modern science fiction."[16] The series includes some historically important titles: Eric Temple Bell's *Before the Dawn*, J. D. Beresford's *The Hampden-shire Wonder*, Jack London's *The Scarlet Plague*, Mark Wicks's *To Mars Via the Moon*, and Sidney Fowler Wright's *Deluge* will be of interest to scholars. A special feature of the collection, and unique to the reprint series published thus far, is the nonfiction section, which includes bibliographies, checklists, and literary criticism. All of these titles have been out of print for many years, and works, such as Bradford M. Day's *The Supplemental Checklist of Fantastic Literature* and *The Checklist of Fantastic Literature in Paperbound Books*, W. R. Cole's *A Checklist of Science-Fiction Anthologies*, and R. Reginald's *Contemporary Science Fiction Authors*, will be welcome aids to researchers in the field.

The Garland Library of Science Fiction, published in 1975, is edited by Lester del Rey, a well-known science fiction writer and editor. Many of the series' forty-five titles are from the genre's formative years: Alfred Bester's *The Demolished Man*, George U. Fletcher's *The Well of the Unicorn*, Edgar Pangborn's *Davy*, Edward E. Smith's *The Skylark of Space*, A. E. Van Vogt's *Slan*, and Jack Williamson's *The Legion of Space*. The series also includes works by some of the field's newest writers, such as Samuel R. Delany's *The Einstein Intersection*, Ursula K. Le Guin's *Planet of Exile*, and Roger Zelazny's *This Immortal*.

The Gregg Press Science Fiction Series, published in 1975, is a diversified collection of twenty titles, chosen with care by David G. Hartwell and L. W. Currey. Each of the titles is unique or significant in one way or another, and the series represents an intelligent and thoughtful survey of the themes that form the essential subject matter of early and modern science fiction: imaginary voyages (Charles Romyn Dake's *A Strange Discovery*), interplanetary travels (George Tucker's *A Voyage to the Moon*), utopias (Mary Bradley Lane's *Mizora*), dystopias (Eugene Zamiatin's *We*), inventions (Jules Verne's *An Antarctic Mystery*), future wars (G. McLeod Winsor's *Station X*), lost races (William N. Harben's *The Land of the Changing Sun*), and post-catastrophic civilizations (Van Tassel Sutphen's *The Doomsman*). Each of the works contains an introductory essay written especially for the series by a noted writer, collector, or scholar. This critical apparatus provides a valuable historical commentary and perspective for the series as a whole.

The reprint activity has continued with Hyperion Press issuing a nineteen-volume Series II in 1976. Gregg Press issued a Series II in 1976 and a Series III in 1977, totaling fifty-five volumes. In addition, Gregg has recently released *The Witch World Novels of Andre Norton*. This seven-volume set constitutes the first hardcover edition of these popular works by one of the most enduring writers of fantasy and science fiction. In their continuing efforts to provide quality reprint editions of noteworthy titles in the field, Gregg published *The Space Adventure Novels of Andre Norton, The Worlds of Poul Anderson*, and Fritz Leiber's *Fafhrd and the Gray Mouser Saga* in 1978.

In a related area, Arno Press has published a sixty-four volume Supernatural and Occult Fiction series, edited by R. Reginald and Douglas Menville. Arno has also issued three Gothic Novels series totaling thirty volumes, under the editorship of Devendra P. Varma, and has announced a Lost Race and Adult Fantasy Fiction series. These series provide important background titles for researchers and historians.

NOTES

1. James Gunn, "From the Pulps to the Classroom," *Algol*, 14 (Winter 1977), p. 10.

2. I would like to thank Garland Publishing, Inc. for allowing me to adapt portions of *A Research Guide to Science Fiction Studies* (1977) for use throughout this essay. I would also like to acknowledge my enormous debt to Roger C. Schlobin and L. W. Currey, who were co-compilers with me on the Garland volume. This essay is as much theirs as it is mine.

3. In June 1976, James Gunn offered his second annual Intensive Institute on the Teaching of Science Fiction at the University of Kansas. My own Conference on Teaching Science Fiction is held annually at Eastern Michigan University.

4. ISFHE is an organization of teachers of science fiction in junior colleges, colleges, and universities. It was founded in 1973 by Dr. Charles Waugh at the University of Maine, primarily to present awards for those works of fiction pub-

lished each year that seemed to be, from the point of view of instructors, very distinguished works. The Jupiter Award is intended to represent for ISFHE what the Hugo Award represents for fans and what the Nebula Award represents for writers.

5. For an annotated list of these special issues, see *A Research Guide to Science Fiction Studies,* ed. Marshall B. Tymn, Roger C. Schlobin, and L. W. Currey (New York: Garland Publishing Co., 1977).

6. Jack Williamson, "Science Fiction: Emerging from Its Exile in Limbo," *Publishers Weekly,* July 5, 1971, p. 17.

7. My sincere appreciation goes to my wife Darlene, for compiling the section, "Historic Outline," thereby allowing me more time to research the other sections in this essay.

8. "Science Fiction Revisited," *Choice,* 10 (1973), p. 924.

9. "Library Collections of Science Fiction and Fantasy," in *Anatomy of Wonder,* ed. Neil Barron (New York: R. R. Bowker, 1976), p. 393.

10. A brochure describing the collection may be obtained by writing Doris Mehegan, Head of Collection, Spaced-Out Library, Toronto Public Libraries, 40 St. George St., Toronto, Ontario, M5S 2E4 Canada.

11. For further information about the Science Fiction Oral History Association, write Lloyd Biggle, Jr., 469 Dubie, Ypsilanti, MI 48197.

12. "Anatomy of Wonder: A Bibliographic Guide to Science Fiction," *Choice,* 6 (1970), 1537.

13. "consumers' guide to recent writing on sf," *Foundation,* no. 11-12 (1977), pp. 171-72.

14. *Teaching Tomorrow: A Handbook of Science Fiction for Teachers* (Dayton, Ohio: Pflaum/Standard, 1972), p. 37.

15. Much of the information discussed here is taken from my article, "Revisiting Possible Worlds: A Look at Four Science Fiction Reprint Series," *Choice,* 12 (1976), pp. 1411-413.

16. Excerpt from the Arno Press brochure.

BIBLIOGRAPHY

BOOKS AND ARTICLES

Aldiss, Brian W. *Billion Year Spree: The History of Science Fiction.* London: Weidenfeld and Nicolson, 1973.

Amis, Kingsley. *New Maps of Hell: A Survey of Science Fiction.* New York: Harcourt, Brace, 1960. Reprint. New York: Arno Press, 1975.

Anderson, Poul. *The Worlds of Poul Anderson.* 6 vols. Boston: Gregg Press, in press.

Armytage, W. H. G. *Yesterday's Tomorrows: A Historical Survey of Future Societies.* London: Routledge and Kegan Paul, 1968.

Ashley, Michael, ed. *The History of the Science Fiction Magazine.* 3 vols. London: New English Library, 1974-76.

Bailey, J. O. *Pilgrims Through Space and Time: Trends and Patterns in Scien-*

tific and Utopian Fiction. New York: Argus Books, 1947. Reprint. Westport, Conn.: Greenwood Press, 1972.

Barron, Neil, ed. *Anatomy of Wonder: Science Fiction*. New York: R. R.
Bowker, 1976.

Baxter, John. *Science Fiction in the Cinema*. London: Zwemmer, 1970.

Bleiler, Everett F. *The Checklist of Fantastic Literature: A Bibliography of
Fantasy, Weird and Science Fiction Books Published in the English Lan-
guage*. Chicago: Shasta, 1948. Reprint. West Linn, Oreg.: FAX Collector's
Editions, 1972.

Bretnor, Reginald, ed. *Modern Science Fiction: Its Meaning and Its Future*.
New York: Coward-McCann, 1953.

————, ed. *Science Fiction, Today and Tomorrow*. New York: Harper and
Row, 1974.

Briney, Robert E., and Edward Wood. *SF Bibliographies: An Annotated Bibliography of Bibliographical Works on Science Fiction and Fantasy Fiction*.
Chicago: Advent Publishers, 1972.

Carter, Lin. *Imaginary Worlds: The Art of Fantasy*. New York: Ballantine, 1973.

Clareson, Thomas D., ed. *Many Futures, Many Worlds: Theme and Form in
Science Fiction*. Kent, Ohio: Kent State University Press, 1977.

————. *Science Fiction Criticism: An Annotated Checklist*. Kent, Ohio: Kent
State University Press, 1972.

————, ed. *SF: The Other Side of Realism: Essays on Modern Fantasy and
Science Fiction*. Bowling Green, Ohio: Bowling Green University Popular
Press, 1971.

————, ed. *Voices for the Future: Essays on Major Science Fiction Writers*.
Bowling Green, Ohio: Bowling Green University Popular Press, 1976.

Cole, Walter R. *A Checklist of Science-Fiction Anthologies*. Brooklyn, N.Y.:
W. R. Cole, 1964. Reprint. New York: Arno Press, 1975.

Contento, William G. *An Index to Science Fiction Anthologies and Collections*.
Boston: G. K. Hall, in press.

Day, Bradford M. *The Checklist of Fantastic Literature in Paperbound Books*.
Denver, N.Y.: Science-Fiction & Fantasy Publications, 1965. Reprint. New
York: New York Times/Arno Press, 1975.

————. *The Supplemental Checklist of Fantastic Literature*. Denver, N.Y.:
Science-Fiction & Fantasy Publications, 1963. Reprint. New York: New
York Times/Arno Press, 1975.

Day, Donald B. *Index to the Science-Fiction Magazines 1926-1950*. Portland,
Ore.: Perri Press, 1952.

De Camp, L. Sprague. *Literary Swordsmen and Sorcerers: The Makers of
Heroic Fantasy*. Sauk City, Wisc.: Arkham House, 1976.

Franklin, H. Bruce, ed. *Future Perfect: American Science Fiction of the Nineteenth Century*. New York: Oxford University Press, 1966.

Gunn, James. *Alternate Worlds: The Illustrated History of Science Fiction*.
Englewood Cliffs, N.J.: Prentice-Hall, 1975.

Heins, Henry Hardy. *A Golden Anniversary Bibliography of Edgar Rice Burroughs*. West Kingston, R.I.: Donald M. Grant, 1964.

Irwin, W. R. *The Game of the Impossible: A Rhetoric of Fantasy*. Urbana: University of Illinois Press, 1976.

Johnson, William, ed. *Focus on the Science Fiction Film*. Englewood Cliffs, N.J.: Prentice-Hall, 1972.

Ketterer, David. *New Worlds for Old: The Apocalyptic Imagination, Science Fiction, and American Literature*. Bloomington: Indiana University Press, 1974.

Lee, Walt. *Reference Guide to Fantastic Films: Science Fiction, Fantasy & Horror*. 3 vols. Los Angeles: Chelsea-Lee Books, 1972-74.

Leiber, Fritz. *The Fafhrd and the Gray Mouser Saga*. 6 vols. Boston: Gregg Press, in press.

Lewis, Anthony. *Index to the Science Fiction Magazines 1966-1970*. Cambridge, Mass.: New England Science Fiction Association, 1971.

Lovecraft, Howard Phillips. *Supernatural Horror in Literature*. New York: Ben Abramson, 1945. Reprint. New York: Dover Publications, 1973.

Metcalf, Norm. *The Index of Science Fiction Magazines 1951-1965*. El Cerrito, Calif.: J. Ben Stark, 1968.

Miller, Marjorie M. *Isaac Asimov: A Checklist of Works Published in the United States, March 1939-May 1972*. Kent, Ohio: Kent State University Press, 1972.

Moskowitz, Sam. *Explorers of the Infinite: Shapers of Science Fiction*. Cleveland, Ohio: World Publishing, 1963. Reprint. Westport, Conn.: Hyperion Press, 1974.

————, ed. *Science Fiction by Gaslight: A History and Anthology of Science Fiction in the Popular Magazines, 1891-1911*. Cleveland, Ohio: World Publishing, 1968. Reprint. Westport, Conn.: Hyperion Press, 1974.

————. *Seekers of Tomorrow: Masters of Modern Science Fiction*. Cleveland, Ohio: World Publishing, 1966. Reprint. Westport, Conn.: Hyperion Press, 1974.

————, ed. *Under the Moons of Mars: A History and Anthology of "The Scientific Romance" in the Munsey Magazines, 1912-1920*. New York: Holt, Rinehart and Winston, 1970.

Mullen, R. D., and Darko Suvin, eds. *Science-Fiction Studies: Selected Articles on Science Fiction 1973-1975*. Boston: Gregg Press, 1976.

Nolan, William F. *The Ray Bradbury Companion: A Life and Career History, Photolog, and Comprehensive Checklist of Writings With Facsimiles From Ray Bradbury's Unpublished and Uncollected Work in all Media*. Detroit: Gale, 1975.

Norton, Andre. *The Space Adventure Novels of Andre Norton*. 7 vols. Boston: Gregg Press, in press.

Olander, Joseph D., and Martin Harry Greenberg, eds. *Writers of the 21st Century*. New York: Taplinger. In press.

Owings, Mark, with Jack L. Chalker. *The Revised H. P. Lovecraft Bibliography*. Baltimore: Mirage Press, 1973.

Penzoldt, Peter. *The Supernatural in Fiction*. London: Peter Nevill, 1952. Reprint. New York: Humanities Press, 1965.

Philmus, Robert M. *Into the Unknown: The Evolution of Science Fiction from Francis Godwin to H. G. Wells.* Berkeley: University of California Press, 1970.

Pieratt, Asa B., Jr., and Jerome Klinkowitz. *Kurt Vonnegut, Jr.: A Descriptive Bibliography and Annotated Secondary Checklist.* Hamden, Conn.: Archon Books, 1974.

Rabkin, Eric S. *The Fantastic in Literature.* Princeton, N.J.: Princeton University Press, 1976.

Reginald, Robert. *Stella Nova: The Contemporary Science Fiction Authors.* Los Angeles: Unicorn & Son, 1970. Reprint. *Contemporary Science Fiction Authors.* New York: New York Times/Arno Press, 1975.

Rovin, Jeff. *The Fabulous Fantasy Films.* Cranbury, N.J.: A. S. Barnes, 1977.

Schlobin, Roger C. and Marshall B. Tymn. "The Year's Scholarship in Science Fiction and Fantasy." Annually in *Extrapolation*.

Scholes, Robert. *Structural Fabulation: An Essay on the Fiction of the Future.* Notre Dame, Ind.: University of Notre Dame Press, 1975.

Siemon, Frederick. *Science Fiction Story Index: 1950-1968.* Chicago: American Library Association, 1968.

Spelman, Richard C. *A Preliminary Checklist of Science Fiction and Fantasy Published by Ballantine Books (1953-1974).* North Hollywood, Calif.: Institute for Specialized Literature, 1976.

————. *Science Fiction and Fantasy Published by Ace Books (1953-1968).* North Hollywood, Calif.: Institute for Specialized Literature, 1976.

Strauss, Erwin S. *The MIT Science Fiction Society's Index to the S-F Magazines, 1951-1965.* Cambridge, Mass.: The MIT Science Fiction Society, 1965.

Strick, Philip. *Science Fiction Movies.* London: Octopus Books, 1976.

Swigart, Leslie Kay. *Harlan Ellison: A Bibliographical Checklist.* Dallas, Tex.: Williams, 1973.

Tuck, Donald H. *The Encyclopedia of Science Fiction and Fantasy Through 1968.* 2 vols. Chicago: Advent Publishers, 1974.

Tymn, Marshall B. *American Fantasy and Science Fiction.* 2 vols. West Linn, Oreg.: FAX Collector's Editions, in press.

————, ed. *Masters of Science Fiction and Fantasy.* Boston: G. K. Hall, in press.

————. *The Science Fiction Reference Book.* West Linn, Oreg.: FAX Collector's Editions, in press.

————, Roger C. Schlobin; and L. W. Currey. *A Research Guide to Science Fiction Studies.* New York: Garland Publishing Co., 1977.

————, et al. *Index to Thematic Anthologies of Science Fiction.* Boston: G. K. Hall, in press.

Willis, Donald C. *Horror and Science Fiction Films: A Checklist.* Metuchen, N.J.: Scarecrow Press, 1972.

PERIODICALS

Algol: The Magazine about Science Fiction. New York, 1963-.

Amra. Philadelphia, 1956-.

Ariel. New York, 1976-.

Cinefantastique. Oak Park, Ill., 1970-.

CSL: The Bulletin of the New York C. S. Lewis Society. Ossining, N.Y., 1969-.

Delap's F&SF Review. West Hollywood, Calif. 1975-.

Extrapolation. Wooster, Ohio, 1959-.

Foundation: The Review of Science Fiction. Essex, England, 1972-.

Locus: The Newspaper of the Science Fiction Field. San Francisco, 1968-.

Luna. Oradel, N.J., 1969-.

Mythlore: A Journal of J. R. R. Tolkien, C. S. Lewis, and Charles Williams. Los Angeles, 1969-.

Orcrist: A Journal of Fantasy in the Arts. Madison, Wisc., 1966-67-.

Riverside Quarterly. Gainesville, Fla., 1964-.

The Science-Fiction Collector. Calgary, Alberta, Canada, 1976-.

Science Fiction Review. Portland, Oreg., 1972-.

Science-Fiction Studies. Terre Haute, Ind., 1973-.

SF Commentary. Melbourne, Australia, 1969-.

Whispers. Chapel Hill, N.C., 1973-.

Xenophile. St. Louis, Mo., 1974-.

CHAPTER 12 Sports
Robert J. Higgs

What is sport? The truth is that no one knows, and the challenge to define it, or at least to describe its characteristics, has engaged the attention of some of the best scholars of our time, always with beneficial results but never with answers that satisfy completely. Says Johan Huizinga in *Homo Ludens*, a book that is *sine qua non* on any aspect of the subject of sport, "In our heart of hearts we know that none of our pronouncements is absolutely conclusive."[1] Like Tennyson's flower in the crannied wall, we know that sport *is*, but we do not know with certainty what it is. Nevertheless, we are compelled to seek understanding of anything that so engages the interest of mankind as sport or play. In fact, play has become so important that it can no longer be left exclusively to the players. The influence of games on societies, from "the bloody Roman spectacles" to the staged demonstrations of the modern Olympiad and the Super Bowl, is simply staggering. Sport, as one observer has claimed, is the new opiate of the masses, as it has probably always been, though never so freely administered as in the modern world.

Drawing upon earlier works, Paul Weiss in *Sport: A Philosophic Inquiry* has grappled admirably with the problem of definitions and provided worthwhile distinctions among sport, play, and game, but does not, and indeed cannot, remove the overlap that exists in the common understanding of the terms. Since time and space do not allow me to delve into the nuances that Weiss establishes, I must, out of necessity, proceed, not on differences of opinion between him and others, but upon some common ground of agreement, with an invitation to the interested scholar to go directly to the sources himself.

" 'Sport', 'athletics', 'games', and 'play'," says Weiss, "have in common the idea of being cut off from the workaday world."[2] Here he is in agreement with Huizinga as he is with Roger Caillois who claims that play is *free, separate, uncertain, unproductive*, and governed by both *rules* and *make-believe*.[3] "Sport," as Weiss reminds us, "means" to disport, "that is, to divert and amuse." Hence in this study I regard sport as that aspect of culture by which men divert themselves from labor as opposed to work. This important distinction between labor and work is well made by Hannah Arendt in *The Human Condition* in her discussion of the difference between *animal laborans*, laboring animal, and *homo faber*, man the maker or artist, which is so succinctly implied in the phrase "the work of our hands and the labor of our body."⁴ Today it is essential to realize that in professional sports, especially in professional sports, the athlete is quite often player, laborer, and artist all, one who laboriously sculpts a life of meaning out of his physical nature. Though lines between different activities frequently become blurred, in this chapter I regard sport as a diversion from labor. I am considering sport as "unnecessary" action in the sense that it is not *required* for survival as are forms of labor, such as farming. I must also add that I regard sport as an activity that requires the expenditure of a substantial amount of physical energy, more than that needed to play a game of bridge or checkers, though these too are certainly forms of play and diversions from labor.

HISTORIC OUTLINE

"What is play? What is serious?" Huizinga asks. The Puritans would have had far less difficulty in answering these questions than we would today. For them, any effort not devoted to the good of the colony was to be eschewed, and games did not seem to lend themselves to the general welfare. In 1621 Governor Bradford rebuked the young men he found "in ye streete at play, openly; some pitching ye barr and some at stooleball, and shuch like sports." There should not be, in the governor's view, any "gameing or revelling in ye streets" nor if we are to judge from the incident of the maypole of Merry Mount any reveling in the country either. "Had the leaders at Plymouth, Salem, and Boston been in Parliament in 1643 they would have voted with the majority that all copies of the *Book of Sports* be seized and burned."⁵

The Puritan hostility to games took the form of official prohibition and even punishment. In 1647 in Massachusetts Bay a court order was issued against shuffleboard, and in 1650 the same injunction was extended against "bowling or any other play or games in or about houses of common entertainment."⁶ In 1693 in eastern Connecticut a man "was fined twelve shillings and sentenced to six hours in the stocks for playing ball on the Sabbath. . . . Apparently, either he was playing alone or his teammates were let go with a warning, since he was the only man convicted."⁷ The Puritan attitude toward fun and games in the view of many is perhaps best illustrated in Macaulay's remark that bear-baiting was stopped not because it gave pain to the bear but because it provided pleasure to the spectators.

The "Detestation of Idleness" was not confined to New England. In Vir-

ginia in 1619 "the assembly decreed that any person found idle should be
bound over to compulsory work; it prohibited gaming at dice or cards,
strictly regulated drinking, provided penalties for excess in apparel and
rigidly enforced Sabbath observance."[8] Interdictions against racing within
the city limits of New Amsterdam were issued in 1657, and two years later
Governor Peter Stuyvesant proclaimed a day of fast on which would be
forbidden "all exercise and games of tennis, ball-playing, hunting, fishing,
plowing, and sowing, and moreover all unlawful practices such as dice,
drunkenness—."[9] Restrictions of activities in some form on Sunday could
be found wherever the new American civilization was extended on the
frontier.

As John A. Krout, Foster Rhea Dulles, and others have pointed out the
theocracy did not represent all of New England, and the narrow sanctions
of the ruling class had in the long run little chance of being obeyed. The
human propensity to play could not be stilled. Sport grew not only in New
England but all along the frontier. Hunting and fishing flourished frequently as a means for gaining food but also as a form of diversion. Forests and rivers seemed to contain an endless supply of game and fish, and
many availed themselves of the abundance. "Even Cotton Mather fished.
Samuel Sewall tells of the time when the stern old Puritan went out with
line and tackle and fell into the water at Spy Pond, 'the boat being tick-
lish'."[10] For those who have read Mather's prose, this is a pleasing image
indeed.

The growth of recreation, even during the latter part of the seventeenth
century, can be inferred from the journal of Sarah Kembell Knight, who
wrote of her travels through Connecticut in 1704: "Their diversions in
this part of the country are on lecture days and training days mostly: on
the former there is riding from town to town . . . and on training days
the youth divert themselves by shooting at the targets, as they call it (but
it very much resembles a pillory). When he that hits nearest the white
has some yards of red ribbon presented to him, which being tied to his
hattband, he is led away in triumph, with great applause, as the winners of
the Olympiak Games."[11]

At the beginning of the nineteenth century there was a wide diversity
of amusements in the North, at least as reported by President Timothy
Dwight of Yale: "The principal amusements of the inhabitants are visiting, dancing, music, conversation, walking, riding, sailing, shooting at a
mark, draughts, chess, and unhappily, in some of the larger towns, cards
and dramatic exhibitions. . . . Our countrymen also fish and hunt. Journeys
taken for pleasure are very numerous, and are a very favorite object. Boys
and young men play at foot-ball, cricket, quoits, and at many other sports
of an athletic cast, and in the winter are peculiarly fond of skating. Riding
in a sleigh, or sledge, is also a favorite diversion in New England."[12]

Ninepins, skittles, and bowls were common at inns in the North for the convenience of the guests,[13] while in the South shooting matches were preferred, with "beef shooting" being one of the favorite forms.[14]

The sports that seemed to attract the most attention in the South, however, were cockfighting and horse-racing. According to Hugh Jones in 1724, "the common planters don't much admire labour or any other manly exercise except Horse racing, nor diversion, except Cock-Fighting, in which some greatly delight." In tones suggestive of William Byrd, he adds, "This Way of Living and the Heat of the Summer make some very lazy, who are then said to be Climate-struck."[15]

While the foreign traveler, especially the English, as Henry Adams notes, "charged the Virginians with fondness for horse-racing and cock-fighting, betting and drinking, . . . the popular habit which most shocked them, and with which books of travel filled pages of description was the so-called rough and tumble fight. The practice was not one on which authors seemed likely to dwell; yet foreigners like Weld, and Americans like Judge Longstreet in 'Georgia Scenes' united to give it a sort of grotesque dignity like that of the bull-fight, and under their treatment it became interesting as a popular habit."[16]

The rough and tumble, Adams argues, did not originate in Virginia, but came to America from England, as did, according to Jennie Holliman, most American sports, excepting those practices learned from the Indians, such as methods of hunting and trapping deer and bear, the use of bows and arrows, fishing at night with lights on canoes, lacrosse, and even rolling the hoop. Still the predominant influence was from abroad. The gun itself is a good example. "Up to 1830," says Holliman, "a few fine guns had been made in America, but they did not sell to an advantage simply because they were not imported." The same was true for fishing equipment, twine, tackles, hooks, flies, and rods, which came from Holland as well as England. Sleighs also came from Holland while bridles, harness, and saddles came from England.[17]

Cockfighting eventually disappeared in the South except in a few isolated areas but horse-racing, as everyone knows, has grown into both a major sport and industry with interest in the Triple Crown equaling that of the World Series and the Super Bowl. Wagering for the 1977 Kentucky Derby exceeded $3,500,000, breaking all previous records.

The history of horse-racing has to a large extent been the history of selective breeding of which Diomed and Messenger provide excellent examples. Diomed was brought to Virginia in 1789 and came to be held in such esteem that his death in 1808 caused almost as much mourning as that for Washington in 1799.[18] Messenger, bred by the Earl of Grosvenor on his Yorkshire farm, was brought to America a few years after the Revolution by Thomas Berger of Pennsylvania. Prized as a stud, Messenger was the sire of a long line of racing immortals, including American Elipse, who defeated Sir Henry of Virginia at the Union course on Long Island in 1823, the first intersectional race that illustrated once and for all the popular appeal of the sport. Another offspring of Messenger was Hambletonian, the horse that turned harness racing into a national mania. "In the 1850's, the nation worshipped Hambletonian. It bought commemorative plates on which his likeness was inscribed. Children talked about him as if he were human."[19] Spurred on by the creation of jockey clubs, the establishment of race courses, and support of the aristocracy, horse-racing became America's first organized sport and has remained unquestionably one of its most popular.

The wide interest in the turf helped to bring about the rise of sporting literature in the three decades before the Civil War. The first sporting magazine in America was the *American Turf Register*, published in Baltimore in 1829 by John Stuart Skinner. Ten years later Skinner sold the *Register* to William Trotter Porter who had already begun his own weekly sporting publication called *Spirit of the Times*, one of the most famous of all American publications and a reservoir of history of American popular culture from 1831 to 1861. Prominent among contributors to this magazine was Thomas B. Thorpe, who inaugurated "the Big Bear school of humor," and the Englishman Henry William Herbert who wrote under the pen name of "Frank Forester" and who introduced "something of the English point of view of sport for sport's sake."[20]

Baseball, like horse-racing, has its roots in the nineteenth century and also like horse-racing owes more perhaps to the English than we are inclined to admit. The myth that Abner Doubleday invented baseball is totally without foundation. "The rules of baseball attributed to Doubleday in 1839 were identical to those in a rule book for the English game of rounders published in London in 1827."[21] In America rounders became known as town ball and was played at Harvard as early as 1829. In *The Book of Sport* (1827) Robert Carver related that many Britons, like the Americans, were calling the game by a new name, "base ball," and that it was "becoming a distinct threat to cricket."[22] Both the game and the new name caught on quickly in America, and by the 1850s the *Spirit of the Times* was calling it "The National Game."[23] By the 1880s daily attendance at the games was some sixty thousand. It has become "far and away the leading spectator sport."[24]

As Foster Rhea Dulles has observed, the role of colleges in the rise of sports in the decades after the Civil War was not one of leadership. The only sport that undergraduates developed was football, and again the English influence is incontrovertible. Basketball, in fact, is the only popular American ball game whose origins are not English, being invented by James A. Naismith in Springfield, Massachusetts, in 1891.

American football evolved from soccer to Rugby to "American" Rugby and finally to the game we know today. While the basic forms derived from England, the Americans had long demonstrated a fondness for games of mayhem. Harvard, for example, "had a festival in the early 1800's which qualified vaguely as football. It was called Bloody Monday, but the upperclassmen mostly kicked the freshmen and only occasionally the ball."[25] Though it was essentially soccer instead of Rugby, what is called the first intercollegiate football game took place in 1869 between Princeton and Rutgers at New Brunswick. Rutgers won, no thanks to the player who, becoming confused and endearing himself to all future generations, kicked the ball through Princeton's goal. The first contest was played before a small crowd but approximately twenty years later Princeton played Yale before a crowd of almost forty thousand.[26] Thus long before the turn of the century football was well established as a mass spectator sport.

The one overriding fact concerning sport in America is its phenomenal growth. From William Bradford's injunction against games on Christmas Day in 1621 to Super Sunday 1977 there has been a complete reversal of attitudes. A few facts on salaries of the super stars tell much of the story. Fran Tarkenton estimates his net worth at $7,000,000, Kareem Abdul-Jabar is earning $2,500,000 for five years with the Lakers, Jim "Catfish" Hunter $1,000,000 more than that for the same period of time with the Yankees, and Muhammad Ali grossed over $16,000,000 in 1976.[27]

How did such changes occur? No one seems to be able to offer any conclusive answers except the human love of sport and the need for heroes. One thing is undeniable, however, and that is the contention that the widespread acceptance of sport was brought about in part by the revolution in technology in the decades after the Civil War. Says John R. Betts, "Ante-bellum sport had capitalized on the development of the steamboat, the railroad, the telegraph, and the penny press, and in succeeding decades the role of technology in the rise of sport proved even more significant."[28]

Of major importance in the promotion of sports has been the press, a major product of technology. Following the lead of the *Spirit of the Times*, new periodicals drawing attention to sport began to appear after the war. Among these were *Baseball Magazine*, *Golfer's Magazine*, *Yachting*, and *Saturday Evening Post*. Newspapers from coast to coast began to devote more and more space to sports until finally they had a section of their own. "Frank Luther Mott designated the years 1892-1914 as a period in newspaper history when sporting news underwent remarkable development, being segregated on special pages, with special makeup pictures, and news writing style."[29] Books, too, continued to arouse interest, especially among the younger generation. Among the many writers bringing dreams of fair play and heroism to millions of American youth were Gilbert Patten (Burt L. Standish), Henry Barbour, Zane Grey, and Edward Strate-meyer.[30] The champion producer of all in this group of juvenile writers was Gilbert Patten who wrote a Frank Merriwell story once a week for nearly twenty years and had only one nervous breakdown. Estimates of the sales of Merriwell novels run as high as five hundred million copies.[31]

The press helped bring together heroes and hero worshippers, but other developments also played crucial roles in the expansion of sports. It would be hard, for example, to overestimate the importance of the railroad and the telegraph in the spread of games. Because of the growing rail network, the Cincinnati Red Stockings could travel from Maine to California, and John L. Sullivan could go on a grand tour of athletic clubs, opera houses, and theaters. Revolution in mass transit meant mass audiences, and for those who could not come to the games the telegraph provided instant news of results. The Atlantic cable, electrification, radio, and television all influenced sport in profound ways that are still only vaguely under-stood. Because of technology the city of New Orleans could build in 1974 a bronzed-topped stadium with a gigantic screen for instant replays at a total cost of over $285,000,000. As Wells Twombly asks, "Was this only the beginning . . . or was it the end?"

REFERENCE WORKS

A basic reference work that librarians will find indispensable and re-searchers in sport very helpful is *Biography Index*, a ten-volume cumula-tive index of biographical material in books and magazines dating from 1946 to the present. In the area of sport almost one hundred categories and associated fields are listed, and further distinction is made between adult and juvenile items. Literally hundreds and perhaps thousands of biographies and autobiographies have been written on American sports figures. Most of the autobiographies are co-authored and seem to follow the same general pattern describing the hero's or heroine's childhood, early promises and disappointments, and the subsequent rise to fame and suc-cess. Joseph Campbell's theory of the monomyth is no doubt confirmed in every issue. Because of the generally youthful audience that sports biog-raphies are slanted toward, the style is generally simplistic, but the stu-dent of popular culture would not want to overlook biographical items relating to the subject of his research.

The need for basic information in any research is unending, and in sport the best source is Frank G. Menke's *The Encyclopedia of Sport*. The fifth edition of this work is over one thousand pages long and contains a listing of records in both amateur and professional sports as well as at-tendance figures, all-American teams, money won on horse and dog rac-ing, and other data. *Webster's Sports Dictionary* is well designed to serve another recurring need, that for a quick explanation of the many terms that saturate the world of sport. Other helpful features of the dictionary are diagrams of courts and fields (with measurements), action illustrations, as well as referee signals and methods of keeping score. *The Oxford Companion to World Sport and Games*, edited by John Arlott, also contains such information in even more detail. Both are extremely useful.

RESEARCH COLLECTIONS

The booming popularity of sport and the quiet dedication of librarians, scholars, and sports enthusiasts have led to a number of fine collections of sporting materials in libraries in various parts of the country. One of the most comprehensive is that of the Citizens Savings Athletic Foundation in Los Angeles. The foundation maintains both a sports museum, which contains perhaps the most complete collection in the world of Olympic Games awards and memorabilia, and a sports library, which is especially strong on Olympic games publications. It has a large number of sports films, available on a loan basis, and thousands of sports photographs, files of sports magazines, and souvenir programs dating back many years. The foundation also instituted Halls of Fame, excepting baseball, in various sports. The sites of these institutions, many of which house libraries as well as museums, can be obtained by writing the foundation.

One of the most extensive collections on sporting materials of all kinds is in the Applied Life Studies Library at the University of Illinois at Urbana-Champaign. The library's card catalog of approximately fifty-one thousand entries was published by G. K. Hall and Co. in 1976. Fields included in this impressive listing are sports history, the sociology of sport, sports medicine, recreation materials, theories of play, health and safety, and dance, to mention only a few of the various categories. The Chicago Historical Society has a general collection of about two thousand volumes concerned primarily with team sports in the areas of biography, history, and statistics. Collection efforts of the society in the future will be limited to the Chicago area.

HISTORY AND CRITICISM

A study of the history of sport attempts to tell us what role sport has actually played in our lives; a study of the issues attempts to understand what roles sport *should* play. Among these many issues are the questions of emphasis, mind/body relationship, professionalism and amateurism, religion, racism, women in sports, language, and aggression. Before the interested scholar begins study in these or other aspects of sports, however, he needs some knowledge of what has already occurred on the

American sporting scene, and the few books that I have already referred to are indispensable in this regard.

The basic book to start with is John A. Krout's *Annals of American Sport*, the first full-length study of the subject. The influence of Krout is acknowledged in one way or another by the authors of other important histories, Jennie Holliman in *American Sports* (*1785-1835*), Foster Rhea Dulles in *America Learns to Play*, and John R. Betts in his invaluable *America's Sporting Heritage 1850-1950*. Betts's work grew out of his 1951 dissertation at Columbia University and is without question the most comprehensive work ever done in the history of American sport. It is a mine of information and the extensive references are probably the most exhaustive ever published on the popular aspects of sport. An excellent bibliography of sources through the 1850s is Robert W. Henderson's *Early American Sport*, and a good general bibliography can be found in the appendix to Robert Boyle's *Sport: Mirror of American Life*.

Another section of Boyle's book worthy of notice is the chapter on Frank Merriwell entitled "The Unreal Ideal." Merriwell's influence as a hero has been pervasive, and another more detailed look at this phenomenon can be found in Patten's autobiography, *Frank Merriwell's "Father."* Another work that sheds a great deal of light on juvenile sports literature is Robert Cantwell's article on Ralph Henry Barbour and William Heyliger called "A Sneering Laugh with the Bases Loaded" in *Sports Illustrated*.

I might mention one oversight in almost all bibliographies and that is certain sections in Henry Adams' *History of the United States during the Jefferson and Madison Administrations*, especially chapters I-VI. Not only does Adams offer humorous and penetrating insights of his own, but he summarizes effectively the opinions of a number of foreign travelers commenting upon American culture.

A student of American sport will frequently find it desirable to know something of attitudes toward sport in other times and places, especially ancient Greece and Rome and nineteenth-century England. E. Norman Gardiner's *Athletics of the Ancient World* is a seminal work on sport in classical times and still of great worth, especially if supplemented by such works as *The Olympic Games: The First Thousand Years*, by M. I. Finley and H. W. Plecket, an impressive work that challenges many of the traditional assumptions on ancient sports. An invaluable aid and a work that is out of print and unlisted in most bibliographies is Rachel Sargent Robinson's *Sources for the History of Greek Athletics*. For a background on English sport an indispensable book is Joseph Strutt's *The Sports and Pastimes of the People of England*. A good treatment of sport during the later Victorian period, especially as dealt with in the literature of the period, is Bruce Haley's 1963 University of Illinois dissertation, "The

Cult of Manliness in English Literature: A Victorian Controversy, 1857-1880," a portion of which has been published under the title "Sports and the Victorian World" in *Western Humanities Review*. Parallels between trends in ancient and modern sports have been noted by a number of contemporary observers, most notably perhaps by Arnold Toynbee in *The Breakdown of Civilizations, Volume 4, A Study of History*.

Though an entire session of the American Historical Association's annual convention in 1971 was devoted to papers on sport, the subject has not been regarded seriously enough by historians. The same is generally true of philosophers though the situation may be changing. Paul Weiss's *Sport: A Philosophic Inquiry* may be considered a pioneer work, as Weiss claims, though Howard Slusher's *Man, Sport, and Existence*, published two years earlier, is a more penetrating work from a philosophical point of view. Both deal with myriad aspects of the mind/body problem but Slusher in the earlier work begins in effect where Weiss leaves off in his last chapter called "A Metaphysical Excursus." Weiss concentrates on "the athlete in his athletic role," the athlete's pursuit of excellence, sport, and war, and women in sport; Slusher, as his title implies, has, instead of narrowing his subject, broadened it to include the cosmos with the central focus being the sporting endeavor. Weiss's book opens up the possibilities of philosophic interpretation of sport; Slusher's illustrates what some of those possibilities can become. Either work would well engage the time and thought of a graduate seminar in sport or philosophy.

One chapter in Slusher's book is entitled "Sport and the Religious," a subject that has attracted the attention of a number of writers over the years, including Thorstein Veblen who, in *Theory of the Leisure Class*, sees sport and religion as two of the four occupations of the leisure class and predatory culture, the other two being government and warfare. Veblen's argument is a compelling one and, as far as I know, has never been successfully refuted. Sports and religion was the subject of a three-part series in *Sports Illustrated* in 1977 by Frank Deford who coined the term *sportianity* and examined the growing phenomenon with the perceptive eye of the reporter. Michael Novak's highly readable *The Joy of Sports* is not only a ringing defense of sports but a compelling argument that sports inevitably spring from a religious commitment, regardless of the form that commitment may take.

To what extent sport and religion are allied or ought to be is open to question, but that sports generate and reflect social and cultural attitudes and hence values there seems to be little doubt. The commercialism that helped to bring about the proliferation of sports has ironically precipitated a widespread criticism of the athletic establishment. At least by the 1920s and probably much earlier, observers were questioning the commercialism of mass sports, and by the 1960s and 1970s the concern had grown to a type of outrage as seen in such works as Paul Hoch's *Rip Off the Big Game: The Exploitation of Sports by the Power Elite* and Jack Scott's *The Athletic Revolution*. Athletes too jumped on the bandwagon. Dave Meggyesy in *Out of Their League* and Gary Shaw in *Meat on the Hoof* voiced trenchant criticism over the way athletes were being exploited for materialistic ends. While football was the sport generally singled out for attack, baseball has not been completely immune. Even such a devoted fan as Roger Angell in *Five Seasons: A Baseball Companion* has registered regret over promotional practices that tend to rob the game of its traditional appeal. *Jock Culture, USA*, by Neil D. Isaacs, examines not only the exploitation of the athlete but questions the pervasiveness of sports in our society and warns against the dangers as far as values, institutions, and modes of thought are concerned.

A recurring theme in the "plethora" (to use a favorite term of Howard Cosell) of books critical of the direction of modern sport has been the status of the black athlete. Notable works on this subject are Harry Edwards' *The Revolt of the Black Athlete* and Jack Olsen's *The Black Athlete: A Shameful Story*. Since much of the controversy over the black athlete has centered around not only forms of exploitation but also on arguments of racial superiority, the researcher should not overlook John Lardner's *White Hopes and Other Tigers*, Martin Kane's *Sports Illustrated* article, "An Assessment of 'Black Is Best,'" Harry Edwards' rebuttal in "The Myth of the Racially Superior Athlete," and the *Time* article, "The Black Dominance."

The role of women in sports has been a frequently debated issue in recent years and has led to the passage of Title IX of the Education Amendments Act of 1972 which stipulated the withholding of federal funds from any school or college that discriminated on the basis of sex in school programs, including physical education and athletics. Conceivably, this act in and of itself could revolutionize athletics in the schools, but that is not likely to happen without a wider understanding of the role and possibilities of women in sport. Important works in this area are those by Pearl Berlin et al., *The American Woman in Sport*, Eleanor Metheny, *Connotations of Movement in Sport and Dance*, and Donna Mae Miller and Katherine R. E. Russell, *Sport: A Contemporary View*. A number of anthologies contain sections on the subject and/or rather extensive references and bibliographies. Among these are *Sport and American Society*, edited by George H. Sage, and *Sport in the Socio-Cultural Process*, edited by Marie M. Hart.

One of the most interesting developments in recent years has been the establishment of the Esalen Institute in San Francisco and Big Sur, California. Co-directed by Michael Murphy and George Leonard, the institute "explores those trends in education, religion, philosophy and the physical and behavioral sciences which emphasize the potentialities and values of human existence." The purpose is not so much to criticize the current sports establishment as to point to new directions in mind/body relationships. Two engaging works published in the Esalen-Viking series are Michael Murphy's *Golf in the Kingdom* and George Leonard's *The Ultimate Athlete*. Both examine the concept of the "inner body" and build cases for a revaluation if not of all values then at least of all clichés that have tyrannized not only the world of sport but society as well. Leonard's book contains an appendix listing seven new games for the "Sports Adventurers."

Both Leonard and Murphy reflect a strong element of Eastern influence as does the whole Esalen project, and the classic work on the Oriental approach to sport, indeed the precursor of many others, is Eugen Herrigel's *Zen in the Art of Archery*, which is generally praised but which comes under an extensive attack by Arthur Koestler in *The Lotus and the Robot*. In the Zen mastery of archery Koestler finds not the spirit of the Buddha but the basic principles of modern behaviorism. Whether science or religion (or both) is a work in the Zen way, the impact it has had upon American culture in recent years has been immeasurable not only upon Americans sitting still and meditating but upon those in action and not just in Aikido. The principles, the theory goes, apply to any undertaking. Hence, a number of recent books have appeared in which Eastern methods are extended to essentially Western sports, for example, Fred Rohe's *Zen of Running*. A good discussion of this marriage of East and West is "Sport Is Western Yoga" in *Powers of Mind*, by Adam Smith.

Michael Murphy's work is so convincing that it has been classified as nonfiction, but it is actually a novel, one of many on sports to come off the press in recent years. Though the number of works of adult fiction on sport is proliferating at a staggering rate, the subject has long been a favorite of American writers. In fact, every significant American author from Holmes and Poe to Updike and Philip Roth have written to one degree or another on some aspect of sport, and some, such as Lardner, Fitzgerald, Hemingway, Anderson, and Farrell, so much so that it would be difficult to interpret their works without some understanding of their view of sports. Still, the study of this whole area of American literature has barely been touched, and it remains a frontier fraught with possibilities of discoveries about ourselves and our culture. To the best of my knowledge only one book has been published to date on sports in American literature, and this is Wiley Lee Umphlett's *The Sporting Myth and the American Experience* in which the author suggests through an examination of sporting fiction "some of the reasons for the increased polarization" of American society in recent years.

Movies, like novels of sport, are coming out in a seemingly endless stream as they have been for several years, with boxing being the favorite subject, as might be surmised from recent releases, *The Great White Hope, Fat City, Rocky,* and also *The Greatest.* The inherent drama and spectacle in boxing make it a natural for the movie maker and the movie goer.

The student of popular culture and especially the teacher of English will more than likely be interested in the relationship between sports and language since the abuse of language, especially superlatives, is a daily occurrence. Again, on this subject, as on many others, a good place to start is with John Betts in the section entitled "Lingo, Lexicon, and Language," in *America's Sporting Heritage, 1850-1950.* Helpful sources are referred to in his notes. A good article on sports and mass communications is "Sportuguese: A Study of Sports Page Communication," which is included in one of the best anthologies on the sociological aspects of sports, *Sport, Culture and Society,* edited by John W. Loy, Jr. and Gerald S. Kenyon. Also included in this work is an article on sport in mass society from a seminal book on mass media and popular culture, Reuel Denney's *The Astonished Muse.*

The aggressive aspect of sport has been the subject of much debate in recent years, stirred on in part by the use of such terms on the sports pages as *scalp, throttle, blast,* etc. Again the matter of definitions is crucial. What is aggression? A wide range of answers can be found in the following works: *Aggression: A Social Psychological Analysis,* by Leonard Berkowitz, *Frustration and Aggression,* by John Dollard et al., and *On Aggression,* by Konrad Lorenz. In *Sports in America,* James Michener has a good discussion of violence as it relates to competition. Michener also has an informative section on women in sport as well as a very enlightening chapter on the financing of sport in contemporary America.

On the matter of aggression, the central unsolved question seems to be: do sports enhance aggression or relieve it? When does aggression cease to be good and become destructive? These are difficult questions but compelling ones in a world where violence in sport is part of our daily scene.

The pervasiveness of sport throughout American society has led to the creation of courses in literature and popular culture in high schools and colleges. In response to the new interest, a number of articles on the methodology of teaching the literature of sport[32] are beginning to appear as well as a number of texts, all with various approaches and emphases. Three recent texts are *Sports Literature,* edited by John Brady and James Hall, *Sports in Literature,* edited by Henry B. Chapin, and *The Sporting Spirit: Athletes in Literature and Life,* edited by Robert J. Higgs and Neil D. Isaacs.

Considering the ubiquitous nature of sports in American society and the increasing awareness of its significance by scholars in various disciplines, one is probably safe in predicting that within a few years the study of sport as an aspect of popular culture will be as commonplace in the universities as the study of languages is now. If this does not happen, it will not be for lack of material. Whether or not sport becomes an area of intensive investigation in the humanities, there is little doubt that it will continue to influence our lives in both obvious and subtle ways, for one thing is certain—man will play. Hopefully he may cease to go to war, but he will never cease to play as long as there is time called leisure after labor is done.

NOTES

1. Johan Huizinga, *Homo Ludens: A Study of the Play Element in Culture* (Boston: Beacon Press, 1960), p. 212.

2. Paul Weiss, *Sport: A Philosophic Inquiry* (Carbondale: Southern Illinois University Press, 1969), p. 134.

3. Roger Caillois, *Man, Play, and Games,* trans. Meyer Barash (New York: Free Press, 1961), pp. 9-10.

4. Hannah Arendt, *The Human Condition* (Chicago: University of Chicago Press, 1958), p. 85.

5. John A. Krout, *Annals of American Sport*, Vol. 15, *The Pageant of America* (New Haven: Yale University Press, 1929), p. 10.

6. Herbert Manchester, *Four Centuries of American Sport, 1490-1890* (1931; rpt. New York: Benjamin Blom, 1968), p. 16.

7. Wells Twombly, *200 Years of Sport in America* (New York: McGraw-Hill, 1976), p. 18.

8. Foster Rhea Dulles, *America Learns to Play: A History of Popular Recreation, 1607-1940* (New York: Peter Smith, 1952), p. 5.

9. Manchester, p. 17.

10. Dulles, p. 25.

11. *Private Journal* (Albany, 1865), pp. 52-53. Quoted in Dulles, p. 29.

12. Quoted in Henry Adams, "The United States in 1800," *Henry Adams: The Education of Henry Adams and Other Selected Writings,* ed. Edward N. Saveth (New York: Washington Square Press), pp. 72-3.

13. Jennie Holliman, *American Sports (1785-1835)* (1931; rpt. Philadelphia: Porcupine Press, 1975), p. 81.

14. Ibid., p. 23.

15. Quoted in Dulles, p. 35.

16. Adams, p. 74.

17. Holliman, pp. 6-7.

18. Ibid., p. 108.

19. Twombly, p. 30.

20. Manchester, p. 77.

21. Twombly, p. 43.

22. Twombly, p. 46.

23. Manchester, p. 127.

24. Dulles, pp. 223-224.

25. Ivan N. Kaye, *Good Clean Violence: A History of College Football* (Philadelphia: Lippincott, 1973), p. 17.

26. Dulles, p. 198.

27. Jay Rosenstein, "Sweating Gold," *Playboy*, April 1977, pp. 106, 112, 238-240.

28. John R. Betts, *America's Sporting Heritage, 1850-1950* (Reading, Mass.: Addison-Wesley, 1974), p. 69.

29. Ibid., p. 68.

30. Ibid., p. 237.

31. Gilbert Patten (Burt L. Standish), *Frank Merriwell's "Father": An Autobiography* (Norman: University of Oklahoma Press, 1964), p. 181.

32. See, for example, Connie Brannen, Mary F. Vincent, and Teri Walton, "Sports in the English Classroom," *English Journal*, 64 (February 1975), 104-105; Louie Crew, "A Humanistic Physical Education Course," *Journal of Physical Education*, 71 (January/February 1974), 70-71; and Barbara J. Kelley, "Getting It All Together: The Integrated Learning Semester," *Journal of Health, Physical Education, and Recreation*, 45 (October 1974), 32-35.

BIBLIOGRAPHY

Adams, Henry. *Henry Adams: The Education of Henry Adams and Other Selected Writings*. Edited by Edward N. Saveth. New York: Washington Square Press, 1963.

Angell, Roger. *Five Seasons: A Baseball Companion*. New York: Simon and Schuster, 1977.

Arendt, Hannah. *The Human Condition*. Chicago: University of Chicago Press, 1958.

Arlott, John, ed. *Oxford Companion to World Sports and Games*. London: Oxford University Press, 1975.

Berkowitz, Leonard. *Aggression: A Social Psychological Analysis*. New York: McGraw-Hill, 1962.

Berlin, Pearl, et al. *The American Woman in Sport*. Reading, Mass.: Addison-Wesley, 1974.

Betts, John R. *America's Sporting Heritage, 1850-1950*. Reading, Mass.: Addison-Wesley, 1974.

Biography Index. New York: H. W. Wilson, 1946-1976.

"The Black Dominance." *Time* (May 9, 1977), 57-60.

Boyle, Robert. *Sport: Mirror of American Life*. Boston: Little, Brown, 1963.

Brady, John, and James Hall, eds. *Sports Literature*. New York: McGraw-Hill, 1975.

Brannen, Connie, Mary F. Vincent, and Teri Walton. "Sports in the English Classroom." *English Journal*, 64 (February 1975), 104-05.

Caillois, Roger. *Man, Play, and Games*. Translated by Meyer Barash. New York: Free Press, 1961.

Cantwell, Robert. "A Sneering Laugh with the Bases Loaded." *Sports Illustrated* (April 23, 1962), 68-76.

Chapin, Henry B. *Sports in Lit.rature.* New York: David McKay, 1976.

Crew, Louie. "A Humanistic Physical Education Course." *Journal of Physical Education,* 71 (January/February 1974), 70-71.

Deford, Frank. "Religion in Sport." *Sports Illustrated* (April 19, 1976), 88-102; see also "Endorsing Jesus" (April 26, 1976), 54-69; and "Reaching for the Stars" (May 3, 1976), 42-60.

Denney, Reuel. *The Astonished Muse.* Chicago: University of Chicago Press, 1975.

Dictionary Catalog of Applied Life Studies Library. Boston: G. K. Hall, 1977.

Dollard, John, et. al. *Frustration and Aggression.* New Haven, Conn.: Yale University Press, 1974.

Dulles, Foster Rhea. *America Learns to Play: A History of Popular Recreation, 1607-1940.* New York: Appleton-Century, 1940.

Edwards, Harry. "The Myth of the Racially Superior Athlete." *Black Scholar* 3 (1971): 16-28.

———. *The Revolt of the Black Athlete.* New York: Free Press, 1969.

Finley, M. I., and H. W. Pleket. *The Olympic Games: The First Thousand Years.* New York: Viking, 1976.

Gardiner, E. Norman. *Athletics of the Ancient World.* London: Oxford University Press, 1930.

Haley, Bruce. "Sports and the Victorian World." *Western Humanities Review* 22 (1968), 115-25.

Hart, Marie, ed. *Sport in the Socio-Cultural Process.* Dubuque, Iowa: William C. Brown, 1972.

Henderson, Robert W. *Early American Sport.* New York: The Grolier Club, 1937. Reprint. Cranbury, N.J.: Associated University Presses, 1977.

Herrigel, Eugen. *Zen in the Art of Archery.* Translated by R. F. C. Null. 1953. Reprint. New York: Pantheon Books, Inc., 1971.

Higgs, Robert J. and Neil D. Isaacs. *Sporting Spirit: Athletes in Literature and Life.* New York: Harcourt Brace Jovanovich, 1977.

Hoch, Paul. *Rip Off the Big Game: The Exploitation of Sports by the Power Elite.* New York: Doubleday, 1972.

Holliman, Jennie. *American Sports (1785-1835).* 1931. Reprint. Philadelphia: Porcupine Press, 1975.

Huizinga, Johan. *Homo Ludens: A Study of the Play Element in Culture.* Boston: Beacon, 1960.

Isaacs, Neil D. *Jock Culture, USA.* New York: W. W. Norton, 1978.

Kane, Martin. "Assessment of 'Black is Best.'" *Sports Illustrated* (January 18, 1971), 72-76.

Kaye, Ivan. *Good Clean Violence: A History of College Football.* Philadelphia: Lippincott, 1973.

Kelley, Barbara J. "Getting It All Together: The Integrated Learning Semester." *Journal of Health, Physical Education, and Recreation,* 45 (October 1974), 32-35.

Koestler, Arthur. *The Lotus and the Robot.* New York: Macmillan, 1961.

Krout, John A. *Annals of American Sport,* Vol. 15, *Pageant of America Series.* New Haven, Conn.: Yale University Press, 1929.

Lardner, John. *White Hopes and Other Tigers.* Philadelphia: Lippincott, 1956.

Leonard, George. *The Ultimate Athlete.* New York: Viking, 1974.

Lorenz, Konrad. *On Aggression.* New York: Harcourt Brace and World, 1966.

Loy, John W. and Gerald S. Kenyon, eds. *Sport, Culture and Society.* London: Macmillan, 1969.

Manchester, Herbert. *Four Centuries of American Sport, 1490-1890.* 1931. Reprint. New York: Benjamin Blom, 1968.

Meggyesy, Dave. *Out of Their League.* Berkeley, Calif.: Ramparts Press, 1970.

Menke, Frank G. *The Encyclopedia of Sport.* 5th ed. Cranbury, N.J.: A. S. Barnes, 1975.

Metheny, Eleanor. *Connotations of Movement in Sport and Dance.* Dubuque, Iowa: William C. Brown, 1965.

Michener, James. *Sports in America.* New York: Random House, 1977.

Miller, Donna Mae, and Katherine Russell. *Sport: A Contemporary View.* Philadelphia: Lea and Febiger, 1971.

Murphy, Michael. *Golf in the Kingdom.* New York: Viking, 1972.

Novak, Michael. *The Joy of Sports.* New York: Basic Books, 1976.

Olsen, Jack. *The Black Athlete: A Shameful Story.* New York: Time-Life Books, 1968.

Patten, Gilbert (Burt L. Standish). *Frank Merriwell's "Father": An Autobiography.* Norman: University of Oklahoma Press, 1964.

Robinson, Rachel S. *Sources for the History of Greek Athletics.* Cincinnati, Ohio: University of Cincinnati Press, 1955.

Rohe, Fred. *Zen of Running.* New York: Random House, 1975.

Rosenstein, Jay. "Sweating Gold." *Playboy* (April 1977), 106, 112, 238-40.

Sage, George H., ed. *Sport and American Society; Selected Readings.* Reading, Mass.: Addison-Wesley, 1970.

Scott, Jack. *The Athletic Revolution.* New York: Free Press, 1971.

Shaw, Gary. *Meat on the Hoof.* New York: Dell, 1973.

Slusher, Howard S. *Man, Sport, and Existence: A Critical Analysis.* Philadelphia: Lea and Febiger, 1967.

Smith, Adam. *Powers of Mind.* New York: Ballantine, 1975.

Strutt, Joseph. *The Sports and Pastimes of the People of England.* 1833. Reprint. New York: A. M. Kelley, 1970.

Toynbee, Arnold. *The Breakdown of Civilizations,* Vol. 4, *A Study of History.* New York: Oxford University Press, 1939.

Twombly, Wells. *200 Years of Sport in America.* New York: McGraw-Hill, 1976.

Umphlett, Wiley Lee. *The Sporting Myth and the American Experience.* Lewisburg, Pa.: Bucknell University Press, 1975.

Veblen, Thorstein. *Theory of the Leisure Class.* 1899. Reprint. New York: Macmillan, 1953.

Webster's Sports Dictionary. Springfield, Mass.: G. and C. Merriam, 1976.

Weiss, Paul. *Sport: A Philosophic Inquiry.* Carbondale: Southern Illinois University Press, 1969.

CHAPTER 13 Stage Entertainment*
Don B.Wilmeth

HISTORIC OUTLINE

Other than the occasional staged variety show, the lone stand-up comic attempting to eke out a living in the few surviving night clubs or cabarets, or the spectacular revues of Las Vegas, popular live stage entertainment appealing to a large mass of Americans is a phenomenon of the past, replaced today by spectator sports, mass media, and rock concerts. In 1932, when the movies took over the Palace Theatre in New York, vaudeville symbolically died, although its slow death began in the 1890s as the motion picture slowly assimilated vaudeville and then replaced it as a more efficient and inexpensive medium. When the Minsky brothers introduced full-fledged strippers into their burlesque empire in the 1930s, burlesque as a unique and significant form of stage entertainment began its slow death. As Charles West, manager of his wife/stripper Evelyn "$50,000 Treasure Chest" West, recently commented as he observed the death of St. Louis's last burlesque house, burlesque's American decline began when taped music replaced bands, elaborate settings were eliminated, and comedians were canned. The decline, of course, began earlier, but he was correct when he added, "All that was left were the strippers." Each major American form of stage entertainment underwent a similar demise or merged into newer forms and vanished.

In the nineteenth century, however, the climate was right for live entertainment to prosper. Prior to the late eighteenth century, it was not possible for popular stage entertainments to appeal to large audiences, for it was necessary that there be a more concentrated society and the incorporation of the majority of the population into that society in order to foster popular entertainment. In this country, with the rise of technology and the rapid expansion of the frontier during the nineteenth century, Americans found increased time for leisure activities and de-

*Portions of this chapter appeared as "American Popular Entertainment," *Choice,* 14 (October 1977), 987-1004. Reprinted by permission.

veloped a hunger for entertainment to fill what was for many a dreary and difficult existence. As cities grew and Americans were concentrated into cohesive urban or near-urban units with common social, economic, and cultural characteristics, a huge market for entertainment was created.

Although often similar in structure and form to the more legitimate, mainstream theatrical forms, popular stage entertainment offered the ordinary man a vital and appealing alternative theater that satisfied his needs and desires. Professional showmen quickly perceived what would be accepted and consciously attempted to appeal to the majority, creating entertainment that was neither complex nor profound but readily comprehended, thus popular in the sense that the majority of people liked and approved it, with few deviations from its standards and conventions. Hundreds of professional troupes and individual performers emerged during the mid-nineteenth century to provide a variety of entertainment forms, some new, some adaptations of earlier forms, but all aimed at a new audience seeking amusement. Urban centers developed theaters and "palaces" of entertainment; rural America depended upon the traveling troupe, be it a circus, a wild west show (not within the province of this essay), a repertoire company playing town halls, an opera house, or even a tent, Lyceum and Chautauqua troupes performing under the guise of religion or culture, and variety companies of all sorts and descriptions.

DIME MUSEUMS AND MEDICINE SHOWS

Prior to the American Revolution, strolling exhibitors of curiosities operated in the colonies along with numerous other mountebanks and itinerant entertainers. They presented crude and disorganized entertainments —animals, freaks, mechanical and scientific oddities, wax figures, peep shows, and the like. By the beginning of the nineteenth century showmen had begun to organize such exhibits into "museums" or "cabinets of curiosities," with little competition from legitimate or serious museums. By mid-century the dime museum was established as a major form of American entertainment, and the first formidable American showman emerged, Phineas T. Barnum, entrepreneur of the American Museum in New York, beginning in 1841.

Barnum's museum established the ultimate pattern for the museum rage, with exhibits of every sort and a so-called lecture room where visitors witnessed extra "edifying" attractions running the gamut from jugglers and dioramas to comics, musicians, and popular theater fare, such as *The Drunkard*. The museums, operating under the thin veneer of culture and learning, soon spread to every medium-sized city in America and survived as a uniquely American institution until World War I. The dime museum filled an important void; unsophisticated Americans and recent immigrants could find here cheap and comprehensible entertainment that was acceptable on moral and religious grounds.

Like the itinerant pre-Revolutionary mountebank, the roving, performing quack selling his tonics and elixirs evolved into a major form of American entertainment, the medicine show, which, with the phenomenal growth of the American patent medicine industry in the nineteenth century, became a major business. Before the turn of the nineteenth century, the traveling medicine show, with its pitchman and frequent humbug Indian spectaculars, was a flourishing form of entertainment, borrowing everything that was taking place in the American theater and adapting it to its own needs.

THE MINSTREL SHOW

Of the major forms of stage entertainment, the first unique American show business form was the minstrel show, which, beginning in the 1840s, literally swept the nation, producing in time a tremendous impact on subsequent forms, in particular vaudeville and burlesque. Using what they claimed were credible black dialects, songs, dances, and jokes, white showmen in blackface created extremely popular and entertaining shows while at the same time perpetuating negative stereotypes of blacks that endured in American popular thought long after the show had vanished. The popularity of the black native character dates from about 1828 when Thomas D. Rice created his "Jim Crow" song and dance routine. Evolving out of the "Ethiopian delineators" of the 1820s, the name for blackfaced white entertainers, four performers calling themselves the Virginia Minstrels and organized by Dan Emmett developed the first full-length example of the new entertainment in 1843; soon a flood of competitors followed. In 1846 E. P. Christy gave the minstrel show its distinctive three-part structure: repartee between the master of ceremonies, or interlocutor, and the endmen (Bruder Tambo and Bruder Bones) sitting on either end of a semi-circular arrangement of the company, followed by the "olio" or the variety section, and culminating with a one-act skit.

Minstrelsy was the first major stage entertainment to avoid the elitist reputation of legitimate drama and commit itself to the new common-man audience. It was immediate, unpretentious, and devoted to fun, the emotional outlet that its urban patrons needed so desperately. Its use of music and comedy created its greatest appeal and most lasting influence. With its endmen and interlocutor the audience was engulfed with an endless string of puns, malapropisms, riddles, and jokes, delivered as rapid fire exchanges and carried over into the later urban humor of vaudeville, burlesque, and even radio, motion pictures, and television.

After the Civil War, the minstrel show expanded in diversity and scope, incorporating elements from newer forms of entertainment, reaching its peak in 1870. Although the changes prolonged its life for a short time, its uniqueness was destroyed. By 1896 only ten companies remained, and the minstrel show was no longer America's major stage entertainment; its new replacement was vaudeville.

V A U D E V I L L E

Like the minstrel show, American vaudeville was largely indigenous, the product of American saloon owners' efforts to attract eager and free-spending drinkers by enticing them with free shows. Early variety shows included risqué girlie shows, and their reputation soon became blighted. By the 1890s the older variety had been renamed vaudeville, capitalizing on the more elegant sound of the French word for light pastoral plays with musical interludes but having nothing in common with its French namesake. Instead, vaudeville developed its own brand of a highly organized, nationwide big business. Vaudeville became, after the early efforts of Tony Pastor (1837-1908), a symbol of Americanism; its performer, according to Robert Toll, the constant symbol of individual liberty and pioneer endeavor.

Modern vaudeville's heyday lasted a scant fifty years or so, from the 1880s to the early 1930s, but during its time Americans of all classes were amused and found relief from the relatively new industrial complex. Huge circuits of vaudeville theaters, led by such magnates as E. F. Albee, B. F. Keith, Marcus Loew, Martin Beck, F. F. Proctor, and Alexander Pantages, were in constant competition and, as rivalries blossomed, vaudeville flourished. The Keith-Albee combine, the most prestigious of them all, developel a formula catering to family audiences with continuous shows in luxurious vaudeville palaces. To protect their interests, managements formed conglomerates; performers quickly retaliated by founding the White Rats, modeled on the British music hall performers' union, the Water Rats, but with little success.

Although vaudeville appeared to its audiences as an unstructured collection of dissimilar acts, it was actually a meticulously planned and executed balance of "turns" designed to control the audiences' responses and interest, while enhancing the appeal of each act and providing a smorgasbord of the best available entertainment—magicians, vocalists, jugglers, comics, animal acts, skits, and even recitations and guest appearances by celebrities of the day. In 1913, the international star Sarah Bernhardt opened at the Palace in New York City and collected $7,000 for her talents. Because of its tremendous popularity, vaudeville helped to dictate morals and attitudes, whether consciously or not. Ethnic humor, for example, was a powerful force and, although immigrants were aided in their assimilation into the American populace by ethnic comics, their jokes helped to sustain the stereotyped misunderstandings and mythologies that still permeate American culture.

BURLESQUE

By the turn of the century a new form of stage entertainment had begun to assert its own unique brand of amusement, burlesque. The origins of burlesque are complex and confusing. Its components can be traced to numerous forms: English and American literary burlesque and parody, the circus, the knockabout farces of the medicine show and dime museums, the farces of such popular theater writers as Edward Harrigan and Charles Hoyt, the sketches of the minstrel show, concert saloons and beer gardens, Western honky-tonks, and even the stage Yankee. It is, however, misleading to attach the American form of burlesque to the older and more reputable forms, for American burlesque was clearly rooted in native soil. Historians usually date its true beginnings to the 1860s when a troupe of stranded ballet dancers in 1866 were incorporated into a musical extravaganza called *The Black Crook* at Niblo's Gardens in New York, followed in 1869 by Lydia Thompson and her "British Blondes" appearing in burlesques that emphasized feminine charms more than parody, the previous thrust of burlesque. As significant as these events were, they were less important than the influence of the honky-tonk, half beer hall and half brothel, with its variety entertainments of the most vulgar sort. The audiences were unsophisticated, and the atmosphere was similar to that of the early English music hall, rough and convivial. The first burlesque impresario, A. J. Leavitt, who began his career in 1870, combined the atmosphere of the honky-tonk with the structure of the minstrel show, took it out of the saloon, and put it into theaters. Soon burlesque assumed its standard form: variety acts and "bits" mingled with musical numbers, featuring beautiful women and bawdy humor. By the turn of the century the comedian was the center of the performance, despite the slow but constant increase of interest in the sensuous presence of the female form, made more prominent beginning with Little Egypt's "cooch dancing" in 1904 at the Columbia Exposition in St. Louis. The comic retained his central position, however, until the advent of the striptease in the early 1930s.

The "golden age" of burlesque began in 1905 with the organization of the Columbia circuit or wheel and began to change in the 1920s when the new Mutual Burlesque Association added greater permissiveness. With an increase in its sexual overtones burlesque came to appeal primarily to male audiences, reaching its height of popularity just prior to World War I. As erotic stimulation replaced bawdy humor, burlesque audiences became jaded and bored; burlesque fell on bad days. Without its basically cheerful humor, never bitter or moralistic, burlesque, like the minstrel show before it, lost its identity and its uniqueness.

POPULAR THEATER

From the earliest days of the American theater, a popular fare dominated much of the best of native production, beginning with the stage Yankee, Jonathan, in Royall Tyler's *The Contrast* (1787). As more common people found their way into theaters, the popularization of drama became a necessity. Native actors gained prominence in plays with native themes and types: James Hackett as the Yankee with his common sense and rustic manners; Joseph Jefferson III, as Rip Van Winkle, providing the audience a momentary escape into a world of fantasy and freedom; Frank Mayo as the idealized American hero Davy Crockett; Frank Chanfrau as the Irish volunteer fireman from the Bowery, "Mose the Fire Bhoy." By the late nineteenth century, some versions of all the most popular plays began to reach small-town America. The earlier stock resident company gave way to "combination" traveling companies. During the last thirty years of the century, with the increase of railroad mileage after the Civil War, previously inaccessible towns became important and profitable stops for touring companies. Nearly every village and hamlet began to construct a local "opera house" to accommodate traveling entertainments, creating a vast theatrical network known as "the road." If an "opera house" or "academy of music" was unavailable, traveling shows turned to existing courthouses, schools, town halls, churches, or other large halls.

The most enduring form of theater that appealed to the common people and reflected their desires, needs, and tastes was the melodrama, which dominated the popular stage during its heyday, 1850-1920. Although much of the popular fare, called *10-20-30 melodrama* after its admission prices, was poorly written, its formula was such that it could accommodate any setting, time, or character, and the simplistic dramatis personae were immediately identifiable to the audience. To a public that found its traditional values exalted, melodrama was more real than reality. Although melodrama rarely dealt with social issues or problems, several of the more prominent examples were significant exceptions: *Uncle Tom's Cabin*, ostensibly against slavery but popular because of its emotionally moving, melodramatic scenes and its spectacle, gave rise to dozens of touring companies called *Tommers* or *Tom shows* which toured the nation well into the twentieth century; *Ten Nights in a Barroom* and *The Drunkard*, temperance plays, created patronage for the theater from people who had condemned it as immoral.

The thirst for a nostalgic look at the American past and a reminder of simpler, nobler times, as well as the need for the reinforcement of stable values that were rapidly changing, gave melodrama writers fertile ground for creation, from Denman Thompson's 1876 study of rural America, *The Old Homestead*, to William F. Cody's mythic creations of genuine western heroes in both drama and wild west shows, to Civil War dramas that ignored the broad issues and the causes of the suffering and the divisiveness in the 1880s.

In time, small towns were invaded by too many touring companies, each doing much the same thing. During the season of 1900, 340 theatrical companies were touring; by 1920 the number had dwindled to less than fifty. As the new century began, a trend developed toward outdoor entertainment, and tent show repertoire became very much a part of the movement. As repertoire companies found themselves squeezed out of many opera houses, in part because of the control of established houses by theatrical trusts, they looked toward more remote areas where one-night stand companies never appeared, and where, as William Lawrence Slout points out, audiences could not compare entertainment values, and obscurity was a protection against tightened copyright enforcement. The solution for many was the canvas pavilion used by the circus, as well as medicine shows and other forms of variety entertainment. Ironically, the movement was encouraged by cultural and religious organizations, first the Millerites in 1842 and the most popular of the movements, the Chautauqua, during the first quarter of the twentieth century. Between 1900 and 1910 there were well over one hundred repertoire companies under canvas. By the summer of 1921, faced with a recession, the golden years of tent repertoire ended.

Emerging from the tent tradition was one of the last native stock characters, Toby, a redheaded, freckle-faced, rustic country boy who became a nightly fixture and feature attraction with many tent rep companies. As tent show dramas lost relevance for rural audiences and Toby became so exaggerated as to lose identity with them, a final chapter in American popular theater fell into decline. While it lasted, however, American drama truly belonged to the people. The combined yearly attendance at tent shows exceeded that of the New York theater, despite the makeshift, shabby quality of the performances.

Like virtually every form of stage entertainment, popular theater was ultimately taken over by films which could be brought into America's heartland inexpensively and with a minimum of effort. Americans would never again be able to shape and mold drama in their own image.

EARLY MUSICAL THEATER AND THE REVUE

The nineteenth century spawned one last major form of American stage entertainment, and, in many respects, the last strong effort to create a form of amusement that would appeal to a large popular audience, although cutting across class lines. The American musical theater and the revue grew out of a blend of elitist European culture and American popular entertainment. By the 1890s, after the success of *The Black Crook*, George L. Fox's pantomime extravaganza *Humpty Dumpty* (1868), the parody *Evangeline* in 1874, Kiralfy's production of *Around the World in 80 Days* (1875), and *The Brook*, a production with Nate Salisbury's Troubadors in 1879 incorporating vernacular music and dance, an American form of the book musical slowly began to evolve. Edward Harrigan and Tony Hart, known as the American Gilbert and Sullivan, introduced their city low life and immigrant characters in a series of Mulligan Guard plays beginning in 1879; Charles H. Hoyt and George M. Cohan continued the trend toward a musical theater centered around urban life and people; and Victor Herbert, Jerome Kern, and Irvin Berlin helped to shape a naturalized American form of musical comedy.

Despite the tremendous popularity of American musical comedy, twentieth-century musical theater merged as part of the mainstream. The last true vestige of popular stage entertainment, then, grew out of the same roots as vaudeville and burlesque. The revue's immense popularity dates from the opening in 1905 of the New York Hippodrome, the home of early lavish circusy revues with a $2 top. In 1907 Florenz Ziegfeld unfurled his first Follies, which continued annually until 1932. The 1920s and 1930s saw a wave of revue series cashing in on Ziegfeld's success: The Passing Shows (1912-24), Greenwich Village Follies (1919-28), George White's Scandals (1919-39), The Music Box Revues (1921-24), and Earl Carroll Vanities (1923-32). Despite later efforts to perpetuate the revue, the great days of Ziegfeld and Earl Carroll, mixing radiant showgirls, humor, and spectacle on a level of sophistication and wit but still retaining a popular appeal, could never again be repeated. Instead, the revue propelled artists, especially songwriters and individual stars, into new avenues of show business.

Popular stage entertainments were quickly assimilated into those new media of mass communication, radio, and the motion picture. Modern technology and its new techniques for duplicating and multiplying materials, along with more efficient methods of production and distribution, quickly spread popular culture in this century, while at the same time replacing the need for live, professional entertainment aimed at a large popular audience.

HISTORY AND CRITICISM

The student and scholar of American popular culture has too frequently assumed that live amusements created by professional showmen for profit and aimed at broad, relatively unsophisticated audiences were unworthy of serious attention—if noted at all. The reasons for this oversight can be traced to the anti-commercial bias with which too many scholars have looked at popular entertainment, the apparent unimportance of such areas for investigation, and even the lack of a strong literary base for most popular entertainment forms, for indeed most of these forms depend more significantly on the performer and the audience than a written text. There are legitimate difficulties in investigating popular stage entertainments; throughout history popular forms have appeared, merged, mutated, disappeared, and, in some cases, reappeared in new guises, all the while virtually ignored by scholars and historians.

Although many of the better sources on stage entertainment are what one might call "good bad" books—chatty autobiographies and memoirs, undocumented histories, and the like—the attention paid to popular entertainment has changed drastically in recent years. No longer are forms like vaudeville, burlesque, and popular theater considered insignificant because they are not abtruse, profound, or complicated. Beyond their primary function, to entertain, as important as that is, social scientists and humanists are discovering other values, the reflection and expression of aesthetic and other needs of a large population base, as well as the creation of effective satire or politically motivated comment. Indications of the broader importance can be seen, for example, in American minstrelsy, which spoke for and to huge numbers of common Americans in the nineteenth century and during its heyday provided unique insights into the thoughts, feelings, needs, and desires of the common people who shaped the show in their own image, or in vaudeville, which also spoke to a new audience and if taken seriously, as something more than an idle form of mass amusement, can be seen as a manifestation of psychic and social forces at work in American history.

Underscoring the newfound significance of popular entertainment as a legitimate area of study is the attention paid the subject by scholarly journals and organizations. The Center for the Study of Popular Culture at Bowling Green University publishes significant books under the aegis of the Bowling Green University Popular Press and issues the important *Journal of Popular Culture* which includes, periodically, articles on stage entertainments. In 1971 *Theatre Quarterly* (published in London) issued a number devoted to "People's Theatre," including essays on melodrama, equestrian drama, and American vaudeville. *The Drama Review*, the single best source for essays dealing with the influence of popular entertainment on the avant garde, published an issue in 1974 devoted to "popular entertainments," containing good articles on popular scenography, commedia dell'arte and the actor, stage magic, and other relevant topics, among them an excellent introduction to the subject by Brooks

McNamara which lays out a sensible categorization of forms. The *Educational Theatre Journal* followed in 1975 with an excellent issue featuring articles on early American musical theater, burlesque, revue, and pantomime.

Despite the mediocre nature of much of the literature on stage entertainments, a tremendous amount has been written. The time coverage of a majority of the sources discussed here is limited to the period from the emergence of a huge market for entertainment in the late eighteenth century (paralleling the appearance of a predominantly middle-class civilization in the Western world, which in turn drastically changed the cultural pattern) to the emergence early in the twentieth century of the motion picture, other than works on the revue, early musical theater, and the stand-up comic. The focus throughout will be on the best sources available (both recent and standard works in the field). The categories used are, at best, often artificial divisions because of the overlapping nature of the forms.

REFERENCE AND GENERAL SOURCES

Since serious scholarly research is relatively new in the field of popular stage entertainment, there are currently no comprehensive bibliographies covering all major forms. John Towsen's "Sources in Popular Entertainment" is a useful general guide with a very selective bibliography; bibliographies provided in the standard works, indicated elsewhere under specific categories, furnish the researcher with the best bibliographical data currently available. A definitive glossary of popular entertainment terminology is, likewise, unavailable, although *The Language of Show Biz*, edited by Sherman Sergel, is a fair guide to the special language of vaudeville, burlesque, and Toby shows. Again, specific works on individual forms tend to be the best guides, many with special glossaries.

Few attempts have been made to produce a comprehensive history of popular entertainments. The two best sources are McKechnie's *Popular Entertainments Through the Ages* and Robert Toll's *On with the Show.* Although originally published in 1931, McKechnie offers a good introduction to major forms (with a focus on Europe), including mimes, minstrels, strolling plays, fairs, commedia dell'arte, Punch and Judy, pantomime, and music hall, and thus provides a good background to European roots of American entertainment. Toll's book is the only attempt to chronicle American forms of entertainment, and despite organizational and emphases problems, this volume is a generally excellent introduction to major American forms. It also contains an excellent bibliographical essay and a comparative chronology showing the parallel between the evolution of American society and American show business.

There is not room in this essay to include coverage of the many studies of popular culture relevant to stage entertainments, but a few are too essential for exclusion. Gilbert Seldes's *The 7 Lively Arts* was the first attempt by an American to justify and defend popular entertainments and as such is still stimulating.

Constance Rourke's *American Humour* and *The Roots of American Culture* are especially important for their analysis of American comic stereotypes in the nineteenth century. Jesse Bier's *The Rise and Fall of American Humour* is less significant but still a good study of nineteenth-century American popular culture, as is Carl Bode's *The Anatomy of American Popular Culture, 1840-1861.* Norman Cantor and Michael Werthman's anthology, *The History of Popular Culture,* includes a section of reprinted essays entitled "Popular Entertainments and Recreation" by such authorities as Foster Rhea Dulles and James H. Young. Dulles' *America Learns to Play* remains the best general introduction to early American popular entertainment and includes much more than show business in its coverage of how Americans made use of their leisure time. Russel Nye's *The Unembarrassed Muse* is also an excellent general introduction to the popular arts and includes a good section on popular theater.

American stage entertainments depend a great deal on general histories for investigation. Although it is necessary to exclude most of these here, two are essential for the student of popular entertainment, G. C. D. Odell's *Annals of the New York Stage* and T. Allston Brown's three-volume *History of the New York Stage.* Odell remains the standard history through the 1893-94 season and is written with charm, accuracy, and impressive scholarship; Brown, a theatrical agent and historian, was a devotee of popular entertainment, and his work contains histories of over four hundred New York theaters, opera houses, music halls, circuses, and other places of entertainment. Brooks Atkinson's *Broadway* is a more up-to-date overview of New York entertainment from 1900 to 1974. Edward Bennett Marks's *They All Had Glamour,* although not limited to popular entertainment, is an amusing source for lesser known theater and musical artists and contains a good glossary, "Old-Time Colloquialisms." Allen Churchill, the author of numerous theater studies, offers a survey of Broadway from 1900 to 1919 in *The Great White Way* and during the revue era and the birth of the modern American musical in *The Theatrical Twenties.* Langston Hughes and Milton Meltzer produced a major survey of the black performer in American entertainment in their *Black Magic*; Edith Isaacs' historical survey *The Negro in the American Theatre,* though older, is still recommended. A *Book About the Theater* gives an interesting perspective on popular entertainments by an important early American theater historian, Brander Matthews, as do George Jean Nathan's *Encyclopædia of the Theatre* and Laurence Hutton's *Curiosities of the American Stage.*

In *America Takes the Stage,* Richard Moody traces the development of romanticism in American drama and theater from 1750 to 1900 and deals prominently with the stage Yankee and Negro minstrelsy. McNamara has written numerous essays of a general nature that are extremely valuable, among them "Popular Scenography," a survey of the architecture and design of traditional popular entertainment, and "Scavengers of the Amusement World," in which he shows the indebtedness of early cinema to vaudeville and other stage entertainments. An excellent period source is John Jennings' *Theatrical and Circus Life,* a compendium of popular forms. A useful guide to other general sources is Don B. Wilmeth's *The American Stage to World War I.*

DIME MUSEUMS AND MEDICINE SHOWS

Two significant areas of popular stage entertainment that have received surprisingly scant coverage are dime museums and medicine shows. Indeed, little attention has been given the theatrical format of these two American institutions, although both had long and fascinating histories. The medicine show belongs to a tradition of mountebanks, charletans, and quack doctors selling tonics and elixirs mixed with attention-getting free entertainment that dates back to the Middle Ages. The dime museum, from the Civil War to World War I, provided a variety of entertainment to working-class audiences in virtually every city and town in the United States.

Only one major full-length study can be included on the American medicine show, Brooks McNamara's *Step Right Up: An Illustrated History of the American Medicine Show,* which is not only the sole documented history of the phenomenon but an excellent reference for additional sources on patent medicine and related topics, examples of medicine show skits, and a glossary of pitchmen's terms. His essays on the subject, although to a large extent incorporated into the longer work, are also recommended. Graydon Freeman's *The Medicine Showman,* Thomas Kelley's *The Fabulous Kelley,* and Malcolm Webber's fictionalized reminiscences, *Medicine Show,* are earlier but less effective attempts to record aspects of the medicine show. In Mae Noell's "Some Memories of a Medicine Show Performer" a medicine show artist recalls the best-loved "bits" and life on the rural circuits and provides some additional insights into this American institution. McNamara, however, remains the definitive source. Background on American patent medicines and their relationship to the medicine show are treated in depth by James Young in *The Toadstool Millionaires* and *The Medical Messiahs.*

The dime museum has received even less attention and, again, the major source to date is by Brooks McNamara, " 'A Congress of Wonders':

The Rise and Fall of the Dime Museum," an excellent survey of the origin and development of this uniquely American brand of popular entertainment. The name most closely associated with the dime museum tradition is Phineas T. Barnum. Although the tendency is to lump him into the American circus tradition, where he indeed did make some contributions, Barnum's major involvement was with his New York museum, where he displayed some six hundred thousand items plus live entertainment. John Betts's "P. T. Barnum and the Popularization of Natural History" offers a good critical perspective on Barnum's museum, although the definitive and only documented study of Barnum's career is Neil Harris' *Humbug: The Art of P. T. Barnum*, an excellent analysis of Barnum's contributions in their social, economic, entertainment, and intellectual contexts. Less useful are the two other major standard biographies of Barnum: M. R. Werner's *Barnum* and Irving Wallace's *The Fabulous Showman*, the latter containing an extensive bibliography. Alice Desmond's *Barnum Presents General Tom Thumb* is a pleasant biography of Barnum's famous attraction, Charles Stratton. Barnum himself authored numerous books and, although their total credibility should be questioned, they are still important sources. His *The Humbugs of the World* (1865) and *Struggles and Triumphs* (1869) have both been reprinted recently.

VARIETY FORMS: MINSTRELSY, VAUDEVILLE, AND BURLESQUE

Variety can include all entertainment that depends on a compartmented structure; the three most prominent American examples, minstrel shows, vaudeville, and burlesque, dominated American popular stage entertainment during their heydays. Each grew out of earlier saloon and variety structures and collectively demonstrate the type of mutation that occurred in American popular entertainment.

In-depth study of American variety entertainment still depends a great deal on periodicals of the time and special collections. Of the numerous newspapers of the period, the most valuable are *Billboard* (beginning in 1894), the New York *Clipper* (1900-1918), *Variety* (especially 1905 to 1937), and the New York *Mirror* (1879-1922). Some of the more extensive collections on variety forms are located in well-known libraries: the Library of Congress, the Harvard Theatre Collection, the Hoblitzelle Theatre Arts Library of the University of Texas at Austin, the Library of the Performing Arts at Lincoln Center, and the Boston Public Library. Good minstrel materials are to be found in the Harris Collection, Brown University, and the Buffalo and Erie County Library. Other collections, noted in William C. Young's *American Theatrical Arts*, contain useful holdings of playlets, joke books, sheet music, song books, and similar primary materials.

Robert Toll's *Blacking Up* is the most comprehensive history and analysis of the minstrel show. Toll portrays minstrelsy as an institution that represents an important reflection of American attitudes; he also provides a superb bibliography of primary and secondary sources. Carl Wittke's *Tambo and Bones*, though dated, is still a good basic history and explanation of minstrelsy form. Dailey Paskman's *"Gentlemen, Be Seated!"* (originally published in 1928) has been revised recently by Paskman and updated to include recent offshoots of minstrelsy. It remains, however, a romanticized history but with good examples of music, sample minstrel routines, and good illustrations. For a "how-to" book, Jack Haverly's *Negro Minstrels: A Complete Guide* is an interesting outline by a successful minstrel manager. Edward Rice's *Monarchs of Minstrelsy* supplies biographical sketches of minstrel specialists, an index of minstrels, and a list of minstrel organizations up to 1911. Moody's "Negro Minstrelsy" provides a good appraisal of minstrelsy largely as a romantic invention of Northern whites.

The career of the first blackface comedian, T. D. Rice, is effectively summarized by Molly Ramshaw in "Jump, Jim Crow! A Biographical Sketch of Thomas D. Rice"; Hans Nathan's *Dan Emmett and the Rise of Early Negro Minstrelsy* chronicles the life of this minstrel specialist and the early period of minstrelsy from the point of view of a musicologist. Tom Fletcher's *100 Years of the Negro in Show Business* places minstrelsy, with a focus on individuals, in the context of black performers over a one hundred year period. The tremendous impact of minstrelsy in Great Britain is adequately told by Harry Reynolds in *Minstrel Memories*, covering the period 1836 to 1927. Two good specialized essays are Marian Winter's "Juba and American Minstrelsy" and Jules Zanger's "The Minstrel Show as Theater of Misrule." Two dissertations on minstrelsy and songsters (Frank Davidson's "The Rise, Development, Decline, and Influence of the American Minstrel Show" and Cecil L. Patterson's "A Different Drummer") add scholarly credibility to the topic.

The definitive history of early variety has yet to be written, although the standard works on vaudeville and one recent study, Parker Zellers' *Tony Pastor: Dean of the Vaudeville Stage*, include some coverage of the early years. Zellers' essay, 'The Cradle of Variety: The Concert Saloon," also sheds light on early variety. Myron Matlaw's essay on Pastor's early years, beginning in 1846, is a useful complement to Zellers. Lloyd Morris in his chatty book *Incredible New York* discusses the atmosphere, reputation, and dangers of various concert saloons; Clair Willson, in *Mimes and Miners*, gives a good sense of variety in the West; and Eugene Bristow's scholarly study of variety in Memphis during the late nineteenth century ("Look Out for Saturday Night") provides good social insights.

Of the general histories of vaudeville during its peak period, John Di-Meglio's *Vaudeville U.S.A.* is the best documented and furnishes the most extensive notes and bibliography. Several older histories should still be considered essential: Abel Green and Joe Laurie's *Show Biz from Vaude to Video*, Joseph Laurie's *Vaudeville: From the Honky-Tonks to the Palace*, and Douglas Gilbert's *American Vaudeville: Its Life and Times*. Of more recent investigations, Albert McLean's *American Vaudeville as Ritual* represents the most thorough job of analyzing vaudeville in its social-historical framework and delving below the surface for greater significance. His more recent article, "U.S. Vaudeville and the Urban Comics," is a natural extension of his book. Paul Distler's dissertation, "The Rise and Fall of the Racial Comics in American Vaudeville," and essay, "Exit the Racial Comics," are excellent scholarly studies of racial comedy in vaudeville.

A large number of active participants in vaudeville left autobiographies or memoirs. The following early ones are especially informative: M. B. Leavitt's *Fifty Years in Theatrical Management*, Robert Grau's two volumes of memoirs, *The Business Man in the Amusement World* and *Fifty Years of Observation of Music and the Drama*, and Brett Page's insider's view of vaudeville, *Writing for Vaudeville*. Eugene Elliott's study, *A History of Variety-Vaudeville in Seattle*, though brief, offers a good look at that Northwestern vaudeville capital. William Marston and John H. Fellers's *F. F. Proctor, Vaudeville Pioneer* and Felix Isman's *Weber and Fields* are among the better biographies of vaudeville luminaries. Bernard Sobel's *A Pictorial History of Vaudeville*, recommended for its illustrations, though directed at a popular audience is still an accurate and informative guide. Caroline Caffin's *Vaudeville* is a good source of critical essays on vaudeville as seen by a member of the audience. The efforts to create a union for vaudevillians is detailed by George Golden, one of its major organizers, in *My Lady Vaudeville and Her White Rats*.

Most recent vaudeville studies are offshoots of the nostalgia craze and vary greatly in content and value. Charles and Louise Samuels' *Once Upon a Stage* is an informal and undocumented history and in no way supersedes earlier histories; Bill Smith's *The Vaudevillians* is a sad and wistful look at daily life on the vaudeville circuit via interviews with thirty-one former headliners (and includes a brief glossary of vaudeville terms); and Marcia Keegan's *We Can Still Hear Them Clapping* is a photographic essay, with limited text, recording the impressions and reminiscences of former vaudevillians still living in the Times Square district. A fair account of the final chapter in vaudeville's history is Marian Spitzer's *The Palace*, which covers this pinnacle in vaudeville from its opening in 1913.

Stage magic was a prominent feature of vaudeville and developed into a form of popular stage entertainment in its own right. The literature on magic is extensive and interest in magic has recently burgeoned. Of the more recent publications, the following are of interest to the scholar and student. Robert Gill's *Magic As a Performing Art* is an excellent annotated bibliography of over one thousand books and pamphlets published during the past forty years and a good guide to earlier bibliographies as well. The work of Milbourne Christopher is highly recommended, especially *The Illustrated History of Magic,* one of the most important magic books of modern times, extremely well-illustrated. His biography, *Houdini: The Untold Story,* is the most comprehensive, although William L. Gresham's *The Man Who Walked Through Walls* is generally lively and thorough. Hyla Clark's *The World's Greatest Magic* is a very attractive popular study of magic stars of the present day, and Edward Claflin and Jeff Sheridan's *Street Magic* is the only history concerned with itinerant wandering magicians, several of whom later became vaudeville headliners.

Burlesque has received even less scholarly treatment than other forms of variety and is invariably admixed with the striptease show, which actually spelled the demise of true American burlesque. American burlesque, not to be confused with the literary tradition effectively dissected by V. C. Clinton-Baddeley in *The Burlesque Tradition in the English Theatre After 1600,* has only one fairly comprehensive history, Irving Zeidman's *The American Burlesque Show,* and the latter, terribly biased in an almost Puritanical way, fails to document his investigation. The single best scholarly source, therefore, on the origin and content of burlesque up to the 1930s in Ralph Allen's "Our Native Theatre: Honky-Tonk, Minstrel Shows, Burlesque." The standard sources, generally weak on historical fact and the separation of striptease from true burlesque, are Ann Corio's *This Was Burlesque* and Bernard Sobel's *Burleycue* and *A Pictorial History of Burlesque.* The latter contains an informative text along with excellent photographs. Also useful is Trish Sandberg's "An Interview with Steve Mills," a superb old-time burlesque comic, and Mills's version of one of his "bits," " 'An Artist's Studio': A Comic Scene From Burlesque." Although a fanciful account of burlesque in the 1920s, Rowland Barber's *The Night They Raided Minsky's* provides a sense of the transition from true burlesque to striptease.

The subject of striptease is no longer limited to latter-day burlesque but more appropriately belongs today to the world of carnivals, fairs, strip clubs, and striptease cabarets. Nevertheless, as an offshoot of burlesque it deserves inclusion and, surprisingly, the subject has begun to stimulate intriguing sociological and psychological investigations. Few of the numerous memoirs of strippers are worthy of consideration, although two stand apart from the others: Gypsy Rose Lee's memoirs are coherent and offer good backstage atmosphere; Georgia Sothern's *Georgia: My Life in*

Burlesque is the best of its ilk—witty, entertaining, and provocative. Strip-tease also lacks a comprehensive history, although Richard Wortley's recent *A Pictorial History of Striptease* makes a somewhat feeble effort. Susan Meiselas's *Carnival Strippers* is a more forthright and honest pictorial essay on the stripper, as is Roswell Angier's *A Kind of Life*, which combines pictorial and textual insights into the life of strippers in Boston's "Combat Zone." Investigations into strippers' morality and the sociological/psychological implications of their profession have been undertaken with varying degrees of success by Bernard Lipnitski, James Skipper, Jr. and Charles McCaghy, "Stripteasers," and Marilyn Salutin, "Stripper Morality."

POPULAR THEATER

Popular theater encompasses the largest body of sources of any form of stage entertainments, primarily because of its scripted nature and its overlap with mainstream theater forms. Virtually all American theater histories deal with various aspects of popular theater, such as nineteenth-century melodrama, Tom shows, Toby and Suzy shows, hippodrama, tent theater and touring troupes, mining camp theater, and other topics that use mainstream theater structures and techniques. For the sake of this essay, I have chosen to discuss only major sources; additional relevant material can be found in Don B. Wilmeth's guide to the American stage to World War I. A familiarity with the journal *Nineteeth Century Theatre Research* is a must in this area of study, as are the major theater collections and periodicals of the period.

An excellent overview of popular theater is included in Robert C. Toll's *On with the Show*, along with a good selective bibliography. Toll is especially effective in his analysis of native themes and characters dealt with in American drama. A. H. Quinn's *A History of the American Drama from the Beginning to the Present Day* remains the standard survey of specific plays and playwrights (anthologies of American drama are excluded from this survey but should be consulted as well). Essays on specific performers of the popular theater can be found in William C. Young's *Famous Actors and Actresses on the American Stage*, a disappointing but nonetheless useful collection by or about 225 performers.

For drama, the most important developments in the late nineteenth century took place in small-town America, where versions of most of the popular plays of the day were presented. Basic formulas evolved that virtually guaranteed success. Identifiable, native American characters figure prominently in the evolution of popular theater. Other than general studies already noted, Francis Hodge's *Yankee Theatre*, Richard Moody's essays, "Uncle Tom, The Theater, and Mrs. Stowe" and, with A. M. Drummond, "The Hit of the Century: Uncle Tom's Cabin," and Moody's "Edward Harrigan" (a full-length book, which should be excellent, is projected), Harry Birdoff's *The World's Greatest Hit*, and Willis Turner's "City Low-Life on the American Stage to 1900" are especially recommended. Hodge's book is the definitive history of the stage Yankee type during its peak period, and Birdoff is the only full-length study of "Tommers" and derivatives from the original *Uncle Tom's Cabin*. Richard Dorson has written an excellent essay entitled "Mose the Far-Famed and World Renowned."

The story of the "trouper" and the evolution of traveling companies, culminating in repertoire tent shows, is effectively and comprehensively told in William Slout's *Theatre in a Tent*, also an excellent source on operational practices. An excellent introduction to the entertainment business in small-town America, although one of those "good bad" books is Harlowe Hoyt's *Town Hall Tonight*. Philip Lewis's *Trouping: How the Show Came to Town* is a pleasant but unreliable history of the same subject. A less successful study of the tent show is Marian McKennon's book, *Tent Show*. A more scholarly analysis of touring systems, specifically in California from 1849 to 1859, is Douglas McDermott's fine essay, "Touring Patterns on California's Theatrical Frontier, 1849-1859."

Much of the atmosphere and climate for popular theater is reflected in early Western theater and amusements in the mining frontiers of Arizona, Oregon, California, and Nevada. This aspect is well covered in studies by Robert Ericson, "Touring Entertainment in Nevada During the Peak Years of the Mining Boom"; Alice Ernst, *Trouping in the Oregon Country*; Joseph Gaer, *Theater of the Gold Rush Decade in San Francisco*; Edmond Gagey, *The San Francisco Stage*; Constance Rourke, *Troupers of the Gold Coast*; George MacMinn, *The Theater of the Golden Age in California*; and Margaret Watson, *Silver Theatre*. The importance of the frontier opera house during the last third of the nineteenth century is explored by Ronald Davis, in "Sopranos and Six Guns." Popular theater in New York is revealed with scholarly exactitude in Marvin Felheim's study of the playwright-manager Augustin Daly and Lise Leone-Marker's book on the director-playwright David Belasco. Doris Cook's small book, *Sherlock Holmes and Much More*, is the only documented study of the popular actor-playwright William Gillette, author of a number of popular melodramas. Cody's involvement in melodrama is touched upon in Don Russell's *The Wild West* and summarized by William Coleman, "Buffalo Bill on Stage," and Jay Monaghan, "The Stage Career of Buffalo Bill." The importance and influence of a strictly American institution, the Chautauqua, which included popular entertainment and theater under the guise of culture and religion, is dealt with in detail in Theodore Morrison's history of Chautauqua, Charles F. Horner's *Strike the Tent*, Marian Scott's

Chautauqua Caravan, and Harry P. Harrison's *Culture Under Canvas,* the latter a recounting of the traveling tent shows by the manager of the Redpath Chautaqua.

The American showboat, which included not only floating theaters but circus and medicine show boats, has been most fully explored by Philip Graham, in *Showboats,* although George Ford's *These Were Actors* is an interesting, if fanciful, account of one of the earliest showboat families and should be consulted as well.

Of all dramatic formulas, the melodrama was the most enduring in American popular culture. A penetrating analysis of the cultural milieu in which melodrama developed and thrived is David Grimsted's *Melodrama Unveiled,* a well-documented scholarly work that includes chapters on critics, audiences, stages, and plays, and offers an excellent bibliographical essay on sources. Frank Rahill's *The World of Melodrama* is also an important treatment of the genre, although less perceptive than Grimsted. The home of melodrama in New York during the nineteeth century, the Bowery Theatre, is given detailed treatment in Alvin Harlow's *Old Bowery Days* and Theodore Shank's "Theatre for the Majority." There is a close relationship between English and American melodrama; consequently a number of good English sources are recommended, especially Michael Booth, *English Melodrama;* Maurice Disher, *Melodrama: Plots That Thrilled;* Ernest Reynolds, *Early Victorian Drama, 1830-1870;* and George Rowell, *The Victorian Theatre.*

The stock character Toby has been the subject of several scholarly investigations, in particular those of Larry Clark, "Toby Shows"; Sherwood Snyder, "The Toby Shows"; and Jere C. Mickel, "The Genesis of Toby." Neil E. Schaffner and Vance Johnson's *The Fabulous Toby and Me,* the story of Neil Schaffner, the last of the well-known tent repertoire showmen, is an entertaining and sometimes revealing look at the tag end of an American tradition.

EARLY MUSICAL THEATER AND THE REVUE

The American musical has been the subject of a vast outpouring of books and essays. The best general sources are still the standard works of Cecil Smith, *Musical Comedy in America;* Stanley Green, *The World of Musical Comedy;* and David Ewen. Ewen's *New Complete Book of the American Musical Theatre* is an excellent reference work for the histories of major musicals. A more general reference to American music is Julius Mattfeld's *Variety Music Cavalcade,* which provides a chronological checklist of popular music, including theater music, in the United States from the Pilgrims to 1969. An earlier survey, but still useful, is Edward Marks'

They All Sang: From Tony Pastor to Rudy Vallee. Raymond Mander and Joe Mitchenson's *Musical Comedy*, although concerned primarily with English musicals, is still valuable, especially for its 240 photographs.

The early history of the American musical, prior to 1800, is carefully treated by Julian Mates in his standard history, *The American Musical Stage Before 1800*. He has written also an excellent summary with a useful selected bibiliography in "American Musical Theatre: Beginnings to 1900"; the significance of *The Black Crook* is examined in his "The Black Crook Myth." Joseph Whitton's *"The Naked Truth,"* however, remains a definitive contemporary history of the extravaganza. Roger Hall's examination of *The Brook* is a scholarly essay which questions its importance as "the 'germinal cell' of American musical comedy." The best study of Edward Harrigan and Tony Hart available in E. J. Kahn's *The Merry Partners*, although Richard Moody's projected book on Harrigan should supersede this undocumented volume. Of the several biographies of George M. Cohan available, John McCabe's *The Man Who Owned Broadway* is the most reliable.

The revue, especially Ziegfeld's contributions, has been the subject of a number of popularized studies. Robert Baral's *Revue: The Great Broadway Period* is the sole comprehensive study of New York revue, with a list of revues on Broadway from 1903 to 1945. The only book-length study of the Hippodrome (1905-39) is by Norman Clarke, *The Mighty Hippodrome*. Of the Ziegfeld studies, the most accurate is Randolph Carter's *The World of Flo Ziegfeld*, although both Marjorie Farnsworth (*The Ziegfeld Follies*) and Charles Higham (*Ziegfeld*) cover much the same ground. All three contain magnificent illustrations and together form a reasonably good picture of the "Follies." Patricia Ziegfeld's book, *The Ziegfelds' Girls*, is a curious and sometimes interesting inside view of Ziegfeld's institution. Other revues have received less coverage. Alice Crowley includes a chapter on "The Grand Street Follies" in *The Neighborhood Playhouse*, and Margaret Knapp discusses the tone, subject matter, performers, and history of the same revue series in a more scholarly and incisive manner in the *Educational Theatre Journal*. Ken Murray's recent *The Body Merchant* is ostensibly the life of Earl Carroll but only deals indirectly with his "Vanities." George Jean Nathan's *The Popular Theatre* and *The Entertainment of a Nation* are worth attention for this critic's analysis of Ziegfeld in 1918 and the decline in the 1940s of the revue form.

The collaboration of America's first important black musical theater creators, Noble Sissle and Eubie Blake, is attractively presented with numerous illustrations by Robert Kimball and William Bolcom in *Reminiscing with Sissle and Blake*. The history of the rise and fall of the Shubert empire and their contributions to the musical stage is adequately related by Jerry Stagg in the only full-length study of the brothers, *A Half-Century of Show Business*. Finally, Stanley Green's *Ring Bells! Sing Songs!* is an exhaustive history with casts and credits for 175 musicals from 1930 to 1939.

STAND-UP COMICS

Trevor Griffith's successful Broadway play *Comedians* during the 1976-77 season has brought new attention to an area of popular entertainment that has received little serious study, the stand-up comic. The roots of the American stand-up comic date back to the early talking clown of the American circus, basically a stand-up comic. The most famous of the early clowns was Dan Rice, whose life and times have been written most effectively by John Kunzog (*The One-Horse Show*) and Maria Brown (*The Life of Dan Rice*). An excellent new survey of the history of clowns, not limited to the stand-up comic, is John Towsen's *Clowns*, which is highly recommended. Few general studies deal exclusively with the stand-up comic, although Phil Berger's *The Last Laugh* is a reasonably successful study of the lives, gags, and routines of the major contemporary stand-up comics. William Cahn's *The Laugh Makers* (and the revised version, *A Pictorial History of the Great Comedians*) is one of the better contemporary sources on stand-up comics, although short on analytical text. Abel Green and Joe Laurie's *Show Biz From Vaude to Video* sums up seven great eras of show business up to 1951 and includes selected emphasis on the place of the stand-up comic.

Of specific works by or about individual stand-up comics, most are so chatty and informal as to be almost useless. The writings of Joey Adams, especially his *Encyclopedia of Humor, From Gags to Riches,* and *The Borscht Belt,* are exceptions. Steve Allen's *The Funny Men* is a better than average literary effort, and Art Cohn's *The Joker is Wild* is a fair biography of Joe E. Lewis. Lenny Bruce, the subject of great attention as a controversial and revolutionary stand-up comic, has been given good treatment in Albert Goldman's biography, *Ladies and Gentlemen, Lenny Bruce!,* and John Cohen's *The Essential Lenny Bruce.*

The world of the night club and cabaret has received even less coverage than the performer, although Stanley Walker's *The Night Club Era* is an early effort in that direction, and Lisa Appignanesi's *The Cabaret* is the first useful historical survey and analytical account in English of the cabaret from its Parisian beginnings to its most recent manifestations in London and the United States.

BIBLIOGRAPHY

BOOKS AND ARTICLES

Reference and General Sources

Atkinson, Brooks. *Broadway*. Rev. ed. New York: Macmillan, 1974.

Bier, Jesse. *The Rise and Fall of American Humour*. New York: Holt Rinehart and Winston, 1968.

Bode, Carl. *The Anatomy of American Popular Culture, 1840-1861*. Berkeley: University of California Press, 1959.

Brown, T. Allston. *History of the New York Stage*. 3 vols. 1903. Reprint. New York: Benjamin Blom, 1963.

Cantor, Norman F., and Michael S. Werthman, eds. *The History of Popular Culture*. New York: Macmillan, 1968.

Churchill, Allen. *The Great White Way*. New York: E. P. Dutton, 1962.

————. *The Theatrical Twenties*. New York: McGraw-Hill, 1975.

Dulles, Foster Rhea. *America Learns to Play: A History of Popular Recreation, 1607-1940*. New York: Appleton-Century, 1940.

Fletcher, Tom. *100 Years of the Negro in Show Business*. New York: Burdge, 1954.

Hughes, Langston and Milton Meltzer. *Black Magic, A Pictorial History of the Negro in American Entertainment*. Englewood Cliffs, N.J.: Prentice-Hall, 1967.

Hutton, Laurence. *Curiosities of the American Stage*. New York: Harper and Brothers, 1891.

Isaacs, Edith J. R. *The Negro in the American Theatre*. New York: Theatre Arts Books, 1947.

Jennings, John J. *Theatrical and Circus Life; or, Secrets of the Stage, Green-Room and Sawdust Arena*. St. Louis, Mo.: Herbert and Cole, 1882.

McKechnie, Samuel. *Popular Entertainments Through the Ages*. 1931. Reprint. New York: Benjamin Blom, 1969.

McNamara, Brooks. "Popular Scenography." *The Drama Review*, 18 (March 1974), 16-25.

————. " 'Scavengers of the Amusement World': Popular Entertainment and the Birth of the Movies." In *American Pastimes*. Brockton, Mass.: Brockton Art Center, 1976. Catalog to exhibition.

Marks, Edward Bennett. *They All Had Glamour*. New York: Messner, 1944.

Matthews, Brander. *A Book About the Theater*. New York: Charles Scribner's Sons, 1916.

Moody, Richard. *America Takes the Stage*. Bloomington: Indiana University Press, 1955.

Nathan, George Jean. *Encyclopaedia of the Theatre*. New York: Alfred A. Knopf, 1940.

Nye, Russel B. *The Unembarrassed Muse: The Popular Arts in America*. New York: Dial, 1970.

Odell, G. C. D. *Annals of the New York Stage*. 15 vols. New York: Columbia University Press, 1927-49.

"People's Theatre." *Theatre Quarterly*, 1 (October-December 1971), 112 pp.
"Popular Entertainments." *The Drama Review*, 18 (March 1974), 122 pp.
"Popular Theatre." *Educational Theatre Journal*, 27 (October 1975), 108 pp.
Rourke, Constance. *American Humour: A Study of the National Character*. New York: Harcourt, Brace, 1931.
————. *The Roots of American Culture*. New York: Harcourt, Brace, 1942.
Seldes, Gilbert. *The 7 Lively Arts*. Rev. ed. New York: Sagamore Press, 1957.
Sergel, Sherman Louis, ed. *The Language of Show Biz*. Chicago: The Dramatic Publishing Co., 1973.
Toll, Robert C. *On with the Show*. New York: Oxford University Press, 1976.
Towsen, John. "Sources in Popular Entertainment." *The Drama Review*, 18 (March 1974), 118-23.
Wilmeth, Don B. *The American Stage to World War I: A Guide to Information Sources*. Detroit: Gale, 1978.

Dime Museums and Medicine Shows

Barnum, Phineas T. *The Humbugs of the World*. 1865. Reprint. Detroit: Gale, 1970.
————. *Struggles and Triumphs; or, The Life of P. T. Barnum*. 1869. Reprint. New York: New York Times/Arno Press, 1970.
Betts, John R. "P. T. Barnum and the Popularization of Natural History." *Journal of the History of Ideas*, 20 (1959), 353-68.
Desmond, Alice C. *Barnum Presents General Tom Thumb*. New York: Macmillan, 1954.
Freeman, Graydon Laverne. *The Medicine Showman*. Watkins Glen, N.Y.: Century House, 1957.
Harris, Neil. *Humbug: The Art of P. T. Barnum*. Boston: Little, Brown, 1973.
Kelley, Thomas. *The Fabulous Kelley: He Was King of the Medicine Men*. New York: Pocket Books, 1968.
McNamara, Brooks. " 'A Congress of Wonders': The Rise and Fall of the Dime Museum." *Emerson Society Quarterly*, 20 (1974), 216-32.
————. "The Indiana Medicine Show." *Educational Theatre Journal* 23 (1971), 431-45.
————. "Medicine Shows: American Vaudeville in the Marketplace." *Theatre Quarterly*, 4 (1974), 19-30.
————. *Step Right Up: An Illustrated History of the American Medicine Show*. Garden City, N.Y.: Doubleday, 1976.
Noell, Mae. "Some Memories of a Medicine Show Performer." *Theatre Quarterly*, 4 (May-July 1974), 25-30.
Wallace, Irving. *The Fabulous Showman*. New York: Alfred A. Knopf, 1959.
Webber, Malcolm. *Medicine Show*. Caldwell, Idaho: Caxton Printers, 1941.
Werner, M. R. *Barnum*. New York: Harcourt, Brace, 1923.
Young, James Harvey. *The Medical Messiahs*. Princeton, N.J.: Princeton University Press, 1967.
————. *The Toadstool Millionaires*. Princeton, N.J.: Princeton University Press, 1961.

Variety Forms: Minstrelsy, Vaudeville, and Burlesque

Allen, Ralph G. "Our Native Theatre: Honky-Tonk, Minstrel Shows, Burlesque." In *The American Theatre: A Sum of Its Parts.* Edited by Henry B. Williams. New York: Samuel French, 1971.

Angier, Roswell. *A Kind of Life: Conversations in the Combat Zone.* Boston: Addison House, 1976.

Barber, Rowland. *The Night They Raided Minsky's.* New York: Simon and Schuster, 1960.

Bristow, Eugene. "Look Out for Saturday Night: A Social History of Professional Variety Theatre in Memphis, Tennessee, 1859-1880." Ph.D. dissertation, State Univ. of Iowa, 1956.

Caffin, Caroline. *Vaudeville.* New York: Michell Kemerley, 1914.

Christopher, Milbourne. *Houdini: The Untold Story.* New York: Thomas Y. Crowell, 1969.

————. *The Illustrated History of Magic.* New York: Thomas Y. Crowell, 1973.

Claflin, Edward, and Jeff Sheridan. *Street Magic: An Illustrated History of Wandering Magicians and their Conjuring Arts.* Garden City, N.Y.: Doubleday, 1977.

Clark, Hyla M. *The World's Greatest Magic.* New York: Tree Communications Edition (Crown Publishers), 1976.

Clinton-Baddeley, V. C. *The Burlesque Tradition in the English Theatre After 1600.* London: Methuen, 1952.

Corio, Ann, with Joe DiMona. *This Was Burlesque.* New York: Grosset and Dunlap, 1968.

Davidson, Frank C. "The Rise, Development, Decline, and Influence of the American Minstrel Show." Ph.D. dissertation, New York University, 1952.

DiMeglio, John E. *Vaudeville U.S.A.* Bowling Green, Ohio: Bowling Green University Popular Press, 1973.

Distler, Paul A. "Exit the Racial Comics." *Educational Theatre Journal,* 18 (1966): 247-54.

————. "The Rise and Fall of the Racial Comics in American Vaudeville." Ph.D. dissertation, Tulane University, 1963.

Elliott, Eugene C. *A History of Variety-Vaudeville in Seattle.* Seattle: University of Washington Press, 1944.

Fletcher, Tom. *100 Years of the Negro in Show Business.* New York: Burdge and Co., 1934.

Gilbert, Douglas. *American Vaudeville: Its Life and Times.* 1940. Reprint. New York: Dover Publications, 1968.

Gill, Robert. *Magic As a Performing Art: A Bibliography of Conjuring.* New York: R. R. Bowker, 1976.

Golden, George Fuller. *My Lady Vaudeville and Her White Rats.* New York: Broadway Publishing Co., 1909.

Grau, Robert. *The Business Man in the Amusement World.* New York: Broadway Publishing Co., 1910.

————. *Fifty Years of Observation of Music and the Drama.* New York: Broadway Publishing Co., 1909.

Green, Abel, and Joe Laurie, Jr. *Show Biz from Vaude to Video.* Garden City, N.Y.: Permabooks, 1953.

Gresham, William L. *Houdini: The Man Who Walked Through Walls.* New York: Henry Holt, 1959.

Haverly, Jack. *Negro Minstrels: A Complete Guide.* Chicago: Frederick J. Drake, 1902.

Isman, Felix. *Weber and Fields: Their Tribulations, Triumphs, and Their Associates.* New York: Boni and Liveright, 1924.

Keegan, Marcia. *We Can Still Hear Them Clapping.* New York: Avon Books, 1975.

Laurie, Joseph. *Vaudeville: From the Honky-Tonks to the Palace.* 1953. Reprint. Port Washington, N.Y.: Kennikat, 1972.

Leavitt, M. B. *Fifty Years in Theatrical Management, 1859-1909.* New York: Broadway Publishing Co., 1912.

Lee, Gypsy Rose. *Gypsy: A Memoir.* New York: Harper and Bros., 1957.

Lipnitski, Bernard. "God Save the Queen." *Esquire,* 72 (August 1969), 104-07.

McLean, Albert F., Jr. *American Vaudeville as Ritual.* Lexington, Ky.: University of Kentucky, 1965.

————. "U. S. Vaudeville and the Urban Comics." *Theatre Quarterly,* 1 (October-December 1971), 50-57.

Marston, William, and John H. Fellers. *F. F. Proctor, Vaudeville Pioneer.* New York: Richard R. Smith, 1943.

Matlaw, Myron. "Tony the Trouper: Pastor's Early Years." *Theatre Annual,* 24 (1968), 70-90.

Meiselas, Susan. *Carnival Strippers.* New York: Farrar, Straus, and Giroux, 1976.

Mills, Steve. " 'An Artist's Studio': A Comic Scene From Burlesque." *Educational Theatre Journal,* 27 (October 1975), 342-44.

Moody, Richard. "Negro Minstrelsy." *Quarterly Journal of Speech,* 30 (October 1944), 321-28.

Morris, Lloyd. *Incredible New York.* New York: Random House, 1957.

Nathan, Hans. *Dan Emmett and the Rise of Early Negro Minstrelsy.* Norman: University of Oklahoma Press, 1962.

Page, Brett. *Writing for Vaudeville.* Springfield, Mass.: The Home Correspondence School, 1915.

Paskman, Dailey. *"Gentlemen, Be Seated!" A Parade of the Old-Time Minstrels.* Rev. ed. New York: Clarkson N. Potter, 1976.

Patterson, Cecil L. "A Different Drummer: The Image of the Negro in Nineteenth Century Popular Song Books." Ph.D. dissertation, University of Pennsylvania, 1961.

Ramshaw, Molly Niederlander. "Jump, Jim Crow! A Biographical Sketch of Thomas D. Rice." *Theatre Annual,* 17 (1960), 36-47.

Reynolds, Harry. *Minstrel Memories: The Story of Burnt Cork Minstrelsy in Great Britain From 1836-1927.* London: Alston Rivers, 1928.

Rice, Edward LeRoy. *Monarchs of Minstrelsy, from "Daddy" Rice to Date.* New York: Kenny Publishing Co., 1911.

Salutin, Marilyn. "Stripper Morality." *Transaction,* 8 (June 1971), 12-22.

Samuels, Charles and Louise. *Once Upon a Stage: The Merry World of Vaudeville.* New York: Dodd, Mead, 1974.

Sandberg, Trish. "An Interview with Steve Mills." *Educational Theatre Journal,* 27 (October 1975), 331-41.

Schaffner, Neil E. and Vance Johnson. *The Fabulous Toby and Me.* Englewood Cliffs, N.J.: Prentice-Hall, 1968.

Skipper, James K., Jr., and Charles H. McCaghy. "Lesbian Behavior as an Adaptation to the Occupation of Stripping." *Social Problems,* 17 (Fall 1969), 262-70.

————. "Stripteasers: The Anatomy and Career Contingencies of a Deviant Occupation." *Social Problems,* 17 (Winter 1970), 391-405.

Smith, Bill. *The Vaudevillians.* New York: Macmillan, 1976.

Sobel, Bernard. *Burleyque: An Underground History of Burlesque Days.* New York: Farrar and Rinehart, 1931.

————. *A Pictorial History of Burlesque.* New York: G. P. Putnam's Sons, 1956.

————. *A Pictorial History of Vaudeville.* New York: Citadel Press, 1961.

Sothern, Georgia. *Georgia: My Life in Burlesque.* New York: Signet Books, 1972.

Spitzer, Marian. *The Palace.* New York: Atheneum, 1969.

Toll, Robert C. *Blacking Up: The Minstrel Show in Nineteenth Century America.* New York: Oxford University Press, 1974.

Willson, Clair. *Mimes and Miners: Theater in Tombstone.* Tucson: University of Arizona Press, 1935.

Winter, Marian Hannah. "Juba and American Minstrelsy." *Dance Index,* 6 (1947), 28-47.

Wittke, Carl. *Tambo and Bones. A History of the Minstrel Stage.* 1930. Reprint. Westport, Conn.: Greenwood Press, 1968.

Wortley, Richard. *A Pictorial History of Striptease: 100 Years of Undressing to Music.* Seacaucus, N.J.: Chartwell Books, 1976.

Young, William C. *American Theatrical Arts: A Guide to Manuscripts and Special Collections in the United States and Canada.* Chicago: American Library Association, 1971.

Zanger, Jules. "The Minstrel Show As Theater of Misrule." *Quarterly Journal of Speech,* 60 (February 1974), 33-38.

Zeidman, Irving. *The American Burlesque Show.* New York: Hawthorn Books, 1967.

Zellers, Parker. "The Cradle of Variety: The Concert Saloon." *Educational Theatre Journal,* 20 (December 1968), 578-85.

————. *Tony Pastor: Dean of the Vaudeville Stage.* Ypsilanti: Eastern Michigan University Press, 1971.

Popular Theater

Birdoff, Harry. *The World's Greatest Hit—Uncle Tom's Cabin.* New York: S. F. Vanni, 1947.

Booth, Michael R. *English Melodrama.* London: Jenkins, 1965.

Clark, Larry Dale. "Toby Shows: A Form of American Popular Theatre." Ph.D. dissertation, University of Illinois, 1963.

Coleman, William S. E. "Buffalo Bill on Stage." *Players, Magazine of American Theatre,* 47 (December-January 1972), 80-91.

Cook, Doris E. *Sherlock Holmes and Much More.* Hartford: Connecticut Historical Society, 1970.

Davis, Ronald L. "Sopranos and Six Guns: The Frontier Opera House as a Cultural Symbol." *The American West,* 7 (November 1970), 10-17.

Disher, Maurice Willson. *Melodrama. Plots That Thrilled.* London: Rockliff, 1954.

Dorson, Richard M. "Mose the Far-Famed and World Renowned." *American Literature,* 15 (November 1943), 288-300.

Ericson, Robert Edward. "Touring Entertainment in Nevada During the Peak Years of the Mining Boom." Ph.D. dissertation, University of Oregon, 1970.

Ernst, Alice Henson. *Trouping in the Oregon Country.* Portland: Oregon Historical Society, 1961.

Felheim, Marvin. *Theater of Augustin Daly.* Cambridge, Mass.: Harvard University Press, 1956.

Ford, George D. *These Were Actors.* New York: Library Publishers, 1955.

Gaer, Joseph, ed. *Theater of the Gold Rush Decade in San Francisco.* 1935. Reprint. New York: Burt Franklin, 1970.

Gagey, Edmond M. *The San Francisco Stage.* New York: Columbia University Press, 1950.

Graham, Philip. *Showboats. The History of an American Institution.* Austin: University of Texas Press, 1951, 1969.

———. "Showboats in the South." *The Georgia Review,* 12 (Summer 1958), 174-85.

Grimsted, David. *Melodrama Unveiled: American Theatre & Culture, 1800-1850.* Chicago: University of Chicago, 1968.

Harlow, Alvin F. *Old Bowery Days.* New York: Appleton, 1931.

Harrison, Harry P., as told to Karl Detzer. *Culture Under Canvas: The Story of Tent Chautauqua.* New York: Hastings House, 1958.

Hodge, Francis. *Yankee Theatre: The Image of America on Stage, 1825-1850.* Austin: University of Texas Press, 1964.

Horner, Charles F. *Strike the Tents, The Story of the Chautauqua.* Philadelphia: Dorrance and Co., 1954.

Hoyt, Harlowe. *Town Hall Tonight.* New York: Bramhall House, 1955.

Leone-Marker, Lise. *David Belasco: Naturalism in the American Theatre.* Princeton, N.J.: Princeton University Press, 1975.

Lewis, Philip C. *Trouping: How the Show Came to Town.* New York: Harper and Row, 1973.

McDermott, Douglas. "Touring Patterns on California's Theatrical Frontier, 1849-1859." *Theatre Survey,* 15 (May 1974), 18-28.

McKennon, Marian. *Tent Show.* New York: Exposition Press, 1964.

MacMinn, George R. *The Theater of the Golden Age in California.* Caldwell, Idaho: Caxton Printers, 1941.

Mickel, Jere C. "The Genesis of Toby." *Journal of American Folklore,* 80 (October-December 1967), 334-40.

Monaghan, Jay. "The Stage Career of Buffalo Bill." *Journal of the Illinois State Historical Society*, 31 (December 1938), 411-23.

Moody, Richard. "Edward Harrigan." *Modern Drama*, 19 (December 1976), 319-325.

————. "Uncle Tom, the Theater and Mrs. Stowe." *American Heritage*, 6 (October 1955), 29-33, 102-03.

————, and A. M. Drummond. "The Hit of the Century: Uncle Tom's Cabin." *Educational Theatre Journal*, 4 (1952), 315-22.

Morrison, Theodore. *Chautauqua*. Chcago: University of Chicago, 1974.

Quinn, Arthur Hobson. *A History of the American Drama from the Beginning to the Present Day*. 2 vols. New York: Appleton-Century-Crofts, 1943.

Rahill, Frank. *The World of Melodrama*. University Park: Pennsylvania State University Press, 1967.

Reynolds, Ernest. *Early Victorian Drama, 1830-1870*. Cambridge, Eng.: Heffer, 1936.

Rourke, Constance. *Troupers of the Gold Coast, or the Rise of Lotta Crabtree*. New York: Harcourt, Brace, 1928.

Rowell, George. *The Victorian Theatre*. London: Oxford University Press, 1956.

Russell, Don. *The Wild West, or, A History of the Wild West Shows*. Fort Worth, Tex.: Amon Carter Museum of Western Art, 1970.

Schaffner, Neil E., with Vance Johnson. *The Fabulous Toby and Me*. Englewood Cliffs, N.J.: Prentice-Hall, 1968.

Scott, Marian. *Chautauqua Caravan*. New York: Appleton-Century, 1939.

Shank, Theodore J. "Theatre for the Majority: Its Influence on a Nineteenth-Century American Theatre." *Educational Theatre Journal*, 11 (1959), 188-89.

Slout, William Lawrence. *Theatre in a Tent: The Developement of a Provincial Entertainment*. Bowling Green, Ohio: Bowling Green University Popular Press, 1972.

Snyder, Sherwood, III. "The Toby Shows." Ph.D. dissertation, University of Minnesota, 1966.

Toll, Robert C. *On with the Show*. New York: Oxford University Press, 1976.

Turner, Willis L. "City Low-Life on the American Stage to 1900." Ph.D. dissertation, University of Illinois, 1956.

Watson, Margaret. *Silver Theatre, Amusements of the Mining Frontier in Early Nevada, 1850-1864*. Glendale, Calif.: A. H. Clark, 1964.

Young, William C. *Famous Actors and Actresses on the American Stage*. 2 vols. New York: R. R. Bowker, 1975.

Early Musical Theater and the Revue

Baral, Robert. *Revue: The Great Broadway Period*. New York: Fleet Press, 1962.

Carter, Randolph. *The World of Flo Ziegfeld*. New York: Praeger, 1974.

Clarke, Norman. *The Mighty Hippodrome*. Cranbury, N.J.: A. S. Barnes, 1968.

Crowley, Alice Lewinsohn. *The Neighborhood Playhouse*. New York: Theatre Arts Books, 1959.

Ewen, David. *New Complete Book of the American Musical Theatre.* New York: Holt, Rinehart, 1970.

Farnsworth, Marjorie. *The Ziegfeld Follies.* New York: Bonanza Books, 1956.

Green, Stanley. *Ring Bells! Sing Songs! Broadway Musicals of the 1930's.* New York: Galahad Books, 1971.

———. *The World of Musical Comedy.* Rev. ed. Cranbury, N.J.: A. S. Barnes, 1968.

Hall, Roger Allan. "The Brook: America's Germinal Musical?" *Educational Theatre Journal,* 27 (October 1975), 323-29.

Higham, Charles. *Ziegfeld.* Chicago: Henry Regnery, 1972.

Kahn, E. J., Jr. *The Merry Partners: The Age and Stage of Harrigan and Hart.* New York: Random House, 1955.

Kimball, Robert, and William Bolcom. *Reminiscing with Sissle and Blake.* New York: Viking, 1973.

Knapp, Margaret M. "Theatrical Parody in the Twentieth-Century American Theatre: The Grand Street Follies." *Educational Theatre Journal,* 27 (October 1975), 356-63.

McCabe, John. *George M. Cohan: The Man Who Owned Broadway.* Garden City, N.Y.: Doubleday, 1973.

Mander, Raymond, and Joe Mitchenson. *Musical Comedy.* New York: Taplinger, 1969.

Marks, Edward B., as told to Abbott J. Liebling. *They All Sang: From Tony Pastor to Rudy Vallee.* New York: Viking, 1935.

Mates, Julian. *The American Musical Stage Before 1800.* New Brunswick, N.J.: Rutgers University Press, 1962.

———. "American Musical Theatre: Beginnings to 1900." In *The American Theatre: A Sum of Its Parts.* Edited by Henry B. Williams. New York: Samuel French, 1971.

———. "The Black Crook Myth." *Theatre Survey,* 7 (May 1966), 31-43.

Mattfeld, Julius. *Variety Music Cavalcade: Musical-Historical Review, 1620-1969.* New York: Prentice-Hall, 1971.

Murray, Ken. *The Body Merchant: The Story of Earl Carroll.* Pasadena, Calif.: Ward Ritchie Press, 1976.

Nathan, George Jean. *The Popular Theatre.* 1918. Reprint. Rutherford, N.J.: Fairleigh Dickinson University Press, 1971.

———. *The Entertainment of a Nation; or, Three Sheets in the Wind.* 1942. Reprint. Rutherford, N.J.: Fairleigh Dickinson University Press, 1971.

Smith, Cecil. *Musical Comedy in America.* New York: Theatre Arts Books, 1950.

Stagg, Jerry. *A Half-Century of Show Business and the Fabulous Empire of the Brothers Shubert.* New York: Random House, 1968.

Whitton, Joseph. *"The Naked Truth!": An Inside History of The Black Crook.* Philadelphia: H. W. Shaw, 1897.

Ziegfeld, Patricia. *The Ziegfelds' Girls.* Boston: Little, Brown, 1964.

Stand-up Comics

Adams, Joey. *From Gags to Riches.* New York: Frederick Fell, 1946.
————. *Encyclopedia of Humor.* Indianapolis: Bobbs-Merrill, 1968.
————, with Henry Tobia. *The Borscht Belt.* New York: Avon Books, 1967.
Allen, Steve. *The Funny Men.* New York: Simon and Schuster, 1956.
Appignanesi, Lisa. *The Cabaret.* New York: Universe Books, 1976.
Berger, Phil. *The Last Laugh: The World of Stand-up Comics.* New York: William Morrow, 1975.
Brown, Maria Ward. *The Life of Dan Rice.* Long Beach, N.J.: published by the author, 1901.
Cahn, William. *The Laugh Makers: A Pictorial History of American Comedians.* New York: G. P. Putnam's Sons, 1957.
————. *A Pictorial History of the Great Comedians.* New York: Grosset and Dunlap, 1970.
Cohen, John. *The Essential Lenny Bruce.* New York: Ballantine, 1967.
Cohn, Art. *The Joker Is Wild: The Story of Joe E. Lewis.* New York: Random House, 1955.
Goldman, Albert. *Ladies and Gentlemen, Lenny Bruce!* New York: Random House, 1971.
Kunzog, John C. *The One-Horse Show: The Life and Times of Dan Rice, Circus Jester and Philanthropist.* Jamestown, N.Y.: John C. Kunzog, 1962.
Towsen, John N. *Clowns.* New York: Hawthorn Books, 1976.
Walker, Stanley. *The Night Club Era.* New York: Frederick A. Stokes, 1933.

PERIODICALS

Billboard. Los Angeles, 1894-.
The Drama Review, New York, 1955-.
Educational Theatre Journal. Washington, D.C., 1949-.
Journal of Popular Culture. Bowling Green, Ohio, 1967-.
New York Clipper. New York, 1900-1918.
New York Mirror. New York, 1879-1922.
Nineteenth Century Theatre Research. Tucson, Ariz., 1973-.
Theatre Quarterly. London, England, 1971-.
Variety. New York, 1905-.

CHAPTER 14 Television
Robert S. Alley

The angle of vision with which one approaches television will have a marked impact upon the way in which its history is recorded. There is the option of writing a totally technological history with reference to those developments that have taken the television set from the crude model created by John L. Baird in 1926 to the new color consoles that will instantly record broadcasts for replay on twenty-five-inch screens. It is also possible to see television as a form of entertainment and examine its history via its stars, drama, and comedy. Alternatively, as a means of communicating news, television may legitimately be weighed and compared to other news media regarding accuracy and influence. Social scientists have a valid concern for television as a social force with particular emphasis on its impact on children and adults. Indeed, it is in this area that the largest number of monographs have surfaced over the past two decades. Of course, television is a business, and its history may be examined in terms of the rise and success of competing networks. Finally, Marshall McLuhan and others have made us aware of television as an appropriate topic for philosophical discourse. I give notice to significant contributions in all these areas. However, for the purpose of this essay I describe the history of television in humanistic terms, with attention to the ways in which it has become preeminently "the" popular culture and a primary purveyor of values and ideas. It is only recently that the long-held reticence of humanities to see the medium as a proper target of inquiry has been successfully challenged, which accounts for the paucity of literature in several important areas. Nell Eurich has written a stunning essay on the present plight of the humanities in a recent publication *Learning for Tomorrow*, edited by Alvin Toffler. In sum she says,

. . . the materials of the humanities are hardly neutral. . . . even in the humanities we see some teachers, in a desperate attempt to ape the "hard sciences," avoiding the difficult, but critical, issue of values. . . . humanists have retreated from the front line of creative and original thought and become priests of the past.

Today film is a primary medium in which the creative arts are united. Together the writer, musician, artistic director, and actor have made film the means with which to capture the innuendos as well as the reality of human experience. . . . With TV, the combined power (visual and audible) has entered the home and become a formidable antagonist—and potential ally—for the teacher relying on words in the classroom.

Still the humanist has not invited the new creative expressions of artists into his sanctuary. Nor have we, by and large, entertained the large questions that must be raised, if the humanities are to have any influence on the quality of our lives today, much less tomorrow.

To remain ignorant of or aloof to science and technology and the directions they are carrying us, to assume that the past alone can enlighten, is to cripple the humanities and shrink the chances for human survival.[1]

HISTORIC OUTLINE

Technically television is in its fifties, culturally it is in its twenties. In the year 1926 there were practical demonstrations of living scenes viewed the instant they took place by audiences removed from the events. In London, Paris, and New York, the technology was similar and impressive. In 1927 the *New York Times* noted that television "outruns the imagination of all the wizards of prophecy." In that year the movies conquered the sound barrier with *The Jazz Singer*. Radio emerged at the same time as a startling source of instant information and live entertainment. Depression, war, and technical difficulties combined to deter the development of television even as its two media partners flourished. The irony was that television, maturing in the 1950s, radically changed the face both of radio and cinema, thereby challenging the existence of each. Only as the two accommodated themselves to the young upstart did they find hope for survival.

By 1951 the commercial television networks had established their hegemony and were developing means of transmitting signals coast to coast. Beer sales rose as baseball invaded the medium, and at least one doctor dolefully predicted that children would have stunted feet from too little walking. By 1953, television had attracted the likes of Bob Hope, Groucho Marx, Lucille Ball, Fred Allen, Jack Benny, Edgar Bergen, and George Burns and Gracie Allen. Thus radio, which had been a way of life for two generations of children, evaporated by the mid-1950s as quickly as it had burst upon us in the 1930s. Gone were the comedians and the dramas of a rainy afternoon. We were to discover that words, which had carried considerable weight, became conditioned by the visual.

The early 1950s was the era of television hearings—Kefauver and McCarthy—and of the so-called "golden age" of television. That age lasted only a few brief years as it claimed the talents of writers, such as Paddy Chayefsky, Reginald Rose, and Rod Serling; directors, such as Delbert

Mann, Arthur Penn, and Sidney Lumet; and a luxury of talent including Paul Newman, Sidney Poitier, Kim Stanley, Rod Steiger, and Joanne Woodward. The remarkable success of the live anthological drama series that emerged with these personalities was all too short-lived. In the first place, the social comment of a play like *Marty* was in sharp contrast with the shiny world of the burgeoning number of eager sponsors. Second, the very success of television prompted a new breath of fresh air for cinema which began to drain talent from New York and consequently eliminate live television drama. Finally, the growing fear of both network executives and advertisers concerning controversial drama tended to stifle talent. Erik Barnouw dates the decline of these anthologies in the year 1955. Delbert Mann concurs. In a 1975 interview he noted that the early television dramas, starting in the late 1940s, appealed "to a small and rather specialized audience." As sets increased in number, the nature of the audience changed. The need to appeal to the mass audience was stimulated by the growing interest of manufacturers in advertising in the new medium. This coincided with the McCarthy era and the black listing of performers and writers. Mann noted that there was a pressure "not to offend." Thus was developed an inevitable pattern, of "restriction on the kind of material that could be used." Mann, like many other persons in the profession, left television for film by the end of the 1950s.

A great deal more was involved for television in the 1950s than fiction. The accident of technological discovery gave control of the television networks to the radio people. Radio, while deeply involved in entertainment, was a news-oriented medium for much of the public. And it was centered in New York. Quite naturally, then, the use of television after 1950 included a considerable emphasis upon public events. Had the motion picture industry controlled the medium, it is not altogether certain that such emphasis would have been as strong. Located on the East Coast and in close proximity to political and social phenomena which were shaping the nation, network executives promoted the beginnings of a vast news network. (For CBS that meant Edward R. Murrow.) David Halberstam noted in an excellent two-part study of CBS in 1976 that

. . . television arrived simultaneously with the height of McCarthyism probably helped to narrow the parameters of journalistic freedom, but it was bound to happen anyway. Politically, television was simply too powerful a force, too fast, too immediate, with too large an audience, for the kind of easy journalistic freedom that radio and print reporters had enjoyed.[2]

Even in its restricted form television brought living drama into American homes regularly in its first decade. The Estes Kefauver Senate hearings on crime catapulted the senator into the Democratic nomination for vice-president by 1956. ABC moved quickly to televise the activities of the

Army-McCarthy hearings in 1953. Concurrently millions of citizens had become more aware of the political process through the televising of the two party conventions of the previous year.

The first pronouncements of Richard Nixon were televised, and his classic "Checkers" speech was delivered in 1952. Many Americans heard about "old soldiers" from General MacArthur in that same year. In the aftermath of the Supreme Court's decision in *Brown* vs. *Board of Education* in 1955 came Little Rock and Governor Faubus, and a changing domestic scene. From Sputnik to the 1959 "kitchen debate," television provided a window on the world beyond the United States.

The American public felt the influence of television entertainment through language, comic heroes and classic portrayals. The phenomenon of families gathered silently around a small box to watch Milton Berle or Sid Caesar exploded in the 1950s in a dozen different directions. The culture of postwar America was straining under the old melting pot philosophy, and much of the comedy of that decade sought to reestablish the mentality of a secure middle-class picket fence community of the 1930s.

The 1940s gave the American viewers its most enduring television figure, Ed Sullivan in 1948. A less remembered role was that played by E. G. Marshall in "Mary Poppins" in the year 1949. The next year the crucial decade began with Sid Caesar, Jack Benny, Burns and Allen and "Broadway Open House" (forerunner of "Tonight"). Live drama was highlighted by Helen Hayes in *Victoria Regina*. In the early years American cultural roots remained in the radio era, a phenomenon that would disappear by 1955. The classics, "I Love Lucy" and *Amahl and the Night Visitors*, were produced early in 1951. The next year there were more comedians—Ozzie and Harriet, "Mr. Peepers," "Our Miss Brooks," and "My Little Margie." Sunday became the preserve of that special niche of television history called "Omnibus" and the sweaty hand of the forge became as well-known as Snap, Crackle, and Pop with the arrival of the Mark VII production "Dragnet."

Along with the inauguration of President Eisenhower, Red Skelton, Steve Allen, and Danny Thomas took to television. *Marty*, deftly directed by Delbert Mann and consistently described as a high point in television drama, was also produced in 1953. That same year viewers might have caught James Dean in *A Long Time Till Dawn* and Richard Kiley in *P.O.W.*, a drama about brainwashing and the Korean War. The heart of the picket fence era was probably 1954. The new offerings included "Father Knows Best," "Lassie," "Walt Disney Presents," "Love That Bob" (Bob Cummings), and "Private Secretary" with Ann Sothern. Live drama prospered in such offerings as *Twelve Angry Men*, written by Reginald Rose.

Little in the year 1955 warned Americans that their world was changing.

Alfred Hitchcock entertained as did "The Honeymooners" and "Sergeant Bilko." "Captain Kangaroo" entered and became a traditional CBS figure for generations of children with Mr. Green Jeans, Dancing Bear, and Bun Rabbit. Meanwhile, American viewers focused on the past in drama and series. "Wyatt Earp" was the first, but "Gunsmoke" made it official; 1955 was the year the Westerns began. Drama was outstanding—Sidney Potier in *A Man Is Ten Feet Tall*, Raymond Massey and Lillian Gish in *The Day Lincoln Was Shot*, with Jack Lemmon as Wilkes Booth, Barry Sullivan in *The Caine Mutiny*, Maurice Evans in *The Devil's Disciple*, Michael Redgrave in *She Stoops to Conquer*, Lee Grant in *Shadow of the Champ*, and Humphrey Bogart in Delbert Mann's production of *The Petrified Forest*. Rod Serling contributed *Patterns*. Perhaps "never again on this stage" was the television epitaph for 1955.

The election year of 1956 saw the movement to Hollywood gather momentum. Film was replacing live drama, not always directly to its detriment but other effects were more subtle. Dramatically 1956 belonged to Rod Serling and his *Requiem for a Heavyweight*.

In 1957 television offered "Maverick," "Perry Mason," "Wagon Train," "Leave It To Beaver," and "Have Gun, Will Travel." The Westerns were on their way as was Jack Paar, who replaced Steve Allen that year on the "Tonight" show. Avid viewers may recall the maudlin conversations which Paar had with Hollywood personalities about bomb shelters and whether having one was cowardly.

Drama, now mostly on film, continued with high quality in 1958 with *The Bridge of San Luis Rey, The Days of Wine and Roses*, and *Little Moon of Alban*. Most lasting in impact was the "Untouchables," a product of Desilu which was also continuing to provide "I Love Lucy." The era of anthological dramatic shows was coming to an end with the television-film phase of 1955 and the discovery of video tape in 1957. "Studio One" moved to Hollywood in 1958, most other similar ventures faded and died. Even so, the last year of the decade offered some reason for hope that drama was not dead. There was Jason Robards in *For Whom the Bell Tolls*, George C. Scott in *Winterset*, Ingrid Bergman in *The Turn of the Screw*, and Laurence Olivier and Judith Anderson in *The Moon and Sixpence*. However, perhaps a greater harbinger of the 1960s was the debut of "Bonanza" that same year.

In the 1960s the stunning social dramas of the earlier decade became the live newscasts and made television fiction pale in comparison. The 1960 television debates between Richard Nixon and John Kennedy heralded the beginning of the decade of the newsman. A barrage of newsmaking events assailed the television viewer. If the event was not presented "live," it reached us within minutes thereafter—the Berlin Wall, the missile crisis, the assassination of John Kennedy and the subsequent killing of

Lee Harvey Oswald "before our eyes," the reality of the war in Vietnam which every night on the news became more unreal, again assassination, Martin Luther King, Jr. and Robert Kennedy, riots at home from Watts in Los Angeles to Washington, D.C., men landing on the moon, and always the war in Southeast Asia. The Vietnam years were more devastating to our culture than perhaps any other event in our history. Distrust of government was rampant, with arrogance of power, depression and discontent among the dispossessed, fear and loathing to our youth, and destruction of decent models for children. Narcotics became a way of life for men called upon to commit mayhem abroad. Rising expectations and white stupidity created civil disorder from Watts to Washington. Television was there and it recorded a rare second chance in New Hampshire in February 1968 but America, after losing Robert Kennedy and Martin Luther King, Jr. to assassins, chose Richard Nixon. After that came Cambodia, Kent State, Attica, Agnew, Mitchell, Watergate, and pardons. In June 1977 Johnny Carson gave voice to many pent-up feelings when he noted upon the sentencing of John Mitchell and H. R. Haldeman to minimum security prinsons in Alabama that had it been you or I, we would have been put in a cell with Charles Manson. Clearly dramatic and comedic television had considerable competition in those years.

In the history of commercial television there have been four distinct types of comedy. The earliest was the personality, Milton Berle or Jack Benny or George Burns. There followed quickly the situation comedies of the "Leave It to Beaver," "Father Knows Best," and "Ozzie and Harriet" variety. Mild doses of fun were sprinkled among basic Puritan moralisms. By the late 1950s a third type of comedy emerged in "The Real McCoys." The 1960s saw the flowering of this genre with "Car 54 Where Are You?," "Gilligan's Island," and "The Beverly Hillibillies." Each poked fun at an authority symbol—the law, the scientist and socialite, or the banking profession. Some, like "The Munsters" and "The Addams Family," seemed to take on all social conventions, but it would be foolish to make too much out of this because each show was also designed quite obviously to match the public mood which increasingly seemed to desire escape. Lucille Ball interestingly reversed the trend. Her early shows were slapstick. Her comedy of the 1960s was similar to the earlier Ann Sothern efforts. Only with the appearance, largely via CBS, of "The Mary Tyler Moore Show" and "All in the Family" did a fourth comedy type begin to dominate. In style these shows owed much to the earlier "Dick Van Dyke Show" (1961-66). Their substance was probably made possible by the pioneering on CBS of the Smothers Brothers with social and political humor and on NBC by the freedom of "Laugh-In" with its sexual allusions, the former appearing first in 1965, the latter in 1968.

Of course even as the third comedy type dominated during the decade, the networks continued the traditional format with "My Three Sons," "Hazel," "That Girl," and "The Andy Griffith Show." The decline of the stand-up comic was a signal that the insatiable appetite of television, a new sketch every week, was beyond the capacity of comedians and writers. Indeed, this is a primary difficulty which television experiences unlike the theater, night club, or film. People like Johnny Carson have survived by creating a liturgy into which viewers enter as surely as the Sunday communicant. Thus the burden on the writers is largely relieved, but Carson is the exception and in that way has become a symbol of one important segment of the population. Carson makes trends and creates language styles. He is a primal popular cultural force, possibly more powerful than any other figure in the history of entertainment.

The decade of the 1960s was notable for three types of drama—police, Western, and medical. Apart from these types there were only a few dramatic series that survived long enough to remember—"The Defenders" (1962), "Combat" (1962), "Outer Limits" (1963), "East Side, West Side" (1963), "Mr. Novak" (1963), "Slattery's People" (1964), "Twelve O'Clock High" (1964), "Star Trek" (1966), "The Bold Ones" (1969), "Room 222" (1969)—an average of one new series per year.

From their beginnings in 1955 the Westerns expanded to number fifteen by 1960. That number was reduced to five by 1965. By the end of the decade it had diminished to three including "Bonanza" and "Gunsmoke." The history of police-detective drama is less consistent. When Americans entered their second ten years with television, they were watching "Naked City," "Peter Gunn," "Hawaiian Eye," "The Untouchables," and "The Detectives." "Dragnet" appeared and reappeared on the schedule during the same period. By 1964 there was not a single drama of this genre represented in network scheduling. In 1965 Quinn Martin, most persistent purveyor of the police motif, introduced the long-running "FBI," and by 1969 the schedule included no less than seven police-private eye shows. The 1970s saw that proliferate into over twenty in the 1975-76 season. The police dramas have been dominated by three producing giants—Martin, Jack Webb, and Spelling and Goldberg.

Medical drama moved in and out of the television scene in this period with the two long-running series, "Ben Casey" and "Dr. Kildare" debuting in 1961 and departing in 1966. By 1969 a new set, "Marcus Welby," "Medical Center," and "The Bold Ones" gave viewers three opportunities to experience vicariously the treatment of obscure and not so obscure diseases.

Documentaries burgeoned in the 1960s. The networks, spurred on by an obvious interest in public events, focused on social events (national and international) for material from migrant workers to Vietnam. Simultaneously domestic unrest bubbled to the surface and cascaded across the land in 1967 and 1968.

When the history of the 1970s is written, the portion devoted to television will undoubtedly emphasize the enormous success of a new comedy art in the business. Norman Lear, Grant Tinker, and Larry Gelbart will carry the credits along with Carroll O'Connor, Jean Stapleton, Bea Arthur, Mary Tyler Moore, Cloris Leachman, and Alan Alda. The similarities between "M*A*S*H" and "Maude" are more felt than defined, but the commonality was expressed both by audiences and actors. The flowering of the television comic short story may well be a most important cultural phenomenon. Beginning in 1971 the American public became conscious of Archie and Mary and Hawkeye. Every week these and other characters filled the screen with social bite in comic form. We laughed, often with a tear, and experienced what many knew finally to be reality joining hands with fantasy. Whatever new forms emerge for the 1980s, the television comedy of the 1970s had style and class and a social consciousness. Humanism dominated these shows and their companions—"The Bob Newhart Show," "Good Times," "The Jeffersons," "One Day at a Time," "Phyllis," and "The Odd Couple."

We were also deluged in this decade by an ever increasing assortment of gun-toting law enforcers. Television always upholds the law. It may be violent and sometimes in poor taste, but right does prevail. Not so in the movies or on the stage or in novels and magazines—these all offer alternatives to the triumph of the system. Television sustains it. To be sure not without criticism, but support there is, nonetheless. Baretta may condone small-time crime, and Kojak may bend the rules, but from Starsky and Hutch to Barnaby Jones to Charlie's Angels, the message is the same. Television has obviated certain cultural differences and leveled our language and dress. History may also affirm that it was the glue that held the clue to societal survival in the present decade. Certainly we all had television in common, and it has been affirming traditional social values. As early as 1968 the National Advisory Commission on Civil Disorders, commenting upon television coverage in 1967, noted:

Content analysis of television film footage shows that the tone of the coverage studied was more calm and "factual" than "emotional" and rumor-laden. . . . Television newscasts during the periods of actual disorder in 1967 tended to emphasize law enforcement activities, thereby overshadowing underlying grievances and tensions. . . .

In contrast to what some of its critics have charged, television sometimes may have leaned over too far backward in seeking balance and restraint.[3]

Television is a massive power of promotion and persuasion and its immediacy to our every thought makes it a likely target when cultural leaders search for a culprit upon which to blame the general tone of our society. It is new, it is beyond our control, and it is electronic. Television is popular culture. Although many social critics condemn and deride what television offers, for the majority of American people television is a friend, warts and all. It has become, as well, a critic in comedy and, less often, drama, of the flaws in our society. James Brown has written:

The fact that the medium [television] produces several outstanding multi-hour presentations a month deserves more praise than the meager annual productivity of Broadway. Books have been with us since movable type for over 600 years. How many books of true significance and public acceptance are published annually? Daily newspapers have been around for more than a century. Movies have been on the scene three-quarters of a century. But radio was first heard clearly in the land in 1920. Television has elbowed its way through exuberant adolescence and is now just beyond its teens. As a mid-twenty-year-old, it continues to try to find itself, to achieve its proper identity in society.[4]

In the early days the term *educational television* was used to apply to those stations normally expected to be unaffiliated with a commercial network. It was not until February 1950 that the first non-commercial station, WOI-TV in Ames, Iowa, was licensed and began operation. It was the one-hundredth station to begin television broadcasting in America. Because of the slow beginning of educational television, most of the stations occupied UHF channels which the Federal Communications Commission (FCC) had begun to assign in 1952. As late as 1956 there were only twenty-four non-commercial, educational channels on the air, and most of those were struggling. Television set manufacturers completely ignored UHF on early sets, and it was not until a decree from Congress required it, that all sets began to be sold with UHF tuners incorporated. Even then, the technology that allowed snap-lock tuning of VHF channels was not installed with the UHF tuner, and this meant long years of invidious comparison with the ease of tuning Channels 2 through 13. This problem was coupled with the fact that the UHF signal was usually more difficult to receive and had a much more restricted range. As late as 1968 only 55 percent of American families could receive UHF. In 1977 most hotels and motels were still not equipped with sets capable of receiving UHF broadcasts.

The original National Educational Television (NET) network survived through grit and grants from a small number of major foundations. Finally, in 1967, Congress took direct action and established the Public Broadcast System with federal funding. It still required substantial fundraising by the local stations in order to guarantee survival. Since 1967, commercial networks have been quite guarded in their reactions to their new colleagues. Publications, such as *TV Guide,* have generally ignored the PBS activities except in the most obvious instances. Trade papers have tended to focus more attention on public policy regarding the new network than on the contributions it was making to television offerings.

Nevertheless, by 1975, with greater ease of reception becoming a reality for more and more of the viewing public, PBS began to attract more attention. There were two clear reasons—the huge success of "Sesame Street" and the prestige garnered from British offerings, such as "Masterpiece Theatre" and "Upstairs, Downstairs." However, the financial difficulties of PBS affiliates did not abate. Inadequate staffing and generally poor pay characterized many of the less affluent PBS members in comparison with the more prosperous channels in New York, Los Angeles, Pittsburgh, San Francisco, and Boston. Most of the new programming sprang from these more fortunate affiliates. Auctions and scrambling for any size grants became a way of life for most stations. Threatened with economic collapse, the temptation has been real to emulate the commercial networks in their quest for ratings. Further, there is the constant danger of government interference in the affairs of PBS even though every effort is made to eliminate politics from the system. There has been considerable pressure from some lawmakers for PBS to serve broader publics since it uses tax dollars. PBS has continued to offer more and more excellent quality programming to a solid minority of citizens. Properly funded, it can provide a healthy stimulus to the three major commercial networks, as it serves a significant public of its own.

REFERENCE WORKS

Even though directed toward "scientific" study of television, an absolute essential for any research in the area, from whatever perspective, is the three-volume work from the Rand Corporation bearing the general title *Television and Human Behavior: The Key Studies.* The first carries the subtitle *A Guide to the Pertinent Scientific Literature.* It, like the other two volumes, is under the general editorship of George Comstock. The first task of the study was to list some twenty-three hundred citations with a single-word description of any area a particular citation might touch. While focused upon social and behavioral science, most of the important contributions by humanists, critics, and columnists are noted. Unfortunately and predictably, the *Key Studies,* an expanded description of 450 of the most significant "scientific" works, includes almost none of the material on content analysis and ignores writings by humanists and interpreters of popular culture. While it would be foolish to fault the Rand study for its omissions, given its purpose, it is legitimate to call to the attention of social scientists the growing literature on television as art and culture.

George Comstock will bring the 1975 bibliography up to date in 1978 with the publication of his interpretations of the material noted in the Rand trilogy. Again, the emphasis is "scientific" but Comstock, who was the senior research coordinator for the 1972 Report of the Surgeon General's Scientific Advisory Committee on Television and Social Behavior, is a well-balanced scholar whose interpretations of the data point toward the need for content analysis. His writings reflect a recognition of the limitations of interpretation by social scientists of their collected information. He points further to the lack of substantive answers and reminds his readers that alternative methods of examination of the medium are appropriate. Comstock's writings could become a bridge for communication among academics concerned with the study of television. He wrote in 1976,

It is tempting to conclude that television violence makes viewers more anti-socially aggressive, somewhat callous, and generally more fearful of the society in which they live. It may, but the social and behavioral science evidence does not support such a broad indictment.[5]

Another, less elaborate listing, but perhaps of equal significance for the humanities, is *Broadcasting and Mass Media: A Survey Bibliography*, compiled by Christopher Sterling. More restricted in scope but useful, with 619 entries, is an appended bibliography to *Television Economics* by Bruce M. Owen, Jack H. Beebe, and Willard G. Manning, Jr. Finally, *Television and Social Behavior: An Annotated Bibliography of Research Focusing on Television's Impact on Children*, by C. K. Atkin, J. P. Murray, and O. B. Nayman is helpful in the same way as the Rand study, but far less thorough.

As previously stated, this bibliography will concentrate upon contributions to television research by humanists and critics of the culture. A primary emphasis is writing in the area of content analysis. Other notations will be offered that might assist a student of popular culture in new investigations and some "scientific" works will be cited. However, it should be understood that the vast majority of such inquiries have been omitted and can be found in the Rand study.

HISTORY AND CRITICISM

The best and most thorough study of the history of American television is Erick Barnouw's *Tube of Plenty*, a revision of material contained in his trilogy on broadcasting. His approach, while academic, is highly readable and excellent not only as a text but as a volume for general readers as

well. The paper edition has been updated to 1977 and contains a chronological appendix that supplies capsule information on events in telecommunications reaching back one hundred years. One of the most effective presentations is Barnouw's treatment of the days of television black-
listing and the harassment of the creative talent in the medium. The book
is effectively illustrated and fulfills the glowing promise of the publisher's
jacket.

Aside from Barnouw, efforts at telling the story of television have concentrated largely upon nostalgia and popular appeal. In that category the
best is *How Sweet It Was*, by Arthur Shulman and Roger Youman. Arranged topically, interlaced with 1,435 photographs, and quite well written, the book provides a visual display of television history. The chief
problem with the work is that it concludes in 1966. The same authors returned to the task in 1972 with *The Television Years*, a less ambitious
undertaking with only a few pages devoted to each year and made up
primarily of photographs. It is not in a class with the initial effort. Irving
Settel and William Laas are the authors of *A Pictorial History of Television*. Arranged chronologically, the text is not nearly so illuminating as
How Sweet It Was. The quality of paper and photographs is inferior, but
it is a good reference with correct information. A two-volume work, *The
Complete Encyclopedia of Television Programs, 1947-1976*, by Vincent
Terrace, is a welcome addition to the literature even though its usefulness
is limited by a lack of indexing. All shows that appeared at any time on
commercial television or PBS are listed alphabetically with a brief summary of the plot of each. There is information about actors and actresses
who appeared in each series and dates of appearances on the networks.
While the musical score is credited in almost every instance, there is no
reference to producers, directors, and writers. And the failure to provide
a cross index of names makes much of the valuable information contained
in the work irretrievable except if one remembers the exact name of a
series. Another problem appears to be in Terrace's comprehension of
quality drama. In his listing of anthological drama series from the 1950s,
he offers a sample of those performed, but he omits most of those plays
that have come to be recognized as classics.

Newspapers and news magazines provide a primary source for the
progress of television since World War II. This is particularly true of the
New York *Times*, *Time*, and *Newsweek*. The single best source for programming is *TV Guide* which has, since 1952, chronicled every schedule
shift on a weekly basis. In addition, the magazine is a gold mine of opinion
on television over its history. Unfortunately, almost no libraries have seen
fit to save copies, and there are no more than a dozen files of the publication available to the public. Further, the publisher has not, as yet, provided an index even of the articles. Barry Cole made some effort to com-

pensate for these problems when he edited *Television*. It contains the "best" of *TV Guide* articles culled from eleven years of the magazine's existence. The book addresses news, programming, censorship, audience, effects, and the future. It contains an impressive group of contributors including Karl Menninger, Arthur Schlesinger, Jr., Arnold Toynbee, and Eleanor Roosevelt.

Three other works are worthy of mention in passing. There is a somewhat dated, nevertheless useful, account of *Documentary in American Television*, by William Bluem. Paul Michael and Robert Parish have compiled a handy resource, *The Emmy Awards*, that has encyclopedic value. Finally there is the totally disappointing *International Television Almanac*, now in its twenty-first year, edited by Richard Gertner. It contains so many omissions that its use is somewhat questionable. For example, in the 1976 edition listing television personalities, Norman Lear was not included. In other sections the failure to be complete erases the value of the volume. Unfortunately more and more libraries appear to be ordering it under the assumption that it is what it advertises itself to be.

The Center for Cassette Studies in North Hollywood has collected a large selection of taped conversations about the medium, many dating to the early 1960s. Many appear to have been taped from television panel discussions held in New York. The Roper Organization has published *What People Think of Television and Other Mass Media: 1959-1972* and has continued to keep it current. From 1959 to 1974 the percentage of persons considering television performance excellent or good rose from 59 to 71 percent. In 1963 Gary Steiner wrote *The People Look at Television*, a study at the Bureau of Applied Social Research of Columbia University that makes some interesting data available on the different viewing habits of college and non-college graduates. Ten years later Robert Bower wrote *Television and the Public*, an effort to pose the same questions as the Steiner book in order to understand possible shifts in public attitudes. The findings proved inconclusive, offering very little new information.

Variety and *The Hollywood Reporter* contain daily information about the happenings in the entire television industry as well as columns interpreting events. Both are trade papers and as such tend toward advocacy, but are indispensable for the serious historian of television. The archives of NBC, ABC, and CBS are not open to the public, and there is little information as to the amount of material that has been saved, particularly from the 1950s. Rumors persist that most of the memorable moments from those early days have been lost. The networks have not taken seriously a responsibility to establish a central library and indexing facility. Some of the funds expended by them each year on "research" could well be diverted to such an enterprise as an investment in future study. Since 1968, Vanderbilt University has maintained a complete video tape library of all network news broadcasts. The collection is available for study either in Nashville or, at a nominal charge, through library loan. The Vanderbilt authorities maintain that no such record exists anywhere else in the world, including the major networks. The collection is maintained by the Vanderbilt Television News Archives.

Arno Press has preserved two excellent collections through reprints. Christopher Sterling, editor of the *Journal of Broadcasting*, is also the editor of *The History of Broadcasting: Radio to Television*, a collection of thirty-two titles including such vintage works as *First Principles of Television* (1932), *The Outlook for Television* (1932), and *Television: A Struggle for Power* (1938). The second series, also edited by Sterling, is entitled *Telecommunications* and contains some interesting early titles on the technology of the medium.

History begins to blend into criticism with two analyses of CBS, Robert Metz's *CBS: Reflection in a Bloodshot Eye* and David Halberstam's "CBS: The Network and the News and the Power and the Profits." Both authors have been on the staff of the New York *Times*. Metz presents a congenial, if critical, picture of the network. It is a book both of events and personalities, centering upon William Paley. Nicely illustrated, the narrative flows effectively with the facts about growth, censorship, and programming strewn across the pages in journalistic style, no interest in sources being identified. It is a useful book. Halberstam's is better. To be sure, he concentrates on the news and the profits but his analysis is more thoughtful, his evidence more convincing. His study of the Murrow days of "See It Now" weaves a far more complex web of personal involvements, resulting in a stunning presentation that is at once fair and vigorously critical. ABC and NBC still await the same type of devoted attention to the operations of their respective networks. Two highly critical analyses of television, *The TV Establishment*, by Gaye Tuchman, and *The Mind Managers*, by Herbert I. Schillar, are important and offer thoughtful comment.

Writing on the subject of television news has been quite popular for over a decade. Many of these studies have attacked alleged television news bias. Chief among those who have addressed that subject from the conservative perspective have been Edith Efron (*The News Twisters*), Ernst Lefever (*TV and National Defense*), and Joseph Keeley (*The Left-Leaning Antenna*). *TV Guide* inaugurated "Newswatch" several years ago to offer conservative criticism of the news systems in the networks. Were authors of an ultra-liberal point of view to take up the pen against network news, the same arguments could be turned in the opposite direction. In fact, the evidence supports the contention that moderation is the goal of most news reporting. Michael Novak has added some helpful insights at this point in his essay "The People and the News" in a volume in the DuPont-Columbia University Broadcast Journalism series, edited by Marvin Barrett, all five of which are useful means of interpreting events between 1969 and 1975. Novak wrote,

The accusations that the national news is not "objective," has a liberal bias, or a Northeastern bias, are, then, wide of the mark. What really is at stake is that the national news is geared to too high and general a focus. It assumes that there is a national, homogeneous point of view. It does not adequately focus on America's real diversity of soul—a profound diversity of perception and point of view.[6]

An informative, if unquestionably biased, study of news and opinion in the networks, *Due to Circumstances Beyond Our Control . . .*, was written by Fred Friendly as a personal vindication of his rupture of relations with CBS in 1966. Edward Epstein has done a detailed investigation of the news-gathering activities of NBC in *News from Nowhere*. The thesis is that television news is largely controlled by organizational factors. A more satisfying investigation has come from M. L. Stein, author of *Shaping the News*. He points to the many problems that plague reporters and the media in general. A companion volume that should be read in conjunction with the two previously mentioned works is *Power to Persuade*, by Robert Cirino. It is a presentation of dozens of case studies relating to decision making and the news. While not restricted to television, it addresses the medium extremely well. Robert MacNeil, a practicing television journalist, has written a highly critical study of television news reporting, *The People Machine*. He concludes with a call for some government control over network news, a risky suggestion in light of his own discussion on presidential access to television in a previous chapter of his book. Finally, there is an intriguing effort to forecast the future role of news through examination of past history in Edwin Diamond's *The Tin Kazoo*. One of its chief values lies in the account of the activities of television reporters in the later Nixon years.

Documents on news and politics are available from several sources, including many accounts of the Watergate scandal. Two collections from the Nixon years seem particularly useful—Edward Knappman's *Government and the Media in Conflict/1970-74* and a collection entitled *The Mass Media and Politics*.

The Aspen Institute has sponsored a series of workshops that have inspired at least three excellent considerations of the news. Paul Weaver and Michael Robinson each contributed an essay to *Television as a Social Force*, edited by Douglass Cater and Richard Adler. Sharon Sperry provided an outstanding chapter to *Television as a Cultural Force*, edited by Richard Adler. She views news as an extension of the entertainment medium and titled her essay, "Television News as Narrative."

Television as a political force has attracted sufficient attention to provide at least a few first-rate works. The classic is Joe McGinniss' *The Selling of the President 1968*. The author writes from firsthand experience with the Nixon campaign in the fall of 1968 and makes a strong case for the proposition that politicians are being packaged for consumers like soap and toothpaste, and just as effectively. Thomas Patterson and Robert McClure have challenged the effect of television on elections in *The Unseeing Eye*. The book jacket states that the authors will dispute the contention that "television elected John F. Kennedy." In fact the writers do no such thing. They have concentrated on the most unlikely election in many decades—McGovern-Nixon—without any real attention to Watergate related activities. The book fails to examine either the 1960 or 1968 presidential elections, when most observers believe there was a marked impact of television on the outcome. It is unlikely that McGinniss would argue that any amount of neat packaging could have sold McGovern in 1972. In the end the study cannot carry the weight of its rather pretentious subtitle *The Myth of Television Power in National Elections*. A more plausible, less polemical work, is that of Sig Mickelson, *The Electric Mirror*. It is a thoughtful, well-documented study that poses pertinent questions related to politics in the age of television. For comparison, the book by Jay Blumler and Denis McQuail, *Television in Politics*, offers a thoroughly engrossing look at television in British politics. A much needed area of inquiry was addressed by Newton Minow, John Martin, and Lee Mitchell in *Presidential Television*. Serious problems are indentified respecting the power of the president to control television and turn it to his advantage. A related public issue is confronted rather well by Fred Friendly in *The Good Guys, the Bad Guys and the First Amendment*.

Any appreciation of television as a force in the culture cannot afford the elimination of the business side of the industry. While numerous sources already referred to touch upon that aspect, there are some that concentrate directly on the economics of the medium. One of the best and most informative is *Television Economics*, by Bruce Owen, Jack Beebe, and Willard Manning, Jr. It is intended to elaborate for the general public the economic theory and policy of television. Another excellent tool is *Broadcast Management: Radio and Television*, edited by James Brown and Ward Quaal. A particularly thorny problem for broadcasters involves government regulations, and the Brookings Institution has sponsored a study entitled *Economic Aspects of Television Regulation*, by Roger Noll, Merton Peck, and John McGowan, that is exceptionally well-balanced in its treatment of a most difficult subject. A book that addresses itself to the specific regulations involving the FCC by Erwin Krasnow and Lawrence Longley bears the title *The Politics of Broadcast Regulation*. Sydney Head's *Broadcasting in America* is something of a classic in the industry and is thoroughly reliable as a major source of information on the business of broadcasting. Alan Pearce, former staff member of the House Committee on Interstate and Foreign Commerce and the Federal Communications Commission, has written a first-rate analysis, "The Television Networks."

There are some other excellent books that attempt to deal with the economic aspects of television within the broader framework of the society. One of the best of these is Les Brown's impressive account of *Television: The Business Behind the Box*. The personal knowledge brought to the book by this veteran journalist adds life and sparkle to the accounts of the rating wars of the 1960s. It is a New York insight into the network operations. While critical, Brown is sympathetic to the problems he addresses. In a similar vein, with a bit more polemic, is Martin Mayer's *About Television*, an engaging inquiry into the entire range of activities that compose the business, along with a well-directed barb or two at the academic critics of the medium. It is good reading. From an author directly involved in television administration has come a "how-to" book by Bob Shanks entitled *The Cool Fire*. An instruction manual for anyone interested in pursuing television as a career, it is, as well, a fine primer for anyone wishing to understand the workings of the networks.

As early as 1956 W. Y. Elliott was raising significant questions about the medium in a cultural context. He wrote,

More than any other medium of communication, [television is] symbolic in its own development and trends of much that is of basic importance to American culture, and serves more than the movies to reflect that culture—even if the mirror is distorted. Can it serve to educate as well as to entertain? How?[7]

While Elliott's volume, *Television's Impact on American Culture*, has most to do with educational television, the study is suggestive for students of culture. One essay by Eugene Glynn, a psychiatrist, points to most of the issues that emerged in the succeeding two decades. He asserted,

Television can produce a people wider in knowledge, more alert and aware of the world, prepared to be much more actively interested in the life of their times. Television can be the great destroyer of provincialism. Television can produce a nation of people who really live in the world, not in just their own hamlets.[8]

More recent critics, such as Michael Novak, or Herbert Gans in *Popular Culture and High Culture*, have challenged this trend as to its desirability in what continues to be a primary debate about the role of television for the future.

Neil Postman, who has a habit of being on the mark before most other observers, wrote an exciting volume in 1960 titled *Television and the Teaching of English*.

But beyond the products of "high culture" which television makes available, what are the effects on society of the more typical programs, the western, the "private eyes," the family shows, the adventures? Although these programs do not have the same status or high purpose of classic literature, we may discover, in the best of them, a "literature" that may be used in much the same way as traditional forms have been and are used. We may use these programs as pleasant and intelligent entertainments or diversions, as a means of increasing our knowledge of ourselves and other people, as criticisms of the social order, and, perhaps most important of all, as forms which call forth satisfying aesthetic responses.[9]

Marshall McLuhan took the center of the stage in the early 1960s with his *Understanding Media*. There he developed his thoughts about television as a "cool" medium, one into which the viewer is drawn as a participant. His emphasis upon the literate quality of Western culture and the consequent revolutionary effects of television upon it won him the distinction of becoming for many the first "seer" of television. There have been many critics of McLuhan since, often offering devastating arguments against his theory. Yet he continues to hover over the television scene. Gerald Stearn edited a "critical symposium" that attempted to analyze him in *McLuhan: Hot and Cold*. Individual reflections have often been more effective as in the comments by Brian Groombridge in *Television and the People* and the crisp remarks of Raymond Williams in *Television: Technology and Cultural Form*. Williams notes,

The particular rhetoric of McLuhan's theory of communications is unlikely to last long. But it is significant mainly as an example of an ideological representation of technology as a cause, and in this sense it will have successors, as particular formulations lose their force.[10]

By the mid 1960s Harry Skornia had established himself as a recognized critic of television, quite severe in his judgments. In his *Television and Society*, he struck vigorously against the excessive commercial influences on the medium. He then turned to an agenda for change, including a suggestion that there be created a profession of television broadcasting that would encourage stiff opposition to the largely economic demands of the top executives. In 1966 Patrick D. Hazard edited *TV as Art*, an excellent apologia for television as a work of art.

An important contributor through the years to literate humanistic interpretation of television has been Michael Arlen, both in the *New Yorker* and in several volumes including *The Living Room War* and *View from*

Highway 1. Arlen gave poignant expression to the common cultic experience of Vietnam and in his latest book offers some stunning essays on a diversity of topics from Norman Lear to television violence. His final essay on violence includes this observation.

But if anyone truly wishes to lessen violence in this country, it is hard to believe that more than a cosmetic alteration will be produced by censoring gunfights in television entertainment; or even, or especially, by relying on the "higher realism" of the classic American literary imagination.[11]

Perhaps this is the appropriate place to cite those "scientific" contributions that have led to so much current debate over the subject of the social impact of violence. Chief among the many television critics concerned with the medium's impact is George Gerbner, director of the Annenberg School of Communications at the University of Pennsylvania. Gerbner is knowledgeable and urbane. He is sincerely convinced of the rightness of his views on the role of television violence and its impact on viewers, a perspective that can be examined in a dozen journal essays. Perhaps the best source for understanding the Gerbner thesis is the article "Living with Television: The Violence Profile" that appeared in the *Journal of Communications*; its co-author was Larry Gross. Several recent studies have challenged his conclusions; among them see Robert S. Alley, *Television: Ethics for Hire?*

If one is to understand the violence debate, it is imperative that the Surgeon General's Report be examined as well as the five volumes of research data collected by George Comstock, Eli Rubinstein, and John Murray in *Television and Social Behavior.* There are at least three schools of thought on violence, all based upon "scientific" data. A. Bandura, L. Bogart, and L. Berkowitz are convinced of the deleterious effects of television violence, while Seymour Feshbach and Robert Singer argue that violence has a cathartic, favorable effect. D. Howitt and G. Cumberbatch, two British researchers, believe "the effects of mass media violence on attitudes, if anything, is very slight in terms of the adverse influences." Selected works by each of these individuals are found in the bibliography of this chapter. Comstock has sought to find a rational way through the extreme differences expressed by researchers. All of this suggests an important role for the humanities in addressing television as a popular literary form and investigating the content of programming with humanistic tools.

Perhaps as a result of the changing patterns of comedy programming and the admitted significance of television in relation to the war in Southeast Asia and Watergate, practitioners of the humanities began to be concerned about television as a source of popular culture. One of the earliest, and most provocative, studies was that of Horace Newcomb. In 1974 he wrote *TV: The Most Popular Art*. Well-versed in American studies and capable of examining the medium content from a literary and ethical perspective, Newcomb subjected a whole array of television fare to scrutiny. He pioneered in this area, and professionals, such as Earl Hamner, have expressed admiration for his work. What Newcomb did was to take seriously the television drama and comedy as products of men and women who might quite correctly be described as humanists. He sought to do what Postman had urged over a decade before, see television scripts as art. He, along with academics like David Thorburn of M.I.T., has provided a structure for serious investigation by the humanities of this new art form. Thorburn expressed the sentiments of a growing group of television critics when he wrote,

The aesthetic and human claims of most television melodrama would surely be much weakened, if not completely obliterated, in any other medium, and I have come to believe that the species of melodrama to be found on television today is a unique dramatic form offering an especially persuasive resolution of the contradiction or tension that has been inherent in melodrama since the time of Euripides.[12]

A second volume from Newcomb, a collection of essays entitled *Television: The Critical View*, offers opportunity for the reader to sample some of the better examples of cultural criticism focused on television. Most of the chapters have appeared previously in other formats. Perhaps the best contribution, apart from Newcomb, is one by John R. Silber, "Television: A Personal View" reprinted from a 1967 publication. Silber describes McLuhan as "surely the funniest stand-up comic in the Western Hemisphere." On "Bonanza" he remarks, "the perfect antidote to 'Father Knows Best' and other idiotic shows." Of "The Beverly Hillbillies" he notes, "a wholesome corrective to Goldwater Republicanism and the pseudo thought of Ayn Rand." And concerning the other popular Western of the 1960s, "Wagon Train" is "very good on religion and race" while "Gunsmoke" is a reminder that "it is far easier for a racial bigot to accept enlightenment from Matt Dillon than from Martin Luther King."

Coincident with the work of Newcomb was a series of workshops sponsored by the Aspen Institute for Humanistic Studies and funded in large part by the National Endowment for the Humanities. Emerging from the two years of meetings with dozens of critics, humanists, and broadcast professionals were two volumes, one edited by Douglass Cater and Richard Adler, *Television as a Social Force*, and the other edited by Adler alone, *Television as a Cultural Force*. Essays in these two collections range from an examination of the news to various content-oriented papers on current television comedy and drama. Of particular note are articles by David

Thorburn and Paula Fass. It is a sign that the alienation between the liberal arts and popular arts is being challenged.

Two volumes previously noted as being British contributions—Brian Groombridge, *Television and the People,* and Raymond Williams, *Television: Technology and Cultural Form*—provide valuable insights about an alternative system and suggest applications for American television. Williams offers a strong case for television content study as contrasted with McLuhan.

Over the quarter century of television history, the estrangement between the humanities and popular art has had unfortunate results. The academic study of television was remanded to the social scientists who found little merit in research into content and therefore made few efforts to comprehend the work of the television creative community. Muriel Cantor, herself a sociologist, took some corrective steps in her book *The Hollywood Television Producer.* It is an informative investigation of the "men who shape the intellectual and emotional impact of television." Robert Alley interviewed over forty members of the artistic community of television in order to assess better the content of current television in the area of values and ideas. He published his findings in *Television: Ethics for Hire?*

An early effort to engage a host of television talent from America and Britain in conversation resulted in 1967 in *Television: The Creative Experience,* edited by A. William Bluem and Roger Manvell. It is an outstanding array of creative talent exchanging ideas on the state of the art in the medium. Many television personalities have recorded their feelings about the industry. At least three seem worth noting here. Desi Arnaz has detailed his experiences in a volume simply titled *A Book.* It provides the reader with abundant information about the early days of television programming, something about which Arnaz was concerned not only with "I Love Lucy," but through Desilu, his company that produced such series as "The Untouchables." Interestingly, he is still quite proud of the Eliot Ness years. Dick Cavett has given a more whimsical look at his experiences in *Cavett,* written in cooperation with Christopher Porterfield. Finally there is the autobiography of Milton Berle which supplies some noteworthy information about the earliest days in television and the comic whose name was almost a synonym for the medium.

There have been several fascinating books released dealing with the making of television programs. The most informative is *The Making of Star Trek* by Stephen Whitfield and Gene Roddenberry. P. Elliott, *The Making of a Television Series* provides some helpful information about British television production. Merle Miller and Evan Rhodes have written perhaps the funniest book, *Only You, Dick Daring!,* a hilarious account of a series that never made it.

Among other recent offerings related to television programming is *The Horse, The Gun and The Piece of Property: Changing Images of the TV Western,* by Ralph Brauer. It is an effort to place the Western as a source of the American dream as defined by the author. It is an interesting exercise in interpretation.

Apart from the massive literature of the social sciences on the effect of television on children, there have been some isolated efforts to discuss content and effect from the non-laboratory perspective. William Melody has done a fine service with his examination of the economics of *Children's Television.* Evelyn Kaye has given expression to serious concerns by Action for Children's Television in *The Family Guide to Children's Television.* There is, however, a too easy acceptance of the extreme assumptions about television's effect on children in the area of violence. This tends to create an imbalance in appraisal of various programs. It is an action book and suggests things parents may do to affect children's programming. Marie Winn has the most recent offering, *The Plug-In Drug,* a book that asserts that too much television, whether "Sesame Street" or "Gunsmoke," will tend to mesmerize children. It raises some significant issues but in the end is, as G. William Jones has described it, "more of a propagation of a faith in television's basic culpability than an honest searching for truth." Two efforts have been made to deal with the phenomenon of "Sesame Street." Richard Polsky's *Getting to Sesame Street* relates the organization of the Children's Television Workshop, and Gerald Lesser's *Children and Television* is a personal record of the development of "Sesame Street." And, as a classic, after twenty years, there is the Hilde T. Himmelweit, A. N. Oppenheim, and Pamela Vince book, *Television and the Child,* detailing the study of two groups of children in Britain in 1958, one of which was exposed to television, the other denied it. The results pointed to a far less significant effect than many modern observers would suggest. For several years the networks have been commissioning research efforts to promote a positive image of their own programming. One of the most extensive has been that of CBS. In a short pamphlet, five special studies are described in *Learning While They Laugh.* Probably the most instructive of these is *A Study of Messages Received by Children Who Viewed an Episode of "Fat Albert and the Cosby Kids."*

There have been numerous efforts to recount the activities of the Public Broadcasting System and its predecessor, National Educational Television. Some of the best work has been done by Wilbur Schramm, a sampling of whose inquiries include *The Financing of Public Television, The Impact of Educational Television, The People Look at Educational Television,* and *Quality in Instructional Television.* The foundations of PBS are best understood by reading the report of the Carnegie Commis-

sion on Educational Television, *Public Television: A Program for Action.*
Both Action for Children's Television (ACT) and the work of Nicholas
Johnson have paid major attention to the growth of PBS and Johnson's
National Citizens' Committee publication, *access*, is an extremely useful
critique and source of information, as is his strong polemic, *How to Talk
Back to Your Television Set.*

As far as the public is concerned, the frontier still appears to be cable
television. Its slow growth and the problems it has faced from government and networks make it an area still in need of exploration. Richard
Adler and Walter Baer have edited a volume dealing with the humanities and cable television, *The Electronic Box Office.* The Sloan Commission published a most optimistic appraisal entitled *On the Cable: The
Television of Abundance.* Concern for public involvement in content is
expressed in the Monroe Price and John Wicklein book *Cable Television:
A Guide for Citizen Action.*

The religious community has been rather silent on the subject of content analysis, preferring to retreat into Sunday morning trivia and volleys
aimed at violence and sex. Even the more responsible religious leaders
have resorted to dismissal of television, as was the case in Kyle Haselden's
Morality and the Mass Media. One monthly publication has promise; it is
Arts in Context from the St. Clement's Film Association of New York,
edited by Stanford Sommers. A positive perspective is expressed by
Spencer Marsh, *God, Man and Archie Bunker.* It seeks to relate the religious community positively to the social concerns of Norman Lear.

Some of the most interesting and able writing on television has been
appearing in various journals and newspapers over the past quarter century. Columns by excellent critics have occupied space in the *New Yorker*,
the *Saturday Review of Literature, Playboy, T.V. Key,* the Washington
Post, and the New York *Times*. A wide range of subjects too numerous to
catalog makes these primary sources for a look at television and culture.
Among the most able critics one must include John Leonard, Robert
Shayon, Steve Scheuer, John O'Connor, and G. William Jones, who bring
serious reflection to programming. The scholarly world has had access to
*Journal of Communications, Journal of Broadcasting, Columbia Journal-
ism Review, Television Quarterly, Journal of Popular Culture,* and *Public Opinion Quarterly*, all of which have directed attention to the emerging technological marvel. The most recent publication to address television
is *American Film* published by the American Film Institute, now devoting
a major portion of each month to consideration of television writing. It is
first rate.

Commercial television has failed to examine itself critically over its
twenty-five years, and that failure of self-criticism has been the more
noticeable since it claims to be an important news medium. There have

been exceptions, such as the 1976 NBC special on violence or the occasional interview on "Who's Who" or "60 Minutes." For the most part, however, the competition for audience has tended to minimize any serious self-evaluation. A PBS film broadcast in 1977, "Television For Better or For Worse," brought nine creators (writers, producers, actors, directors) to the screen to discuss the medium and its relation to values, censorship, and violence. The half-hour program was produced by Robert Alley and Ernest Skinner. Another film from the same producers, *How Dare These Little Half Hour Comedies . . . ?* was made in late 1977. It includes interviews with Alan Alda, Norman Lear, and Jim Brooks discussing their professions and the role of values in program content.

There are several general books addressing popular culture that have good articles about television. These include W. M. Hammel, *The Popular Arts in America: A Reader*, F. Rissover and D. C. Birch, *Mass Media and the Popular Arts*, David M. White and Richard Averson, *Sight, Sound and Society: Motion Pictures and Television in America*, and Herbert Zettl's *Sight, Sound, Motion*. Edward Fischer has written a helpful guide to film and television in *The Screen Arts*.

There are literally hundreds of paperback volumes containing stories either related vaguely or not at all to particular series. These include books claiming attachment to such shows as "Star Trek," "Kojak," and "The Waltons." Some were done with cooperation of the television writers and producers, many were not. Any newsstand has available as many as thirty magazines on television in any given month, most of them gossip sheets that parallel the movie fan magazines. There are a dozen different publications dealing with daytime television, all gossip in the style of Rona Barrett or worse.

Any serious consideration of television content and culture must address the "soaps" and the game shows. At present there is almost no solid material on them other than a few isolated essays in journals, magazines, and newspapers. One volume that could prove beneficial is *The Soaps: Daytime Serials of Radio and TV*, by Madeleine Edmondson and David Rounds. A final note on syndication is in order. Both through reruns and such popular shows as "Lawrence Welk" and "Hee Haw," the public is experiencing a dimension of television not as yet addressed for study by anyone.

NOTES

1. Nell Eurich, "The Humanities Face Tomorrow," in Alvin Toffler, ed., *Learning for Tomorrow* (New York: Random House, 1974), pp. 150-51.

2. David Halberstam, "CBS: The Network and the News and the Power and the Profits," *The Atlantic Monthly*, 237 (January 1976), p. 63.

3. *Report of the National Advisory Commission on Civil Disorders* (New York: New York Times, 1968), p. 373.

4. Ward Quaal & James Brown, *Broadcast Management* (New York: Hastings House, 1976), p. 440.

5. George Comstock, *The Evidence on Television Violence* (Santa Monica, Calif.: The Rand Corporation, 1976), p. 5.

6. Michael Novak, "The People and the News," in Marvin Barrett, ed., *Moments of Truth* (New York: Thomas Crowell, 1975), p. 200.

7. William Y. Elliott, *Television's Impact on American Culture* (East Lansing: Michigan State University Press, 1956), p. xvi.

8. Ibid., p. 181.

9. Neil Postman, *Television and the Teaching of English* (New York: Appleton-Century-Crofts, 1961), p. 38.

10. Raymond Williams, *Television: Technology and Cultural Form* (New York: Schocken Books, 1975), p. 128.

11. Michael Arlen, *The View From Highway 1* (New York: Farrar, Straus, Giroux, 1976), p. 293.

12. David Thorburn, "Television Melodrama," in Richard Adler, ed., *Television as a Cultural Force* (New York: Praeger Publishers, 1976), p. 87.

BIBLIOGRAPHY

BOOKS AND ARTICLES

Adler, Richard, ed. *Television as a Cultural Force.* New York: Praeger, 1976.
————, and Walter S. Baer, eds. *The Electronic Box Office: Humanities and Arts on the Cable.* New York: Praeger, 1974.
Alley, Robert S. *Television: Ethics for Hire?* Nashville, Tenn.: Abingdon, 1977.
————. "How Dare These Little Half Hour Comedies . . . ?" Half-hour film. Charlottesville: Virginia Foundation for the Humanities and Public Policy, 1977.
————, and Ernest Skinner. "Television, For Better or for Worse." Half-hour film. Charlottesville: Virginia Foundation for the Humanities and Public Policy, 1976.
Arlen, Michael. *Living Room War.* New York: Tower Publications, 1969.
————. *The View from Highway 1, Essays on Television.* New York: Farrar, Straus, Giroux, 1976.
Arnaz, Desi. *A Book.* New York: Warner Books, 1976.
Atkin, C. K.; J. P. Murray; and O. B. Nayman. *Television and Social Behavior: An Annotated Bibliography of Research Focusing on Television's Impact on Children.* Washington, D.C.: U.S. Government Printing Office, 1972.
Bandura, A. *Aggression: A Social Learning Analysis.* Englewood Cliffs, N.J.: Prentice-Hall, 1973.
Barnouw, Erik. *The Image Empire: A History of Broadcasting in the United States from 1953.* New York: Oxford University Press, 1970.

————. *Tube of Plenty: The Evolution of American Televsion.* New York: Oxford University Press, 1975.

Barrett, Marvin, ed. *The Alfred I. DuPont-Columbia University Survey of Broadcast Journalism, 1968-1969.* New York: Grosset and Dunlap, 1969.

————. *The Alfred I. duPont-Columbia University Survey of Broadcast Journalism, 1969-1970. Year of Challenge, Year of Crisis.* New York: Grosset and Dunlap, 1970.

————. *The Alfred I. duPont-Columbia University Survey of Broadcast Journalism, 1970-1971. A State of Siege.* New York: Grosset and Dunlap, 1971.

————. *The Alfred I. duPont-Columbia University Survey of Broadcast Journalism, 1971-1972. The Politics of Broadcasting.* New York: Thomas Y. Crowell, 1973.

————. *The Alfred I. duPont-Columbia University Survey of Broadcast Journalism. Moments of Truth?* New York: Thomas Y. Crowell, 1975.

Berkowitz, L. *Aggression: A Social Psychological Analysis.* New York: McGraw-Hill, 1962.

Berle, Milton. *An Autobiography.* New York: Delacorte, 1974.

Bluem, A. William. *Documentary in American Television.* New York: Hastings House, 1965.

————, and Roger Manvell, eds. *Television: The Creative Experience. A Survey of Anglo-American Progress.* New York: Hastings House, 1967.

Blumler, Jay G., and Denis McQuail. *Television in Politics, Its Uses and Influence.* Chicago: University of Chicago Press, 1969.

Bogart, L. *The Age of Television.* 3rd ed. New York: Frederick Ungar, 1972.

Bower, R. T. *Television and the Public.* New York: Holt, Rinehart and Winston, 1973.

Brauer, Ralph. *The Horse, The Gun and The Piece of Property: Changing Images of the TV Western.* Bowling Green, Ohio: Bowling Green University Popular Press, 1975.

Brown, James A., and Ward L. Quaal. *Broadcast Management: Radio and Television.* New York: Hastings House, 1975.

Brown, Les. *Television: The Business Behind the Box.* New York: Harcourt, Brace, Jovanovich, 1971.

Cantor, Muriel G. *The Hollywood Television Producer: His Work and His Audience.* New York: Basic Books, 1971.

Cater, Douglass, and Richard Adler, eds. *Television as a Social Force: Approaches to TV Criticism.* New York: Praeger, 1975.

Cavett, Dick, and Christopher Porterfield. *Cavett.* New York: Bantam, 1975.

Center for Cassette Studies, North Hollywood, Calif. See catalog.

Cirino, Robert. *Power to Persuade: Mass Media and the News.* New York: Bantam, 1974.

Cole, Barry G., ed. *Television: A Selection of Readings from TV Guide Magazine.* New York: Free Press, 1970.

Comstock, George. *Effects of Television on Children: What is the Evidence?* Santa Monica, Calif.: Rand Corporation, 1975. Paper #P-5412.

————. *The Evidence on Television Violence*. Santa Monica, Calif.: The Rand Corporation, 1976. Paper #P-5730.

————. *The Long-Range Impact of Television*. Santa Monica, Calif.: The Rand Corporation, 1976. Paper #P-5750.

————. *Television and Human Behavior: The Key Studies*. Santa Monica, Calif.: The Rand Corporation, 1975.

————. *Television and Its Viewers: What Social Science Sees*. Santa Monica, Calif.: The Rand Corporation, 1976. Paper #P-5632.

————. *Television and the Teacher*. Santa Monica, Calif.: The Rand Corporation, 1976. Paper #P-5734.

————, and Marilyn Fisher. *Television and Human Behavior: A Guide to the Pertinent Scientific Literature*. Santa Monica, Calif.: The Rand Corporation, 1975.

————, and George Lindsey. *Television and Human Behavior: The Research Horizon, Future and Present*. Santa Monica, Calif.: The Rand Corporation, 1975.

————; Eli Rubinstein; and John Murray, eds. *Television and Social Behavior: Media Content and Control*. Vol. 1. Washington, D.C.: U.S. Government Printing Office, 1972.

————. *Television and Social Behavior: Television and Adolescent Aggressiveness*. Vol. 3. Washington, D.C.: U.S. Government Printing Office, 1972.

————. *Television and Social Behavior: Television in Day-to-Day Life, Patterns of Use*. Vol. 4. Washington, D.C.: U.S. Government Printing Office, 1972.

————. *Television and Social Behavior: Television's Effects, Further Explorations*. Vol. 5.Washington, D.C.: U.S. Government Printing Office, 1972.

————. *Television and Social Behavior: Television and Social Learning*. Vol. 2. Washington, D.C.: U.S. Government Printing Office, 1972.

Diamond, Edwin. *The Tin Kazoo: Television, Politics and the News*. Cambridge, Mass.: M.I.T. Press, 1975.

Edmondson, Madeleine, and David Rounds. *The Soaps: Daytime Serials of Radio and TV*. New York: Stein and Day, 1973.

Efron, Edith. *How CBS Tried to Kill a Book*. New York: Manor Books, 1973.

————. *The News Twisters*. Los Angeles, Calif.: Nash Publishing, 1971.

Elliott, P. *The Making of a Television Series: A Case Study in the Sociology of Culture*. New York: Hastings House, 1973.

Elliott, William Y. *Television's Impact on American Culture*. East Lansing: Michigan State University Press, 1956.

Epstein, Edward Jay. *News from Nowhere: Television and the News*. New York: Random House, 1973.

Feshbach, Seymour, and Robert Singer. *Television and Aggression*. San Francisco: Jossey-Bass, 1971.

Fischer, Edward. *The Screen Arts: A Guide to Film and Television Appreciation*. New York: Sheed and Ward, 1969.

Friendly, Fred W. *Due to Circumstances Beyond Our Control . . .* New York: Random House, 1968.

———. *The Good Guys, the Bad Guys and the First Amendment: Free Speech vs. Fairness in Broadcasting*. New York: Random House, 1976.

Gans, Herbert J. *Popular Culture and High Culture: An Analysis and Evaluation of Taste*. New York: Basic Books, 1974.

Gerbner, George, and Larry Gross. "Living with Television: The Violence Profile." *Journal of Communications*, 26 (Spring 1976), 172-199.

Gertner, Richard, ed. *1976 International Television Almanac*. New York: Quigley Publishing, 1976.

Groombridge, Brian. *Television and the People: A Programme for Democratic Participation*. New York: Penguin Books, 1972.

Halberstam, David. "CBS: The Network and the News and the Power and the Profits." *The Atlantic Monthly*, 237 (January 1976), 33-71; (February 1976), 52-91.

Hammel, W. M., ed. *The Popular Arts in America: A Reader*. New York: Harcourt Brace Jovanovich, 1972.

Haselden, Kyle. *Morality and the Mass Media*. Nashville, Tenn.: Broadman, 1968.

Hazard, Patrick D., ed. *TV as Art: Some Essays in Criticism*. Champaign, Ill.: National Council of Teachers of English, 1966.

Head, Sydney W. *Broadcasting in America: A Survey of Television and Radio*. 2nd ed. Boston: Houghton Mifflin, 1972.

Himmelweit, Hilde T.; A. N. Oppenheim; and Pamela Vince. *Television and the Child: An Empirical Study of the Effect of Television on the Young*. London: Oxford University Press, 1958.

Howitt, D. "Television and Aggression: A Counterargument." *American Psychologist*, 27 (October 1972), 969-70.

———, and G. Cumberbatch. *Mass Media Violence and Society*. New York: John Wiley & Sons, 1975.

Johnson, Nicholas. *How to Talk Back to Your Television Set*. New York: Bantam, 1970.

Kaye, Evelyn. *The Family Guide to Children's Television: What to Watch, What to Miss, What to Change and How to Do It*. New York: Pantheon Books, 1974.

Keeley, Joseph. *The Left-Leaning Antenna: Political Bias in Television*. New Rochelle, N.Y.: Arlington House, 1971.

Knappman, Edward W., ed. *Government and the Media in Conflict/1970-74*. New York: Facts on File, 1974.

Krasnow, Erwin G., and Lawrence D. Longley. *The Politics of Broadcast Regulation*. New York: St. Martin's, 1973.

Learning While They Laugh. Studies of Five Children's Programs on the CBS Television Network. New York: CBS Broadcast Group, 1976.

Lefever, Ernst. *TV and National Defense: An Analysis of CBS News, 1972-1973*, Boston, Va.: Institute for American Strategy Press, 1974.

Lesser, Gerald S. *Children and Television: Lessons from Sesame Street*. New York: Random House, 1974.

McGinniss, Joe. *The Selling of the President 1968*. New York: Pocket Books, 1970.

McLuhan, Marshall. *Understanding Media: The Extensions of Man*. New York: McGraw-Hill, 1964.

MacNeil, Robert. *The People Machine: The Influence of Television on American Politics*. New York: Harper and Row, 1968.

Marsh, Spencer. *God, Man, and Archie Bunker*. New York: Harper and Row, 1975.

The Mass Media and Politics. New York: New York Times/Arno Press, 1972.

Mayer, Martin. *About Television*. New York: Harper and Row, 1972.

Melody, William. *Children's Television: The Economics of Exploitation*. New Haven, Conn.: Yale University Press, 1973.

Mendelsohn, H. A. *Mass Entertainment*. New Haven, Conn.: College and University Press, 1966.

Metz, Robert. *CBS: Reflections in a Bloodshot Eye*. Chicago: Playboy Press, 1975.

Michael, Paul, and Robert Parish. *The Emmy Awards: A Pictorial History*. New York: Crown, 1971.

Mickelson, Sig. *The Electric Mirror: Politics in an Age of Television*. New York: Dodd, Mead, 1972.

Miller, Merle, and Evan Rhodes. *Only You, Dick Darling! or How to Write One Television Script and Make $50,000,000, a True-life Adventure*. New York: William Sloan, 1964.

Minow, Newton N.; John Bartlow Martin; and Lee M. Mitchell. *Presidential Television*. New York: Basic Books, 1973.

Newcomb, Horace. *TV: The Most Popular Art*. New York: Doubleday, 1974.

————, ed. *Television: The Critical View*. New York: Oxford University Press, 1976.

Noll, Roger G.; Merton J. Peck; and John J. McGowan. *Economic Aspects of Television Regulation*. Washington, D.C.: The Brookings Institution, 1973.

Owen, Bruce M.; Jack H. Beebe; and Willard G. Manning, Jr. *Television Economics*. Lexington, Mass.: D. C. Heath, 1974.

Patterson, Thomas E., and Robert D. McClure. *The Unseeing Eye: The Myth of Television Power in National Elections*. New York: G. P. Putnam's Sons, 1976.

Pearce, Alan. "The Television Networks." Paper presented at National Conference of Black Lawyers Convention, 1975, Washington, D.C.

Polsky, Richard M. *Getting to Sesame Street: The Origins of the Children's Television Workshop*. New York: Praeger, 1974.

Postman, Neil. *Television and the Teaching of English*. New York: Appleton-Century-Crofts, 1961.

Price, Monroe E., and John Wicklein. *Cable Television: A Guide for Citizen Action*. Philadelphia: Pilgrim Press, 1972.

Public Television: A Program for Action. The Report of the Carnegie Commission on Educational Television. New York: Bantam, 1967.

Rissover, F., and D. C. Birch, eds. *Mass Media and the Popular Arts*. New York: McGraw-Hill, 1971.

The Roper Organization. *What People Think of Television and Other Mass Media: 1959-1972*. New York: Television Information Office, 1973.

Schiller, Herbert I. *The Mind Managers*. Boston: Beacon, 1973.

Schramm, Wilbur. *The Impact of Educational Television*. Urbana: University of Illinois Press, 1960.

————, ed. *Quality in Instructional Television*. Honolulu: University of Hawaii Press, 1973.

————, and L. Nelson. *The Financing of Public Television*. Palo Alto, Calif.: Aspen Institute, 1972.

————; J. Lyle; and I. deSola Pool. *The People Look at Educational Television*. Stanford, Calif.: Stanford University Press, 1963.

Settel, Irving, and William Laas. *A Pictorial History of Television*. New York: Grosset and Dunlap, 1969.

Shanks, Bob. *The Cool Fire: How to Make It in Television*. New York: W. W. Norton, 1976.

Shayon, Robert Lewis. *The Crowd-Catchers*. New York: Saturday Review Press, 1973.

Shulman, Arthur, and Roger Youman. *How Sweet it Was, Television: A Pictorial Commentary*. New York: Bonanza Books, 1966.

————. *The Television Years*. New York: Popular Library, 1973.

Skornia, Harry J. *Television and Society: An Inquest and Agenda for Improvement*. New York: McGraw-Hill, 1965.

————, and J. Kitson, eds. *Problems and Controversies in Television and Radio: Basic Readings*. Palo Alto, Calif.: Pacific Books, 1968.

Sloan Commission on Cable Communications. *On the Cable: The Television of Abundance*. New York: McGraw-Hill, 1971.

Stearn, Gerald. *McLuhan: Hot and Cold*. New York: Dial Press, 1967.

Stein, M. L. *Shaping the News: How the Media Function in Today's World*. New York: Washington Square Press, 1974.

Steiner, G. A. *The People Look at Television*. New York: Alfred A. Knopf, 1963.

Sterling, Christopher, ed. *Broadcasting and Mass Media: A Survey Bibliography*. Philadelphia: Temple University Press, 1974.

————, ed. *History of Broadcasting: Radio to Television*. Reprint of 32 volumes. New York: New York Times/Arno Press, 1972.

————, ed. *Telecommunications*. Reprint of 34 books. New York: New York Times/Arno Press, 1974.

A Study of Messages Received by Children Who Viewed an Episode of "Fat Albert and the Cosby Kids." New York: CBS Broadcast Group, 1974.

Television and Growing Up: The Impact of Televised Violence. Report to the Surgeon General. Washington, D.C.: U.S. Government Printing Office, 1972.

Terrace, Vincent. *The Complete Encyclopedia of Television Programs, 1947-1976*. 2 vols. Cranbury, N.J.: A. S. Barnes, 1976.

Toffler, Alvin, ed. *Learning for Tomorrow*. New York: Random House, 1974.

Tuchman, Gaye, ed. *The TV Establishment: Programming for Power and Profit*. Englewood Cliffs, N.J.: Prentice-Hall, 1974.

White, David M., and Richard Averson, eds. *Sight, Sound and Society: Motion Pictures and Television in America*. Boston: Beacon, 1968.

Whitfield, Stephen, and Gene Roddenberry. *The Making of Star Trek*. New York: Ballantine, 1968.

Williams, Raymond. *Television: Technology and Cultural Form*. New York: Schocken Books, 1975.

Winn, Marie. *The Plug-In Drug*. New York: Viking, 1977.

Zettl, Herbert. *Sight, Sound, Motion: Applied Media Aesthetics*. Belmont, Calif.: Wadsworth, 1973.

PERIODICALS

access. Washington, D.C., 1969-.

American Film: Journal of the Film and Television Arts. Washington, D.C., 1975-.

Arts in Context. New York, 1974-.

Broadcasting: The Businessweekly of Television and Radio. Washington, D.C., 1931-.

Columbia Journalism Review. New York, 1962-.

The Hollywood Reporter. Los Angeles, 1930-.

Journal of Broadcasting. Philadelphia, 1956-.

Journal of Communications. Philadelphia, 1951-.

Journal of Popular Culture. Bowling Green, Ohio, 1967-.

Journalism Quarterly. Minneapolis, 1924-.

Public Opinion Quarterly. New York, 1937-.

Television Quarterly: The Journal of the National Academy of Television Arts and Sciences. Beverly Hills, Calif., 1963-.

TV Guide. Radnor, Pa., 1953-.

Variety. New York, 1905-.

CHAPTER 15 The Western
Richard W. Etulain

HISTORIC OUTLINE

Until the 1950s little had been written about the Western, for it, like most types of American popular culture, was not considered worthy of scholarly scrutiny. The rise of the American studies movement in the 1950s and the birth of the Popular Culture Association in the late 1960s have encouraged students and teachers to examine the form and content of popular literary genres, such as the Western. It is now acceptable in many English, history, and American studies departments for a student to undertake a study of the Western for a thesis or dissertation. As yet, however, not much of this new interest in the Western has found its way into published articles and books; systematic study of the popular genre is still in its infancy.

The following essay deals with the popular Western, the formula fiction of such authors as Owen Wister, Max Brand, Zane Grey, Ernest Haycox, Luke Short, and Louis L'Amour. These writers follow the patterns of action, romance, and the clash of heroes and villains familiar to the Western. Their plots are predictable; they confirm rather than challenge or satirize American culture. Writers of Westerns do not produce the less stylized western novels of Willa Cather, John Steinbeck, Wallace Stegner, and Larry McMurtry. To make these distinctions between the *Western* and the *western novel* is not to denigrate the former and praise the latter but to make clear the subject of the following pages.

In recent treatments of the Western, two points of view about its historical development have emerged. One group argues that the Western is strongly tied to several nineteenth-century sources: the *Leatherstocking Tales* of James Fenimore Cooper, dime novels, and western local color writing. Another group asserts that though these early roots are significant for a large understanding of popular literature about the West, the Western is primarily the product of the dynamic climate of opinion surrounding 1900. The present account leans toward the second point of view while trying not to overlook the earlier influences upon the Western.

Many Americans did not take a positive view of the frontier until the

last decades of the eighteenth century. Before that time, the earliest settlers and their descendants saw the frontier as a region for expansion but
also as a forbidding and evil wilderness. As Richard Slotkin has recently
pointed out in his book *Regeneration Through Violence*, it was not until
John Filson published his legend-making volume, *The Discovery, Settle-
ment and Present State of Kentucke* (1784), that Americans were provided with a western hero in the author's account of Daniel Boone.

In the fifty years following the publication of Filson's work, other information necessary for the creation of a western literature became available. Even before Thomas Jefferson became president, he was encouraging
exploration of the West, and after he was elected, he sent Lewis and Clark
to traverse the West and to provide written records of what they saw and
experienced. The publication of their journals and the accounts of such
travelers as Josiah Gregg, Jedediah Smith, and Stephen H. Long convinced many Americans that the empty spaces beyond the frontier were
indeed a "passage to India" and part of the nation's "untransacted destiny."

The stage was set for an imaginative writer who could synthesize the
information available about the West and the emotions that these facts
and rumors had inspired. James Fenimore Cooper was able to use these
materials to create the earliest full-blown hero of western fiction in Natty
Bumppo (or Leatherstocking, the Long Rifle, or the Deerslayer). Many
interpreters argue that Cooper produced the first widely read novels
about the West and hence deserves to be called the father of the western novel.

Cooper used many ingredients in his fiction that later became standard
parts of the Western. In the first place, his hero, Leatherstocking, em-
bodied several of the virtues of the Romantic hero. He was a man of
nature who loved animals, forests, and good Indians (Cooper made sharp
distinctions between what he considered good and bad Indians) and was
at home himself in the wilderness. Although Natty was interested in the
women his creator provided for him, when he had the opportunity to
choose between these heroines and his forest home, he selected the frontier rather than hearth, home, and domesticity. On numerous occasions
Leatherstocking conflicted with white men or Indians who challenged his
sense of territory or what he thought to be his rights. These conflicts foreshadowed the famous walkdowns that appeared later in such novels as
The Virginian. And anyone acquainted with the modern Western will
recognize its indebtedness to the chase-and-pursuit plot that Cooper
utilized in his *Leatherstocking Tales*.

Cooper's western novels attracted thousands of readers throughout the
world, and thus it is not surprising that several American authors rushed
in to imitate his work. Such writers as James Hall, Charles Webber, Mayne
Reid, and Emerson Bennett turned out dozens of adventure novels set in

the West. By the Civil War, American readers were widely acquainted with the frontier West through the fiction of Cooper and other novelists. Then, in the next three decades, two developments changed the content and direction of western fiction and helped pave the way for the rise of the modern Western.

The first of these innovations was the appearance of the earliest dime novels shortly before the Civil War. Sales of the dime novel rose spectacularly until the late 1880s. And, as one might expect, authors of this new popular fiction, in their search for salable materials, made wide use of themes and formats contained in earlier writing about the West. Some writers sensationalized the deeds of historical persons, such at Kit Carson and Buffalo Bill; others like Edward Wheeler and Edward S. Ellis created the fictional characters Deadwood Dick and Seth Jones. As demands for the dime novel increased, writers were less inclined to stick to the Leatherstocking figure inherited from Cooper and fashioned instead heroes more adventurous and less reflective. Gradually the actions of these heroes—and heroines—were melodramatized beyond belief, and the potential power of the western setting was lost in the drive to turn out hundreds of dime novels in which action and adventure were paramount. The dime novel popularized the West, but its lurid sensationalism revealed a lack of serious intent in dealing with the western materials introduced earlier in the nineteenth century.

The other development that influenced writing about the West was the rise of the "local color" movement after the Civil War. In the first decades following Appomattox many American writers began to emphasize local dialect, customs, and settings in their fiction. Bret Harte was a well-known participant in this movement; indeed, his stories about Californian mining camps and prostitutes and hard-bitten miners with hearts of gold were path-breaking developments in the local color movement. Other writers like Joaquin Miller, Mary Hallock Foote, and Alfred Henry Lewis wrote poems, stories, and novels about explorers, engineers, and cowpunchers. These authors, whose works never sold as widely as those of the dime novelists, were more serious of purpose and proved that literary treatment of the West need not fall victim to sensationalism.

In addition to the rise of the dime novel and the local color movement, several other developments in late nineteenth-century America prepared the way for Owen Wister and the Western. Not the least of these was the realization of many Americans that the frontier was gone or rapidly disappearing. As the wide-open spaces vanished, cities, industrialism, and numbers of immigrants seemed to increase; and writers, sensing the public's desire to hold onto the frontier, began to write about the cowboy and other symbols of an older West. The same nostalgic mood helped popularize Buffalo Bill's Wild West Show, which played to large audiences in the United States and abroad. The show included real Indians, cowboys, and sharpshooters, and it aided in keeping alive an era that was rapidly disappearing. Probably the most important of the cultural "happenings" leading to the birth of the western novel was the discovery of the cowboy. A few dime novelists, journalists, and travelers mentioned the cowboy before 1890, but during the 1890s the fiction of Wister and the illustrations of Frederic Remington helped to make the cowboy a new cultural hero worthy of a major literary treatment.

And Wister was the man worthy of the task. Philadelphia-born and Harvard-educated, Wister first saw the West in the 1880s during a series of trips designed to relieve his boredom and restore his health. At first, he was satisfied to wander throughout the West as a dilettantish sightseer, but at the suggestion of his friends he began to record in his journals what he saw and experienced. Wister was a keen observer and talented writer—he had already published on a variety of subjects—and his first western stories published in magazines in the early 1890s attracted a good deal of attention. By the turn of the century, Wister was known as a prominent writer about western subjects.

Wister's position in 1900 was similar to Cooper's in 1820: he had at his disposal the materials necessary for a significant work of fiction, and his previous writings proved he could produce work that attracted readers. His first western books *Red Men and White* (1896) and *Lin McLean* (1897) dealt with cowboys, although these heroes were most often picaresque protagonists who were not as adventurous and winsome as many Romantic heroes. But in *The Virginian*, published in 1902, Wister put his brand on the most popular Western ever written, and after its publication western writing was never the same.

The Virginian occupies the central position in the historical development of the Western. The novel not only contains the action, adventure, romance, and good-versus-bad characters that had become standard parts of nineteenth-century western fiction; the work also reveals how much its creator was a participant in several cultural currents at the turn of the century. Wister's novel is shot through with nostalgia. From the prefatory note to the closing pages of the book, the tone is elegiac. The Virginian and the other cowboys are dealt with as symbols of a vanishing frontier. Wister also treats the West as another (perhaps the final) arena in which Anglo-Saxons can prove their superiority through vigorous competition with other people and the environment. In *The Virginian*, the hero and setting are used to illustrate these ideas: the Virginian is the Anglo-Saxon protagonist who wins his competition with others and who proves his superiority through conflict.

And yet there is an ambivalent strain in the novel. Though Wister seems drawn to the openness, the challenge, and the romance of the West, he also implies that life in Wyoming may turn men brutal and careless in their treatment of land, horses, and people. And it is necessary for Molly Wood, the Eastern schoolmarm, to bring civilization (as Eastern women had often done in earlier western fiction) to the West in the form of literature and culture. Finally, the marriage of the East (Molly) and West (the Virginian) is a union of the best qualities of each region and a union that bodes well for the future of America.

If Wister provided in *The Virginian* a paradigm for the modern Western, B. M. Bower (Bertha Sinclair), Zane Grey, Max Brand (Frederick Faust), and Clarence Mulford followed his lead and produced hundreds of novels that hardened the ingredients of Wister's novel into a durable formula. Although each of these writers turned out numerous works—most of which were notable for their predictable plots, stereotyped characters, and conventional morality—they exhibited individual talents and tendencies.

B. M. Bower, the only woman to produce a string of notable Westerns, is best known for her characters in *Chip of the Flying U*. She dealt authentically with the details of cattle ranching, and reviewers noted her use of humor and her varied plots. Like Wister, she used East-versus-West conflicts and tried to capture the complexities of a closing frontier. Her heroines were more convincing than those of her contemporaries, but the organization of her novels was often choatic, and conflicts between characters were too easily resolved. Even more damaging to her reputation was the fact that she seemed unable to deal with serious cultural or social issues and during her long career was reluctant to make changes in her plots and ideas.

Zane Grey was a much more well-known writer than Mrs. Sinclair. In fact, between 1910 and 1930 he did more than any other writer to popularize the Western. Not only did several of his works top the bestseller lists, he also portrayed a West of picturesque and restorative power that appealed to Americans increasingly distraught with urban, industrial, and international problems. The public seemed convinced that Grey's West, which was pictured as able to redeem effete Easterners, was a marvelous and wonderful place. His descriptive and narrative abilities were particularly alive in novels such as *Riders of the Purple Sage* (1912), *The U. P. Trail* (1918), and *The Vanishing American* (1925). Grey's popularity has endured, and many readers when asked to define the Western point to Grey's works as epitomizing the elements of the formula Western.

Max Brand (the most popular of Frederick Faust's seventeen pen names) was much less interested than Grey in specific settings, natural or historical, and Brand never placed a high value on his Westerns. While Grey was convinced that his novels should place him among the leading writers of his time, Brand referred to his novels set in the West as "Westtern stuff" or "cowboy junk." He was interested, however, in showing human nature in conflict, and to enlarge the significance of these battles he frequently made his heroes titan-like. Between the early twentieth century and his death in 1944, Brand turned out more than five hundred books, more than one hundred of which were Westerns.

Another writer, Clarence Mulford, was more serious than Faust in his approach to writing Westerns. Mulford prided himself on his careful research into the historical backgrounds of his fiction. He gathered a large library and boasted of knowing intimately the West even though most of his writing was carried out in Maine. Early in his career he introduced Hopalong Cassidy, a wise, humorous, and appealing cowboy, who appeared later in many of Mulford's Westerns and became one of the well-known series characters in western fiction. Hopalong was a working cowboy and rancher—much different from the image of Cassidy that William Boyd depicted in western movies.

By the early 1930s these novelists, in addition to such writers as Stewart Edward White, Emerson Hough, W. C. Tuttle, and Eugene Manlove Rhodes, had helped to identify the Western as a separate fictional type. Reviewers and readers were now aware of what the term *Western* meant when it was applied to a novel. Unfortunately, for many critics *Western* denoted a subliterary type that they considered beneath their scholarly interests.

Part of this negative reaction arose because the Western was associated with the pulp magazines of the 1920s and 1930s. Publishers found that after the demise of the dime novel and the popular story weeklies in the years surrounding the turn of the century, there was still a large audience for adventure fiction about the West. Firms such as Munsey's, Doubleday, and Street and Smith capitalized on this huge market. *Love Story, Detective Story, Western Story,* and *Adventure* were four of the most widely read pulps, but western stories and magazines were the most popular. By 1930, more than thirty western magazines were on the market, and writers like Frank C. Robertson, Frank Richardson Pierce, W. C. Tuttle, and Max Brand, especially dominated the pulp western scene.

From the middle 1930s until his death in 1950, Ernest Haycox was the premier figure among another group of writers of Westerns. Haycox had served his apprenticeship in the pulps during the 1920s, and by the mid-1930s his stories and serials were appearing in *Collier's*, which, along with *Saturday Evening Post*, was considered the leading slick magazine. When Zane Grey lost his place in the major serial markets in slick magazines, Haycox quickly moved into his vacated slot and won the attention of editors and many readers. Several writers of Westerns who began their careers in the 1940s and 1950s were later to testify that they learned their craft by reading and studying the Haycox serials in *Collier's*.

Haycox was interested in producing more believeable Westerns. Not only did he try to create more persuasive characters, he also tinkered with the stereotyped characterizations of the Western by using two or more heroes and heroines and thereby added a measure of complexity to an uncomplex genre. In addition, Haycox began to people his Westerns with what one interpreter calls *Hamlet heroes*. These protagonists were reflective men who often wrestled with their consciences in deciding what was the right course of action. These heroes were far more serious and contemplative than the leading men in the Westerns of Grey and Brand.

Finally, Haycox added a historical dimension to several of his Westerns. He was convinced that by resting his fiction on historical events he could increase the realism of the Western. In such novels as *The Border Trumpet* (1939), *Alder Gulch* (1942), and particularly in his novel on General Custer, *Bugles in the Afternoon* (1944), he carefully gathered data on historical occurrences and based his plots on recorded events. Because of his tinkerings with and his additions to the format of the Western, Ernest Haycox occupies a large niche in the development of the popular genre.

No single writer can be said to have inherited Haycox's mantle, but three authors of the last three decades have attracted more attention than other writers of Westerns. Henry Wilson Allen, who writes under the pen names of Will Henry and Clay Fisher, has adhered closely to the historical Western that Haycox popularized in the 1940s. Particularly in his Will Henry Westerns, Allen demonstrates an experienced hand in joining history and fiction to produce high caliber Westerns. His Clay Fisher Westerns, on the other hand, emphasize action and adventure and rarely deal with specific historical events. Among the best of the Will Henry novels are *From Where the Sun Now Stands* (1959), *The Gates of the Mountains* (1963), and *Chiricahua* (1972).

Frederick Glidden, better known by his *nom de plume*, Luke Short, was probably the most popular writer of Westerns during the 1950s and 1960s. Short emphasizes action, and he packs his Westerns with suspense. His novels are tightly written with carefully structured adventure. In several of his works, Short draws upon his knowledge of frontier and western occupations to make his characters more believeable. Sometimes he sets a Western in a twentieth-century mining town, but most of his settings are frontier communities of no specific location. Short frequently deals with town life, although he seems little interested in using historical characters or events in his novels. He is skillful in handling women and knows how to picture some of his heroes as good men who have made a mistake in the past and are now bent on redeeming themselves. In the 1950s Short's Westerns began to appear as original paperbacks after markets for magazine serials had disappeared. Since that time most Westerns have been printed as original paperbacks.

The third of the triumvirate of contemporary writers of Westerns is Louis L'Amour. During the early 1970s L'Amour reportedly became the bestselling living author of Westerns. Readers of L'Amour's novels praise his abilities as a storyteller. His speedy narratives seem to contain fresh stories within the familiar format of the Western. One survey of nearly two dozen of L'Amour's Westerns (he has written about sixty novels, more than four hundred stories, and about one hundred television scripts) noted a pattern in L'Amour's fiction: his emphasis on families, their origins and characteristics, and their historic roles in settling the West. Another critic stressed L'Amour's use of violence; in ten randomly selected Westerns, 156 persons were killed, not counting those destroyed in massacres and other mass killings. The same commentator observed that most of the heroes of L'Amour's Westerns are self-made men who espouse traditional and popular causes. It seems clear that L'Amour has gained his audience primarily because he produces Westerns that contain predictable characters, plots, and endings. His narrative skills hold his readers while he relates stories strongly tied to the familiar structure of the Western.

If Allen, Short, and L'Amour have made, at the most, tinkering changes with the content and format of the Western, other writers and film producers have given the popular genre a total overhaul. These people appear certain that the Western—like much of popular culture of the 1960s and 1970s—has not been very relevant to an understanding of America. Yet they also seem convinced that because the nature of the Western is so well-known, parodies of its tone, structure, and focus could be used to reveal dangerous tendencies in the formula Western and the popular genre's inadequacies as a moral and ethical base for American ideology.

In the 1960s such books and films as *The Rounders* (Max Evans, 1960), *Little Big Man* (Thomas Berger, 1964), *Cat Ballou* (1965), *North to Yesterday* (Robert Flynn, 1967), and *Soldier Blue* (1970) satirized the Western. Some of the treatments were gentle: *The Rounders* dealt with a pair of cowpokes cavorting about as drunken and lusting failures; *Cat Ballou* pictured a renowned western gunslinger as a drunk (Lee Marvin) and utilized a pretty and naive schoolmarm (Jane Fonda) as protagonist; *North to Yesterday* described a cattle drive which arrived two decades late in a Mid-western cattle town. (The novels of Richard Brautigan also seem, in part, gentle satires of the ingredients of the popular Western.) Other accounts are more biting: *Little Big Man* portrays General Custer as a vicious killer of Indians and suggests, on the other hand, that the Indians were *the* western heroes (the film based on Berger's novel was even more harsh and pro-Indian than the book); *Soldier Blue* implied that the army on the frontier was little more than a pack of killers who slaughtered Indians.

In 1960, E. L. Doctorow prefigured this attack on the Western in his first novel *Welcome to Hard Times*. Through his narrator-historian, Blue, Doctorow hints that early western experiences were, at best, depressing and more often savage. Most of the residents of Hard Times are grotesques: ludicrous whores, grasping merchants, and violent killers—all of whom rip into one another and show little or no sense of community. Another author, John Seelye, is equally devastating in his attack on the Western in his brief novel *The Kid* (1972). Seelye, who dedicates his work to Leslie Fiedler and who is obviously indebted to the writing of Mark Twain and Herman Melville, pictures a frontier Wyoming town ripe with violence, racism, and perversion. In addition to parodying the usual makeup of the Western, Seelye hints at the detrimental impact that violence, racism, and sexual prejudices have had on America. Thus, *The Kid* undercuts the form and content of the Western while it also attacks what the author sees to be the major weaknesses of American culture.

Finally, there are other small signs the Western is changing. Writers are dealing more explicitly with sex. For example, Playboy Press is publishing its line of Jake Logan Westerns which emphasize the hero's abundant sexual prowess. Other recent Westerns treat homosexuality. Women are playing a more conspicuous role; the protagonists in some Westerns are women (see Jack Bickham's novels dealing with a female character named Charity Ross), and more and more writers are avoiding picturing their heroines as merely pawns of their men. Moreover, the treatment of Indians, blacks, and Mexican-Americans is more balanced than in earlier Westerns. Indians, for example, are often described in these recent novels as embodying a culture different from white society, and it is obvious that these differences will lead to conflict, but the Indians who fight their white enemies are not portrayed as inferior people or as savages.

These innovations suggest that the Western is reflecting the changing ideas and customs of the United States during the last decade or so. If this surmise is true, the Western remains a valuable source for attempting to understand the American popular mind.

REFERENCE WORKS

The lack of extensive bibliographical guides to the Western is one illustration of the small amount of material available on the popular genre. No compilation of secondary sources dealing with the Western was published until the 1960s, and there is still no adequate listing of works by the leading writers of Westerns. Bibliographies have been compiled on a few individual writers, but a comprehensive checklist of Westerns has not been published.

One useful source for information on the Western is Clarence Gohdes,

Literature and Theatre of the States and Regions of the U.S.A.: An Historical Bibliography. This state-by-state listing also includes a special section on the Western. A few entries are annotated. Some overlapping occurs among the sections on western states, regionalism, and the Western; and Gohdes' definition of the Western is fuzzy, but if one is acquainted with the names of writers of Westerns, this bibliography will be useful. For articles and books that have been published since Gohdes' volume, one should consult two listings in the winter issues of *Western American Literature,* the scholarly journal of the Western Literature Association. The "Annual Bibliography of Studies in Western American Literature" lists books and essays about specific topics and individual writers, and "Research in Western American Literature" notes theses and dissertations. These bibliographies are particularly helpful because most research and writing about the Western has been so recent.

Richard W. Etulain has provided two other brief bibliographies. His "Western American Literature: A Selective Annotated Bibliography" emphasizes secondary works published since 1960. Divided into four sections (Bibliographies, Anthologies, History and Criticism—Books, and History and Criticism—Articles), this list contains brief annotations on more than sixty items, about fifteen of which deal with the popular Western. More extensive are the listings in Etulain's *Western American Literature: A Bibliography of Interpretive Books and Articles.* This book-length compilation contains sections on bibliography, anthologies, general works, a specific listing on the Western, and lists of secondary materials available on more than two hundred writers. The part dealing with the Western enumerates nearly one hundred items—books, essays, theses, dissertations, and book review essays. Notable among the listings on specific writers are those on Owen Wister, Ernest Haycox, Max Brand, and Zane Grey. Etulain's bibliography includes works published through 1971 with stress on recent publications. Though the bibliography is not annotated or exhaustive, it does attempt to be comprehensive and to bring "together in one volume for the first time the most important research on the literature of the American West."

In "The Western: A Selective Bibliography," Michael D. Gibson lists twenty-six books and dissertations and eighty-one essays. He includes general items on Western fiction and film as well as materials on specific authors. His entries are not annotated, and he includes materials published through 1972. Some of the same items are listed in "Suggestions for Further Research" in *The Western Story: Fact, Fiction, and Myth,* edited by Philip Durham and Everett L. Jones. The most recent brief bibliography of interpretive treatments of western literature is that in Rodman Paul and Richard W. Etulain, *The Frontier and American West.*

The section on western writing contains nearly one hundred unannotated items, a good portion of which treat the popular Western.

Except for the scattered listings on individual authors in the National Union Catalogue, there is no comprehensive bibliography of Westerns. The most extensive checklist—other than the brief listings in the NUC— is that of Jack VanDerhoff, *A Bibliography of Novels Related to American Frontier and Colonial History*. VanDerhoff deals with areas other than the trans-Mississippi frontier, and his definition of the Western includes such unlikely choices as Walter Van Tilburg Cla.k's *The City of Trembling Leaves*. Sometimes he lists but one or two novels to illustrate an author's works, but the major writers of Westerns are well represented: Zane Grey (fifty items), Ernest Haycox (twenty-seven), and Max Brand (seventy-nine). Another incomplete listing of Westerns is that Philip Durham and Everett L. Jones. Published from 1969 to 1970 in *The Roundup*, the house organ of the Western Writers of America, their bibliography includes only the works of then-present members of WWA. Thus, Wister, Grey, Brand, and Haycox are not cited, but Nelson Nye and Luke Short are among those who are. Most of the items listed are novels, but nonfiction works are included for authors who have written little or no fiction.

Although there is no comprehensive bibliography of Westerns, check-lists on individual writers are available. Dean Sherman provides the most useful published listing of Owen Wister's fiction, nonfiction, shorter pieces, and books in "Owen Wister: An Annotated Bibliography." Most of the annotations are summary in nature. Complementing Sherman's work is Sanford E. Marovitz's outstanding compilation "Owen Wister: An Annotated Bibliography of Secondary Material." Reliable and thoroughly annotated, Marovitz's listing is arranged chronologically from 1887 to 1973. This bibliography, which contains hundreds of items and a very useful author index, will remain *the* source for commentary on Wister's life and writings.

On Frederick Faust (Max Brand), Darrell C. Richardson has provided an extensive bibliography in his *Max Brand: The Man and His Work*. Richardson's bibliography is an exhaustive listing of Faust's writings including work he published under several pen names. Noted are books, novelettes, short stories, other magazine and newspaper work, and several magazine articles about Faust. Meant to be complete through 1950, the checklist contains enormous amounts of information, but it is a bit disorganized and difficult to follow. Less extensive but easier to use is the bibilography contained in Robert Easton, *Max Brand: The Big "Westerner."* Organized chronologically, this list contains American original publications only and includes books and magazine and newspaper writings, as well as work published under his numerous pseudonyms. Helpful listings of essays and books about Faust and Faust's works used in film, radio, and television are included.

The most significant works on Zane Grey also include bibliographies. In *Zane Grey*, Carlton Jackson lists novels, manuscripts, and articles in periodicals (the latter contains only six items). In addition, he produces a helpful map indicating the settings of Grey's Westerns. Jackson lists but eleven items on Grey. Another writer, Frank Gruber (*Zane Grey: A Biography*), includes a listing of Grey's numerous novels with an indication of prior appearances as magazine serials, and he provides a more extensive listing of magazine pieces (largely nonfiction and juveniles) than Jackson. The only annotated bibliography of Grey's works appears in Jean Karr's *Zane Grey: Man of the West*. These annotations, which deal with novels, juveniles, and outdoor books, are not analytical but provide useful information on settings and plots. Karr does not list Grey's numerous short stories. The most recent brief bibliography is contained in Ann Ronald's pamphlet, *Zane Grey*, in the Boise State Western Writers Series. She lists the novels alphabetically and also notes juveniles, outdoor books, and general and specific studies about Grey.

There are no published bibliographies dealing with Luke Short and Louis L'Amour, but Ernest Haycox's writings are conveniently listed in Jill Haycox and John Chord, "Ernest Haycox Fiction—A Checklist." This excellent compilation contains information on novels, anthologies, paperback anthologies and reprints, short stories in periodicals, and includes a helpful index. The authors provide dates for serial appearances and further information on each novel.

RESEARCH COLLECTIONS

The three largest research collections pertaining to the Western are those at the university libraries of Oregon, Wyoming, and UCLA. For at least two decades these libraries have been collecting the manuscripts and correspondence of writers of Westerns. In addition, they have useful collections of western novels.

The University of Oregon Library houses several manuscript collections dealing with the Western. Not only does it have a growing assemblage of the papers of Ernest Haycox and Luke Short, it also has numerous letters concerning the origin and development of the Western Writers of America (WWA). Some of these letters are contained in the correspondence of Charles Alexander, Brian Garfield, Dwight Newton, John and Ward Hawkins, Thomas Thompson, and Robert O. Case.

An even larger number of writers are represented at the University of Wyoming Library. The Western History Center in the library at Laramie contains numerous small collections of letters and manuscripts. The Jack

Schaefer Collection is particularly useful, as is the correspondence dealing with the Western Writers of America. And the original western journals of Owen Wister are on deposit at Wyoming.

The UCLA Library houses a large collection of Westerns, and it too contains useful information about the WWA. The collections at this library and those at Bowling Green University in Ohio, the New York Public Library, and the Library of Congress are the most notable gatherings of Westerns. The Huntington Library in San Marino, California, has a large collection of dime novels.

The papers of other leading writers of Westerns are scattered throughout the United States. The Max Brand collection is at the Bancroft Library in Berkeley, and the largest collection of Owen Wister correspondence is on file at the Library of Congress. The Huntington Library contains the papers of Eugene Manlove Rhodes and Eugene Cunningham. Most of Emerson Hough's letters are housed in the Iowa State Department of History and Archives in Des Moines. Nearly all of Zane Grey's manuscripts and correspondence are in the private collection of Zane Grey, Inc., in Pasadena, California.

Other useful materials are still in the hands of publishers. Little, Brown and Company holds a sizeable collection of Haycox's letters, and some of Grey's correspondence is on file with Harper and Row. Dodd, Mead and Condé Nast Publications (successor to Street and Smith) have Brand letters, and Houghton Mifflin has some of the correspondence of Andy Adams and Jack Schaefer. Unfortunately, many of the papers of Street and Smith, *Collier's*, *Saturday Evening Post*, and Doubleday and Company are not available or easily accessible. These collections will be necessary sources for a full-scale history of the Western.

HISTORY AND CRITICISM

Although a few authors dealt with facets of the Western prior to the appearance of Henry Nash Smith's *Virgin Land*, that book has stimulated more research and writing about popular western literature than any other volume. First of all, Smith was one of the first scholars willing to study, as literature, several types of writing that previous scholars had relegated to the nonliterary categories of history, propaganda, and pulp novels. Through careful analysis of a wide variety of fiction and nonfiction about the West, Smith outlined what Americans came to believe about the western frontier. Second, he described the symbols and myths about the West that fascinated Americans. He was able to show how the West as a "passage to India," as a stage for the "sons of Leatherstocking," and as a desert and a garden, was a large part of Americans' mental image of the West in the nineteenth century. Third, Smith demonstrated one way that scholars could approach popular literature in his probing discussion of dime-novel Westerns. No scholar who aims at completeness in his research on western writing can afford to overlook Smith's brilliant book.

If Smith opened the door for early studies of western writing, John Cawelti has recently marked out one corridor students could follow in pursuing the Western. First in *The Six-Gun Mystique* and then in *Adventure, Mystery, and Romance,* he has encouraged systematic thinking about the nature of popular fiction about the West. He urges scholars to study the Western as a species of formula literature (he defines formulas as "structures of narrative conventions which carry out a variety of cultural functions in a unified way") to see how these patterns change over time as they respond to the culture that produces them. Although Cawelti provides useful sketches of the historical development of the Western, he is more concerned with the social and cultural implications of the formulas he finds in Westerns. In Cawelti's volumes, the plots and characters of novels by Cooper, Wister, and Grey are scrutinized and used to illustrate what Cawelti believes to be the major themes of the authors' cultural environments. *Adventure, Mystery, and Romance,* which in addition to dealing with the Western treats crime novels, detective stories, and social melodramas, incorporates much information from Cawelti's earlier volume, but it also includes extensive treatments of nineteenth-century Western fiction and recent Western films. In fact, Cawelti is satisfied to break off discussion of the fictional Western after his treatment of Zane Grey. One wishes he had chosen to deal with Haycox, Short, and L'Amour. Still, his books are necessary beginning points for all serious study of the Western.

The volume that comes nearest to being a brief history of the twentieth-century Western is *The Popular Western: Essays Toward a Definition,* edited by Richard W. Etulain and Michael Marsden. The book contains, in addition to brief introductory and concluding sections, eight essays and a selective bibliography. Some of the articles deal with individual topics and writers, such as the dime-novel Western, B. M. Bower, Zane Grey, Clay Fisher, Will Henry, Luke Short, and Jack Schaefer; another essay traces the historical development of the Western, and in a superb piece Don D. Walker argues for more rigorous application of standard methods of literary criticism to the Western. The authors of the essays approach their subjects from their training in history, literature, and American studies, but their major emphasis has been to show how their topic or author contributes to an understanding of the development of the Western. The editors are now preparing a full-scale history of the Western that will supersede this slim volume.

In addition to these books on the Western, several other volumes offer useful background information on the popular genre. Two of these books —Richard Slotkin's *Regeneration Through Violence* and Edwin Fussell's *Frontier: American Literature and the American West*—do not focus on the Western but provide lengthy discussions of the treatment of the frontier in American imaginative literature published before 1870. Slotkin's massive volume—nearly seven hundred pages—traces Americans' feelings about the frontier from the first settlers to the middle of the nineteenth century. He is particularly interested in writers' attitudes toward land, Indians, and pioneers who moved West. Fussell centers on the major American authors of the Romantic era and shows how they wrote about their complicated responses to the frontier. His chapters on Cooper, Thoreau, and Whitman are particularly stimulating.

In his book *The Western Hero in History and Legend*, Kent Steckmesser offers another perspective for students of the Western. He outlines how four historic characters—Kit Carson, Billy the Kid, Wild Bill Hickok, and George Armstrong Custer—became legendary figures. Working his way through large amounts of history, literature, and propaganda, Steckmesser points out what writers, ideas, and events shaped the "legendary" lives of these four men. Along the way, he discusses the role of a few Westerns in helping to make these reputations, but, more importantly, his book outlines the manner in which historical figures can and have been used in popular literature. Joseph G. Rosa does the same for one western type in his study, *The Gunfighter: Man or Myth?* Both of these authors—in research method and findings—owe a great deal to *Virgin Land*.

Two other studies comment upon the early historical and literary treatments of the cowboy. E. Douglas Branch's *The Cowboy and His Interpreters* was a pioneer work and has been largely superseded in J. B. Frantz and Julian E. Choate, *The American Cowboy: The Myth and the Reality*. Although these authors employ a narrow and misleading definition of myth—that is, the opposite of historical fact—they do provide useful summaries of cowboy novels published from about 1890 to 1920. Another volume that collects eight essays about the images of cowboys in early movies, recent films, and music and their associations with Indians and dude ranching is the lively book edited by Charles W. Harris and Buck Rainey, *The Cowboy: Six-Shooters, Songs and Sex*. None of these works, unfortunately, is the full-scale study we need of the roles of the cowboy in the Western and other kinds of American literature.

Russel Nye's brief history of the Western in *The Unembarrassed Muse* is the best brief account of the roots of the popular genre. In fact, Nye's succinct chapter should be the starting point for students of the Western interested in its origins and its historical development. Cooper's role in the rise of the Western is covered in *Virgin Land*, in James K. Folsom's *The American Western Novel*, and in a host of other essays and books.

The classic study of the dime novel is Albert Johannsen, *The House of Beadle and Adams and Its Dime and Nickel Novels*. Additional information is found in Daryl Jones's recent essays and his dissertation on the dime novel Western. No complete study of the pulp Western has been published, but Quentin Reynolds offers a helpful volume on Street and Smith Company in The *Fiction Factory*. Narrower in focus and more personal in tone is Frank Gruber's *The Pulp Jungle*.

In the past half dozen years or so more scholarship has appeared on the film Western than on Western fiction, and several of these recent studies are useful for scholars undertaking research on writers. The standard history of the film Western is George N. Fenin and William K. Everson, *The Western: From Silents to the Seventies*, which is comprehensive, detailed, and well-illustrated. Jenni Calder attempts to discuss the myths and reality of Western films in her book *There Must Be a Lone Ranger*. Along with treatments of such filmmakers as John Ford, Sam Peckinpah, and Howard Hawkes, she includes analyses of the Westerns of Brand, Grey, Haycox, and Short. A sociologist who employs the structural insights of Vladimir Propp and Lévi-Strauss, Will Wright deals with such well-known films as *Stagecoach, Shane, High Noon, Rio Bravo, Butch Cassidy and the Sundance Kid*, and *True Grit* in his *Sixguns and Society*. His comments about narrative formats are illuminating for those interested in the formulas endemic to many Westerns. Another fine example of the numerous recent studies of Western films is *Horizons West* by Jim Kitses, who analyzes the films of Anthony Mann, Budd Boetticher, and Sam Peckinpah. In an adjacent field, Ralph and Donna Brauer have provided the first book-length study of the television Western in their volume, *The Horse, The Gun and The Piece of Property*. For a full listing of publications about Western films, one should consult John G. Nachbar, *Western Films: An Annotated Critical Bibliography*.

The select number of scholars who have dealt with larger topics of western American literature have not devoted much attention to the Western. Among the overviews of western fiction, James Folsom's The *American Western Novel* is the best summary. His chapters are largely topical in nature with emphases on Indians, western heroes, and agrarian novels. He treats major writers like Cooper, Garland, and Clark, and he discusses the Westerns of Wister, Grey, and LeMay; but he does not reveal how the writings of the latter group differ from the works of major western novelists like Cather and Steinbeck. His handy book would have been even more stimulating had he chosen to make some of these distinctions. Richard W. Etulain discusses several other interpretations of western literature and the Western in his long essay "The American Literary West and Its Interpreters: The Rise of a New Historiography."

Although a book-length study of the Western has not been published,

several studies of individual writers have appeared. No scholar has completed a literary biography of Owen Wister, but Ben M. Vorpahl's *My
Dear Wister* contains a lively account of Frederic Remington's friendship
with and influence upon Wister. Even more useful as a model for understanding Wister as a man, a writer, and a cultural figure is G. Edward
White's penetrating book, *The Eastern Establishment and the Western
Experience*. White reveals how Wister became an integral part of a cultural consensus of the East and West in the decades surrounding 1900.
A short summary of Wister's life and western writings is presented in
Richard W. Etulain, *Owen Wister*. Two or three scholarly studies currently under way should provide the full-length monographs that are
needed on Wister.

Judged solely on the numbers of studies published, Zane Grey has fared
much better with scholars than Wister. Jean Karr, Frank Gruber, and
Carlton Jackson have written books on Grey, but the first two are weak
on interpretation and the third lacks sufficient critical insights to be
labeled a major study. Karr and Gruber are much too sympathetic to
Grey to see his shortcomings, and Jackson, an intellectual historian, is
unacquainted with recent research and writing on the Western and popular culture and is guilty of including too much plot summary in his book.
Another writer, Gary Topping, provides a more searching analysis of
Grey's Westerns in his essays and his recently completed dissertation.

Frederick Faust's son-in-law, Robert Easton, has produced a fine biography in his *Max Brand: The Big "Westerner."* No one will need to cover
that ground again, but, unfortunately, Easton does little with Faust as a
writer of Westerns. He is reluctant to evaluate Faust's novels and is unaware of the scholarship available on western writing. Eugene Manlove
Rhodes is the subject of W. H. Hutchinson's lively book, *A Bar Cross Man*.
Hutchinson is more interested in biography and in presenting long sections of Rhodes's valuable letters than he is in evaluating Rhodes as a
writer, but the book is nonetheless rewarding reading. Other writers, such
as B. M. Bower, Clarence Mulford, and Stewart Edward White, merit
extended monographs, but no published studies on their lives or works
have appeared.

More than a decade ago, Richard W. Etulain prepared the first literary
study of a writer of Westerns in his unpublished dissertation on Ernest
Haycox. Chapters of the dissertation have been published as essays, but
Haycox, like Alan LeMay, Luke Short, and Louis L'Amour, deserves a
full-length volume that is yet unwritten. In fact, no writer of Westerns
whose career reached its peak after the 1930s (with the exception of Jack
Schaefer) has received much attention from scholars. Gerald Haslam's
pamphlet on Schaefer summarizes the writer's life and major works.

The paucity of extended analyses of Westerns and their creators may

soon be at an end. Theses and dissertations on Zane Grey, Stewart Edward
White, Clarence Mulford, and Emerson Hough have been recently completed, and the Popular Press of Bowling Green University is making
plans to publish a series of monographs on writers of Westerns. These
are encouraging signs for students and scholars interested in pursuing
the Western.

ANTHOLOGIES AND REPRINTS

There are few collections of Western stories in print—largely because
little demand exists for such books among general readers and for use in
classrooms. In addition, short story collections most often lose out in the
stiff competition with reprints of older novels and the new paperback
originals. If one wishes to make money writing Westerns, he must turn out
novels; neither the skimpy remuneration available to short story writers
nor the moderate interest of general readers in short fiction is enough to
encourage the publication of many collections of short stories. There are,
however, a few anthologies of stories worthy of mention.

The best anthology currently in print is one edited by Philip Durham
and Everett L. Jones, *The Western Story: Fact, Fiction, and Myth*. This
collection was designed as a text for college courses—for freshman composition courses and for classes concentrating on the Western. The book
is divided into three sections: *fact*—five primary essays dealing with cowboys, cattlemen, and the cattle country dating from the time of Theodore
Roosevelt to the present; *fiction*—sixteen stories from Bret Harte's "Tennessee's Partner" to Walter Van Tilburg Clark's "The Indian Well"; *myth*
—six interpretive essays on western fiction and films. This is a useful
anthology even though the authors' reasons for selecting the stories are
not clear. The editors include the works of popular Western writers, such
as Mulford, Grey, Haycox, Short, and Thomas Thompson, but, strangely,
they also have chosen stories by Jack London, Vardis Fisher, and Walter
Van Tilburg Clark that are not good examples of the Western. A brief
introduction and lists of discussion questions after each selection will help
students and teachers to reflect on the nature of the Western.

Another notable collection is J. Golden Taylor's *Great Short Stories of
the West*, which appeared originally as a hardcover book, *Great Western
Short Stories*. Taylor has organized his anthology into ten divisions that
move chronologically from Indians to contemporary Westerners. The editor wishes "to emphasize the diversity of life that has characterized the
West from earliest times and to show the variety of themes and techniques
various writers have used in the past century to represent Western life."
Among the twenty-eight stories are works by Will Henry, Emerson Hough,
Max Brand, Owen Wister, E. M. Rhodes, and Conrad Richter. Wallace

Stegner's essay "History, Myth, and the Western Writer" is a first-rate introduction. Unfortunately, Taylor's book has been too often out of print. Another fine collection currently not in print is Harry Maule's *Great Tales of the American West*. Maule, who edited pulp magazines in the 1920s and 1930s and later became an executive with Doubleday and Random House, appreciates the historical development of the Western (as his brief Introduction demonstrates) and senses which authors have made the largest contributions to the popular genre. His book contains eighteen stories from Harte to Clark and includes works from Wister, Rhodes, Grey, Raine, Mulford, Short, Haycox, and Brand. The stories are judiciously chosen; Maule has selected the best stories from the most important writers of Westerns.

Two other anthologies reprint stories that appeared first in two periodicals. E. N. Brandt has edited *The Saturday Evening Post Reader of Western Stories*, and Ned Collier has collected short stories from the pulp magazine *West* in his book *Great Stories of the West*. Brandt's volume, which contains eighteen stories and two novelettes from leading Western writers, demonstrates how well the *Post* did in securing the best Western fiction for its pages. Collier reprints fourteen pieces that are not as well written as those in Brandt's volume, but the *West* stories illustrate the kinds of fiction that appeared in a leading pulp periodical of the 1920s and 1930s.

Three other earlier anthologies should be mentioned because they reprint stories from the best Western writers of the first half of the twentieth century. They are William Targ's *Western Story Omnibus*, William MacLeod Raine's *Western Stories*, and Leo Margulies' *Popular Book of Western Stories*.

The most up-to-date anthologies of short western fiction are the collections published by the Western Writers of America. From 1953 through 1976, members of the WWA have sponsored thirty-two anthologies. The first books in the series used reprinted stories, but the more recent anthologies contain original pieces written by members of the WWA for specific collections. These volumes reflect changing trends in western fiction of the last twenty-five years, but one cannot say the anthologies always contain the best Western writing, for the works of Luke Short and Louis L'Amour, for example, have not appeared in recent volumes. A new collection that attempts to illustrate the accomplishments of the WWA is edited by August Lenninger, *Western Writers of America: Silver Anniversary Anthology*. The editor has chosen twelve novelettes and stories and two poems. Most of his selections appeared first in the 1940s and 1950s, but two stories are original publications. Among the authors included are Luke Short, S. Omar Barker (author of the two poems), Elmer Kelton, and Nelson Nye. The Introduction contains a brief account of the WWA's dealings with outlets for the publications of western fiction in the 1940s, 1950s, and 1960s.

BIBLIOGRAPHY

BOOKS AND ARTICLES

Branch, E. Douglas. *The Cowboy and His Interpreters*. New York: D. Appleton, 1926, 1961.

Brandt, E. N., ed. *The Saturday Evening Post Reader of Western Stories*. Garden City, N.Y.: Doubleday, 1960; New York: Popular Library, 1962.

Brauer, Ralph (with Donna Brauer). *The Horse, The Gun and The Piece of Property: Changing Images of the TV Western*. Bowling Green, Ohio: Bowling Green University Popular Press, 1975.

Calder, Jenni. *There Must Be a Lone Ranger: The American West in Film and in Reality*. New York: Taplinger, 1975.

Cawelti, John G. *Adventure, Mystery, and Romance: Formula Stories as Art and Popular Culture*. Chicago: University of Chicago Press, 1976.

———. *The Six-Gun Mystique*. Bowling Green, Ohio: Bowling Green University Popular Press, 1971.

Collier, Ned, ed. *Great Stories of the West*. Garden City, N.Y.: Doubleday, 1971.

Durham, Philip, and Everett L. Jones, eds. *The Western Story: Fact, Fiction, and Myth*. New York: Harcourt Brace Jovanovich, 1975.

Easton, Robert. *Max Brand: The Big "Westerner."* Norman: University of Oklahoma Press, 1970.

Etulain, Richard W. "The American Literary West and Its Interpreters: The Rise of a New Historiography." *Pacific Historical Review*, 45 (August 1976), 311-48.

———. "The Literary Career of a Western Writer: Ernest Haycox, 1899-1950." Ph.D. dissertation, University of Oregon, 1966.

———. *Owen Wister*. Western Writers Series, No. 7. Boise, Idaho: Boise State University, 1973.

———. *Western American Literature: A Bibliography of Interpretive Books and Articles*. Vermillion, S. Dak.: University of South Dakota Press, 1972.

———. "Western American Literature: A Selective Annotated Bibliography." In *Interpretive Approaches to Western American Literature*. Edited by Daniel Alkofer, et al. Pocatello: Idaho State University Press, 1972.

———, and Michael T. Marsden. *The Popular Western: Essays Toward a Definition*. Bowling Green, Ohio: Bowling Green University Popular Press, 1974.

Fenin, George N., and William K. Everson. *The Western: From Silents to the Seventies*. New York: Grossman, 1973.

Folsom, James K. *The American Western Novel*. New Haven, Conn.: College and University Press, 1966.

Frantz, Joe B., and Julian E. Choate, Jr. *The American Cowboy: The Myth and the Reality*. Norman: University of Oklahoma Press, 1955.

Fussell, Edwin. *Frontier: American Literature and the American West.* Princeton, N.J.: Princeton University Press, 1965.

Gibson, Michael D. "The Western: A Selective Bibliography." In *The Popular Western.* Edited by Richard W. Etulain and Michael T. Marsden. Bowling Green, Ohio: Bowling Green University Popular Press, 1974.

Gohdes, Clarence. *Literature and Theatre of the States and Regions of the U.S.A.: An Historical Bibliography.* Durham, N.C.: Duke University Press, 1967.

Gruber, Frank. *The Pulp Jungle.* Los Angeles: Sherbourne Press, 1967.

———. *Zane Grey: A Biography.* Cleveland, Ohio: World, 1970.

Harris, Charles W., and Buck Rainey, eds. *The Cowboy: Six-Shooters, Songs, and Sex.* Norman: University of Oklahoma Press, 1976.

Haslam, Gerald. *Jack Schaefer.* Western Writers Series, No. 20. Boise, Idaho: Boise State University, 1975.

Haycox, Jill, and John Chord. "Ernest Haycox Fiction—A Checklist." *The Call Number* [University of Oregon] 25 (Fall 1963/1964), 5-27.

Hutchinson, W. H. *A Bar Cross Man: The Life and Personal Writings of Eugene Manlove Rhodes.* Norman: University of Oklahoma Press, 1956.

Jackson, Carlton. *Zane Grey.* New York: Twayne Publishers, 1973.

Johannsen, Albert. *The House of Beadle and Adams and Its Dime and Nickel Novels.* 2 vols. Norman: University of Oklahoma Press, 1950; Supplement, 1962.

Jones, Daryl E. "The Dime Novel Western: The Evolution of a Popular Formula." Ph.D. dissertation, Michigan State University, 1974.

———. "Of Few Days and Full of Trouble: The Evolution of The Western Hero in the Dime Novel." In *New Dimensions in Popular Culture.* Edited by Russel B. Nye. Bowling Green, Ohio: Bowling Green University Popular Press, 1972.

Karr, Jean. *Zane Grey: Man of the West.* New York: Greenberg Publishers, 1949.

Kitses, Jim. *Horizons West: Anthony Mann, Budd Boetticher, Sam Peckinpah: Studies of Authorship Within the Western.* Bloomington: Indiana University Press, 1969.

Lenniger, August, ed. *Western Writers of America: Silver Anniversary Anthology.* New York: Ace Books, 1977.

Margulies, Leo, ed. *Popular Book of Western Stories.* New York: Popular Library, 1948.

Marovitz, Sanford E. "Owen Wister: An Annotated Bibliography of Secondary Material." *American Literary Realism 1870-1910,* 7 (Winter 1974), 1-110.

Maule, Harry E., ed. *Great Tales of the American West.* New York: Random House, 1945.

Nachbar, John G., ed. *Western Films: An Annotated Critical Bibliography.* New York: Garland Publishing Co., 1975.

Nye, Russel. "Sixshooter Country," *The Unembarrassed Muse: The Popular Arts in America.* New York: Dial Press, 1970.

Paul, Rodman W., and Richard W. Etulain. *The Frontier and American West.*

Goldentree Bibliographies in American History. Arlington Heights, Ill.: AHM Publishing Corporation, 1977.

Raine, William MacLeod, ed. *Western Stories*. New York: Dell, 1949.

Reynolds, Quentin. *The Fiction Factory*. New York: Random House, 1955.

Richardson, Darrell C., ed. *Max Brand: The Man and His Work*. Los Angeles: Fantasy Publishing Company, 1952.

Ronald, Ann. *Zane Grey*. Western Writers Series, No. 17. Boise, Idaho: Boise State University, 1975.

Rosa, Joseph G. *The Gunfighter: Man or Myth?* Norman: University of Oklahoma Press, 1969.

Sherman, Dean. "Owen Wister: An Annotated Bibliography." *Bulletin of Bibliography*, 28 (Jaunary-March 1971), 7-16.

Slotkin, Richard. *Regeneration Through Violence: The Mythology of the American Frontier, 1600-1860*. Middletown, Conn.: Wesleyan University Press, 1973.

Smith, Henry Nash. *Virgin Land: The American West as Symbol and Myth*. Cambridge, Mass.: Harvard University Press, 1950.

Steckmesser, Kent Ladd. *The Western Hero in History and Legend*. Norman: University of Oklahoma Press, 1965.

Targ, William, ed. *Western Story Omnibus*. Cleveland, Ohio: World, 1945. (An abridged edition appeared as *Great Western Stories*, New York: Penguin Books, 1947.)

Taylor, J. Golden, ed. *Great Stories of the West*. 2 vols. New York: Ballantine, 1971. (The American West Publishing Co. printed the hardcover version as *Great Western Short Stories*, Palo Alto, Calif., 1967.)

Topping, Gary. "Zane Grey's West." In *The Popular Western*. Edited by Richard W. Etulain and Michael T. Marsden. Bowling Green, Ohio: Bowling Green University Popular Press, 1974.

———. "Zane Grey's West: Essays in Intellectual History and Criticism." Ph.D. dissertation, University of Utah, 1977.

VanDerhoff, Jack. *A Bibliography of Novels Related to American Frontier and Colonial History*. Troy, N.Y.: Whitston, 1971.

Vorpahl, Ben M. *My Dear Wister: The Frederic Remington-Owen Wister Letters*. Palo Alto, Calif.: American West Publishing Co., 1972.

White, G. Edward. *The Eastern Establishment and the Western Experience: The West of Frederic Remington, Theodore Roosevelt, and Owen Wister*. New Haven, Conn.: Yale University Press, 1968.

Wright, Will. *Sixguns and Society: A Structural Study of the Western*. Berkeley: University of California Press, 1975.

PERIODICALS

The Roundup. Bradenton, Fla., 1953-.

Western American Literature. Logan, Utah, 1966-.

Proper Name Index

Index

About the Contributors

ROBERT S. ALLEY is professor of humanities and director of American studies at the University of Richmond. His recent research has concentrated on television and values in American society. He is the author of *Television: Ethics for Hire?* and the producer of two half-hour films concerned with values in the television creative community. One of the films, *Television, For Better or Worse,* was aired in the Spring of 1977 over PBS.

ROBERT A. ARMOUR is associate professor of English at Virginia Commonwealth University. He is especially interested in interdisciplinary teaching and research; his continuing principal research effort concerns the relationship between poetry and film. His articles on film have appeared in the *English Journal,* the *Journal of the University Film Association,* and *Literature/Film Quarterly,* and he has just completed a book-length manuscript on Fritz Lang for Twayne's Theatrical Arts Series.

BILL BLACKBEARD is founder and director emeritus of the San Francisco Academy of Comic Art. He has edited, annotated, and introduced over fifty volumes in the narrative arts field in 1976 and 1977, notably the Hyperion Press series of classic comic strip reprints and the *Smithsonian Collection of Newspaper Comics,* and he has written the forthcoming Oxford University Press study, *The Literature of the Comic Strip.* He plans a similar cycle of collections and studies in the area of the pulp magazine.

MARK W. BOOTH is assistant professor of English at Virginia Commonwealth University. He has written essays on eighteenth-century

English literature and on the art of song verse. He is presently at work on a book about the functions of words in songs.

MAURICE DUKE is professor of English and director of Graduate Studies in English at Virginia Commonwealth University. He is a founder and continuing editor of *Resources for American Literary Study* and the co-editor of a major two-volume study entitled *Black American Writers: Bibliographic Essays.* The author of numerous articles on American and southern literature, he is also a licensed automobile racer and competes several times yearly on tracks on the East Coast.

RICHARD ETULAIN is professor of history at Idaho State University. He has authored or co-edited several books on western history and literature and written more than 150 essays and reviews for scholarly journals. He is currently at work on a guide to Western American literature and is co-editing a history of the Western. From 1978 to 1979 he served as president of the Western Literature Association.

ROBERT J. HIGGS is professor of English at East Tennessee State University. He has been engaged in research on the literature of sport and human values for several years and is co-editor of *The Sporting Spirit: Athletes in Literature and Life.* He is also co-editor of *Voices from the Hills* and author of a number of articles on the literature of Southern Appalachia.

THOMAS W. HOFFER is associate professor in mass communication, College of Communication, the Florida State University, Tallahassee. His teaching and research interests include empirical and historical aspects of film, broadcasting, cable, and international communication, and he has contributed to several scholarly journals and books. He is currently in the fourth year of a long-term project indexing knowledge about American and world mass media derived from trade and industrial journals published in the United States.

M. THOMAS INGE is professor and chairman of the Department of English at Virginia Commonwealth University, and he has taught also at Michigan State University, Vanderbilt University, the University of Salamanca in Spain, and at several schools in Buenos Aires, Argentina. He has published books on William Faulkner, American humor, southern literature, and ethnic American writing, and he is a founding editor of two publications: *Resources for American Literary Study* and *American Humor: An Interdisciplinary Newsletter*. In addition to editing several series of reference guides in popular culture for Greenwood Press, he is engaged in research on the history, development, and appreciation of American comic strips and comic books.

R. GORDON KELLY is associate professor in the American Studies Department at the University of Maryland. He was previously in the Department of English at Virginia Commonwealth University and the American Civilization Department at the University of Pennsylvania. His extensive writings on American children's literature include the seminal study of late nineteenth-century periodical fiction for children, *Mother Was a Lady*.

LARRY LANDRUM is assistant professor of English at Michigan State University, where he teaches a series of courses in popular culture. He is bibliographer for the Popular Culture Association and *Journal of Popular Film* and is co-editor of *Challenges in American Culture, Theories and Methodologies in Popular Culture*, and *Dimensions of Detective Fiction*.

KAY J. MUSSELL is director of the American Studies Program at the American University and was formerly a member of the Department of English at George Mason University. Her research interests are primarily in the area of women in American popular culture, and she is currently completing a study of women's romantic novels in the mid-twentieth century.

NICHOLAS A. SHARP has a joint appointment as assistant professor in the Department of English and as coordinator of Non-Traditional Studies in the Office of Continuing Education at Virginia Commonwealth University. His primary interest is in the relationship between literature and values. He has published critical articles and reviews in the fields of Renaissance literature, American literature, children's literature, science fiction, and adult education.

MARSHALL B. TYMN is associate professor of English at Eastern Michigan University, where he directs the largest conference on teaching science fiction held in the United States. He is an active researcher in the science-fiction field and an officer in the Science Fiction Research Association. He is the co-editor of *A Research Guide to Science Fiction Studies* and *The Year's Scholarship in Science Fiction and Fantasy* and editor of *American Fantasy and Science Fiction* and *The Science Fiction Reference Book*.

DON B. WILMETH is professor of English and theatre arts and executive officer of the Theatre Arts Program at Brown University. He serves on the Executive Committee of the American Society for Theatre Research, is theater editor for *Intellect*, an advisory editor for *Nineteenth Century Theatre Research*, book review editor for the *Educational Theatre Journal*, chairman of the George Freedley Memorial Book Award Committee of the Theatre Library Association, and author of numerous articles and reviews in major theater journals. He is the author of the recently published volume *The American Stage to World War I: An Information Guide*.